Past and Present Publications

Peasants, Knights and Heretics

Past and Present Publications

Past and Present Publications will comprise books similar in character to the articles in the journal *Past and Present*. Whether the volumes in the series are collections of essays — some previously published, others new studies — or monographs, they will encompass a wide variety of scholarly and original works primarily concerned with social, economic and cultural changes, and their causes and consequences. They will appeal to both specialists and non-specialists and will endeavour to communicate the results of historical and allied research in readable and lively form. This new series continues and expands in its aims the volumes previously published elsewhere.

The first volumes to be published in the series by Cambridge University Press are:

Family and Inheritance: Rural Society in Western Europe 1200-1800, edited by Jack Goody, Joan Thirsk and E. P. Thompson

French Society and the Revolution, edited by Douglas Johnson

Peasants, Knights and Heretics: Studies in Medieval English Social History, edited by R. H. Hilton

Volumes previously published with Routledge & Kegan Paul are:

Crisis in Europe 1560-1660, edited by Trevor Aston

Studies in Ancient Society, edited by M. I. Finley

The Intellectual Revolution of the Seventeenth Century, edited by Charles Webster

Peasants, Knights and Heretics

Studies in Medieval English Social History

edited by
R. H. HILTON
Professor of Medieval Social History, University of Birmingham

CAMBRIDGE UNIVERSITY PRESS

Cambridge
London · New York · Melbourne

Published by the Syndics of the Cambridge University Press
The Pitt Building, Trumpington Street, Cambridge CB2 IRP
Bentley House, 200 Euston Road, London NW1 2DB
32 East 57th Street, New York, NY 10022, USA
296 Beaconsfield Parade, Middle Park, Melbourne 3206, Australia

First published in this form 1976

Printed in Great Britain
at the
University Printing House, Cambridge
(Harry Myers, University Printer)

Library of Congress Cataloguing in Publication Data

Main entry under title:

Peasants, knights, and heretics.

(Past and present publications)

Essays previously published in Past and present.

Includes index.

1. Great Britain – Economic conditions – Addresses, essays, lectures.   2. Great Britain – Social conditions – Addresses, essays,
lectures.   3. Great Britain – Civilization - Medieval period, 1066-
1845 – Addresses, essays, lectures.   4. Robin Hood – Legends –
History and criticism – Addresses, essays, lectures.   I. Hilton,
Rodney Howard.   II. Past and present.

HC254. P4   309.1′42′03   76–1137

ISBN 0 521 21276 6

Contents

Introduction

R. H. HILTON

THE ESSAYS IN THIS VOLUME WERE PUBLISHED IN *PAST AND PRESENT* between 1958 and 1973. They therefore illustrate the type of article which has appeared at different times, ranging from the relatively short and deliberately provocative presentation of a thesis for debate (as in the earliest of the contributions to the Robin Hood ballads) to the long and well-researched examination of a major theme, of which there are several in this volume. The latter type of article has become more common in the journal although some critics persist in propagating the view that it is the first type of contribution which characterizes the journal as a whole.[1]

The essays in the present volume have been selected from a much larger available pool of articles on medieval subjects in order to illustrate a number of important themes in the history of later medieval England (that is, from the twelfth to the fifteenth centuries). In some cases two or more are connected as part of a debate but in general they are not deliberately linked thematically. There is, however, a rational element in their choice and grouping. We first present a group of articles in which certain crucial phases in the economic history of the period are considered; next a group in which the changing relationships between the main social classes are examined; and finally some explorations which touch on problems of social consciousness, social mentality and the history of ideas. It is, however, clear to any reader of these articles that this division of themes into the economic, the social and the ideological is, to a certain extent, a matter of convenience. The interconnection of themes is obvious throughout: social problems are so intimately affected by economic developments that one could say that if these writings prove anything it is that the attempt to separate economy and society is not only bound, but deserves, to fail. It is also evident that the ideas and feelings expressed in the ballads, the theological manifestoes and the heretical programmes, which are the subject matter of the last group of papers, only make sense in their contemporary socio-political context.

One of the most important themes in our collection emphasizes the crucial character of the decades before and after 1200. The key article here is that of Dr. Paul Harvey on the inflation of 1180-1220 — a key article in spite of the fact that it is the latest to be printed in the pages

[1] Denys Hay, "The historical periodical: some problems", *History*, liv (June, 1969), pp. 174-5.

of *Past and Present*. However, as Dr. Harvey has made clear, what he has done is thoroughly to document and to attempt to explain a phenomenon to which previous writers had referred as underlying certain other features of this period of history, but without the exploration in detail which Dr. Harvey has given us. Thus, Dr. Sally Harvey has examined in her pioneer article on the knight and the knight's fee in twelfth-century England the economic and social process in the course of which the class of knights was polarized and transformed. At the end of the eleventh century the majority of knights were professional fighters of a social status which seemed hardly to lift them beyond the upper ranks of the peasantry, at any rate as far as income was concerned. Their position in society was, of course, sharply different even from the better-off peasants, these knights being specialists who lived off an income composed of peasant surplus, meagre though that income might be. Those of them who were not household knights permanently in the retinues of the greater feudatories had been enfeoffed, not so much by the greater barons as by a middling aristocratic group, with petty holdings on the periphery of the great manorial enterprises, averaging above one hide in extent, only about four times the size of the average holdings of the middle peasantry.

By the middle of the thirteenth century even five times the amount of land, or landed income, of the earlier period was insufficient to maintain a knight, so much had basic military costs escalated, not to speak of the rising costs of the display which was more and more necessary to a group with the social and religious prestige which had accrued to it during the course of the twelfth century. By now the "knight", or perhaps in view of the reluctance of even some well endowed individuals to enter the order of knighthood, we should say the "knightly families", were fully members of a county nobility. As such they had local administrative powers and responsibilities, political muscle, military expertise and a chivalrous life style which they shared with the magnates with whom they had many direct personal contacts. All this, of course, because the knightly class had largely, though not entirely, shed those lesser members who had not been able to survive the inflation and its side effects (such as new methods of estate management) which Dr. Paul Harvey describes in his article.

One must, however beware of attributing too much to this single economic phenomenon. Dr. Paul Harvey believes that the inflation was confined to England, the consequence of an influx of silver resulting from a favourable balance of trade. Whether this is so or not it is worth while mentioning that over the Channel the rise to social prestige of the class of knights from a similarly depressed origin as low-status professionals had occurred considerably earlier, the rise beginning around the year 1000 and reaching its completion, according to G. Duby, by the year 1200,[2] though when one considers the literary apotheosis of knighthood in the writings of Crétien de Troyes one must assume that they had arrived socially at least a quarter of a century earlier. Was this explicable by inflation? Surely a complex of other factors, such as the devolution down to the level of petty lords of banal jurisdiction with its cash rewards[3] and the political wooing of the military groups by the crusading church must have played a considerable rôle. Perhaps England imported not only silver but continental cultural patterns, diffused not only downwards but laterally.

Another important social shift of the thirteenth century was linked with the rise in prices and the associated changes in estate management. This affected a much greater section of the rural population than the knights and operated through the development of the direct management of the demesnes on the lords' estates. As is well-known, this led to the stepping up of rent demands in the form of labour services, whether actually performed or "sold" on an annual basis. This seems to have been part of a general attempt to increase the volume of transfers of surplus from the peasant economy to the lords, not only in the form of rent of one kind or another, but in increased profits of jurisdiction. Aristocratic and state expenditure was expanding considerably, almost certainly more than production, and there could only be one ultimate source to sustain it, peasant labour. This, it is suggested below, was the explanation for the definition of villeinage as servile. However, we must once again be cautious in our linking of cause and effect. The rise in prices was contemporaneous with, but not necessarily the only cause of, a range of social and political developments which could not but lead to the increased demands on the peasant economy referred to above. These include both the development of the judicial and fiscal machinery of the Crown and the strengthening of the economic and political base of the higher nobility, developments which at the level of feudal politics might be contradictory, but from the standpoint of the peasant producer in relation to the rest of society were convergent.

There is a problem about these changes in the relations of lords and peasants which is analogous to that which we have noted in discussing the knights. Just as the development of the knightly class was

[2] This theme, to be found in several of Duby's books and articles, is also outlined in an article "The diffusion of cultural patterns in feudal society", *Past and Present*, No. 39 (April, 1968).

[3] Several regional studies have illustrated this point, an interesting recent example being that of Guy Devailly, *Le Berry du Xe siècle au milieu du XIIIe* (Paris, 1973).

diachronic as between England and the Continent, so we find a similar lag in the evolution of serfdom. It is noted below that the thirteenth-century descriptions of the larger English estates mention much more frequently than their counterparts a century earlier, such obligations as merchet and heriot which, like labour services were frequently used as tests of servile villeinage in the king's courts. It was suggested that, although these obligations were not invented during the period when the screws were being turned on the peasantry, it was then that they became generalized. It was also suggested that this generalization could well have been influenced by the widespread imposition of *formariage* and *mainmorte* on the peasantry across the Channel.

There is some irony here as well as a lesson perhaps concerning the realities of serfdom. We now know that *formariage*, *mainmorte* and many other charges were being imposed, through the generalization of the *seigneurie banale*, on wide sections of the French rural population, more or less as juridical serfdom, and the use of the term *serf* was being abandoned. In the eyes of the law the subjected *vilein* was free while his English counterpart was now servile. But the free *vilein*, subjected to the *seigneurie banale*, was not necessarily "freer" than the English villein who was also subjected, for most things that mattered in rural life, to the private jurisdiction of the manorial court. Whilst it would be wrong to pretend that legal distinctions were irrelevant, we must bear in mind that serfdom as a general phenomenon affecting the medieval peasantry has more to do with the level of non-economic compulsion in the transfer of surplus labour, or the product of labour, than it has to do with the nice distinction of the lawyers. In England as in France there was an evening out as well as a raising of the level of surplus transfer from the mass of the peasantry. In England this was guaranteed in law by the unfreedom of villeinage, in France by the generalization of *juridiction banale*, which could be imposed without making subjects into serfs. The consequences were not dissimilar.

There is then a considerable emphasis in this collection of articles on the problems of the medieval English peasantry. In spite of an occasionally expressed view that only the history of the "political" classes is a worthy topic of study there is good reason for this emphasis. One could point to the fact that this class constituted the overwhelming majority of the population, a majority still greater if one also includes that other (and much less well known) plebeian mass, the urban artisans. In any case peasant studies are well established in medieval English historiography, from J. E. Thorold Rogers, through Maitland, Vinogradoff, those historians who published with Vinogradoff in the *Oxford Studies in Social and Legal History* and a host of worthy successors in the inter-war years. Peasant studies have taken many interesting new paths in recent years, in particular under the influence of sociological and socio-anthropological studies. Inter-action within peasant communities is quite rightly emphasized and a new approach to well-tried types of evidence is yielding good results. It would be unfortunate, however, if such studies ignored that aspect of the peasant economy which was devoted to producing income for landowners. Indeed it would be impossible to isolate peasants from the context of the estate and its demands. But this was by no means an unchanging relationship. We have seen that there was a period of great pressure associated with the changing conjuncture of the late twelfth and early thirteenth centuries. Mr. Dyer shows us that two centuries later there was a movement of countervailing pressure, almost a reversal of what had happened in the thirteenth century. For not only was there a general reduction in the amount of surplus transferred from the peasant economy to the landowners, there was apparently a conscious selection by the peasants on the bishop of Worcester's estate of those elements of rent and other payments which could be thought to represent a tribute to seigneurial domination rather than a fair rent for the landed holding. If the historian regarded all forms of peasant payment as one form or other of transferred surplus for the support of the ruling class and its state, the distinction in the conditions of the medieval economy between a real and a personal payment might seem illusory. But the fact that this distinction was now insisted upon by the peasants themselves is quite significant because it suggests that experience of the production of commodities for the market may have persuaded them that land was not so much the natural condition of their existence as a factor of production which had its price.

When had the balance of forces begun to swing against the land-owner and in favour of the peasant? The usual answer is that the shortage of tenants and of labourers resulting from the mortality of the second half of the fourteenth century created a situation in which rents had to fall and wages to rise; in other words, to use Mr. Dyer's phrase, there was a redistribution of incomes in favour of the ruled and at the expense of the rulers. But Mr. Dyer's redistribution postdated the population collapse by many years: other factors, of which the subjective attitudes of the exploited must be to the forefront, must have played their part. Another debate is closely connected, namely the chronology of the break of the equilibrium of the medieval economy. The older view was that if there was a breaking point it was with the Black Death of 1348-9. Other historians have lately tended to push the crises of the agrarian economy, and therefore of the whole of the medieval economic system, back, some to the second half of the thirteenth century when, it is argued, overpopulation caused soil exhaustion, others to the famine of the years, 1315-17.   A French historian indeed has gone so far as to suggest that the late medieval fall in grain prices, often attributed to the post-1348-9 population collapse dates back to the *crise frumentaire* of those famine years.[4]

Dr. Kershaw's article, the most detailed study we have of the 1315-17 crop failure, famine, and human and animal disease, puts it into a comprehensible perspective.   He shows that the crisis was much more prolonged than has been supposed, since crop failure as well as sheep and cattle murrain persisted into the 1320s.   Land went out of cultivation for shortage of tenants, land values fell, demesnes were leased, rich peasants took advantage of the amount of land coming on the market to enlarge their holdings, all the familiar symptoms of social dislocation, in fact, which are usually associated with the decades after the Black Death.   What is striking, however, is that although already backward areas were very badly hit, the more densely populated and more prosperous cereal-producing areas recovered remarkably quickly, demonstrating that enormous recuperative power of arable farming communities which has been noticed in those areas on the Continent which were devastated during the fourteenth-century wars and pillagings.[5]

It is interesting that what Dr. Kershaw considers to be the most serious agrarian crisis since the eleventh century seems not to have triggered off on a significant scale the sort of agrarian discontent which is often associated with famine conditions.   However, as he points out, this period seems to have been one which produced a crop of verse outpourings complaining not of natural calamity but of human injustice. The dating of such verses is, of course, a problem, but even if in the end insoluble, it is considerably less complex than the dating of a tradition which also bears the character of a myth.   Such is the puzzle presented in the group of contributions which centre on the question of the historicity and social rôle of the ballads of Robin Hood.

This debate suffers perhaps by being somewhat too narrowly situated in the familiar terms of discourse of the professional historian.   This is exemplified by the title of one of the contributions, "Robin Hood —

[4] G. Fourquin, *Les campaignes de la région parisienne à la fin du moyen-âge* (Paris, 1964), pp. 191-208. Cf. R. and L. Fossier, "Aspects de la crise frumentaire du XIVe siècle" in *Receuil de travaux offert à M. Clovis Brunel* (Paris, 1955), where the wars rather than the weather are blamed for the crisis.

[5] J. M. Pesez and E. Le Roy Ladurie, "Le cas français: vue d'ensemble", in *Villages désertés et histoire economique* (Paris, 1965), p. 213.

Peasant or Gentleman?" It is almost certain that any attempt to identify and thus to locate the "actual" hero of a popular ballad, either as an individual or even as a member of a social group, though not without importance, risks diverting the investigator from what should be true object of his search. Ballads, in common with many other products of oral tradition, may be derived from an insignificant happening or from a literary work. They may, like fairy tales, be composed of a combination of traditional motifs, or they may narrate an actual or imagined sequence of events. What is of interest to the historian of social mentality is not the origin or even the formal content, but the function of the ballad for the singer and for his audience. If, therefore, we are to interpret the significance of the Robin Hood ballads in social terms, we have to think primarily of the audience and to try to see what the singer will present to it, knowing the audience's prejudices and its aspirations. Whilst paying careful attention to the details of the story our attention should be focused principally on the problem: What social message is given? And this problem does, of course, pose the further problem of dating, for the social message of one time would not be the same as that of another.

Within the ballads it is tempting to identify historical features of a specific period, such as the pre-eminence of the sheriff as the law enforcer, the indebtedness of the poor knight to the great landowner or the theme of the forest. These may well be features of thirteenth-century origin whereas the marked anti-clerical atmosphere could be of a later date. But the social message is most likely to be that conveyed by the latest bearers of the oral tradition before it was put down in writing (and henceforth became something else).[6] Every indication suggests that this would be at the latest the latter part of the fourteenth century. This is the period in which all the earliest references to Robin Hood cluster, including the remark about the predilections of Sloth in Piers Plowman; the guess by the late fourteenth-century chronicler, Fordun, that the ballad referred to the period of the Barons' Wars; Daw Topias' remark about Robin's bow; the use of the names of the ballad outlaws as nicknames by actual outlaws and rebels. It is, of course, in the fifteenth century that Professor Holt suggests a bifurcation of the audience of these ballads, one continuing to be aristocratic, the other now plebeian.

The argument for knightly patronage of the ballads in the earlier period, apart from details which may or may not be irrelevant (for instance the absence of specific reference to villeinage cases) seems to

[6] Cf. Jan Vansina, *Oral Tradition* (Harmondsworth, 1973), pp. 91-5.

rest broadly on the view that the actual life of outlaws portrayed in the earlier ballads corresponded to the actions of the unruly county gentry such as can be deduced from the legal records, that is poaching, robbing, kidnapping, murdering. Apart from the fact that the principal authority on this topic, Professor John Bellamy, whilst seeing some of these correspondences, rejects the identification of the ballad heroes within the gentry,[7] the theory of Robin Hood as simply an archetypal aristocratic brigand seems to ignore many of the moral resonances of the legends, as told through the ballad medium. This ballad hero, like the "social bandit" throughout European folk legend, may not rob the rich to give to the poor but he rights wrongs while standing against the law and its official enforcers.[8] Unlike Gamelyn (and unlike many of the unruly county gentry) he does not alternate between fighting sheriffs and becoming a sheriff himself. The message, in spite of its royalism, is basically subversive. Whatever the stories implied in the thirteenth century (*if* they were then current), by the late fourteenth and fifteenth centuries when we *know* that they were current, that subversive message must have met a highly receptive audience. The loss of plebeian respect for the traditional élites has, in the past, been obscured by the factional politics of the nobility between the 1370s and the 1460s, but its reality is now recognized more and more, not only in the events of 1450, but in such episodes, by no means isolated, as those described below by Mr. Dyer.[9]

The papers reprinted in this volume finish on another note of subversion. Dr. Aston's important paper emphasizes the fears of the secular and clerical rulers who, quite naturally, associated heretical questionings of established religious doctrine with designs on the stability of the established social order. There would seem to have been exaggeration on all sides. If disendowment proposals and plots by artisans to become dukes and earls seem to reveal extremes of fantasy on the part of some of the Lollards, one cannot help suspecting that unlikely aims, such as the community of goods, were attributed to them by their accusers. Whatever Froissart may have learned from his aristocratic informants some years after 1381, the community of goods, supposedly advocated by John Ball, and later a frequent charge against the Lollards, seems an unlikely peasant or artisan aspiration. In other words, between one set of fantasies and another it is not easy to estimate

---

[7] *Crime and Public Order in England in the Later Middle Ages* (London, 1973), pp. 87-8.

[8] See the chapter entitled "The noble robber" in E. J. Hobsbawm's *Bandits* (London, 1969).

[9] For other examples see my *English Peasantry in the Later Middle Ages* (Oxford, 1975), pp. 64-73.

the extent or the radical character of genuine lower class social and political discontent in the fifteenth century. One suspects that there is here a relatively unexplored field for research with a fresh eye into the records of rural estates and urban communities, as well as into the still relatively unexplored mass of records of royal and ecclesiastical courts.

1. *The Common Fields*[1]

JOAN THIRSK

IT IS NOW NEARLY FIFTY YEARS SINCE H. L. GRAY PUBLISHED HIS detailed study of *English Field Systems*, and nearly twenty-five years since the first appearance of *The Open Fields* by C. S. and C. S. Orwin.[2] Both books made an attempt to explain the origin of the common-field system, Gray regarding it as a ready-made scheme of cultivation imported by the Anglo-Saxons from the Continent, the Orwins considering it as a common-sense method of farming in pioneer conditions when cooperation was the best insurance against hunger and famine. Both theories still command a certain measure of support for the simple reason that no alternatives have yet been offered in their place. But in the last two decades and more, a number of studies on agrarian subjects have contained evidence that does not fit comfortably in the old framework, and a fresh appraisal of the subject is overdue. Moreover, since all countries in western Europe have the same problem to solve — they have all had experience of common-field systems existing side by side with enclosed farms — it behoves us to take account of the large amount of foreign literature that has accumulated in recent years, since it may not be irrelevant to the English situation.

But first a definition of the common-field system is necessary. It is composed of four essential elements. First, the arable and meadow is divided into strips among the cultivators, each of whom may occupy a number of strips scattered about the fields. Secondly, both arable and meadow are thrown open for common pasturing by the stock of all the commoners after harvest and in fallow seasons. In the arable fields, this means necessarily that some rules about cropping are observed so that spring and winter-sown crops may be grown in separate fields or furlongs. Thirdly, there is common pasturage and waste, where the cultivators of strips enjoy the right to graze stock and gather timber, peat, and other commodities, when available, such as stone and coal. Fourthly, the ordering of these activities is regulated by an assembly of cultivators — the manorial court, in

---

[1] For many helpful comments and criticisms I wish to thank Mr. Trevor Aston, Dr. A. R. H. Baker, Mr. T. M. Charles-Edwards, Dr. Cunliffe Shaw, Professor Rodney Hilton, Dr. W. G. Hoskins, and Professor M. M. Postan, and most of all Professor H. P. R. Finberg, who has read every one of the innumerable drafts of this paper.

[2] H. L. Gray, *English Field Systems* (Cambridge, Mass., 1915); C. S. and C. S. Orwin, *The Open Fields* (Oxford, 1938).

most places in the Middle Ages, or, when more than one manor was present in a township, a village meeting.

Since all four elements — strips, common rights over the arable and meadow, common rights over the pasture and waste, and disciplinary assemblies — are necessary to make a fully-fledged common-field system, it is unthinkingly assumed that they have always existed together. This, however, is almost certainly not the case. The oldest element in the system is in all probability the right of common grazing over pasture and waste. It is the residue of more extensive rights which were enjoyed from time immemorial, which the Anglo-Saxon and later Norman kings and manorial lords curtailed, but could not altogether deny. By the sixteenth century we are familiar with commons that were enjoyed by one township alone. But even at this date there are examples of commons which were still enjoyed by two or three townships, such as Henfield common, grazed by the commoners of Clayton-le-Moors, Altham, and Accrington, Lancashire. Earlier still we have examples of commons that were used by the townships of a whole Hundred, such as the common called Kentis Moor in Kentisbeare, which belonged to the Hundred of Hayridge, Devon, in the early fourteenth century, and the common of the Hundred of Colneis, Suffolk, so described in 1086. A century earlier than this we hear of commons which were reserved to the inhabitants of a whole county: thus, the men of Kent had common rights over Andredsweald, and the men of Devon over Dartmoor. There is some reason to think, then, that common rights over pasture and waste were ancient, were once extensive, but underwent a process of steady erosion, which even in the sixteenth century was not everywhere complete.[3]

The existence of strips in the arable fields and meadows is first attested in one of the laws of King Ine of Wessex, issued between A.D. 688 and 694. Since the interpretation of the passage is of some importance, it must be quoted in full:

> If ceorls have a common meadow or other shareland to enclose, and some have enclosed their share while others have not, and cattle eat their common crops or grass, let those to whom the gap is due go to the others who have enclosed their share and make amends to them.

The meaning of the passage is not crystal clear, and with our knowledge of later common-field systems in mind, it is, of course, tempting to assume that one such is depicted here. In fact, there is nothing in this law to prove the existence of a mature common-field

---

[3] L. Dudley Stamp and W. G. Hoskins, *The Common Lands of England and Wales* (London, 1963), pp. 5–13; *Trans. Devon Assoc.*, xxxii (1900), p. 546. I wish to thank Prof. H. P. R. Finberg for this reference.

system. It states explicitly that peasants could have shares in arable and meadow, bearing "common crops or grass", but it does not say that all the fields of the community were organized together for the purposes of cropping and of grazing when the land lay fallow. It is perfectly possible that one set of parceners or neighbours shared one field, while another group shared another field. Indeed, this is the meaning taken for granted by Vinogradoff, who described the law as one imposing on parceners the duty of maintaining the hedges of a meadow. If this interpretation is correct, then such arrangements as parceners may or may not have made about cultivating and grazing their land in common were likely to be their own private concern.[4]

There is nothing in Ine's law, then, to support the idea that in the late seventh century common grazing after harvest was practised in common fields or meadows on a village basis. And where no evidence exists, there is no place for assumptions. There are examples from the later Middle Ages onwards, in the fens of south Lincolnshire and in Kent, of strip fields in which there were no common rights of pasture and none were felt to be necessary. If and when cultivators grazed their arable, they tethered their beasts on their own parcels. In another county, where common rights over the arable were customary in the later Middle Ages, there are hints that they had been established only recently. It is the opinion of Dr. Cunliffe Shaw that when, in the period 1250-1320, manorial lords began to make grants of common rights over ploughland in the Royal Forest of Lancaster, such rights were an innovation. Before this, common grazing had been confined to the *Moors* — the relatively small pastures attached to every Lancashire vill. In short, there is a case for thinking that in the earliest strip fields cultivators may not have enjoyed common rights over all the arable fields of the township. If so, an essential ingredient of the mature common-field system was missing.[5]

Early evidence of communally-agreed crop rotations is also elusive. The authors of some detailed studies of medieval estates as late as the fourteenth and fifteenth centuries have confessed themselves com-

---

[4] Ine's laws, c. 42 (ed. Liebermann, i, pp. 106-9). This law is translated and discussed in F. M. Stenton, *Anglo-Saxon England*, 2nd edn. (Oxford, 1947), p. 277; P. Vinogradoff, *The Growth of the Manor* (London, 1905), p. 174. See also H. R. Loyn, *Anglo-Saxon England and the Norman Conquest* (London, 1962), pp. 156-7.

[5] Joan Thirsk, *English Peasant Farming*, p. 14; A. R. H. Baker, "The Field Systems of Kent" (London Ph.D. thesis, 1963), pp. 23-6. See also A. R. H. Baker, "The Field System of an East Kent Parish (Deal)", *Archaeologia Cantiana*, lxxviii (1963), pp. 96-117; "Open Fields and Partible Inheritance on a Kent Manor", *Econ. Hist. Rev.*, 2nd ser., xvii (1964), pp. 1-23; "Field Systems in the Vale of Holmesdale", *Agric. Hist. Rev.*, xiv (1966), pp. 1-24. Dr. Cunliffe Shaw in correspondence with the author.

pletely unable to disentangle any system of cropping, despite the presence of fields divided into strips. In some cases, it is clear that the lands of the demesne were subject to a rotation while tenants' lands lack any signs of having been similarly organized. In other cases, even the demesne lands seem to have been cropped haphazardly. Miss Levett's study of the manors of St. Albans Abbey, for example, showed that in 1332 the demesne fields were divided into three main groups (*prima, secunda, et tertia seisona*), presumably for the purpose of a three-course rotation, but there was no indication that the tenants' lands were similarly grouped. She concluded her study of all the manors of St. Albans with the judgement that the three-field system was imperfectly developed or else decaying. Professor Hilton, writing of the distribution of demesne arable on the manor of Kirby Bellars, Leicestershire, and observing the variety of crops, both spring and winter sown, which were grown in the same field, was driven to conclude that "the lord of the manor had a flexible agricultural system within the framework of the supposedly rigid three-field system." On the estates of Stoneleigh abbey at Stone-leigh, Warwickshire, he concluded that there was no regular division of the common fields into two, three, or four large fields, that widely separated furlongs were cropped together, and that tenants' holdings were unevenly distributed throughout the fields. Miss Davenport in her study of Forncett manor, Norfolk, thought that "probably Forncett was a three-course manor", but at the same time admitted that there were no clear indications of three great fields, cultivated in rotation. On the contrary, there were abundant references to fields which were numerous and small. A more recent study of the fields of Church Bickenhill, Warwickshire, has shown "not the classic arrangement of two or three large open fields; instead . . . we are confronted by a bewildering complexity of many small open fields or furlongs . . . there is no way of discovering whether the six or seven apparently independent open fields were separate cropping units in the fourteenth century, and if so how they were related to each other." Moreover, in all but one of the few deeds in which the holdings of tenants were specified in detail, there was no equality in the acreage which each tenant held in each field. From all these examples, then, we have to conclude that another ingredient of the common-field system — regulated crop rotations — was missing from at least some villages in the later Middle Ages.[6]

[6] A. E. Levett, *Studies in Manorial History* (Oxford, 1938), pp. 338-9, 184; R. H. Hilton, *The Economic Development of some Leicestershire Estates* (Oxford, 1947), p. 152; R. H. Hilton, *The Stoneleigh Leger Book* (Dugdale Soc. Publications, xxiv, 1960), p. lv; F. G. Davenport, *The Economic Development of*

The account of Church Bickenhill carries us a stage further, however, because its authors pursue the problem beyond 1500, and demonstrate how the field pattern was later immensely simplified. A deed of 1612 and a survey of 1677 show that Church Bickenhill's ploughland then consisted of three common arable fields, whose many furlong names had been discarded. In short, a simplification of field lay-out and/or nomenclature had occurred somewhere between the fourteenth and seventeenth centuries.[7]

Our knowledge of the origins of the common-field system is woefully incomplete, but what there is does not support the view that the four elements composing the system were present in all villages from the very beginning of settlement. In many places, some of the essential elements seem still to be missing in the later Middle Ages. Yet from the sixteenth century onwards manorial documents contain more and more explicit rules and regulations about the workings of the system until in the seventeenth and eighteenth centuries they are at their most emphatic and lucid. On the eve of Parliamentary enclosure some maps of common-field villages present a more orderly pattern of strips, furlongs, and fields than anything available earlier. Here then are grounds for the hypothesis that the system evolved slowly. Common rights of pasture on the waste were ancient; arable fields seem to have been divided into strips before any village agreements were reached to regulate rotations and graze the stubble and fallow in common. The careful supervision exercised by manorial officers over all aspects of common-field farming is not everywhere apparent in early manorial documents, and in some manors not until the sixteenth century: court roll material survives from the thirteenth century onwards, and although there is much evidence of penalties imposed on those who damaged the property of others, particularly at harvest time, there are few hints of crop rotation or common pasture rights. Since this view of the common-field system as a gradual development is already the considered opinion of German scholars, has won the assent of Scandinavian and Yugoslavian colleagues, and is now being more seriously considered by the French, it is worth paying some attention to their argument and the evidence for it. While some of the steps in the argument have to rest upon the balance of probability, most lie upon a sound foundation of archaeological and documentary evidence.[8]

a *Norfolk Manor, 1086-1565* (Cambridge, 1906), p. 27; V. H. T. Skipp and R. P. Hastings, *Discovering Bickenhill* (Dept. of Extra-Mural Studies, Birmingham Univ., 1963), pp. 15-18.

[7] Skipp and Hastings, *op. cit.*, pp. 20, 22.

[8] I wish to thank Professor W. O. Ault for allowing me to see his manuscript, since published (1965), on early agrarian by-laws. It is mainly on his very full

In Germany the first farms for which there is archaeological proof from the later Iron Age were farms in severalty. Some were isolated, some were grouped in hamlets. By the sixth century of our era German settlements were still small, consisting not of twenty or thirty households, as Meitzen once supposed, but of two or three families with perhaps twenty inhabitants all told. As population increased, new households were at first accommodated in the old settlements. It was this increase which led to the emergence of nucleated villages. Other changes accompanied the growth of population. Farms were split up to provide for children, and fields were divided again and again. Ancient field names, such as *Spalten*, i.e. splinters, point to this development, while later documents and plans amply prove it. A multitude of German examples can be cited of townships consisting at one stage of large, undivided, rectangular fields, which became subdivided into hundreds of strips in two centuries or less. There are Yugoslavian examples, authenticated by detailed maps, which show this transformation taking place in the nineteenth and twentieth centuries in an even shorter period.[9]

If it be asked why the division of holdings resulted in the creation of long strips rather than small rectangular fields, then the answer of German scholars is that the strip was a more convenient shape for cultivation by the plough. It did not, as English historians have sometimes argued, influence the lay-out of fields at the time of colonization, but it did influence the method of partitioning holdings at a later date.[10]

As farms were divided into smaller units and population rose, the production of food had to be increased. The arable land was enlarged by assarts and the fields became more numerous. The waste diminished, and the arable had to be worked more intensively. The former field-grass economy, under which land had been used alternately for arable crops and then left for years under grass, gave

collection that the above remarks about court rolls are based. For Continental literature on common-field systems, see Gunner Bodvall, "Periodic Settlement, Land-Clearing, and Cultivation with Special Reference to the Boothlands of North Hälsingland", *Geografiska Annaler*, xxxix (1957), pp. 232, 235; Svetozar Ilešič, *Die Flurformen Sloweniens im Lichte der Europäischen Forschung* (Münchner Geogr. Hefte, xvi, 1959), *passim*; E. Juillard, A. Meynier and others, *Structures Agraires et Paysages Ruraux* (Annales de l'Est, Mémoire xvii, 1957), p. 54.

[9] W. Abel, *Geschichte der deutschen Landwirtschaft* (Stuttgart, 1962), pp. 15-16, 27, 70-74; Annaliese Krenzlin, *Die Entstehung der Gewannflur nach Untersuchungen im nördlichen Unterfranken* (Frankfurter Geogr. Hefte, xxxv, 1961), part 1, p. 110; A. Krenzlin, "Zur Genese der Gewannflur in Deutschland", *Geogr. Annaler*, xliii (1961), pp. 193-4; S. Ilešič, "Die jüngeren Gewannfluren in Nordwestjugoslavien", *ibid.*, pp. 130-7.

[10] Krenzlin, *Die Entstehung der Gewannflur*, p. 96; Abel, *op. cit.*, p. 72.

way gradually to a more intensive rotation of arable crops and fewer
years of grass until finally a two- and later a three-course rotation,
allowing only one year of fallow, was arrived at.   It is unlikely,
however, that in the first instance this system of cropping was
communally organized.   More probably it was adopted by individuals
or by parceners cooperating for mutual convenience in one field.[11]

Eventually, as fields multiplied whenever new land was taken into
cultivation from the waste, and as the parcels of each cultivator
became more and more scattered, regulations had to be introduced
to ensure that all had access to their own land and to water, and that
meadows and ploughland were protected from damage by stock.
The community was drawn together by sheer necessity to cooperate
in the control of farming practices.   All the fields were brought
together into two or three large units.   A regular crop rotation was
agreed by all and it became possible to organize more efficiently the
grazing of stubble and aftermath.   Thereafter, the scattering of strips,
which had at one time been a handicap, became a highly desirable
arrangement, since it gave each individual a proportion of land under
each crop in the rotation.   Some exchanges of land took place to
promote this scattering.   The partition of holdings was in future
contrived to preserve the same effect.   And when new land was
colonized in the Middle Ages by the inhabitants of old-established
settlements, it was not uncommon for this too to be divided into
strips.   Indeed, such was the force of example that the inhabitants
of some East German villages, colonized for the first time in the high
Middle Ages under lordly direction, allotted their arable from the
start in intermingled strips.[12]

German scholars also recognize the possibility that, when cropping
regulations were introduced and peasants did not have adequate
representation in all the fields, a complete re-allotment of strips may
have taken place, and a new pattern of occupation introduced to
replace the old.   One case of re-allotment occurred in unusual
circumstances in 1247 when the abbot of the monastery owning the
village of Isarhofen ordered a fresh apportionment of holdings on the
grounds that war and the desertion of farms had caused such confusion

---

[11] Krenzlin, *op. cit.*, pp. 104-7, 111-7.
[12] Abel, *op. cit.*, p. 75; F. Steinbach, "Gewanndorf und Einzelhof",
Historische Aufsätze Aloys Schulte zum 70 Geburtstag gewidmet (Düsseldorf,
1927), p. 54; Krenzlin, *op. cit.*, p. 114; *Kolloquium über Fragen der Flurgenese
am 24-6 Oktober, 1961, in Göttingen*, ed. H. Mortensen and H. Jäger (*Berichte
zur deutschen Landeskunde*, xxix, 1962), p. 313.   I wish to thank Dr. Karl
Sinnhuber for drawing my attention to this report of the latest German
conference on the origin of common fields.

that no one knew the boundaries of his land. Similar re-arrangements in more peaceful circumstances may perhaps be inferred from fourteenth-century documents showing tenants' holdings that were more or less equally distributed throughout the fields.[13]

The evolution of common fields in Germany was a long-drawn-out process. Many came into existence gradually after sites, deserted in the Middle Ages, had been re-occupied. It is possible to observe the gradual parcelling of rectangular fields into strips as late as the seventeenth and even the eighteenth centuries. But for our purpose, of comparing German with English experience, it is more important to be able to date the earliest examples of a complete common-field system. Unfortunately, the German evidence is, if anything, more scanty than the English in the Middle Ages. There is enough to suggest the existence of fields, divided into strips, in the high Middle Ages. Examples of crop rotations are found on monastic demesne as early as the eighth century and may be assumed to have spread to tenants' holdings by 1300 when rising population compelled people to use their land with the utmost economy. A rotation on tenants' lands may be inferred from documents from the Wetterau *circa* 1300 showing tenants' holdings that were divided more or less equally between three fields. Finally, since the multiplication of strips seems to be associated in Germany with periods of increasing population, in the sixteenth, and again in the eighteenth and nineteenth centuries, it is argued by Dr. Annaliese Krenzlin that the first complete common-field systems probably developed in the previous period of rising population, somewhere between the tenth and thirteenth centuries. It will be noticed that, in answering this final and most important question of all, the documents fail and German scholars are driven to an assessment of probability.[14]

With the steps of this argument in mind, it is now time to review the English evidence, looking for clues to the gradual evolution of the common-field system. The task is difficult because so many of the

[13] Abel, *op. cit.*, p. 75. It has been suggested that the Swedish re-organization of strips, known as *solskifte*, was also associated with the introduction of a communal crop rotation: Staffan Helmfrid, *Östergotland "Västanstång"*, *Geogr. Annaler*, xliv (1962), p. 260.

[14] Abel, *op. cit.*, p. 75; Krenzlin, *op. cit.*, pp. 102–7, 111; *Kolloquium, op. cit.*, pp. 232, 246. Controversy still rages among German scholars, but the main differences of opinion concern explanations for the different shapes of common fields, a subject which is almost totally ignored by English scholars. One exception, however, is *Valley on the March* (London, 1958) by Lord Rennell of Rodd, chapter iv. See also Harald Uhlig, "Langstreifenfluren in Nordengland, Wales, und Schottland", *Tagungsbericht und Wissenschaftliche Abhandlungen, Deutscher Geographentag, Würzburg, 29 Juli bis 5 August 1957*, pp. 399–410.

earliest references impart only scraps of ambiguous information, and it is tempting when the presence of one element of the common-field system is proved, to take the others for granted. This temptation must be resisted.

Nucleated villages and common fields are generally believed to have been an innovation of the Anglo-Saxons, who introduced to England a system of farming with which they were already familiar in their homeland. This theory could only prevail so long as German scholars adhered to the argument, put forward in its clearest form by August Meitzen in 1895 in *Siedelung und Agrarwesen der Westgermanen und Ostgermanen, der Kelten, Römer, Finnen, und Slawen*, that the field systems portrayed in German maps of the eighteenth and nineteenth centuries, so strongly reminiscent of English common-field villages of the same period, were a more or less faithful representation of the lay-out of fields from the time of original settlement. Modern German scholars who have consulted earlier maps and plans than those available to Meitzen, however, no longer hold this view. As we have seen, they now regard the common-field system as the outcome of a long and slow process of development. In these circumstances, it is no longer possible for English scholars to argue that the Anglo-Saxons brought from Germany in the sixth century a fully-fledged common-field system.

Anglo-Saxon laws refer to parceners, to "common meadow", and "shareland", the charters to land lying "acre under acre", to land lying in "common fields", "in common land", in "two fields of shareland", to headlands and gores. The significance behind these terms and phrases is uncertain, but it is just as legitimate to interpret them as a description of lands in which parceners were associated as to conclude that a mature common-field system embracing the whole village was in existence. With even more reason, this interpretation can be put upon the chapter in the "Venedotian" lawbooks, which has frequently been used to illustrate the cooperative method of farming from which emerged the common-field system in Wales. This chapter on co-tillage (*cyfar*) describes how land, when ploughed with a team assembled by a group of cultivators, was then divided between them, one strip being allotted to the ploughman, one to the irons, one to the exterior sod ox, one to the exterior sward ox, and one to the driver. Since we are also told about "whoever shall engage in co-tillage with another", and about "tillage between two co-tillers", it is reasonable to assume that these laws refer to partnerships between a few cultivators, such as parceners, and not to a system of cultivation involving the whole township. But in any

case, these Welsh regulations can no longer be safely used as evidence
for tenth-century conditions, since most if not all of them are of much
later date.[15]

If laws and charters fail to establish the existence of a mature
common-field system, they nevertheless give ample evidence of the
division of land into strips. Was this due to division of land at
death, or, as Continental scholars assume, to the effects of partible
inheritance? Almost nothing is known from any period as yet about
the customs of the English peasantry when devising land by will.
But there were few manors in the Middle Ages, whatever the official
manorial custom of inheritance, which did not allow customary
tenants to create trusts on their death beds and so dispose of their
land in any way they pleased, and at all times freeholders were
entitled to dispose of their land freely. Primogeniture was never
popular with the peasantry: it was the subject of adverse comment by
pamphleteers during the Interregnum, when it was called "the most
unreasonable descent." Even in the nineteenth century, a writer on
primogeniture in England was constrained to remark that "primogeniture is not rooted in popular sentiment or in the sentiment of any
large class except the landed aristocracy and those struggling to enter
their ranks". We are left with a shrewd suspicion that the English
peasant preferred, if he could, to provide for more than one of his
children.[16]

As for the influence of partible inheritance, this is a subject almost
totally neglected by English historians, who have been too readily
persuaded of the supremacy of primogeniture by the lawyers and by
medieval evidence from the later twelfth century onwards from a few
highly manorialized and carefully administered ecclesiastical estates
where partible inheritance did not find favour with the landlord. It
is generally thought that partible inheritance was once the dominant
custom in England. Domesday Book shows that it was still a common
custom among members of the upper classes in the eleventh century.
It is usual to argue that the custom began to be displaced after the
Conquest when land held by knight service was made subject to the
rule of primogeniture. By the end of the thirteenth century lawyers

[15] Vinogradoff, *op. cit.*, p. 262, note 29; H. P. R. Finberg, *Gloucestershire*
(London, 1955), pp. 39-40; F. Seebohm, *The English Village Community*
(Cambridge, 1926 edn.), pp. 118-21; *The Welsh History Review*, 1963, "The
Welsh Laws", *passim*, esp. p. 55; J. G. Edwards, "The Historical Study of the
Welsh Lawbooks", *Trans. Roy. Hist. Soc.*, 5th ser., xii (1962).
[16] Margaret James, *Social Problems and Policy during the Puritan Revolution,
1640-60* (London, 1930), pp. 26, 98, 310 (I wish to thank Mr. Christopher Hill
for drawing my attention to these references); J. W. Probyn, ed., *Systems of
Land Tenure in Various Countries* (London, 1876), p. 375.

applied the rule of primogeniture to all free land unless special proof was given of a custom of partibility. Primogeniture thus became the law of England in cases of intestacy. So far the argument is unexceptionable. But it would be a mistake to pay too much attention to the lawyers' assertions concerning the subsequent supremacy of primogeniture, particularly among the peasantry. Partible inheritance was still the custom of the manor in the sixteenth century in many of the less densely-settled pastoral areas of the north — Furness, Rossendale, highland Northumberland and the West and North Yorkshire dales — as well as in parts of Kent and the East Anglian fenland. Indeed, I have argued elsewhere that it was liable to persist in all weakly-manorialized areas where the lord's authority was frail, and land was plentiful — usually only pastoral regions by the Tudor period.[17]

But even if we concede only a small place in our calculations for the effects of inheritance in partitioning land, we have to be prepared for large consequences. H. L. Gray has demonstrated its effects in a township of 205 acres in Donegal, Ireland, which was at one time divided between only two farms. In 1845, after two generations of partitioning, these two farms had dissolved into twenty-nine holdings consisting of 422 separate parcels. The plan of the township without accompanying explanation would suggest a common-field township on the way to being enclosed. In fact, it was an enclosed township on the way to becoming a common-field one. Similar effects were described by the inhabitants of the Welsh lordship of Elvell, Radnorshire, before the statute of 27 Hen. VIII put an end, in law if not in practice, to the custom of gavelkind in Wales. It was not unusual, declared the natives, for a small tenement to be divided into thirty, forty, and sometimes more parcels in three or four generations. They had seen the lordship, numbering 120 messuages, increase to 400.[18]

If the partition of inherited land could have the effect of dividing

[17] Professor G. C. Homans and Dr. H. E. Hallam are honourable exceptions to this generalization at the beginning of this paragraph; T. H. Aston, "The Origins of the Manor in England", *Trans. Roy. Hist. Soc.*, 5th Ser., viii (1958), pp. 78-9; W. Holdsworth, *History of English Law*, iii (London, 1903), p. 173; Joan Thirsk, "The Farming Regions of England", in *The Agrarian History of England and Wales*, vol. iv, *1500-1640*, ch. I.

[18] H. L. Gray, *op. cit.*, pp. 190-1; E. G. Jones, *Exchequer Proceedings (Equity) concerning Wales, Henry VIII-Elizabeth* (Univ. of Wales, History and Law Series, iv, 1939), p. 313; I owe this reference to the kindness of Mr. Glanville Jones. For a discussion showing that this custom of inheritance had exactly the same effect upon land in China, see Hsiao-Tung Fei, *Peasant Life in China* (London, 1943), pp. 194-5.

fields into a multitude of strips, what evidence is there to show that it had this effect in England? There are some illustrations to show single fields which became subdivided into strips: an example, cited by Professor Hilton, concerns Swannington, Leicestershire, where an assart, *Godebertes Ryding*, held in severalty by Roger Godeberd in the thirteenth century, was found later subdivided among several tenants and incorporated in the common fields. In this case the reason for the partition is unknown. More conclusive is the example of a number of villages in the East Riding of Yorkshire in which the creation of strips led on to the emergence of a complete common-field system. These villages lay in a district that was devastated in 1069 and lay waste for almost a century. When the land underwent reclamation in the mid-twelfth century, charters show that the tenants occupied farms in severalty. They provided for their sons by dividing their lands and, when necessary, reclaiming more. Their assarts bore the names of those who first cleared the land, and by the end of the thirteenth century they too were divided among several occupiers, all heirs of the original tenant. Indeed, the townships were full of selions and bovates. And although this is not adequate evidence by itself of a fully-fledged common-field system, it was well established by the sixteenth century. Here then is convincing proof that when farms in severalty are divided among heirs, fields of arable strips can emerge in a comparatively short time out of farms in severalty, and eventually become absorbed into a full common-field system.[19]

These examples from the East Riding carry us silently over several vital stages in the evolution of the common-field system. They explain the appearance of intermingled arable strips, but they do not tell us how and when the cultivators resolved upon rationalizing this complex arrangement by adopting a common crop rotation and agreeing to share common rights after harvest throughout the village fields. To illuminate this phase of development we have to examine evidence from other places and periods.

When once the number of tenants and the number of arable fields in a village increased substantially, the problem of ensuring access to land and water and of preventing encroachments must have become acute. Our knowledge of assarting which took place in the thirteenth century tells us much if we have imagination enough, for many

---

[19] *Vict. County Hist. of Leicester*, vol. ii, p. 158; T. A. M. Bishop, "Assarting and the Growth of the Open Fields", *Econ. Hist. Rev.*, vi (1935-6), pp. 13 ff. For the effects of partible inheritance on Kentish fields, see articles by A. R. H. Baker cited in note 5.

assarts were divided into strips at the outset, others in the course of several generations. But we can also illustrate the problem more exactly. Professor Finberg has drawn attention to an unusual charter, probably belonging to the early eleventh century, which describes the boundaries of an estate at Hawling, Gloucestershire. It defines the area of *feld*, or pasture, in the south of the parish, and the area of woodland in the north. These boundaries exclude a piece of land in the centre occupied by the village and its arable. Thus, we are able to compare the arable land of Hawling in the early eleventh century with the lay-out of the parish some seven hundred years later, when in 1748 a new plan of the common fields of Hawling was drawn. There were then three arable fields. The original nucleus of arable was now Middle Field, the smallest of the three; the West Field was part of the former *feld*, and stretched to the parish boundary; the East Field was also an assart from the *feld* in the south-east of the parish. The arable was some five or six times its size in the eleventh century, and we may guess that the parcels or strips of individual tenants were perhaps ten or even twenty times as numerous.[20]

Ine's law hints at cooperation between parceners or neighbours who possessed strips in the same fields. And it may be that (as the later Welsh evidence suggests), such cooperation extended to choice of the crops to be grown in a particular field and assistance in cultivation. If men cooperated to this extent, did they also pasture their fields in common after harvest, and if so, how? We cannot attempt to answer these questions until we have considered whether the stubble was grazed at all. It afforded useful feed for animals but was not indispensable if pasture and waste were plentiful. The fields needed the manure to keep them in good heart and it was obviously more convenient to graze stock on the fields than to cart the manure from elsewhere. But the need for manure might not be urgent until the fields were fairly intensively cropped. Under a rotation of crops and long years of grass, men could have managed without. Thus, until population grew and land had to be used economically, we can envisage the possibility that the stubble in the arable fields was not grazed. But by the thirteenth century, certainly, and how much earlier we do not know, the value of dung was fully recognized and received due attention in Walter of Henley's treatise on husbandry.[21]

[20] H. P. R. Finberg, *The Early Charters of the West Midlands* (Leicester, 1961), pp. 188-96.

[21] *Walter of Henley's Husbandry . . .* , ed. E. Lamond (London, 1890), pp. 18-23.

We must now consider the second question: when and how was the stubble grazed? When once parceners and neighbours cooperated in cultivating their fields, *and* also recognized the need to graze the stubble, we may assume that in some places, at least, common grazing would suggest itself naturally. It may not always have happened this way: the example of Kentish fields, in which stubble was always grazed in severalty, springs to mind. But grazing in common was obviously convenient, for it eliminated the tedious and always unsatisfactory business of hurdling strips to contain the sheep and of tethering great cattle.

We are still dependent on Ine's law (apart from the dubious later Welsh evidence) for our assumption that cultivation of the arable and the grazing of the fields in common concerned only parceners and neighbours who were sharing fields, and did not necessarily involve the whole community of tenants. This belief is strengthened by Bracton's treatise on the *Laws and Customs of England*, written in the mid-thirteenth century, which also discusses rights of common pasture on the same basis, that is, as a grant of a right from one person to another or between members of a small group who are parceners or neighbours. Indeed, his examples make it abundantly clear that the word *common* had a more restricted meaning than that which historians normally accord it.[22] Medieval charters and court rolls lend further support to this view by yielding examples of such agreements between neighbours possessing intermingled or adjoining land. The charters of Missenden Abbey, Buckinghamshire, record a grant of land in Missenden in 1161 from Turstin Mantel. With it Mantel granted rights of common over all his own land, presumably because it lay intermingled with, or adjoining, that newly granted to the abbey. In 1284 each side agreed to forgo rights over the other's arable, and the monks received permission to build a dyke and hedge to divide their land from Mantel's. In another charter from the same cartulary, dated 1170-79, Alexander de Hampden confirmed a grant to the monks of Missenden Abbey of a virgate of land in Honor, minus four acres which Alexander kept for himself. He substituted in their place four acres from his demesne elsewhere. He allowed the monks to pasture a certain number of animals on his land "in wood and field (*in bosco et plano*)", and in return Alexander received rights of common over the third field of the abbey grange, which lay next to Alexander's land, when it was not in crop. Another agreement (1240-68) recorded in the same cartulary was between

[22] Henry de Bracton, *De Legibus et Consuetudinibus Angliae*, ed. G. C. Woodbine (New Haven, 1915-22), vol. iii, pp. 129-30, 166-70, 182, 184. The Welsh evidence seems to come from rather the same period (above, n. 15).

Thomas Mantel and Robert Byl. Thomas held land within the bounds of Robert Byl's estate and agreed to enclose his portion with a ditch and not to claim rights of pasture beyond it. Here, then, are three agreements, each of which refer to the grant of rights of common over arable between two parties. Bearing in mind the possibility that such agreements between neighbours might continue in some places long after they had given way in others to a common-field system on a village basis, we may treat as equally relevant other examples from later periods.[23]

In the Wakefield manor court rolls of 1297 a dispute between Matthew de Bosco and Thomas de Coppeley concerning grazing rights in open time (i.e. after harvest) was settled by an agreement that in open time "they ought to intercommon". Another quarrel at Alverthorpe in the same manor in December 1307 concerning common rights in a certain *cultura* of the arable fields was set down in the court rolls not as a quarrel between the complainant, Quenylda de Alverthorpe, and the whole township but between her and four other named persons. In 1299 in the manor court of Hales, Worcestershire, Richard de Rugaker made amends to Geoffrey Osborn because he drove off Geoffrey's animals from a field which was common between themselves *and others* (not, it should be noted, between them and the whole township). Similarly, when German Philcock of Stanley, in Wakefield manor, was accused in November 1306 of making a fosse in the fields of Stanley, he said it was not to the injury of *his neighbours*, because it was always open in open time. Yet again, Prior Walter and the canons of Selborne Priory, Hampshire, granted in 1326 to Henry Wyard and his wife Alice common pasture for all their beasts except pigs and goats in the field (described in detail) belonging to the Prior, in exchange for a release from Henry and Alice of all their right in sixteen acres of land in Theddene and in the common pasture above *La Bideldone*. Finally, another citation from a later period, from the court orders of Lowick, Furness, in 1650, wherein it was laid down that Christopher Harries, Bryan Christopherson, and James Penny "shall stint their after grass when their corn is gotten equally according to their share".[24]

[23] E. C. Vollans, "The Evolution of Farm Lands in the Central Chilterns in the Twelfth and Thirteenth Centuries", *Trans. Institute of British Geographers*, xxvi (1959), pp. 204-5, 208, 222, citing charters from *The Cartulary of Missenden Abbey*, part i, ed. J. G. Jenkins (Bucks. Arch. Soc., Records Branch, ii, 1938), pp. 66-8, 184-5, 128.

[24] *Court Rolls of the Manor of Wakefield*, vol. ii, *1297-1309* (Yorks. Arch. Soc. Rec. Ser., xxxvi, 1906), pp. 20, 131, 58; *Court Roll of the Manor of Hales, 1270-1307*, part ii (Worcs. Hist. Soc., 1912), p. 391; *Calendar of Charters and Documents relating to the Possessions of Selborne and its Priory* (Hants. Rec. Soc.,

Alongside the early grants of common pasture rights between individuals and small groups, we must set examples of grants of wider scope, some embracing all tenants, though not, so far as our evidence extends, embracing all fields, others proving conclusively that all tenants commoned all fields. In a grant dated between 1235 and 1264 Roger de Quincy forbade his tenants in Shepshed to pasture their animals on the fields of the monks of Garendon "except in the open season when neighbours common with neighbours". This saving clause — "set in seysona quando campi aperti sunt et vicini cum vicinis communicare debent" — stresses once again the rights of neighbours to common with one another. Nevertheless, it is significant that the right of common pasture mentioned here is a grant to *all* tenants to pasture the fields of the monks. A custumal of the late thirteenth century (temp. Edward I) tells us that tenants of land in Crowmarsh, Oxfordshire, had common of pasture on the stubble of the lord's land as soon as the grain had been gathered. A custumal of Laughton, Sussex, dated 1272, declared that rights of common pasture over the demesne were the privilege of the free tenants in return for services to the lord. Finally two convincing examples of tenants' common rights over all fields. According to the customs of Stanbridge and Tilsworth, Bedfordshire, in 1240 "when a field of Tilsworth lies out of tillage and to fallow, then likewise a field of Stanbridge ought to lie out of tillage and fallow, so that they ought to common horn under horn"; the court roll of Broughton, Huntingdonshire in 1290 lists the names "of those who sowed in the fallow where the freemen and bondmen ought to have their common pasture". If we assimilate these examples into one generalization, we may say that rights of grazing over arable land were still being shared by neighbours in the twelfth century, but before the middle of the thirteenth century there were villages in which all tenants shared common rights in all fields. Further search, of course, may well produce evidence of the latter in the twelfth century. Alternatively, we may reach the same goal by approaching the problem from another direction.[25]

The grazing of all the fields of a village in common could not take

1894), p. 41 — see also p. 38, and Hants. Rec. Soc., 1891, pp. 38-9, 49, 64; G. Youd, "The Common Fields of Lancashire", *Trans. Hist. Soc. Lancs. and Cheshire*, cxiii (1962), p. 10.

[25] L. C. Lloyd and D. M. Stenton, *Sir Christopher Hatton's Book of Seals* (Northants. Rec. Soc., xv, 1950), p. 14; *Custumals of Battle Abbey in the Reign of Edward I and Edward II*, ed. S. R. Scargill-Bird (Camden Ser., N.S., xli, 1887), pp. 89, xxxv; *Custumals of the Manors of Laughton . . .*, ed. A. E. Wilson (Sussex Rec. Soc., lx, 1961), pp. 3-4; G. C. Homans, *English Villagers of the Thirteenth Century* (Cambridge, Mass., 1942), pp. 422, 57-8.

place until they were all incorporated into a scheme of cropping which ensured that all the strips in one sector lay fallow at the same time, that all the strips in another were sown in autumn, or in spring, and that the fields were harvested and cleared at the same time. Thus, in places where common rights over the arable were still a matter of agreement between neighbours, we should not expect to find crop rotations organized on a village basis. We need not be surprised, then, that many villages in the Middle Ages appear to have contained numerous fields, not apparently arranged in any orderly groups, and that no distinction was preserved between furlongs and fields. In such cases, it is likely that the distinction was of no practical significance.

Not all manors, however, exhibit the same puzzling appearance of disordered cultivation even in the thirteenth century. Some early references to cropping imply that an intensive rotation of one or two crops and a fallow was observed on ecclesiastical demesne in the twelfth century. A lease of Navestock manor, Essex, in 1152, for example, mentions winter and spring corn and a season of fallow. An extent of 1265-6 shows that some lands of the monastery of St. Peter at Gloucester, situated in Littleton and Linkenholt, Hampshire, were cropped for two years out of three. In 1299 a two-course rotation, including one year of fallow, prevailed on various Worcester episcopal estates. And, indeed, since three thirteenth-century treatises of husbandry imply that a regular two or three-course rotation was an essential of good farming, we may guess that it was fairly commonplace practice among responsible farmers by that time.[26]

None of these examples, however, can be taken as proof that tenants' lands were subject to the same rotation, or, indeed, any rotation. But on Lincolnshire manors in the twelfth and thirteenth centuries we find clues to the division of all the village land into two halves for cropping purposes, and here we are on firmer ground: tenants' lands must have been drawn into the same field courses as that of their lords. Sir Frank Stenton assures us that the practice of dividing the land of the village into two halves was not unusual in Lincolnshire: it was common in every part of Lindsey, and less frequently found in Kesteven; it has not been found in Holland, but we should not expect this, for there is no evidence of a common-field

[26] *The Domesday of St. Paul's . . .* , ed. W. H. Hale (Camden Ser., 1858), p. 133; *Historia et Cartularium Monasterii Sancti Petri Gloucestriae*, ed. W. H. Hart (Rolls Series, 1863-7), vol. iii, pp. 35-6, 41; *The Red Book of Worcester*, ed. Marjory Hollings (Worcs. Hist. Soc., lxxii, lxxiv, 1934), pp. 125, 126, 151; *Walter of Henley's Husbandry*, pp. 6-9, 66-7, 84-5.

system ever having developed in the fens. To illustrate this arrangement, two of Sir Frank Stenton's earliest examples must suffice. Early in Henry II's reign (between 1154 and 1170) Thorald, son of Warin, gave to the nuns of Bullington in East Barkwith "15 acres of arable land on the one side of the village and as much on the other side and half the meadow which belongs to all my land of the same village, and pasture for a hundred sheep with all things pertaining to the same land". In 1156-7 Peter Cotes granted to Catley priory 20 acres of land on one side of the village of Cotes and 20 acres on the other. The purpose of equally dividing the land between two halves of the village is made clear in at least two leases which said that the land was to be cropped in alternate years.[27]

If we now discount the possibility that these holdings had been equally divided between the two halves of the village from the time of original settlement, we have to explain how this equal division had been brought about. German scholars, as we have mentioned already, envisage the possibility that at some stage in the evolution of a common-field system a radical re-distribution of land was necessary in order to facilitate the introduction of new common-field regulations on a village basis. Such a re-organization is not inconceivable in English villages; it would not have been repugnant to tenants. We are already familiar with the annual re-apportionment of meadow by lots, which was customary in many English villages. The re-allotment of arable land was a common, though not, of course, annual, practice in Northumberland — a normal common-field county — in the sixteenth century and later: in a number of villages the fields were divided into two halves and the strips re-allocated in order to give tenants land in one half or the other and reduce the distances they had to walk to their parcels. It was also customary in parts of the northern counties, possessing an infertile soil, to change the arable fields at intervals by putting the old ploughland back to common pasture and taking in a new field from the common. It is clear that people did not always cling tenaciously to their own plots of land.[28]

---

[27] *Transcripts of Charters relating to the Gilbertine Houses . . .* , ed. F. M. Stenton (Lincs. Rec. Soc., xviii, 1920), pp. 94, 83; *Registrum Antiquissimum . . . of Lincoln*, vol. iv, ed. C. W. Foster (Lincs. Rec. Soc., xxxii, 1937), pp. 69-70, 233. Other possible twelfth-century examples are listed in H. L. Gray, *op. cit.*, pp. 450-509, but the evidence given there is not sufficient to prove anything either way.

[28] M. W. Beresford, "Lot Acres", *Econ. Hist. Rev.*, xiii (1943), pp. 74-9; Lord Ernle, *English Farming Past and Present* (London, 1961 edn.), pp. 26, 230; R. A. Butlin, "Northumberland Field Systems", *Agric. Hist. Rev.* xii (1964), pp. 99-120; H. L. Gray, *op. cit.*, pp. 208-9.

HPK

Clues to the re-allotment of land in the Middle Ages are not explicit, but indirect. They are of two kinds. Some documents show holdings comprising strips that lay in a regular order between the strips of other tenants. Professor Homans has cited several examples from the thirteenth and fourteenth centuries. Seebohm drew attention to an outstanding example from Winslow, Buckinghamshire, where in 1361 John Moldeson held seventy-two half-acre strips, of which sixty-six had on one side the strips of John Watekyns, while on the other side forty-three lay next to the strips of Henry Warde and twenty-three next to those of John Mayn. However, knowing as we do from the experience of German, Welsh, and Irish villages that, in a matter of two generations, a pattern of land occupation could be changed out of recognition through conveyances of pieces and the division of fields among parceners, we cannot believe that this orderliness dates from the time of original settlement. Indeed, we could say with some confidence that the allotment of land, depicted in a document in 1361, had taken place not more than one hundred years before. Do these examples, then, denote deliberate re-allotments of village land in the not very distant past for the sake of facilitating common-field regulations? It is possible. But there are equally plausible, alternative explanations. They may be the result of a redistribution of land following the Black Death, for many new tenancies had to be created after this calamity. Alternatively they may represent isolated examples in their villages of the partition among heirs of one holding comprising scattered fields. Such an effect can be demonstrated from English documents occasionally, from German records frequently. In short, none of these cases is any use for clinching an argument.[29]

Other clues to the re-distribution of village land lie in the evidence of holdings that were equally divided between two or more sectors of the village lands. But when we look for such examples, they turn out to be far from numerous. The vast majority of tenants' holdings did not consist of strips evenly divided between two or more cropping units. The distribution was more often highly irregular, and this fact has been a constant source of bewilderment to historians. Even the examples from Lincolnshire of estates comprising equal amounts of land in two halves of the village prove to be less tidy than we

[29] G. C. Homans, "Terroirs ordonnés et Champs orientés: une Hypothèse sur le Village anglais", *Annales d'histoire économique et sociale*, viii (1936), pp. 438-9; Seebohm, *op. cit.*, p. 27; P. F. Brandon, "Arable Farming in a Sussex Scarp-foot Parish during the late Middle Ages", *Sussex Arch. Coll.*, c (1962), p. 62.

imagined. Peter Cotes's grant of land in Cotes, already quoted, consisted of forty acres divided into two equal halves. But the details of the parcels composing it are as follows: 13½ acres lay on the north side of the village upon Lechebek, 3 acres less one rood upon Northills; on the south side 9 acres lay upon Lekbek, 8 acres upon Rodewale, 3 acres next Gilbert's court, and a further selion on the other side of the trench opposite the toft. Far from indicating an orderly allocation of tenants' lands throughout the village, the composition of this estate strongly suggests a collection of pieces, deliberately selected at this date or earlier to make an estate that conformed to some prior division of all the village lands. It prompts the suggestion that the division of village fields into halves, and later into thirds or quarters was intended to facilitate cultivation and grazing, but was implemented without much regard to the distribution of individual tenants' strips. After all, it would not have been difficult, within a generation, for the individual to rectify any irksome imbalance of crops by buying, leasing, or exchanging land. Moreover, additional land was being assarted at the same time: some of it was held in severalty; some of it was assarted by cooperative effort and immediately divided into strips and added to the existing field courses. There were plenty of occasions for re-shaping a lop-sided holding, even though many peasants did not apparently deem it necessary to do so. If this is a reasonable hypothesis, it removes some of the problems of explaining how field courses could be re-organized from time to time without any elaborate preliminaries or consequences. When we encounter a decision in the court roll of the manor of Crowle, Isle of Axholme, in 1381 to divide the fields into four parts in order to fallow a quarter each year, and when the villagers of Marton, north Yorkshire, in the fourteenth century appointed men "to do and ordain as best they can to cast the field into three parts so that one part every year be fallow", we do not have to look for a wholesale re-allocation of tenants' land.[30]

This survey of some of the early evidence of common-field practices does not allow us to say with any certainty when the first village took a decision to organize the cultivation *and* grazing of its arable fields on a village basis. A much more thorough examination of all the evidence will be necessary before this stage is reached. All we have been able to do so far is to recognize in documents of the twelfth and

[30] Lincs. Archives Office, Crowle manor 1, 34; Homans, *English Villagers*, p. 56.

thirteenth centuries some of the steps in the development of a common-field system. The earliest case cited here of regulated cropping by the whole village is dated 1156-7. It may have involved common grazing as well, but we cannot be certain. The first unmistakable statement about commoning by a whole village dates from 1240. With some assurance, then, we can point to the twelfth and first half of the thirteenth centuries as possibly the crucial ones in the development of village-organized common-field systems.

To reach this stage of our argument, we have been obliged to use scraps of information from many different manors and villages, and it may not have escaped the notice of the observant reader that some of the illustrations used here are drawn from districts of England in which the final system did not usually contain two or three arable fields on the classic model, but one or many fields. Some explanation is called for. The distinction between the two- and three-field system, on the one hand, and systems with other numbers of fields on the other, is not, I submit, a fundamental one that indicates a different origin, as H. L. Gray maintained. The two systems coincide with, and arise out of, the distinction between arable and pasture farming types. The two- and three-field system characterized arable, that is mixed farming districts. Villages with more or fewer common fields were mainly pasture-farming communities. I have argued elsewhere that the principal difference between the communal farming practices of the forest and pastoral areas, on the one hand, and the arable areas on the other was that in the latter the common-field system reached a more mature stage of development. In the pastoral areas, common arable fields were not unknown, but they were small in comparison with the acreage of pastures. Grassland was the mainstay of the economy and arable crops were grown for subsistence only. Hence the arable fields did not have to be cropped with the utmost economy; their small area lessened the problems of ensuring access to all tenants' parcels; and the stubble did not have to be economically grazed owing to the abundance of other pasture. For these reasons, there was no urgent necessity to control rigorously the cultivation of the ploughland. In the pastoral villages of the Lincolnshire fenland, for example, no attempt was ever made to order the strip fields on a village basis.[31]

If pastoral areas were slow to regulate their ploughland as a village

[31] Thirsk, "The Farming Regions of England," cited in note 17. The importance of arable husbandry in forcing the growth of the common-field system is also stressed in Ilešič, *op. cit.* (cited in note 8 above), pp. 73, 75, 114.

concern, we begin to understand why enclosure was for them a painless and peaceful process. For agreements between two persons or a small group to extinguish common rights over the arable were far more easily reached, as the charters of Missenden abbey readily demonstrate, than agreements between all the inhabitants of the village. Far-reaching conclusions follow from this argument if it is pursued to its logical end. The areas of England which we are accustomed to label as "early enclosed" — central Suffolk, most of Essex, Hertfordshire, parts of Shropshire, Herefordshire, Somerset, Devon, and Cornwall — were pastoral districts in the sixteenth century, and were more easily enclosed because they had never known a fully developed common-field system.

Finally, it is necessary to revert again to the unanswered question, posed in this paper, namely the date of the earliest complete common-field system to be found in England. It is clear that the mature system was liable to come into operation at different times in different parts of the kingdom. Professor Hilton's introduction to the Stoneleigh Leger Book shows that common fields in this forest area were in process of creation in the period 1250-1350. Mr. Elliott's study of Cumberland common fields hints at an even later process of evolution, as well as supplying some excellent examples of one phase in gestation when closes were shared between several tenants. Mr. Glanville Jones has recently argued that Welsh bond hamlets with their open field share-lands are well documented in the Middle Ages and go back to the Early Iron Age; if the argument presented here is at all acceptable, then we may recognize in this case too the first signs of a field pattern that might evolve later into a common-field system. For there is no reason to regard Wales, or England, for that matter, as a special case. One point is established beyond reasonable doubt by the comparisons drawn here between English and Continental experience, namely, that in those West and East European countries in which field systems have been analysed with some care, the evolution of the common fields appears to have followed much the same course. In all cases the presence of a sufficiently large and growing population, compelled to cultivate its land more intensively, was a pre-condition of growth. It should also be said that there is no reason to think that the social framework in which common-field systems emerged necessarily influenced their form. They could evolve in a thoroughly authoritarian society, in which the lord allotted land to his men — there are German examples to show this occurring in a pioneering community under the close surveillance of the lord. They could just as well take shape in a society of free colonists, such as that depicted in the East Riding of Yorkshire in the twelfth and thirteenth centuries.[32]

[32] Hilton, *The Stoneleigh Leger Book*, p. liv; G. Elliott, "The System of Cultivation and Evidence of Enclosure in the Cumberland Open Fields in the Sixteenth Century", *Trans. Cumb. and Westm. Antiq. and Arch. Soc.*, N.S., lix (1959), pp. 85, 87, 95, 99; Glanville Jones, "Early Territorial Organization in England and Wales", *Geogr. Annaler*, xliii (1961), pp. 175-6.

2. *Medieval England and the Open-Field System*[*]

J. Z. TITOW

IN A RECENT ARTICLE ON "THE COMMON FIELDS",[†] DR. THIRSK ATTACKED the orthodox view — for long embodied in the Gray-Orwin exposition of the subject[1] — on the origins and early history of the open-field system in England. Her views are novel and stimulating but they should not be left unchallenged. In this discussion I intend to deal broadly, and briefly, with the more controversial aspects of her argument.

I

Dr. Thirsk's article opens with the following definition of the open-field system:

> It is composed of four essential elements. First, the arable and meadow is divided into strips among the cultivators, each of whom may occupy a number of strips scattered about the fields. Secondly, both arable and meadow are thrown open for common pasturing by the stock of all the commoners after the harvest and in fallow seasons. In the arable fields, this means necessarily that some rules about cropping are observed so that spring and winter-sown crops may be grown in separate fields or furlongs. Thirdly, there is common pasturage and waste, where the cultivators of strips enjoy the right to graze stock and gather timber, peat and other commodities, when available, such as stone and coal. Fourthly, the ordering of these activities is regulated by an assembly of cultivators — the manorial court, in most places in the Middle Ages, or, when more than one manor was present in a township, a village meeting (pp. 10-11).

This definition is quite unobjectionable, though it could be argued that its third element — common rights over the waste — admittedly a usual concommitant of the open-field system is not, strictly speaking, essential to it. It is quite possible to envisage a situation whereby a certain manor, at a certain time, had used up all its waste but nevertheless exploited its arable on the open-field basis. But this is a minor point in no way affecting subsequent arguments.

[*] I am grateful to Professor M. M. Postan and Professor A. W. Coats for their valuable comments on the original draft of this paper.

[†] J. Thirsk, "The Common Fields", reprinted as chapter 1 above. All subsequent page references refer to that chapter. Dr. Thirsk uses the phrase "common-field" instead of the more usual "open-field" throughout; I have reverted to the more common usage since, in the past, all the major studies of English medieval field systems regarded the two terms as freely interchangeable.

[1] H. L. Gray, *English Field Systems* (Cambridge, Mass., 1915); C. S. and C. S. Orwin, *The Open Fields* (Oxford, 1938: 2nd edn., 1954).

To have defined the system, however, is not enough. It is not sufficient to define at the start the "what" of our search; it is equally essential to define the "where" of it, as well. Unless this is done it must be assumed that attempts to show that the open-field system as it is normally understood did not come into being until the later middle ages relate only to those parts of England which are commonly held to have practised the system. Scraps of information gathered from areas which are not usually held to have practised it, such as Kent, East Anglia, Northumberland or Wales, must be ruled out as clearly irrelevant when used as arguments about the existence of the open-field system over other parts of the country. In what follows, therefore, I am confining my arguments to those parts of the country which are commonly held to have been under the open-field system in the Middle Ages.

Likewise the discussion of developments in Germany or Yugoslavia is irrelevant to the English case. Many English battles have been won in the past on the soil of Europe but I fail to see why all the engagements of this particular battle have to be fought on the fields of Germany, especially when, as Dr. Thirsk herself admits, "the German evidence is . . . , if anything, more scanty than the English in the Middle Ages" (p. 17).

Two other preliminary general points must be made. The phrase "there is no evidence" runs — quite rightly — like a *leitmotif* through the whole article; but it would no doubt be agreed that this can be a misleading argument. First the mere fact that certain features are not recorded in extant documents does not necessarily mean that they were not present at the time. There are many features which the documents were not intended to record but which we know did exist from accidental glimpses of them. For example, most information about the distribution of peasant holdings in the fields is purely accidental to the main purpose of medieval documents. Second, if one moves beyond the eleventh century (or in some cases even beyond the thirteenth century) the amount of evidence on the subject of field systems in operation is so scanty as to be virtually non-existent. This total lack of any evidence at all is certainly no proof that the open-field system existed at the time; but it is *equally no proof that the alternative system of cultivation in severalty* was practised.

In fact, at some points, Dr. Thirsk shows herself aware of the difficulty of arguing from silence of documents. Thus, when commenting on an important passage in Ine's Laws, clearly referring to common grazing rights over arable, Dr. Thirsk concludes that "there is nothing in . . . [it] . . . to support the idea that in the late seventh century common grazing after harvest was practised in common fields or meadows on a village basis", and she goes on to say that "where no evidence exists there is no place for assumptions" (p. 12). One could not disagree more with the latter statement. Where *conclusive* evidence exists there is no need for assumptions. But where such evidence is lacking, assumptions may indeed be made. And this is precisely what Dr. Thirsk herself is doing, here and elsewhere. She interprets this passage from Ine's Laws as evidence of the existence of common rights of coparceners over fields held by them in severalty and cultivated jointly. Why should this interpretation be considered less of an "assumption" than the orthodox interpretation of the same passage? Similarly, much of her discussion is highly speculative, for it concerns itself with an *assumed* system of cultivation in severalty, with what it might have looked like, and how it might have arisen.

In the course of her article Dr. Thirsk makes a number of useful observations the limitations of which, however, may not be necessarily as self-evident to others as they are to medieval specialists. The early pages of the article add up to a conclusion which is obviously crucial: namely, that in the twelfth and thirteenth centuries essential elements of the open-field system were absent in many parts of England. The argument proceeds in three stages. Firstly, known references to common grazing rights are dismissed as inconclusive. Second, the existence of strips — an undisputed feature of the open-field system when it can first be studied in its entirety — is taken to represent something other than a feature of the open-field system. Third, lack of conclusive evidence of communally agreed rotation of crops is represented as absence of such rotation. It is my contention that these arguments, in the form in which they are presented, do not add up to the crucial general conclusion *except with an amended definition of the open-field system in mind.*

Let us look at these arguments a little more closely. First, a few early pieces of evidence referring to common grazing rights or to orderly distribution of strips in the fields are dismissed as instances of special arrangements between coparceners; and it is suggested "that in the earliest strip-fields cultivators may not have enjoyed common rights over *all* the arable fields of the township. If so, an essential ingredient of the *mature* common-field system was missing" (p. 12; italics mine). Next, a few quotations from studies of individual estates or manors are brought in to show that even on demesne land there is often no clear evidence of a regulated crop rotation. It is then concluded that if this is so then "another ingredient of the common-field system — regulated crop rotations — was missing from at least some villages in the later Middle Ages" (p. 13). Is this conclusion valid on the basis of the examples quoted?

The citation from Miss Levett (p. 13) clearly shows that she believed that on the St. Albans' estates a three-field system existed except that it was "decaying or imperfectly developed". That from Professor Hilton's study of the manor of Kirby Bellars (p. 13) clearly postulates a frame-work of a three-field system except that he qualifies it as being flexible. The second quotation from Professor Hilton's study of the manor of Stoneleigh (p. 13) clearly mentions the existence of common-fields and merely explains that they were not divided into two, or three, great fields. The same point is illustrated by the quotations (p. 13) from the studies by Miss Davenport of the manor of Forncett and by Mr. Skipp and Mr. Hastings of the manor of Church Bickenhill. This is a far cry from saying that they add up to evidence that "essential elements" of the open-field system are missing, unless, of course, it is maintained that the open-field system must: (i) include all the arable, (ii) be rigid, (iii) involve all villagers, (iv) have the arable in the form of two or three great fields only. But such qualifications form no part of the original definition of the system; and the citing of these cases as evidence that "essential elements" are missing clearly implies too narrow or too rigid a definition.

The clues to Dr. Thirsk's real definition are to be found, I think, in such adjectives as "complete", "fully-fledged", or "mature" which occur throughout the text to describe the open-field system whenever it is under attack. It is difficult to escape the impression that what she understands by the open-field system is not the definition with which she begins, but the picture of the system as it was in the late sixteenth or seventeenth centuries, that is, at the earliest time when documents permit us to see it in its entirety. Such a criterion is clearly inadmissible. Her opening definition is useful because it concentrates on essentials. But if absolute identity in every respect with the open-field system as it is depicted in much later documents is to be used to determine the presence, or absence, of the system in the Middle Ages, then the whole exercise is unnecessary. It is quite unhistorical to expect to find no changes in the agrarian system of the country over a period of several centuries; in fact it would be very surprising if no such changes were to be found. The fact that the open-field system as operated in the Middle Ages differed from the system as present in later centuries is as one would expect it to be. The real issue is whether it differed in essentials or accidentals.

Among the non-essentials at least three major points deserve mention. It is not essential: (i) that all, or even most of the arable land should be in the common fields; (ii) that the strips should be distributed equally among the fields or nearly so; (iii) that the two or three "rotational" fields[2] should correspond on the ground to two or three great fields — they may represent permanent groupings of more than one real field each. None of these points contradicts Dr. Thirsk's opening definition. She talks there of the "arable . . . divided into strips" not all the arable, of "strips scattered about the fields" not equally divided among the fields, of crops grown "in the arable fields . . . in separate fields or furlongs" not of crops grown in two or three great fields only. In fact, all the proven points in Dr. Thirsk's arguments so far cited merely show that the open-field system as it existed in the Middle Ages differed in non-essentials from its later version.

II

It has been necessary to dwell on these points because the first part of the article is crucial. What follows are not so much conclusions forced upon us by an examination of relevant evidence, as logical necessities consequent on the acceptance of the general conclusion that the open-field system was not present, in all its essentials, before the twelfth or thirteenth centuries. If it is accepted that the open-field system only emerged during the twelfth and thirteenth centuries, then two things follow: on the one hand, it becomes necessary to discover some alternative system presumably in operation before then; on the other hand, it becomes necessary to discover wholesale and general re-allocations of land over the crucial period to explain those regularities manifest in the documents which are clearly too orderly to have arisen by some haphazard process of natural evolution.

How well do these logical necessities stand up to historical investigation? The need to explain away all medieval features which resemble open-field features too closely for comfort immediately encounters two major difficulties: first, the references to common grazing rights; and second, the evidence of holdings being distributed among the fields.

The various Anglo-Saxon references to rights of common, or, to strips, are explained as referring to coparceners. Such an interpretation is perfectly legitimate since these early references are

---

[2] A lot of unnecessary confusion would be eliminated if Professor Homans' terminology on the basic division of the village arable under the open-field system could be adopted: i.e. division not into two or three *fields*, but into two or three *sectors*. G. C. Homans, *English Villagers of the Thirteenth Century* (Harvard, 1942).

never explicit enough to preclude alternative interpretations.   The twelfth- and thirteenth-century references to rights of common, on the other hand, present a more intractable problem.   Since there is no logical obstacle to the acceptance of post-medieval references to common grazing rights as referring to features of the open-field system, these are accepted as such.   But the twelfth- and thirteenth-century references to similar rights cannot be so accepted since it has already been concluded that the system did not exist at the time. Dr. Thirsk overcomes this difficulty by arguing that there is an essential difference in such rights before, and after *c.* 1250. A number of twelfth- and thirteenth-century examples is cited, followed by the conclusion that "if we assimilate these examples into one generalization, we may say that rights of grazing over arable land were still being shared by neighbours in the twelfth century, but before the middle of the thirteenth century there were villages in which *all* tenants shared common rights in *all* fields" (p. 25; italics mine).

If the argument, that there was a change-over from rights of common held individually to rights of common enjoyed by all tenants over all arable about 1250, could be proved, it would undermine the belief that the open-field system existed earlier. But the instances quoted by Dr. Thirsk do not support such a sweeping conclusion.   They fall into two categories: cases of transfers of rights of common between individuals, and cases of disputes in the manorial courts.   As to the former, her conclusion rests on the fact that common rights were exchanged between *individuals*; and as to the latter, it depends on a peculiar interpretation of the phraseology of the court roll entries.

With the former category it is necessary, in the first place, to remember that all rights of common were *tenant* rights, i.e. that they were not rights enjoyed by everybody but rights entered upon on acquisition of a holding.   Dr. Thirsk herself seems to be aware of this distinction, for in her opening definition of the open-field system she talks of common rights enjoyed by "cultivators- of the strips" or "commoners", not all villagers.   There is, therefore, nothing unusual in transfers of land with rights of common between individuals, and to construe such transfers as implying that rights of common were only enjoyed by certain individuals over their own land is to misread the evidence.   The second point to notice is that, nominally, all the land of the manor was under the lord's control and he could, therefore, grant away holdings with rights of common. There is nothing special or unusual about this.   The case of the grants of land and pasture rights between Selbourne Priory and Henry Wyard and his wife, cited by Dr. Thirsk (p. 24), is a straightforward example of such a grant.

All the examples in the second category support Dr. Thirsk's conclusion only under very strained interpretation. The case from the manor of Wakefield (p. 24) shows that the complainant had a quarrel with *four other persons*. In the next example from the manor of Hales the complainant had a quarrel with one named person *and others*. In yet another example from the manor of Wakefield German Philcock was restrained from behaving in a way injurious to *his neighbours*. And why not? Why cannot a man quarrel with some persons having rights of common without entailing the conclusion that others did not have them? Why must we assume that the expression "neighbours" excludes everybody except neighbours in the literal sense when even nowadays we are often exhorted to do our neighbours no harm without meaning only the chaps in the houses to the left and to the right of us? The term "neighbours" is constantly used in medieval manorial documents as a synonym for the more cumbersome phrase "and other persons concerned", and although the narrow literal use is not precluded such an interpretation seems to me unnecessarily constricted. What other phrases could the documents have used; *homagium*, "the whole township", or some such descriptive phrase as "all those who have rights of common in the aforesaid fields"? Surely, the two former terms would be quite inappropriate since they would, by definition, include persons without such rights, while the latter would be too cumbersome and unnecessarily precise.

The second difficulty which the acceptance of Dr. Thirsk's crucial conclusion requires us to explain is the undisputed evidence of the presence of strips in the fields in the medieval period. So coparcenage, conveyance of pieces of land, and partible inheritance, are brought in to explain them. We are told that the orderly distribution of strips in the fields *cannot* be a feature of the original settlement. But why not? Because we know "from the experience of German, Welsh, and Irish villages that, in a matter of two generations, a pattern of land occupation could be changed out of recognition through conveyances of pieces and the division of fields among parceners" (p. 28). Surely, this is totally irrelevant. Is there any evidence that in those parts of England which are generally taken to be open-field territory, (i) coparcenage was a general feature, (ii) composition of holdings was being constantly altered out of recognition, and (iii) partible inheritance was widespread? These are the relevant questions and the answer to them is quite unequivocal. Coparcenage and partible inheritance — which we are told are responsible for the presence of the strips in the fields — are conspicuously absent from the manorial documents of the relevant areas; their presence, consequently, has to be inferred, contrary to indisputable evidence to the contrary, in order to satisfy a logical necessity in a preconceived argument. In so far as customary land is concerned, and whatever may have been the original position, undivided inheritance — primogeniture or ultimogeniture (Borough English) — was, unquestionably, the rule in the relevant parts of England in the twelfth and thirteenth century. The fact that the *"pamphleteers during the Interregnum"* thought primogeniture "the most unreasonable descent", or that partible inheritance was practised *"in the sixteenth century* in many of the less densely-settled *pastoral areas of the north"* (pp. 19–20; italics mine) cannot be seriously taken as proofs to the contrary.

The well-known example of colonization in Yorkshire which Dr. Thirsk quotes (p. 21)[3] is interesting but its true significance seems to me to be different from that suggested by her. No one would expect to find the open-field system in a place where a few straggling settlers cultivated a few acres of assart. The real lesson of the Yorkshire example seems to be that as soon as a settlement increased in size to become a village community, it tended to adopt the open-field system of cultivation, presumably because this seemed to the settlers the most appropriate system for community farming — and it must have been a system known to them from their general knowledge or their experience in whatever place they came from. The Yorkshire evidence provides a clear example of what happened when arable cultivation was started completely from scratch. But the time when villages in other parts of England had their first acres carved out of the waste by their original settlers was not for the most part the twelfth century but some time in the far distant past. If cultivation elsewhere had followed the same pattern as in Yorkshire the open-field system must have been established long before.

We come now to the last major difficulty which must be disposed of if Dr. Thirsk's original conclusion is to be accepted. If we agree that the more or less equal distribution of strips among the fields — an essential feature of the open-field system — is absent up to a relatively late date, then it becomes imperative to discover widespread and all-embracing reshaping of holdings. I do not know of any evidence

[3] After T. A. M. Bishop, "Assarting and the Growth of the Open Fields", *Econ. Hist. Rev.*, vi (1935-6).

for such re-shuffling. It could, of course, be argued that since there are no documents emanating from the peasants, inter-peasant arrangements could not be expected to appear in manorial documents. But would such an argument really be valid? In the thirteenth century, in most villages of the open-fields zone, the bulk of tenant land consisted of standard holdings, each representing a unit of clearly defined duties and obligations to the manorial lord. Are we to believe that an upheaval involving the totality of peasant holdings would have left no traces in the manorial documents of the thirteenth and fourteenth century? It hardly seems likely.

The more or less even distribution of strips among the fields is not, however, the only regular feature whose presence cannot be explained except by postulating organized and co-ordinated division or redistribution of land. It is an indisputable fact that at least as early as 1086 the bulk of peasant holdings in the relevant parts of the country consisted of certain types of uniform holdings: virgates, half-virgates, fardels and cotlonds in the south, bovates and their multiples in the north. They need not have been created at one go; but the nucleus of these standard holdings may well go back to the time of the original settlement itself and it must have been added to in an organized and co-ordinated fashion to account for the strong pattern of regularity so clearly present in the earliest relevant documents. If we accept Dr. Thirsk's argument, we would have to postulate not one but at least two wholesale redistributions of land: an earlier one which turned the mass of miscellaneous individual plots into a uniform pattern of standard holdings; and a later one which re-arranged the strips of all such holdings more or less evenly among the newly created two or three fields now cultivated on the basis of a newly adopted open-field system. Is it not really much simpler to envisage an original settlement which created the nucleus of the regular elements — the standard holdings, the strips, the even distribution among the rotational fields — and which was expanded in a rational way by succeeding generations of villagers? And why should it be difficult to accept such a solution when we have always been told that England was largely settled by bands of immigrants who would have been faced with the necessity of carrying out some distribution of land from the very start? One could even grant Dr. Thirsk the point that the open-field system might have been developed some time after their arrival. I find it, however, difficult to accept that it did not develop well before the thirteenth century.

Until the gap between the medieval period and the sixteenth- or seventeenth-century evidence, clearly showing the open-field system in existence, can be bridged by a chain of documentary evidence, it is surely best to start an enquiry into the medieval field systems with a careful examination of the contemporary English evidence for the relevant areas.   To start with *a priori* assumptions derived from studies of other societies or other regions is to encourage a search for bits of evidence supporting predetermined theories.   On one point however, Dr. Thirsk is undoubtedly right — in believing that the available factual evidence is too scanty and too equivocal to enable us to prove anything, and that the choice of interpretations must, consequently, depend on the balance of probabilities.

III

Let us then ask a few questions concerning the plausibility of rival interpretations.   What follows is, I believe, a fair summary of the normal position in the relevant parts of England as depicted in countless thirteenth and early fourteenth century documents.   However, before I proceed any further I must digress for a moment to safeguard myself against a possible charge from non-medievalists of failing to substantiate my claims, since I intend to give few references and even those only by way of illustration.

The reason for this is simple.   How does one give references to something which does not exist?   Take for instance the three main-stays of Dr. Thirsk's argument: coparcenage to explain medieval references to common rights, partible inheritance to account for the existence of strips, and free interchange of strips to account for their scattered distribution in the fields.   All these are conspicuously absent from the manorial documents for the relevant areas and yet had they existed the documents would have recorded them.   Similarly, it is very easy to give specific references to the atypical and the exceptional, but it is well nigh impossible to reference adequately the typical and the usual.   It is possible to find for the open-field area single instances of divided inheritance, of holdings held jointly by a number of tenants,[4] or of exchanges of strips between peasants.   But should a single reference to such instances be accorded the same weight as their complete absence in the vast majority of cases?   Take for instance the three estates in south-west England with some of the best series of thirteenth- and early fourteenth-century court fines:

---

[4] The presence in some of the twelfth- and early thirteenth-century surveys of holdings against which a number of names are recorded should not mislead casual readers into believing that these are necessarily instances of true coparcenage.

those of the bishopric of Winchester, of the abbey of Glastonbury and of Saint Swithin's Priory, Winchester. Between them, they cover over a hundred manors scattered throughout the south-west of England and parts of the home counties. The Winchester estates alone have over 50,000 entry fines between 1209 and 1350 with only an exceptional case of divided inheritance here and there; similarly on the other estates. Or take another example. When Professor Homans states categorically that in the champion country of England impartible inheritance was the rule[5] he gives no references. Non-medievalists may shout "unsubstantiated!" but any medievalist will know that Professor Homans is absolutely right. This is why I have said at the beginning that this digression is aimed at forestalling a possible charge from non-medievalists, for it is they who often lack the experience to distinguish between the typical and the exceptional in medieval sources.

The first point to notice about medieval evidence is that we know much more about demesne land than about tenants' land. We have frequently very full information on the distribution of demesne land (Surveys) and on the crop rotation followed on it (Grange Accounts), whereas such information is usually totally lacking for tenant land. This is so because the only type of medieval documents concerned directly with tenant land as such — the Custumals — are concerned exclusively with the size, obligations, and nominal occupants of the holdings, and not with their location or composition. The evidence of charters and court rolls, on the other hand, is usually fragmentary and inconclusive. An important distinction could perhaps usefully be drawn here. A single explicit reference to a piece of land lying "in the common field" (*in communi campo*) is sufficient to indicate the presence of the open-field system, but the reverse does not hold good; even a number of references to pieces of land held in severalty does not disprove the existence of open fields as well. It is true that explicit references to "common" fields are very rare before the end of the fourteenth century.[6] We should however be guilty of a gross misuse of our medieval evidence if we were to jump to the conclusion that the references in the late fourteenth century were due to the evolution of the system at that time. It simply happens that round about that time the documents in question become, in various ways, more informative than they have been hitherto.

[5] Homans, *op. cit.*, pp. 118, 121.
[6] The earliest instance known to me dates from 1332 but I may have over-looked an earlier one: Hampshire Record Office, Ecc. Comm. 2/159344, Bishops Waltham.

In so far as demesne land is concerned a vast amount of late thirteenth- and early fourteenth-century evidence for a regulated crop rotation exists for many localities showing that demesne land was being cultivated on what was basically two- or three-field system. That much is clear from cropping details which by the early fourteenth century are a common feature of manorial accounts, as well as from the actual descriptions of the location of demesne lands in the manorial surveys, in which they are often divided into two or three sectors. While it is true that on many manors a clear-cut two- or three-field system cannot be discerned, it would be wrong to conclude that it did not therefore exist.   Apart from the fact that not all the demesne lands lay in the open fields, the apparent lack of any obvious regularity of rotation may be partly an illusion due to the way in which the documents record the facts.   In my experience the most striking instances of such apparent lack of regular rotation are limited to large manors, small manors usually having very clear-cut arrangements. The explanation for this could be quite simple.   Very large manors nearly always include more than one settlement each with its own field systems.   We have therefore, in such cases, to deal with a cluster of open-field systems rather than with a single all-embracing open-field system; but the demesne which in reality consists of lands forming a part of each of these individual systems is entered in the documents as if it were a single unit.   It is thus obvious that any difference in cropping arrangements between these individual systems will introduce a measure of confusion into the description of cropping arrangements on the demesne.   If, as could sometimes be the case, some of the component systems operated on the two-field basis while others operated on the three-field basis, the rotation of crops on the demesne as depicted in a unitary grange account would quite misleadingly appear distinctly irregular.   It could, of course, be argued that the presence of regulated rotation on demesne land is not by itself sufficient evidence of the presence of a general open-field system.   For such an objection to be valid it must be shown that it was usual for demesne land to be bodily separated from tenant land, for only in such a situation does what happens on the demesne become irrelevant.   The solution to this difficulty must be based on probabilities rather than established facts.   If the two types of land were normally intermingled — and it seems to me that the balance of probabilities favours such a view — proof of regulated rotation on demesne land would automatically constitute conclusive evidence for regulated rotation on tenant land; if they were not intermingled, proof of the presence, or absence, of regulated rotation on tenant land would have to be sought elsewhere. Such evidence does, however, exist. The earliest surviving manorial surveys do contain some evidence that tenant land was also subject to a regulated rotation on the two- or three-field basis for they occasionally record tenants holding land "in one field and the other" (*in uno campo et in alio*), or "in each of the two fields" (*in utroque campo*),[7] or "in one field only" (*in uno campo, in uno campo et non in alio*),[8] or land from which rent was due "every other year" (*in uno anno, in uno anno et non in alio*),[9] or from which higher rent was due in one year than in the other.[10] Such entries, though usually (as one would expect) involving land of demesne or assart origin, are sometimes concerned with standard holdings and constitute clear evidence that regulated crop rotation on the basis of two- or three-field systems was known on tenant land in England in the twelfth century.

So far as the composition and distribution of tenant land is concerned the facts of the case amount to this. There is overwhelming evidence from all over what is usually considered the open-field area, that the bulk of ancient peasant land was already in the form of standard customary holdings at least as early as 1086. This is why the evidence of charters, which is practically the only evidence available to us on the distribution and composition of peasant holdings, should be used circumspectly. For land which is subject to transfer by charter is usually non-customary land, and thus almost irrelevant to our discussion. But even when the grantors of the charters were villeins — as they were in that remarkable Peterborough collection of villein charters, the *Carte Nativorum*[11] —

---

[7] Examples of such instances can be found on the following manors. Glastonbury Abbey: *Liber Henrici de Soliaco*, ed. J. E. Jackson (Roxburghe Club, 1882): Christmalford p. 112, Pilton p. 30, Newton p. 134, Mere p. 28, East Pennard p. 40, Ditcheat p. 36.   Shaftesbury Abbey: Chartulary of Shaftesbury Abbey, Brit. Mus., MS. Harl. 61: f. 86a (name of manor missing).

[8] Glastonbury: *op. cit.*, Nettleton p. 103, Blakeford p. 81, Pilton p. 30. Shaftesbury: *op. cit.*, Ywernia f. 46b.

[9] Glastonbury: *op. cit.*, Pilton p. 30, Ashbury p. 116, Winterbourne p. 123, Blakeford p. 81.   Evesham Priory: "Registrum Cartarum Abbatie de Evesham", Brit. Mus., MS. Cotton Vespasian B. xxiv, Beningthurda f. 34a, Baddesheie f. 50a, Lenewic f. 52b.

[10] Glastonbury: *op. cit.*, Winterbourne p. 123, Ashbury p. 116, East Brent p. 64, Blakeford p. 81.   Shaftesbury: *op. cit.*, Ywernia f. 46a.   These examples are clearly instances of somewhat uneven distribution of land between two cropping units.   Similar arrangements seem to be implied in a statement from yet another twelfth-century survey which informs us that at Hampton Lucy there were "three *bovarii* each of whom has seven acres in one year and eight in the other" (*quorum quisque habet in uno anno septem acras et in alio viii*): *The Red Book of Worcester*, ed. M. Hollings (Worcs. Hist. Soc., 1934), Pt. iii, p. 277.

[11] C. N. L. Brooke and M. M. Postan, eds., *Carte Nativorum, A Peterborough Abbey Cartulary of the Fourteenth Century* (Northants Rec. Soc., xx, 1960).

and the land transferred possibly customary land, the very fact that it consisted of odd acres of land which could be freely transferred shows its unusual character, and one must be very careful when arguing from such cases.   There is also a large body of evidence, from many parts of the country, showing that peasants held their land in strips scattered about the fields, very often in a way clearly implying that a two- or three-field system must have been in operation.[12]   But such evidence being again almost exclusively charter evidence, it could be argued that it does not apply to standard customary holdings and it is thus theoretically possible that these might have constituted compact blocks of arable.   However, in view of the fact that all other land seems to have been in strips scattered about the fields, such a supposition does not appear very convincing, and there is some evidence of standard customary holdings being similarly constituted.[13]

The problem of the even, as opposed to the merely scattered, distribution of strips in the fields is a distinct one and must be treated separately.   This is so because existing evidence almost exclusively concerns odd acres granted away, or exchanged, by a peasant.   If they were merely odds and ends, then they are unrepresentative; if they were parts of standard holdings their evidence may mislead because we do not know how large was the remaining portion of each holding and how it was distributed over the fields.   In view of this it is really quite remarkable how equally — without being pedantically exact — acres so granted were usually distributed over the fields.   Dr. Thirsk's statement that "the vast majority of tenants' holdings did not consist of strips evenly divided between two or more cropping units" (p. 28), admissible as an expression of belief, is unacceptable as a statement of fact.   In the vast majority of cases we simply do not know either way.   Most grants of complete standard holdings do not specify their composition, but when they do I have always found them to be remarkably evenly divided.   Equal division

[12] Even the most perfunctory glance at any of the published collections, or calendars, of thirteenth- and early fourteenth-century charters will produce examples by the dozen.   The following are suggested for their special interest or wide geographical coverage: Brooke and Postan, *op. cit.*; C. D. Ross, ed., *The Cartulary of Cirencester Abbey Gloucestershire* (Oxford, 1964) 2 vols.; N. Denholm-Young, ed., *Cartulary of the Mediaeval Archives of Christ Church, Oxford* (Oxford, 1931).

[13] E.g. Cirencester Abbey, *op. cit.*, no. 392/512, (vol. ii, p. 351): a grant of 1 virg. showing scattered distribution in many strips divided equally between the West Field and the East Field and interspersed among other tenants' lands, *c.* 1242.   Cirencester Abbey, *op. cit.*, no. 383 (vol. ii, p. 342): a grant of 1 virg. distributed over the North Field and the South Field, *c.* 1187.   Brooke and Postan, *Carte Nativorum*, no. 551 (p. 203), no. 555 (p. 217), both showing scattered distribution of virgated holdings though, in other respects, they represent exceptional circumstances.

between two cropping units seems also to be implied in some evidence from the surveys. For instance, when the twelfth-century surveys tell us that on a manor of Evesham Priory there were sixteen virgates and a half virgate *in alio anno*;[14] or that a tenant of Glastonbury Abbey held a virgate of land in *uno campo et non in alio*;[15] or that a tenant of Shaftesbury Abbey paid 18d. for his half-virgate holding every other year (*xviii. d. et nichil in altero*);[16] or a tenant of Glastonbury Abbey paid the rent for his half-virgate every other year (*in uno anno*);[17] or that some tenants of these estates paid higher rents for their holdings in one year than they did in the other;[18] it seems legitimate to assume that such exceptional instances of unequal distribution imply that all the other holdings were equally divided between the fields.

I would certainly not claim that the number of references to scattered distribution of strips over the fields is very great, or that they show that all the holdings of all the tenants in all the places were so distributed, or that the distribution was always even. On the other hand, whereas such references do exist in considerable numbers, and cumulatively add up to evidence for the presence of all the elements of the open-field system, there is no evidence at all that all, or even most, tenant land was held at any time or place exclusively in severalty.

In so far as tenant land is concerned, therefore, the questions to ask are these:

(1) Is it more likely that the regular pattern of the bulk of ancient peasant holdings is the result of organized distribution of the arable carried out well before 1086, or the result of some six centuries of un-coordinated clearance of land, uncontrolled except by the limitations on the individual's ability to clear land, and accompanied by unhampered conveyancing and subdivision of holdings?

(2) Are known instances of scattered distribution of peasant holdings more likely to represent the exception or the rule?

(3) In view of the fact that partible inheritance and dismembering of standard customary holdings by conveyance of pieces are clearly absent from the records of the relevant parts of England from at least 1200 onwards, is it more likely that twelfth- and thirteenth-century evidence of the distribution of holdings over the fields in strips is a sign of the open-field system being

[14] *Op. cit.*, Beningthurda, f. 34a. [15] *Op. cit.*, Nettleton, p. 105.
[16] *Op. cit.*, Melberia, f. 48a. [17] *Op. cit.*, Winterbourne, p. 123.
[18] See above notes 7-10.

operated or the result of the custom of partible inheritance and conveyancing of land which obtained in some remote past?

It is true that the thirteenth-century surveys and court rolls show that on many manors there were odd customary acres in existence, but we must beware of jumping to the conclusion that they must necessarily represent the break-up of old standard holdings. Their origin must obviously be a matter for speculation. Personally, I tend to think that they existed as odd acres from the very beginning rather than that they constitute fragments of broken-up standard holdings. There are numerous instances in the twelfth- and early thirteenth-century surveys of standard customary holdings of explicit assart or demesne origin and it would seem that in the past newly created holdings were looked upon as customary land, unlike the later practice when assarts and land obtained from the demesne were held as just so many acres enjoying a special status half-way between *terra libera* on the one hand and ancient customary land on the other. But even if they do in fact constitute fragments of standard holdings which have been broken up, it is clear, whenever surviving documents permit us to trace or evaluate changes over a period of time, that such fragmentation must have taken place in some remote past. It is equally clear that such fragmentation of standard customary holdings, even if it did take place in some distant past, had not reached any significant proportions by the time of Domesday Book and was probably brought to a halt soon afterwards. For not only are instances of such fragmentation very rare in the twelfth and thirteenth centuries — as any one comparing the number of virgated holdings in Domesday Book with the thirteenth-century manorial surveys, or tracing the fortunes of individual holdings through the manorial court rolls would notice; there are also occasional explicit statements to the effect that such fragmentation was frowned upon.

What lends Dr. Thirsk's case such an air of plausibility at times is the ease with which instances of irregularities can be found in thirteenth- and fourteenth-century documents. But is it right to expect such irregularities to be absent, or to take their presence for a sign of some strange goings-on? Surely, even the most regular, uniform and inflexible system of arable cultivation — and the medieval open-field system was certainly none of these — would have been bound to develop some irregular features after a century of the most active colonization ever recorded in this country.

If one surveys the manorial scene in the thirteenth century one of its most striking features is the presence of strong elements of both regularity and irregularity. The former is represented by what is basically a two- or three-field system of cultivation, by the uniform character of the bulk of the peasant holdings, and by the preservation of the basic unity of such holdings over the course of centuries. And yet some land — both demesne and tenant land — was held in severalty (in closes) and often cultivated outside the ordinary two- or three-field system. And alongside the regular ancient holdings, large numbers of new and irregular holdings of all sizes and shapes, of assart or demesne origin, also appear in the documents.

The crucial question to ask, therefore, is which of the two patterns, the one of regularity or the one of irregularity, is more likely to be the *underlying pattern*. Since most of the regular features seem to be the ancient ones, it seems to me advisable to consider the irregularities as a later overlay brought about by colonization and conveyancing of land not subject to the same extent of manorial control as the old standard holdings.

IV

What is then the final conclusion? It seems to me that the balance of the evidence points to the conclusion that all the essential features of the open-field system can be discerned in the thirteenth century though this evidence is far from being either conclusive or satisfactory. The balance of probabilities seems to be even more strongly in favour of the view that the open-field system, rather than the system of cultivation in severalty, was the dominant form of arable cultivation at the time. One must admit that, taken singly, many of Dr. Thirsk's specific interpretations are not impossible. But are involved explanations necessarily better than simple ones, and should we reject the obvious inference that the documents mean what they say when they mention common rights, common fields, or common practices? If Dr. Thirsk succeeds in showing that the evidence for the existence of the open-field system in the twelfth and thirteenth centuries is far from being conclusive or satisfactory, she does nothing to convince us that the evidence for the widespread prevalence of the alternative system of cultivation in severalty must be regarded as *more conclusive or satisfactory*. But I would like to make it quite clear that in what I have said here I have been not so much defending the orthodox view about the open-field system in medieval England, as trying to show why I find Dr. Thirsk's particular line of attack on that view unconvincing. Let us hope that her article will stimulate new research into the problem. If this happens, whatever the ultimate verdict may be, we shall all be in her debt.

A POSTSCRIPT, 1976

As I have tried to indicate above, the main obstacle to defending successfully the view that the Open Field System existed in, and before, the thirteenth century and, *mutatis mutandis*, the greatest boon to the would-be attackers of the traditionalist position, is the very laconic nature of the references to agricultural practices in the documents of the period. At best we have a number of scattered references to holdings being held "in common" or "in common fields", or to their being scattered in strips throughout some larger units of arable cultivation; at the worst, the subject is passed over in silence.

Whether such references, taken individually, represent elements of the Open Field System, or something else; whether, collectively, they add up to all the essential elements of the Open Field System, is not something that can be settled conclusively without more explicit information. And if the dearth of more explicit information is so great in the relatively well-documented thirteenth century, what hope is there of finding it for the earlier centuries? In my ignorance I thought none.

It was, therefore, with considerable gratification that I have recently come across two pieces of information which, I believe, considerably strengthen my case. The late Professor Finberg in his latest publication draws attention to two facts which have emerged from his extensive studies of late Anglo-Saxon charters: "the unquestionable evidence" of intermixed acres (often described as "lying in common") in tenth-century charters and, more importantly to my argument, an instance in which a tenth-century charter not only describes a holding as "lying in common" but actually defines what this means.[1] And what this means is "that the open pasture is common, the meadow is common, and the arable is common".

This explicit tenth-century explanation provides clear proof of the existence of the Open Field System, in all its essentials, as early as the tenth century, at least in one part of England. It also creates, in my view, a very strong presumption that all the other unexplained references to land "lying in common", from the broad area later clearly associated with the Open Field System, should be interpreted in the same way.

[1] H. P. R. Finberg, *The Formation of England 550-1042* (London, 1974), pp. 200-1.

3. *The Origin of the Common Fields*

JOAN THIRSK

I HAVE TO THANK DR. TITOW FOR GIVING ME A CLAIM TO MORE SPACE IN *Past and Present* and so enabling me to elaborate upon some of the problems raised by my article in No. 29 (December, 1964).* It was intended to open a fresh discussion on the origins of the common-field system. Why, how, and when did it take this form? Dr. Titow offers two different answers to these questions, which are designed to meet all cases. Farmers, founding a settlement for the first time, laid out standard holdings in intermingled strips equally divided between the rotational fields and then expanded the area of land in cultivation in succeeding generations (p. 41). In short, the system was fully worked out in men's minds before they imposed it on the land. The second explanation meets the case of villages in the East Riding where the documents suggest that a group of farmers with ring-fence farms in the mid-twelfth century had turned themselves into a common-field village by the sixteenth century, if not a great deal earlier. Dr. Titow explains the situation thus:

> No one would expect to find the open-field system in a place where a few straggling ["straggling" is surely a gratuitous adjective] settlers cultivated a few acres of assart . . . . As soon as a settlement increased in size to become a village community, it tended to adopt the open-field system of cultivation, presumably because this seemed to the settlers the most appropriate system for community farming — and it must have been a system known to them from their general knowledge or their experience in whatever place they came from (p. 40).

Thus, in the first explanation the common-field system is taken as an idea already fully formulated before it was put into operation. In the second case three vital questions are ignored: first, why did the growth of a village community make people want community farming in place of their existing arrangements; second, how did the change take place, quietly by a process of evolution, or by a decisive break with the past and a fresh start; third, when was the system adopted? Dr. Titow has decided that it was devised long before any documents begin and that all communities who subsequently adopted it were copying the examples of others. This he rightly calls a simple explanation. But it is simple only because it dismisses as insoluble

---

* Joan Thirsk, "The Common Fields", *Past and Present*, no. 29 (December, 1964); J. Z. Titow, "Medieval England and the Open-Field System", *ibid.*, no. 32 (December, 1965). Reprinted as chapters 1 and 2 above.

all the problems which I was trying to explore. Perhaps they *are* insoluble, but I am not yet satisfied that we have to accept this as the final verdict. Most of our documentary evidence has been examined by historians with the same strong preconceptions as Dr. Titow, namely, that the common-field system was in full operation before our documents begin. My article was intended to encourage the re-examination of the evidence without preconceptions. I know this is a difficult exercise, but it may in the end advance our knowledge and for that reason I consider it worth doing. It has led me to incur the charge from Dr. Titow that I have forced my own unorthodox and novel interpretations upon words which have perfectly straight-forward meanings (pp. 39, 49). I admit that my scepticism has grown so great that I question all accepted meanings. But I hoped to show that interpretations other than the orthodox ones are possible. I do not wish my interpretations to become a new orthodoxy unless and until they have been better tested.

I do not propose here to enter into a debate with Dr. Titow about the precise meanings of particular phrases in single documents. These will only be made clear by the re-examination of far more evidence than that which I cited. Instead I wish to take up some of Dr. Titow's more general statements which I consider disputable, and which, if not contested now, may confuse subsequent discussion by others.

1.   I deplore Dr. Titow's statement that evidence from the Continent of Europe is irrelevant to my discussion of the origins of the common-field system. I am tempted to provoke Dr. Titow further by declaring that we may also learn something from the study of peasant cultivation in present-day Asia, Africa, and South America, where examples abound of intermingled strips, though not, I believe, usually accompanied by common rules about rotations and grazing. But if we narrow the scope of our enquiry a little, and agree that the common-field system is not a world phenomenon, it is at least a European one.

2.   Dr. Titow makes several references (pp. 34, 40) to the areas (which he does not himself define) which are commonly held to have practised a common-field system. Northumberland, Wales, East Anglia, and Kent, he says, are not areas of common fields. In fact, of course, there are excellent examples of common-field systems in all these areas except Kent. Moreover, the old generalizations about the geographical distribution of common fields need thorough revision, for much that was once accepted as evidence of common fields merely

illustrates the presence of intermingled strips; it does not necessarily follow that such strips were part of a common-field system. This has been demonstrated in recent studies of the Lincolnshire fenland and of Kent, where intermingled strips were independently cultivated by their occupiers and were not subject to common rules.[1] Since it is essential to make these differences clear by the use of a precise terminology, I have followed the usage recommended in the Glossary of Terms published in the *Agricultural History Review*,[2] and have employed the term *common field* for land worked under a common-field system, reserving *open field* for land lying in strips but not subject to common grazing rights. Dr. Titow's persistence in regarding the terms *open field* and *common field* as freely interchangeable (p. 33, note †) will confuse rather than clarify the interpretation of the evidence.

3. The word *common* which appears so often in medieval documents has for Dr. Titow a perfectly straightforward meaning (p. 43). It describes land worked under the common-field system. But Dr. A. R. H. Baker has demonstrated that in Kent a *common field* simply meant a field of intermingled strips.[3] How can we be certain, without examining the matter again, that in the earliest medieval documents it did not have the same meaning? Professor Hilton has recently traced changes in the meaning of the word "freedom" in the Middle Ages.[4] I suggest that we must be equally watchful for changing meanings of agrarian terms.

4. I agree with Dr. Titow that the rule of impartible inheritance came to dominate customary land in champion areas while partible inheritance persisted in the pastoral regions (p. 43). But this dominance was far from complete in the thirteenth century, and in any case some manors had less customary land and more free land than others. Moreover, within the framework of this broad generalization, changes of emphasis can be observed at different periods. Dr. Faith has suggested that in periods when land was plentiful peasants were less concerned to keep their land in the family than in periods of land shortage when heirs insisted on their inheritance rights.[5] In the thirteenth century when population was increasing, in some places

---

[1] See my original article, p. 22.

[2] R. A. Butlin, "Some Terms used in Agrarian History. A Glossary", *Agric. Hist. Rev.*, ix (1961), pp. 98-104.

[3] A. R. H. Baker, "Field Systems in the Vale of Holmesdale", *Agric. Hist. Rev.*, xiv (1966), pp. 7, 9.

[4] R. H. Hilton, "Freedom and Villeinage in England", *Past and Present*, no. 31 (July, 1965).

[5] Rosamond Faith, "Peasant Families and Inheritance Customs in Medieval England", *Agric. Hist. Rev.*, xiv (1966), p. 89.

very rapidly as Dr. Titow has shown in his excellent description of customary tenancies on the manor of Taunton,[6] a modest revival of partible inheritance could easily have aggravated the organizational problems of cultivation in champion areas by increasing the number of parcels. There are signs in the Tudor period that partible inheritance, coupled with the rise of population, brought to a head a number of problems which were merely latent in periods when numbers were stable or falling: the size of holdings was falling alarmingly, and complaints to this effect were explicit; but implicit in these complaints was also an increase in the number of parcels. This, indeed, may be the reason why descriptions of the workings of the common-field system accumulate at this period — because the organizational difficulties created by increasing numbers of people made stricter rules necessary. Our experience of life in England at the present day does not help much towards the understanding of the common-field system, but it does at least reinforce this point that a rise of population calls forth a host of regulations and restrictions affecting the use of land.

Borough English, the third custom of inheritance, is treated by Dr. Titow as having the same effect as primogeniture, resulting in a holding passing undivided to one son (p. 40). Here again there is some room for doubt about the universal truth of this statement. Dr. Faith has argued persuasively that the descent of land to the youngest son is a "fossilized" form of partible inheritance, for part of the rule of gavelkind was special provision for the youngest son.[7] I would like to be reassured that holdings subject to Borough English always passed intact to the youngest son and were not used before death to provide a nucleus of a holding for other sons. On the manor of Taunton Dr. Titow showed how in a period of acute land shortage sons without an inheritance in prospect married widows with land. This was an admirable solution, but it was only made possible by the custom of the manor relating to widows' rights. Not all widows on all manors could offer the same inviting prospect to land-hungry young men. My suspicions about Borough English are deepened by the fact that it was still a strong custom in forest areas in the sixteenth century, and these were notorious for their many small holdings. Did Borough English have anything to do with it? This

---

[6] J. Z. Titow, "Some Differences between Manors and their Effects on the Condition of the Peasant in the Thirteenth Century", *Agric. Hist. Rev.*, x (1962), pp. 1-13. See also J. Z. Titow, "Some Evidence of the Thirteenth-Century Population Increase", *Econ. Hist. Rev.*, 2nd ser., xiv (1961-2), pp. 218-24.

[7] Rosamond Faith, *op. cit.*

paragraph is full of possibilities and suspicions rather than certainties, but there is some justification here for looking again at the alleged dominance of single-son inheritance in champion areas in the thirteenth century. I would like this door left open despite Dr. Titow's desire to close it.

5. My definition of the common-field system is based on the way things worked in the sixteenth and seventeenth centuries when our documents make the arrangements reasonably clear (p. 36). This is the way our textbooks present it, and the way we are led to believe it worked from the beginning. Dr. Titow thinks it quite unhistorical to believe that changes did not take place over a period of several centuries (p. 36). So do I. But he allows only for a certain untidiness, overlying an original tidy arrangement. I envisage the casual development of a field system which arrived at its most systematic form at varying dates in different villages between about the thirteenth and eighteenth centuries. I do not believe that the emergence of the common-field system necessarily involved a major reallocation of holdings; I endeavoured to make this clear on page 29 of my article. On the other hand I do not exclude the possibility that this happened in some cases. Nor did I argue that all land was held in severalty before the thirteenth century (p. 49).[8] On the contrary, I see evidence of intermingled strips over which neighbours, sharing one or more fields, may have organized their own rotations and common grazing. This is a kind of half-way house between land in severalty and land under a common-field system. It may not involve the intervention of the village community or manorial court. Does this perhaps explain why the first entries (referring to agricultural disputes) in the manor court rolls of the later twelfth and thirteenth centuries are concerned with asserting only the lord's rights against individuals who have damaged *his* crops and injured *his* stock? Claims by other tenants against their neighbours were the exception. This, however, raises the question why, how, and when the manor court took up issues which were really a village concern. If the common-field system, as Dr. Titow envisages it, existed from time immemorial, perhaps a village commune upheld rules of cultivation until its authority was taken over by the manorial court. Or were the rules first taking shape, as I have argued, when the manorial

---

[8] I entirely agree with Dr. Titow that the bulk of ancient peasant land was already in the form of a standard customary holding as early as 1086 (p. 45) But I know no evidence to prove that at this date the virgates and bovates consisted of intermingled strips, as he implies. This is not made clear until the twelfth and thirteenth centuries when we first see them at closer quarters.

court was developing its authority for enforcing them? Questions phrased in this way are perhaps impossible to answer. But an assembly of information about the antiquity of the village commune would contribute helpful circumstantial evidence.

From a desire to make my original article as concise as possible I did not make explicit all the problems that surround this subject. Nor have I done so here. There are questions about the development of the common-field system after the Black Death, for example. Did it collapse in some places, only to revive again in the sixteenth century? Clearly, my questions do not make the path of the agrarian historian easy. But the answers which Dr. Titow puts forward, and which rest, as he admits, on a balance of probabilities, do not seem to me lifelike. I shall continue to search for material by which to test my hypothesis, and hope that medieval historians who are far more conversant with the sources than I, will lend a hand.

4. *The English Inflation of 1180-1220*[*]

P. D. A. HARVEY

HISTORIANS HAVE FOR LONG BEEN AWARE OF THE RISE IN PRICES THAT occurred in thirteenth-century England. In 1908 Sir James Ramsay gave examples to show that "prices were rising steadily and continuously" from 1200 to the death of Henry III.[1] In 1914 S. K. Mitchell, citing Ramsay, considered that "a rise in prices was going on, probably slowly, from about 1190 to 1250".[2] N. S. B. Gras in 1915, writing particularly of the price of corn, discussed the general increases that he found throughout the century for all agricultural commodities and suggested that they were caused by an "increase in the volume of trade due in part to a growing foreign demand and more especially to the growth of the town population, a subject bound up with the evolution of the local market".[3] Three years later Gras also commented on the increase in the price of wine between the reigns of Henry II and Edward I.[4] But it was not until the work of the future Lord Beveridge in 1927, A. L. Poole in 1940 and Dr. D. L. Farmer in 1956-8 that the chronology and scale of these price rises were defined with real precision.[5] Their tables, drawn from the royal

---

[*] I am grateful to Mr. T. H. Aston for some very valuable comments and suggestions which I have taken into account in revising this article for the press and for letting me read the unpublished paper mentioned in note 72. Throughout the notes I have referred to the editions of the Pipe Rolls from 5 Hen. II to 2 Hen. III (1159-1218) published by the Pipe Roll Society (old ser., vols. i-xxxviii, 1884-1925; new ser., vols. i-xxxiv, 1925-72) as *P.R. 5 Hen. II*, etc.

[1] *The Dawn of the Constitution* (London, 1908), p. 301.
[2] *Studies in Taxation under John and Henry III* (Yale Historical Publications, Studies, ii, New Haven, 1914), p. 2.
[3] *The Evolution of the English Corn Market* (Harvard Economic Studies, xiii, Cambridge, Mass., 1915, repr. 1926), pp. 15-16.
[4] *The Early English Customs System* (Harvard Economic Studies, xviii, Cambridge, Mass., 1918), p. 42.
[5] W. H. Beveridge, "The Yield and Price of Corn in the Middle Ages", *Economic History*, i (1926-9), pp. 162-6; A. L. Poole, "Livestock Prices in the Twelfth Century", *Eng. Hist. Rev.*, lv (1940), pp. 284-95; D. L. Farmer, "Some Price Fluctuations in Angevin England", *Econ. Hist. Rev.*, 2nd ser., ix (1956-7), pp. 34-43, and "Some Grain Price Movements in Thirteenth-Century England", *ibid.*, x (1957-8), pp. 207-20. These can now be supplemented by T. H. Lloyd, *The Movement of Wool Prices in Medieval England* (Econ. Hist. Rev. Supplement no. 6, 1973), pp. 38-9, 45, 50, whose series start in 1209. A convenient table of prices of wheat, oxen and wool is given by J. Z. Titow, *English Rural Society, 1200-1350* (London, 1969), pp. 100-1.

Pipe Rolls and from the estate accounts of the bishops of Winchester, show that the prices of corn, livestock and the few other goods for which we have evidence doubled or trebled between 1180 and 1220; they continued to rise slightly until about 1260 but then levelled off, just at the date when manorial accounts start to provide real profusion of evidence on prices, evidence that had been tabulated and analysed by Thorold Rogers as long ago as 1866.[6] The enormous local, seasonal and annual variations make it very difficult to discover long-term price trends from medieval records, but the conclusions that Poole and Dr. Farmer reached have not been questioned. Rapidly rising prices are now well established as a feature of late twelfth- and early thirteenth-century England and have been mentioned among the causes of various phenomena of the time: the increasing legal disabilities of the peasantry, the change from leasing manors to demesne farming on large estates, and the political troubles of the reign of John. It is not now too early to attempt to survey the overall consequences of these price changes, to see what effect they had on the society of the time, what was their economic significance, and to take a fresh look at their possible cause.

In the twelfth century large estate owners drew profits from their lands by leasing them to farmers who would pay an agreed rent in cash or (decreasingly in the course of the century) in produce. In the thirteenth century the lessees had been replaced by the landlords' own local agents — reeves and bailiffs — who tilled the demesne lands on their behalf and were answerable to them for all profits. The change may seem a small one, but, as Mr. E. Miller has recently pointed out, the shift in emphasis from local to seigneurial entre-preneurship in agriculture lay at the root of the "economic contrast" between the twelfth and thirteenth centuries in England.[7] Our only source of general evidence for the chronology of the change is the accounts for estates temporarily in the king's hands that are entered on the Pipe Rolls, and the information these give us is sparse and difficult to interpret. The earliest clear case they provide of part of a substantial estate being run by a local agent as regular practice is in 1171-2, when some small part of the bishop of Winchester's lands were under direct management; the same is found at Peterborough Abbey in 1176-7 and on the honour of Chester in 1181-2, and thence-

---

[6] J. E. T. Rogers, *A History of Agriculture and Prices in England*, 7 vols. (Oxford, 1866-1902), i and ii.
[7] "England in the Twelfth and Thirteenth Centuries: an Economic Contrast?", *Econ. Hist. Rev.*, 2nd ser., xxiv (1971), pp. 1-14.

forward the estates for which there is evidence were turning more and more to demesne farming.[8] By the end of the reign of John there were still some estates of which substantial portions were leased out — probably three-quarters of the manors of Ramsey Abbey were farmed out in 1211-12 — but most were all or nearly all under direct management, like those of Sherborne and Milton Abbeys and Canterbury Cathedral Priory in the same year.[9] The coincidence between the period when estate owners were turning to demesne farming and the period of rapidly rising prices is very striking. At first sight, indeed, it might seem altogether too striking: some delay would be necessary if we are to see them as cause and effect. But this is probably due to the nature of our records; new price levels would have to be well established before the Exchequer would allow them to sheriffs and others, and thus bring them into recorded history on the Pipe Rolls. Given hindsight and an elementary knowledge of economics it is clear that estate owners were taking exactly the right steps to meet the situation; even if rents could be raised to new levels there would always be a time-lag in which the lessees would benefit unduly from the increased prices that their landlords and others would have to pay for the produce they sold and direct management was the only way to avoid this. The failure of the landlords' successors in the sixteenth century to adopt a similar policy in like circumstances meant that some of their lessees made considerable gains at their expense.[10] But it is equally clear that twelfth-century landlords had neither the theoretical knowledge nor the information about contemporary price trends that would enable them to see their position in these terms. If they adopted the correct policy it was for immediate and empirical reasons. Ultimately these reasons all stemmed from the rise in prices,[11] but in practice the form in which the landlords saw the problem probably depended on whether the particular manor was let for a short or a long term.

It is not difficult to find examples from the late twelfth century of manors held on long leases. One is Benfleet (Essex), which the abbot of Westminster leased out at £24 a year for the lifetime of the lessee,

[8] *P.R. 18 Hen. II*, pp. 85-6; *P.R. 23 Hen. II*, pp. 104-5; *P.R. 28 Hen. II*, pp. 148-9; P. D. A. Harvey, "The Pipe Rolls and the Adoption of Demesne Farming in England", *Econ. Hist. Rev.*, 2nd ser., xxvii (1974), pp. 353-8.

[9] *P.R. 14 John*, pp. 6, 40, 121-2; Harvey, *loc. cit.*

[10] P. Bowden in *The Agrarian History of England and Wales*, vol. iv, *1550-1640*, ed. Joan Thirsk (Cambridge, 1967), pp. 687-9.

[11] I thus find myself in full agreement both with the conclusions of C. G. Reed and T. L. Anderson, "An Economic Explanation of English Agrarian Organization in the Twelfth and Thirteenth Centuries", *Econ. Hist. Rev.*, 2nd ser., xxvi (1973), pp. 134-7, and with Mr. E. Miller's refutation of the arguments used to reach them, "Farming of Manors and Direct Management", *ibid.*, pp. 138-40.

an agreement that is enrolled on the first Pipe Roll of Richard I's reign.[12] Another is the Bury St. Edmunds manor of Runcton (Norfolk) which the wife of Herlewin likewise held for life: "Yesterday I would have given sixty marks to free that manor; but now the Lord hath freed it", said Abbot Samson on hearing of her death.[13] In a valuable discussion of the abandonment of leasing in the late twelfth century Mr. Miller shows the drawbacks to contemporary landlords of leases of this type.[14] It was not only that rising prices would before long make the annual rent worth far less in real terms than when the agreement had been made; an increase in the number of peasant sub-tenants, assarting and other improvements on the manor could bring the lessee an income appreciably larger than the landlord had anticipated or bargained for. Moreover there was a real risk that the lease might become hereditary, effectively alienating the manor from the estate: Mr. Miller cites the interesting case of the Ramsey Abbey manor of Over (Cambridgeshire) which, after four generations in the hands of a single family of lessees, was recovered by the abbey only by long litigation.[15] Just what tenures and offices could be inherited was of course much in question at that time, and a landlord may well have been afraid of binding his heirs for ever to an agreement made originally for a limited term. But leasing out manors for cash rents differed from demising them for military or other services that changing social conditions would make nugatory; given an unchanging economy, both locally and nationally, the landlord had little to lose from a lease that was inherited. The only exceptions would be where, for a large initial payment or for some other consideration, a lease had been granted for a particularly low annual rent, but such cases were probably a minority. Otherwise it was only by extensive local development or by a general rise in prices that the lessee would start to make profits so conspicuous (for it is thus that the situation would come to his landlord's notice) that the landlord would see the perpetuation of such leases as a real risk. Certainly assarting, peasant population increase and more intensive husbandry must have brought enhanced profits to some lessees in

[12] *The Great Roll of the Pipe for 1 Richard I*, ed. J. Hunter (Record Commission, London, 1844), p. 230.
[13] Jocelin of Brakelond, *Chronicle*, ed. H. E. Butler (London, 1949), pp. 32-3.
[14] Miller, "England in the Twelfth and Thirteenth Centuries", pp. 8-10.
[15] *Ibid.*, p. 9, citing *Cartularium Monasterii de Rameseia*, ed. W. H. Hart and P. A. Lyons (Rolls Series, 1884-93), i, pp. 120-7. R. V. Lennard, *Rural England, 1086-1135* (Oxford, 1959), pp. 107-11, gives earlier evidence of the same trend; it was not a new phenomenon.

the late twelfth century.[16]   But local developments of this sort had for many generations been part of the background of the leasing of manors,[17] and we have no reason to suppose that at this point they became especially widespread.   The rise in prices, on the other hand, must everywhere have brought immediate benefits to the long-term lessees, benefits that were clearly visible in their effects even if their cause was obscure.   It was probably this that brought home to landlords the disadvantages of so inflexible a method of running their properties, whether or not there was the risk that a long lease might become hereditary.   It is worth noting that in other parts of Europe too there was a tendency at this time for leases to become hereditary, but that only in England was this tendency halted by the introduction of direct management of estates; as we shall see, the rise in prices was probably a purely English phenomenon, and it would satisfactorily explain why the adoption of demesne farming was a development peculiar to England.[18]

But if some manors were let out on long leases by fixed agreement, others, perhaps the majority, were farmed under much more flexible arrangements.   When Abbot Samson of Bury St. Edmunds decided on a policy of direct management of his estates he did not have to wait for the expiry of leases or buy out lessees' rights on most of his manors: he simply waited until the Michaelmas after his installation and then took them into his own hands.[19]   Leases on a short-term, even annual, basis are implied by the pattern of re-stocking manors that were in the king's hands by wardship or escheat: for the most part new stock was bought for them (and, thus, the rents raised) not piecemeal as one would expect if leases had to expire before their conditions were changed, but *en bloc* following the

---

[16] An example of a manor leased for a farm that was well below its true value is provided by Waddington (Lincs.), which in 1185 rendered £22 a year but was said to be worth £40: *Rotuli de Dominabus*, ed. J. H. Round (Pipe Roll Soc., old ser., xxxv, 1913), p. 15.

[17] Lennard, *Rural England*, pp. 182-3, describes arrangements for increasing the amounts of the farm within the term of a lease.

[18] Dorothea Oschinsky, *Walter of Henley and other Treatises on Estate Management and Accounting* (Oxford, 1971), pp. 72-3, 213-14, suggests that the existence in England of well-developed accounting techniques was one cause of the adoption of demesne farming there but not in Germany; but this argument implies that written accounts were in general use by estate owners from the very beginning of the period of demesne farming, an assumption that is open to question.

[19] Jocelin of Brakelond, *Chronicle*, ed. Butler, p. 32; M. M. Postan in *The Cambridge Economic History of Europe*, vol. i, *The Agrarian Life of the Middle Ages*, 2nd edn., ed. M. M. Postan (Cambridge, 1966), p. 586, provides some other examples.

periodic inquiries made by the itinerant justices.[20] Tunstead
(Norfolk) was in the king's hands in the early 1180s; for two years its
custodians received £19 farm, but they then added a hundred sheep
to the manorial stock and it thenceforth produced an extra pound
a year.[21] The lessees in such a case would probably be one or
several of the sub-tenants of the manor or, more vaguely, men of the
vill (*homines ville*) acting jointly or even communally.[22] Certainly
where leases were as flexible as this it cannot have been fears of
lessees' hereditary rights nor even of rents fixed irrevocably at
unrealistic levels that led landlords to turn to direct management.
Jocelin of Brakelond speaks of the dilapidations that had occurred
on the Bury St. Edmunds manors at the hands of their farmers;[23]
this points to the laxity and negligence of Abbot Samson's predecessor, but it was something that had always had to be guarded against in
a system of leasing and it can hardly have suddenly become a universal
problem.   In fact we can again see rising prices as bringing about the
general change to demesne farming, though not in quite the same way
as where manors were let for long terms.   Clearly a rise in prices
would benefit any lessee who had a marketable surplus of produce,
whether he held by a long lease or a short one.   But we must
remember that it would not be a question of gradual, steady
improvement in his position so that each year he did a little better
than the year before.   There would be good harvests and bad ones;
there would be years when local demand was strong and prices high,
but there would be other years when the market was depressed.
There would increasingly be years when the lessee did very well
indeed — outrageously well from his landlord's point of view.   But
there would still be years when he might hardly be able to find the
cash to pay the stipulated farm.   And once rising prices had
introduced a measure of long-term change into the local economy,
making the established farms palpably unrealistic, it was very difficult
to discover what new levels of rent would be fair to landlord and lessee

---

[20] Thus there are many cases of restocking on *P.R. 13 Hen. II* (pp. 36-8,
102-4, etc.) following the judicial visitation of 1166, but hardly any on the Pipe
Rolls for the three following years.

[21] *Rotuli de Dominabus*, ed. Round, p. 48.

[22] *P.R. 27 Hen. II*, pp. 107-9, gives a list (unique on the Pipe Rolls) of the
farmers of the manors of the honour of Rayleigh (lands of Henry of Essex) who
seem in each case to be one or two of the local inhabitants; cf. Lennard, *Rural
England*, pp. 153-5.

[23] Jocelin of Brakelond, *Chronicle*, ed. Butler, pp. 1, 32.   We find that
deterioration or improvement of the manor at the hands of a lessee was one of the
matters on which the jurors of the St. Paul's manors were questioned in the
inquiries of 1222: *Domesday of St. Paul's*, ed. W. H. Hale (Camden Soc., old
ser., lxix, 1858), pp. 1-2, 8, 13-14, etc.

alike. In fact we see just this difficulty arising at this time. The *Rotuli de Dominabus* of 1185 record that when Billingford (Norfolk) came into the hands of the Crown it was sworn to be worth £15 a year, but its custodian for the king was able to let it out at £20.[24] More dramatically, when the archbishop of York acquired Billinghay (Lincolnshire) through a wardship he substantially increased its farm "and as a result, so the jurors say, the vill has been wasted and its men harassed".[25] We can easily see how the landlord might turn to direct management when confronted with recurrent problems of this sort and confronted too with the local resistance that would be aroused by any proposal to increase the annual farm.

The rise in prices, then, provides a simple and straightforward explanation of landlords' replacement of lessees by their own manorial officers in the late twelfth and early thirteenth centuries.[26] We may even conjecture that had a system of food-farms instead of money-rents prevailed until after prices stabilized in the mid-thirteenth century there would have been no period of demesne farming in England, for landlords as well as their lessees would then have benefited directly from the rise in prices. But there was one landlord in England to whom rising prices presented as much of a problem as to any other magnate but who could not turn to direct management as a way out of the difficulty; this was the king, the greatest landowner of all. For the most part the royal estates were run by the sheriff of each county who was in a sense a lessee: he would keep for himself the income from certain of the king's resources in the shire — not only the royal demesne but the dues from certain boroughs and the profits of the hundred and county courts — and he paid to the king simply a fixed sum, the farm of the county. Not only was the sheriff a lessee; he might even become an hereditary lessee, for from John's reign onwards the shrievalties of a few counties were granted or claimed as hereditary, a custom which had been known under William I and his sons but which had lapsed since.[27] But even where, as in most counties, the sheriff held office for only a few years

---

[24] *Rotuli de Dominabus*, ed. Round, p. 57.

[25] "et ideo, ut aiunt juratores, est villa destracta et homines destracti": *ibid.*, p. 3. At Ospringe (Kent) in 1240 we see a later case of difficulty in fixing a fair farm in view of annual variation in profits: R. S. Hoyt, *The Royal Demesne in English Constitutional History, 1066-1272* (Ithaca, 1950), pp. 158-9.

[26] Interestingly, the return to leasing has been associated with the decline of prices in real terms in the fourteenth and fifteenth centuries: Postan in *Cambridge Economic History*, i, 2nd edn., p. 588.

[27] W. A. Morris, *The Medieval English Sheriff to 1300* (Manchester, 1927), pp. 50-2, 76-7, 84, 145, 179-82; S. Painter, *The Reign of King John* (Baltimore, 1949), pp. 40, 59.

at a time the farm of the county could not be increased to accord with changing economic circumstances, for its amount was fixed by custom; with few exceptions the amount of the farm was the same at the end of the thirteenth century as it had been in 1170.[28]   In effect, however, the farms were augmented by making the sheriff answer for a further amount known as the *crementum* or *incrementum*, increase, a practice that first appears in the 1160s; but by 1201-2 this added less than one-tenth, by 1211-12 less than a quarter, to the amounts of the traditional farms, and even this modest supplement was forbidden by Magna Carta.[29]   Another device that Richard I and John used to tap the wealth of their own estates and other resources was to exact a premium from an incoming sheriff for the privilege of holding office; this practice had existed since the eleventh century, but it was now exploited so that a shire could be practically sold to the highest bidder for a sum that might be as much as £2,000.[30]   At best this was a hit-and-miss method of bringing the profits of the shires into the Exchequer, but it points to the value of the office to the sheriff and the amount of revenue that the Crown was losing through having to adhere to custom.   Finally in 1204 John took the step that so many English magnates had already taken on their estates: he appointed sheriffs who, designated keepers (*custodes*), were required to answer not only for the traditional farms of their counties but for for additional profits (*proficua*) as well, so that, in effect, they became bailiffs instead of lessees.   The system was applied to about half the counties, and in its first year it increased their revenues by about one-third, but after four years it was rapidly abandoned and the sheriffs became simple lessees once more.[31]   Both political and administrative reasons have been suggested for its failure.   In fact it

[28] Painter, *op. cit.*, p. 243; G. J. Turner, "The Sheriff's Farm", *Trans. Roy. Hist. Soc.*, new ser., xii (1898), p. 122.

[29] Mitchell, *Studies in Taxation*, pp. 15-16; Mabel H. Mills, "Experiments in Exchequer Procedure (1200-1232)", *Trans. Roy. Hist. Soc.*, 4th ser., viii (1925), pp. 159-60; Morris, *op. cit.*, pp. 128, 144; Painter, *op. cit.*, p. 115.   Both Mitchell and Mabel Mills seem to have misinterpreted the Buckinghamshire increment of £10 and three hawks on the list of county farms given by Turner, *op. cit.*, p. 143; as Morris shows, other increments, some both earlier and larger, are recorded on the Pipe Rolls of Henry II.   The reissues of Magna Carta omitted the prohibition of these increments (*cap.* 25 in Magna Carta of 1215: W. Stubbs, *Select Charters*, 9th edn., ed. H. W. C. Davis [Oxford, 1913], p. 296), and they reappeared after a few years' lapse (Mills, *op. cit.*, pp. 166-7).

[30] Morris, *op. cit.*, pp. 64, 83-4; introduction by Doris M. Stenton to *P.R. 6 Ric. I*, pp. xvii-xviii.

[31] Morris, *op. cit.*, p. 144; Painter, *Reign of King John*, pp. 118-23; J. C. Holt, *The Northerners* (Oxford, 1961), pp. 152-3; introduction by Patricia M. Barnes to *P.R. 16 John*, pp. xx-xxiii.

seems unlikely that it could have been made to work successfully. When magnates turned to direct management of their properties, they appointed bailiffs to have oversight of several manors and stewards who would supervise agriculture over an entire estate, so that the reeve on the individual manor was carefully and closely watched in all his activities; only in the late thirteenth century were accounting techniques developed to the point where it became possible to relax this continual supervision and give greater freedom to the manorial officer who would answer for his actions simply in the searching scrutiny of the annual audit.[32]   Royal Exchequer procedure had certainly not reached this level of sophistication by the reign of John; indeed, compared even with private estate accounts of the same period, its written records, the Pipe Rolls, are clumsy, obscure and riddled with archaic conventions.   The sheriffs were too dispersed and their duties too multifarious for the alternative of close oversight to be practicable, even if the traditions of the shrievalty had permitted it, but it may be that the appointment of a second official to some counties represents an attempt at supervision and that his function was to act as a check on the honesty of the first; the account for Warwickshire and Leicestershire in 1204–5, for instance, is rendered by "Hugh de Chaucumb as keeper and Master Hilary with him".[33]   We do not know how the recorded profits of the keeper-sheriffs were determined,[34] but if they really represent an attempt to set down the total profits from the counties they must have given rise to much bullying and extortion on one side of the Exchequer board, much concealment and fraud on the other; politically, if not financially, the system would soon be self-defeating.

The Crown then, unable to apply contemporary methods of direct management to its own estates and other regular sources of revenue, was powerless to draw from them the greatly increased income that the rise in prices would warrant.   Even on the small but growing number of royal manors that were run directly from the Exchequer, by-passing the sheriffs, conservatism or administrative difficulties seem to have prevented the introduction of demesne farming, though here the annual farms could be and were raised substantially;[35] it is interesting that these properties were specifically excluded from

---

[32] See chaps. iii–v (especially the last two paragraphs of ch. iii) of the introduction to *Manorial Records of Cuxham*, ed. P. D. A. Harvey (Hist. MSS. Commission and Oxfordshire Rec. Soc., 1976).

[33] *P.R. 7 John*, p. 28.

[34] S. Smith in introduction to *P.R. 7 John*, p. xxvi.

[35] Painter, *Reign of King John*, pp. 123–4.

Magna Carta's prohibition of increments.[36]   Eventually the Crown solved the problem for its demesne manors by the reforms of 1236-40 that were probably the work of Peter des Rivaux: the royal estates were all taken from the sheriffs' control and organized centrally by two keepers who in principle let each manor to its own tenants (*hominibus singulorum maneriorum*) under a lease reviewable every five years.[37]   The date is significant, for by the 1230s prices in the long term were becoming steadier so that a policy of leasing was once more compatible with efficient management; the Crown thus passed through the period of massive price increases without gaining direct control of its estates.   Even if the experiment of 1204 had proved workable, turning the sheriffs into bailiffs of the royal estates, it is unlikely that the Crown's profits from this source would have been commensurate with the rise in prices, though, as we have seen, the premiums that men were prepared to pay for appointment show that the office was a profitable one.   We know little of how the sheriffs ran the royal manors in their care, but they probably adhered to a system of leasing.   With frequent changes of sheriff demesne farming would be very difficult to organize and from its opportunities for abuse it is unlikely to have been viewed favourably by the itinerant justices who exercised ultimate control of the royal estates; certainly the instructions for the judicial visitation of 1194 imply a system of leasing.[38]   This meant that the sheriffs suffered the same disadvantages as landlords who leased out their estates: the case of the Ramsey Abbey manor of Over, which its lessees claimed as an inheritance, can be paralleled by that of the royal manor of Matlock (Derbyshire) which its lessee claimed to hold in fee-farm after it had been let to his family for five generations.[39]   The other resources of the Crown for which the sheriff answered in his farm were probably even less amenable than the royal demesne to increased profits corresponding to the rise in prices: the revenues from the boroughs were fixed by custom and so too, very probably, were the fines and amercements of the local courts so that any increase, let alone one of two or three hundred per cent, would appear grossly extortionate.

[36] Presumably because no powerful interest was concerned with them.
[37] Mabel H. Mills, "The Reforms at the Exchequer (1232-1242)", *Trans. Roy. Hist. Soc.*, 4th ser., x (1927), pp. 121-3; F. M. Powicke, *Henry III and the Lord Edward*, 2 vols. (Oxford, 1947), i, pp. 102-3; Hoyt, *Royal Demesne*, pp. 156-61.
[38] *Select Charters*, 9th edn., p. 255; *assisus redditus* here almost certainly means the fixed return or farm from the entire manor (Harvey, "The Pipe Rolls", p. 348). Cf. B. P. Wolffe, *The Royal Demesne in English History* (London, 1971), p. 25.
[39] Hoyt, *Royal Demesne*, pp. 150-1.

As we shall see, the boroughs were probably as capable as the royal demesne lands of paying increased dues exactly related to the rise in prices, and it is in this context that we should see the increasingly heavy tallages that were laid on boroughs and royal demesne in the reigns of Richard I and John:[40] they were attempts not merely to tap wealth that was immune from most other forms of taxation, but to tap wealth that was inaccessible to the king as landlord because his administrative system was unable to take account of economic change. Professor R. S. Hoyt has argued that these tallages had an important consequence: they forced the barons and, in Magna Carta, the king to accept a distinction between the boroughs and the king's manors which amounted in effect to the earliest clear definition of the royal demesne.[41] If this is so, it is one constitutional development that can be closely linked with the rise in prices.

It is by no means the only one. Dr. B. P. Wolffe has recently suggested that for most of the middle ages the royal estates were regarded as a source of patronage rather than of cash, and that the kings lived on the proceeds of taxation and other extraordinary income rather than from their so-called ordinary revenues.[42] The rise in prices certainly ensured that this was so in the reigns of Richard I and John, and it may have tilted the scales in this direction for the next two hundred years. Giraldus Cambrensis says of Henry II and his sons that "what they lacked in fixed returns (*in redditibus*) they made up in casual profits, trusting more to accessories than to principals".[43] Knowledge of price trends gives the comment more significance than its author intended. The kings had no alternative. Their failure to raise the income that reached them through the sheriffs' farms to anything like the level demanded by the rise in prices threw the whole burden of their increased expenditure on other forms of revenue. It was not just that John in 1215 had to pay about three times as much as his father fifty years before when he bought food for his household or livestock and corn for his manors; he also had to pay his troops at three times the earlier rates. Henry II had paid his knights 8d. a day, his foot-soldiers 1d.; by about 1200 the rates were 2s. or 3s. for the

---

[40] Painter, *Reign of King John*, pp. 125-6; S. K. Mitchell, *Taxation in Medieval England* (Yale Historical Publications, Studies, xv, New Haven, 1951), pp. 313-5.
[41] Hoyt, *Royal Demesne*, pp. 144-6.
[42] Wolffe, *Royal Demesne*, p. 10.
[43] Giraldus Cambrensis, "De Principis Instructione Liber" in *Opera*, ed. J. S. Brewer, J. F. Dimock and G. F. Warner (Rolls Series, 1861-91), viii, p. 316, cited by F. M. Powicke, *The Loss of Normandy, 1189-1204*, 2nd edn. (Manchester, 1961), p. 232 n.

knights, 2d. for the foot-soldiers.[44] There is evidence too of increasing standards of luxury or comfort at the royal court, which must also have increased its expenses.[45] How Richard I and John exploited every variety of taxation known to them, every available source of casual profits, is well known and there is no need to rehearse the details here.[46] Despite expensive commitments abroad both kings managed to remain solvent. But in the end the defiance of custom that knew nothing of price trends was too great. Whatever other personal and political factors were involved, it was the king's continual financial exactions of one sort or another that lay at the root of the rebellion of 1215. Certainly, if John's expenditure had been reduced by one-half or two-thirds, enabling him to keep his financial demands within the limits of feudal custom, most of his political difficulties would have vanished. No landmark in English constitutional history was more clearly brought about by economic change than Magna Carta.

Historians' assessments of John's ability as king have exactly kept pace with growing knowledge of the rise in prices and the financial administration of his reign. No one would now say, as F. M. Powicke did in 1913, that "By careful management Henry II had doubled his income; by mismanagement John brought chaos".[47] Even in 1914 S. K. Mitchell remarked that it was likely that the rise in prices "increased the difficulties of the government somewhat".[48] To the late Lady Stenton in 1951, "No king of England was ever so unlucky as John".[49] Dr. W. L. Warren in 1961 described John's government as "enterprising and intelligent" in its attempts to bring more money to the Crown.[50] In a way John's predicament was very like Henry

[44] Sir J. H. Ramsay, *The Angevin Empire* (London, 1903), p. 373, and *A History of the Revenues of the Kings of England, 1066-1399*, 2 vols. (Oxford, 1925), i, pp. 211, 221; Mitchell, *Studies in Taxation*, p. 309. But at the beginning of John's reign a knight's wage could clearly vary a good deal: Doris M. Stenton in introduction to *P.R. 1 John*, p. xiv; cf. A. L. Poole, *From Domesday Book to Magna Carta*, 2nd edn. (Oxford, 1955), pp. 371-2.

[45] Painter, *Reign of King John*, p. 112.

[46] The details are most fully set out in the introductions to the Pipe Roll Society's editions of the Pipe Rolls of their reigns; a general description is given by W. L. Warren, *King John* (London, 1961), pp. 148-52.

[47] *The Loss of Normandy, 1189-1204* (Manchester, 1913), p. 350 (p. 237 in the 2nd edn. [1961], where the author acknowledged that subsequent investigation had shown that John was in fact more business-like than he had supposed).

[48] *Studies in Taxation*, p. 2.

[49] *English Society in the Early Middle Ages* (Pelican History of England, iii, 2nd edn., Harmondsworth, 1952), p. 44.

[50] Warren, *King John*, p. 152. Of modern writers on John and his reign it is Dr. Warren who attaches most weight to the price rises in considering his financial and political difficulties: *op. cit.*, pp. 145-53.

IV's two hundred years later: in a changing economy fiscal custom denied him access to the real wealth of the country.   Certainly when we recognize the extraordinary difficulties he had to meet we must admire his ingenuity and tenacity in managing the royal finances. The Interdict was, of course, financially a piece of great good fortune, enabling the king to take major ecclesiastical revenues into his own hands for up to five years, apparently without serious protest from the laity;[51] this almost certainly staved off the final debacle.   But when we find that for the last year of his reign, when the Exchequer had ceased to function, John was able to subsist largely on the money that he had saved and stored in scattered treasuries,[52] we can only see his financial administration as an astonishing achievement in the face of economic pressures that he was probably unaware of and certainly could not control.   Conversely it is easy for us to condemn the baronial opposition to John.   Having secured their own financial position by direct management of their estates, and enjoying the enlarged incomes that rising prices were bringing them,[53] the magnates combatted every attempt of the king to bring his revenues into line with theirs.   But they could hardly see the position in these terms. Even if they were aware of the problems posed by rising prices it is unlikely that they realized how ruthlessly they were exploiting the Crown's declared respect for custom.   There was probably nothing cynical in their appeals to irrelevant precedent.   And if they were simply unaware of the economic weapon that fate had placed in their hands, this very ignorance would give the weapon added power.

We have seen that soldiers' pay in this period increased in the same proportions as the prices of corn and livestock.   This raises a funda-

[51] Painter, *Reign of King John*, pp. 174-6, 183-4; Poole, *Domesday Book to Magna Carta*, pp. 446-9; Warren, *King John*, pp. 166-8, 173.   This is not to say, however, that the Crown's tenure of these revenues caused no resentment among laymen; cf. Holt, *Northerners*, pp. 235-6.

[52] J. E. A. Jolliffe, "The Chamber and the Castle Treasuries under King John", in R. W. Hunt, W. A. Pantin and R. W. Southern (eds.), *Studies in Medieval History presented to F. M. Powicke* (Oxford, 1948), pp. 125-38; C. F. Slade, introduction to *P.R. 12 John*, pp. xxxi-xxxii.   The king did, however, get some revenue at this period from the confiscated estates of rebels: Painter, *Reign of King John*, pp. 350, 371.

[53] Calculations showing increases in manorial revenues have been made by S. Painter, *Studies in the History of the English Feudal Barony* (Baltimore, 1943), p. 160, who finds an average increase of 60% from 1086 to 1220 and a further 51-64% from 1220 to 1250.   There is some reason to suppose that estates in eastern England were slower to adopt demesne farming than those elsewhere (Harvey, "The Pipe Rolls", pp. 353-4), whence perhaps the opposition to John in this area (Painter, *Reign of King John*, pp. 298, 360; Poole, *Domesday Book to Magna Carta*, p. 469 n.), as landlords there would be less able to meet the king's financial demands.

mental question. So far we have been considering the direct consequences of a rise in prices that is well attested. But what was the significance of this rise in prices? Are we dealing with a simple change in price structure or with a general inflation of the currency? Unfortunately we just have not got the evidence to give an indisputable answer to this question. Virtually all we know of prices at this period concerns agricultural products, and their prices depended not on costs of production but on market levels regulated by supply and demand.[54] Thus they might change quite independently of wage-rates or the prices of other goods and, indeed, we find just this happening in the mid-fourteenth century: the loss of population in the Black Death led to marked rises in wages and in prices that depended on wage-rates, while the prices of agricultural products were unaffected.[55] Was it the reverse process that occurred in the late twelfth century, a sudden vast rise in the value of foodstuffs that might be attributed to population pressure and growing shortage of land? Or are these increases in prices the only clear traces to survive of a general decline in the value of money that affected all prices, wages and other payments? Historians differ in their views. Dr. Warren takes for granted that it was an inflation of the currency: "It was John's misfortune to reign in a period of monetary inflation . . . . There was more silver available, trade was flourishing, and the standard of living was rising; but the productivity of the land was increasing only slowly, so the prices of agricultural produce went up, and labour was dear".[56] Professor Postan in 1944 was prepared to countenance the same view, but by 1952 he had concluded that the price increases affected foodstuffs alone.[57] At first sight, of course, the rise in soldiers' pay might seem conclusive evidence of a general rise in wages. But this could possibly be a special case: the increases may reflect the more elaborate (and thus more expensive) equipment that was becoming necessary,[58] while the military were in a peculiarly strong position to bargain for rates of pay that took into account the

[54] It is a great pity that we have no more evidence of the price of salt in this period; the few examples on the Pipe Rolls from 1171 to 1210 can be interpreted either way: Farmer, "Price Fluctuations", p. 37; cf. Rogers, *History of Agriculture and Prices*, ii, pp. 409-18. The increase in the price of wine, as noted by Gras (above, note 4), is more significant, though there is here the complication that we are dealing with an imported product.

[55] A. R. Bridbury, *Economic Growth: England in the Later Middle Ages* (London, 1962), p. 92.   [56] Warren, *King John*, p. 145.

[57] "The Rise of a Money Economy", *Econ. Hist. Rev.*, 1st ser., xiv (1944), p. 128; *Cambridge Economic History*, vol. ii, *Trade and Industry in the Middle Ages*, ed. M. Postan and E. E. Rich (Cambridge, 1952), p. 167.

[58] As suggested by Mitchell, *Studies in Taxation*, p. 309.

increased cost of living. Other evidence of wages, however, points in the same direction. The presumably skilled workers in charge of the king's vineyards in Herefordshire and at Windsor were paid 1d. a day at the beginning of Henry II's reign;[59] in 1210-11 carpenters working on the bishop of Winchester's residence at Marwell (Hampshire) were paid from 1½d. to 2d. a day, and by the mid-thirteenth century 2½d.-3d. a day seems to have been the normal rate for work of this sort.[60] But twelfth-century examples of civilian wage-rates are very few indeed, and in view of later medieval evidence of wide seasonal and regional variations in wages it would be wrong to attach much importance to them. There are two more cogent arguments that there was a real inflation of the currency. The first is the apparent prosperity of towns at this period. If prices of corn and livestock rose while wages and other prices remained static we would expect the prosperity of towns to diminish. Pressure of population might indeed bring about expansion of old towns and the creation of new ones, which would bring more rent into the pockets of the king or borough-owning magnate, but the individual trader or craftsman, paid the same as before for his own work yet paying two or three times as much for the food he ate, would be much worse off and would have little cash to spare for schemes of municipal improvement or aggrandizement. Yet the evidence suggests that the towns — and that is the burgesses, not the borough-owners — were prospering and were ready to buy the privileges that Richard I and John were offering to sell them in royal charters.[61] Admittedly it was in John's reign that we find the first signs of decline in the urban cloth industry, but this can be traced to causes other than a general decline in the towns' wealth.[62] Their continuing prosperity

[59] *The Great Rolls of the Pipe for 2, 3 and 4 Henry II*, ed. J. Hunter (Record Commission, London, 1844), pp. 18, 51; payments at this rate continued until 1204-5 and at least 1205-6 respectively (*P.R. 7 John*, p. 271; *P.R. 8 John*, p. 226) but this attests the Exchequer's conservatism rather than stability of wage rates.

[60] *The Pipe Roll of the Bishopric of Winchester, 1210-1211*, ed. N. R. Holt (Manchester, 1964), p. 13; W. Beveridge, "Wages in the Winchester Manors", *Econ. Hist. Rev.*, 1st ser., vii (1936-7), pp. 40-1, and "Westminster Wages in the Manorial Era", *ibid.*, 2nd ser., viii (1955-6), p. 27.

[61] J. Tait, *The Medieval English Borough* (Manchester, 1936), pp. 178-9. Admittedly there were delays and difficulties over payment in some cases.

[62] E. M. Carus-Wilson, "An Industrial Revolution of the Thirteenth Century", *Econ. Hist. Rev.*, 1st ser., xi (1941), pp. 39-60; E. Miller, "The Fortunes of the English Textile Industry in the Thirteenth Century", *Econ. Hist. Rev.*, 2nd ser., xviii (1965), pp. 71-4. In the article cited below (note 93) I suggest a way in which the change might, indirectly, be linked with the cause of the inflation.

is a serious difficulty in the way of seeing the rise in prices as something other than an aspect of monetary inflation. The second piece of evidence comes from the countryside. On manors where villeins did labour services in the thirteenth and early fourteenth centuries custom often gave the lord the option of taking in any year a stipulated payment in cash instead of the basic week-work. Sometimes this is specified in a custumal, sometimes it appears only when works were thus commuted and entered as "sold" in the annual account. But when this was done we very often find that the amount paid was much less than the value of the work. At Combe (Hampshire) in the mid-thirteenth century the tenant of a half-virgate was required either to pay 4s. rent or to do some 150 days' labour service in the course of a year, work that at contemporary rates was worth about 12s. 6d.[63] Again, at Cuxham (Oxfordshire) in the early 1330s the week-works of a villein tenant were valued at just over 10s. a year, yet if they were remitted the charge levied was only 5s.[64] These instances can be matched from many other places. The simplest explanation is that these customary charges were fixed at a time when labour was worth rather less than half what it cost by the mid-thirteenth century,[65] and it seems most likely that they date from the twelfth century, when so many landlords were taking money rents as an alternative to the traditional labour services. It

[63] *Select Documents of the English Lands of the Abbey of Bec*, ed. Marjorie Chibnall (Camden Soc., 3rd ser., lxxiii, 1951), p. 43; theoretically his obligation is for 184 days' week-work (three days a week for 38 weeks, five days for 14 weeks) but 30 days seems a reasonable allowance for holidays together with the harvest boon-works which he had to perform even when paying rent and which must have been deducted from his week-work.

[64] P. D. A. Harvey, *A Medieval Oxfordshire Village* (London, 1965), pp. 82-3.

[65] It might be argued, following M. M. Postan, "The Chronology of Labour Services", *Trans. Roy. Hist. Soc.*, 4th ser., xx (1937), pp. 186-9, that the disparity was due to heavy increases in labour services in the thirteenth century. The return to labour services is discussed below, pp. 75-6. I do not question that in the thirteenth century they were sometimes increased above the former customary level. I doubt, however, for three reasons, whether these increases accounted for more than a small part of the disparity between labour services and the alternative money rents: (i) the disparity seems too large and too consistent to be explained thus; (ii) it is difficult to see why an authoritarian doubling or trebling of labour services should not be accompanied by an equivalent increase in the alternative money rent; (iii) there are anomalous cases that will not fit this explanation. Combe (Hants.) in fact provides an example of these last: as already shown, the half-virgaters in the mid-thirteenth century did week-work worth about 12s. 6d. a year or paid 4s. rent, but the full virgaters simply paid 10s. rent; if the need for labour led to doubling or trebling the half-virgaters' works, why were the full virgaters allowed to continue to pay a money rent? More likely the imposition of the half-virgaters' week-work at the customary level produced as much labour as the demesne could use from this source.

follows that agricultural wages rose in this period in very much the same proportion as agricultural prices.[66]

Once we accept that the rise in prices was only one aspect of a general inflation of the currency, other developments of the time start to fall into place as part of a connected pattern of events. In an inflationary period those who would suffer would be those who, like the king, drew their income from fixed charges. Those who paid these fixed charges, of course, stood to gain. In the countryside the most obvious class of beneficiaries was the group of manorial tenants who held land permanently for money rents, with or without other light services, on what was acknowledged to be a contractual basis or even explicitly by written charter. These men, the sokemen of eastern England and the forerunners of the thirteenth-century free tenants found elsewhere, must have greatly strengthened their economic position at this time as the real value of the rents they paid fell by half or two-thirds. This may well have contributed to the growth of the peasant land-market in the thirteenth century:[67] rising prices and static rents gave free tenants both the opportunity and the incentive to improve their holdings by purchase wherever possible. But it was not so much in economic terms that the position of these tenants was visibly improving at this time but rather in legal and social status *vis-à-vis* their fellow manorial tenants; these were the villeins whose tenure was held to be not contractual but customary. They were affected by the inflation in much more complicated ways.

The tenure of the villeins was regulated by immemorial custom of the manor. Our earliest descriptions of their services date from before the Norman conquest and correspond closely to the custumals

[66] I venture here to disagree with the conclusions that Professor M. Postan illustrates from an analysis of wages and labour services at Cottenham (Cambs.) in *The Famulus* (Econ. Hist. Rev. Supplement no. 2, 1955), pp. 41-2. What seems to me particularly significant about the Cottenham evidence is that the allowances of rent made to the tenants for doing their harvest works in the thirteenth century (half-virgaters 12d., cottagers 6d.) were less than half the values attached to their harvest works in 1322 (half-virgaters 2s. 1d., cottagers 18d.) after the reorganization that made it the norm for these works to be performed; I would not, however, attach particular importance to this example in default of evidence that this same reorganization did not increase the number of works demanded: Frances M. Page, *The Estates of Crowland Abbey* (Cambridge Studies in Economic History, ii, Cambridge, 1934), pp. 86-7, 180, 220, 244-6.
[67] G. C. Homans, *English Villagers of the Thirteenth Century* (Cambridge, Mass., 1941), pp. 201-4; Postan in *Cambridge Economic History*, i, 2nd edn., pp. 625-8; P. R. Hyams, "The Origins of a Peasant Land Market in England", *Econ. Hist. Rev.*, 2nd ser., xxiii (1970), pp. 18-31, especially p. 20 on the sources of finance.

of the thirteenth and fourteenth centuries. These custumals sometimes go a little beyond the services of the tenants and mention other customs as well, and we may reasonably suspect that villein tenure was only a part of a vast mass of unwritten, slowly evolving custom that controlled many aspects of life in the medieval village and laid obligations on landlord and lessee, bailiff and villagers alike. In one notable respect the customs of villein tenure were changing in the twelfth century. As already mentioned, the period saw money rents replacing labour services on many manors, either altogether or as an alternative option at the landlord's choice from year to year.[68] This was the equivalent of the contemporary change from food-farms to the money rents paid by the lessees of entire manors; both may well have been made possible by increasing cash sales of surplus produce to the growing towns and other markets. This spread of commutation is often spoken of as if it were wholly to the advantage of the tenants, but in fact the immediate beneficiary may well have been the landlord. We know little of the day-to-day work of a manor in the twelfth century, but from the time detailed records become abundant in the late thirteenth century landlords clearly found it difficult to exact efficient labour services, and they were used only for the most unskilled work of the manorial demesne: the threshing, the ditching, the muck-carting, rather than the ploughing, the sowing or the keeping of animals.[69] Money rents, on the other hand, were easy to collect and difficult to evade, and Mr. Miller has suggested that the lessees of manorial demesnes may well have encouraged their spread;[70] certainly they must have made it much easier for both landlord and lessee to evaluate the tenants' services when negotiating a new lease. In some cases, of course, the change may have come about through a reduction in the demesne lands, which would make labour services redundant, or through a lease of the demesne to the villagers themselves.[71] Nevertheless, this process of commutation does not

---

[68] Postan, "Chronology of Labour Services", pp. 174-85.

[69] A. Elizabeth Levett, *The Black Death on the Estates of the See of Winchester*, in P. Vinogradoff (ed.), *Oxford Studies in Social and Legal History*, 9 vols. (Oxford, 1909-27), v (1916), pp. 35-6, 60, 66-7, 89-94; J. A. Raftis, *The Estates of Ramsey Abbey* (Pontifical Institute of Medieval Studies, Studies and Texts, iii, Toronto, 1957), pp. 190-201; Harvey, *Medieval Oxfordshire Village*, pp. 75-86.

[70] E. Miller, *The Abbey and Bishopric of Ely* (Cambridge Studies in Medieval Life and Thought, new ser., i, Cambridge, 1951), p. 112; Lennard, *Rural England*, p. 198, gives examples of tenants installed in their holdings by the farmer of the manor.

[71] Postan, "Chronology of Labour Services", pp. 173-85, sees a close connection between the reduction of demesnes and the swing to money rents in the twelfth century.

seem to have continued into the thirteenth century. At the very least the swing towards commutation stopped or was drastically reduced. There may even have been a general return to labour services, as Professor Postan suggested in 1937; he argued that where the option of a money rent existed it was often dropped or, as we have seen, allowed exceptionally, while elsewhere money rents were often simply replaced by the labour services that had been commuted in the previous century.[72] Professor Postan accounted for this marked reaction by the increasing areas of manorial demesne lands: larger demesne lands needed more labour to till them, and labour services provided the answer.[73] But there are difficulties in the way of this explanation, which implies a very sensitive connection between labour services and demesne area. By this date labour services can seldom have played a very important part in demesne agriculture. At Cuxham (Oxfordshire), where heavy week-work was normally exacted in full, they provided about one-third (the least skilled third) of all the work done on the demesne at the end of the thirteenth century, and this is probably typical.[74] There was no shortage of labour in the thirteenth century, a period when population was growing fast, and it seems improbable that landlords had to use labour services as the only way — or even the most convenient way — of tilling their lands. More likely the inflation forced labour services upon them. This does not credit the landlords with a precocious knowledge of economics: it would come about very naturally. On manors where an option existed it would become increasingly clear that the value of the services was greater than the alternative money rent, which would gradually fall into near disuse or be dropped altogether.[75] This would serve as an example

[72] *Ibid.*, pp. 186-9. It is likely, though, that the restoration of labour services was much less widespread than is there suggested (cf. Titow, *English Rural Society*, p. 60). The question is a complicated one that badly needs further investigation and re-assessment. I have learned much from Mr. T. H. Aston's unpublished paper of 1953, which deals with this and other aspects of manorial rents and labour.   [73] Postan, "Chronology of Labour Services", p. 186.

[74] Harvey, *Medieval Oxfordshire Village*, pp. 84-5.

[75] A graphic case of the opposite process occurs in the 1366 custumal of Wood Eaton (Oxon.): under a new agreement after the Black Death, the virgater was to do certain services or else pay 13s. 4d. money rent if the lord preferred, to which the writer of the custumal has added the sardonic note "and indeed the lord will prefer this for ever, for the said services are not worth so much": *Eynsham Cartulary*, ed. H. E. Salter, 2 vols. (Oxford Hist. Soc., old ser., xlix, li, 1907-8), ii, p. 20. The alternatives must have been fixed at the time of very high wages immediately after the Black Death. Interestingly, the same custumal gives the pre-plague alternatives (*ibid.*, p. 19): 5s. money rent, plus boon-works totalling 16 man-days, or else about 180 days' week-work (worth about 15s. by the mid-thirteenth century); need we doubt that given this choice it was the latter that the lord would go on preferring "for ever"?

for the restoration of labour services on manors where they had been entirely abandoned.   In this way the inflation may have acted directly in bringing about a return to labour services.

This does not explain, however, why the process of commutation did not advance as it did in the twelfth century, replacing existing labour services with money rents set at new, realistic levels.   In fact commutation now brought a positive disadvantage to the landlord. That it did so was again a consequence of inflation, but indirectly, as part of more far-reaching legal and social change.   In restoring labour services we see the landlords acting with remarkable respect for manorial custom.   They did not invent new burdens for their tenants: they brought back old ones.   It is very likely that in a period of economic change the landlords found themselves as much hampered by custom in their financial relations with their tenants as the king was in his relations with the landlords.   Historians have long recognized that the legal position of the villein changed for the worse in the course of the twelfth century — certainly in relation to other classes of rural society and probably absolutely.   R. V. Lennard, following A. Ballard, referred to these tenants at the beginning of the century as *villans*, so as to make it plain that their Domesday predecessors were legally quite different from the thirteenth-century *villeins*.[76]   The Domesday villan was classed among the free men of society; his landlord could not eject him from his holding if he did the services due for it, and his oath was accepted in the king's court. None of this was true of the thirteenth-century villein, whom the common lawyers were enmeshing in an elaborate net of rulings that in some ways equated him with the slave of Roman law.   In practice the villein was, more often than not, sheltered by manorial custom from the new insecurity of his position, but this was only by the grace of the lord of the manor, who now had the unquestionable right to override this custom in almost every detail if he chose.   Recently Professor R. H. Hilton has argued that the villein's legal status did not decline steadily throughout the twelfth century but changed catastrophically in its last two decades: 1180-1200 was "the crucial period for the depression of the majority of the rural population".[77] This certainly accords well with the suggestion that a fall in the value of money would tend to bring landlords into conflict with manorial custom.   Legal changes in the twelfth century did not come about by formulating rules in the abstract, but from actual decisions reached in

[76] *Rural England*, p. vi.
[77] "Freedom and Villeinage in England", *Past and Present*, no. 31 (July 1965), p. 13; below, p. 184.

the courts. If lords of manors acquired new powers over their tenants, enlarging, defining or wholly setting aside manorial custom, this was because disputes were arising and were being brought to the royal courts for settlement. Professor Hilton connects this with "the rising prices, the intense fiscal pressure" of the time, especially in John's reign, and suggests that it was only natural that "rising costs should be passed on to the basic producer" and that "this must involve a worsening of his legal and social status".[78] But if we accept that there was a monetary inflation we see the decline in villein status as the landlords' response to a situation where manorial custom combined with the decreasing value of money was endangering their income from their tenants. Overall, indeed, the landlords may even have lost financially: in many places labour services were not reimposed and the money rents continued unchanged. But potentially they gained enormously in the clear backing of royal authority for their powers over the lands, goods and persons of their newly unfree tenants, whether these powers were entirely new or just defined and extended. Certainly throughout the next two hundred years we see these powers being exercised, intermittently and with varying severity, but bringing to the landlords advantages that probably lay beyond the reach of their twelfth-century predecessors. In the process, however, their free tenants had undoubtedly gained, and not only economically. For the first time a sharp line of legal definition was drawn between them and the customary tenants, and as this depressed the one group so, correspondingly, it elevated the other, not only legally but socially as well. It was through this new demarcation of villeinage that the inflation served to maintain labour services. Of the various tests that the courts applied to decide whether a man was a villein and unfree, one of the commonest was his obligation to do unspecified work on his lord's demesne.[79] It was thus to the landlord's long-term advantage to have his villeins render labour services rather than money rents since this helped to identify them as unfree tenants. Directly or indirectly the inflation delayed the effective disappearance of labour services from England by some two hundred years. At the same time it brought the class that paid its rents in this way into a legal degradation from which it took even longer to emerge.

To the people of the countryside, then, the inflation brought changes that were profound and long-lasting. In the towns its

[78] *Ibid.*, p. 14; below, p. 185.
[79] F. Pollock and F. W. Maitland, *The History of English Law before the Time of Edward I*, 2nd edn., 2 vols. (Cambridge, 1898), i, p. 372.

direct effects were less dramatic. At the same time it must have contributed much to two long-term developments: the rise of one class, the decline of another. The burgesses certainly did not suffer from the inflation. Whether their town was at farm to them or whether they paid individual rents to the borough-owner their annual payments, similarly fixed by custom, did not rise with the fall in the value of money. Not only did existing rents not increase: the rents charged in new towns and suburbs seem to have kept the same general level. When the bishop of Salisbury founded the new Salisbury in the 1220s he let out the house-plots at 12d. a year each, the same rent as the bishop of Lincoln had charged in his new town of Banbury eighty or ninety years before; when a new suburb of Banbury was laid out in the mid-thirteenth century an annual rent of 6d. was charged for its cottages (the plots were clearly smaller than in the old town).[80] Rents, of course, were only one of the charges on the burgess, who had to meet increases in royal taxation and perhaps in local dues as well. Even so, it was probably cheaper in real terms to be a townsman in the thirteenth century than in the twelfth. But whether or not the burgesses gained financially over this period they certainly gained by the new legal definitions that created an unfree peasantry. The burgesses were set firmly among the classes of free men recognized by the common law. Increasingly the difference between *burgensis* and *villanus* came to mean more than merely the difference between borough-dweller and village-dweller: it implied a great difference in legal status and privilege. It was not merely through the king's need for ready money that the period of inflation began the steady growth of privilege and self-government in the towns; it probably contributed a little to their economic prosperity and it certainly brought a new status to their inhabitants and with it a new self-confidence and self-respect.

Equally it is no coincidence that the same period saw a sharp decline in the position of the Jews in England, a decline that continued down to their expulsion in 1290. There can have been no group in the country that would be worse hit by a fall in the value of money. The wealth of the Jewish community was based almost entirely on money-lending. The dislocation that the inflation caused may at first have brought the money-lenders some extra business from those whose income came from estates farmed out to lessees; we perhaps see an example of this at Bury St. Edmunds, where the abbot and

[80] *Historic Towns*, ed. M. D. Lobel (London, 1969-), i, Salisbury, p. 4, Banbury, pp. 2, 3.

obedientiaries were heavily in debt to Jews by the 1180s.[81] But over some forty years the real value of the Jews' working capital must have fallen by half or two-thirds. Clearly John's tallages on the Jews were aimed at entirely the wrong target: like the king himself they were victims of the economic trends of the time. But neither king nor magnates could be expected to see this, and the Jews seemed an obvious source of revenue to help the Crown in the difficulties that inflation had brought. A very heavy tallage was levied on them in 1210, and the cruelties with which it was exacted may not be entirely the invention of later chroniclers; moreover, as C. Roth put it, this tallage "set a new fashion in the manner of exploiting the Jewish wealth", initiating the crippling series of levies inflicted on the Jews by Henry III.[82] The expulsion of the Jews can reasonably be seen as a natural conclusion to the steady attrition of their wealth throughout the thirteenth century.[83] It was the inflation that began the Jews' financial weakness, and indirectly it contributed to their impoverishment over a much longer period through the new severity of royal taxation and the wealth and growing political power of the landed gentry. There were, of course, many other factors involved. But it is significant that the decline of the Jewish community in England began in the period of inflation and it is not difficult to see why this was so.

The fact of a sharp rise in prices from 1180 to 1220 is generally accepted, and the outlines of its economic and political effects are clear. It is less certain that there was a monetary inflation, but what evidence there is points to this and, as we have seen, it accords well with various social and economic developments of the period and helps to explain them. But in considering not the effects but the cause of this inflation we are straying much further into an area of speculation and hypothesis. However, one possible explanation can be ruled out completely. There was no deterioration in the

[81] Jocelin of Brakelond, *Chronicle*, ed. Butler, pp. 1-3, 5-6, 10, 30-1, 32; cf. D. Knowles, *The Monastic Order in England*, 2nd edn. (Cambridge, 1963), pp. 304-5, 353-4. But many monasteries were chronically in debt throughout the thirteenth century: J. R. H. Moorman, *Church Life in England in the Thirteenth Century* (Cambridge, 1945), pp. 294, 303-4.

[82] C. Roth, *A History of the Jews in England* (Oxford, 1941), pp. 35, 43-50, 270-1 (but cf. Powicke, *Henry III and the Lord Edward*, i, p. 311 n.); Painter, *Reign of King John*, p. 144; Doris M. Stenton in introduction to *P.R. 13 John*, pp. xix-xxi; H. G. Richardson, *The English Jewry under Angevin Kings* (London, 1960), pp. 166-72.   [83] Cf. Roth, *op. cit.*, pp. 84-5; Powicke, *loc. cit.*

standard of the English coinage that would lead to its depreciation. The silver content of the penny, the only coin in normal use, barely altered from A.D. 800 to 1250.[84]   If, then, the real value of money fell, this is to say that silver was worth less than before, and we must see the inflation of 1180-1220 as a catastrophic fall in the value of silver to about one-third of what it had been.   Was this a local phenomenon peculiar to England, or did it occur throughout Europe so that we should look for an explanation in the development of new silver mines and over-production of the metal?   Unfortunately, sparse though our evidence is for twelfth-century prices and wages in England, it is plentiful compared with what we find elsewhere. However in Normandy, where one would most expect a pattern similar to England, at least until 1204, there seems to have been a slight upward movement of prices between the mid-twelfth century and the mid-fourteenth, but there is no trace of changes of the scale or rapidity of those in England.[85]   Nor does there seem to have been any similar rise in prices elsewhere in Europe.[86]   On other grounds too it is unlikely that Europe generally was flooded with silver at this time.   The silver content of the currencies of France and Italy in the early thirteenth century was very low: the *denarii* of Tours, Genoa and Milan contained less than a quarter, those of Venice less than a sixteenth, of the amount of silver in the English penny.[87]   It seems to have been shortage of silver as well as new imports of gold from West Africa that led to the introduction of gold coinage alongside the silver from 1252 on.[88]   In fact England, in the thirteenth century and throughout the middle ages, was quite exceptional in her wealth in silver.   It is attested by the high standard of her silver currency and by the fact that it was not permanently supplemented with gold until 1344.   It is attested too by the comments of contemporaries.   The Venetian diplomat who wrote the *relazione* on England about 1500 was notably impressed by the quantity of silver plate he saw in churches, in private houses, in shops and even in inns.[89]   Even in the

[84] C. M. Cipolla, "Currency Depreciation in Medieval Europe", *Econ. Hist. Rev.*, 2nd ser., xv (1962-3), p. 422.

[85] L. Delisle, *Études sur la Condition de la Classe Agricole et l'État de l'Agriculture en Normandie au Moyen Âge* (Évreux, 1851), pp. 572-626.   The most useful evidence is the prices of livestock (pp. 610-19), as these avoid the variations in local measures though not the variations in the currencies used for payment.   [86] Postan in *Cambridge Economic History*, ii, pp. 165-7.

[87] Cipolla, "Currency Depreciation", p. 422.

[88] R. S. Lopez, "Back to Gold, 1252", *Econ. Hist. Rev.*, 2nd ser., ix (1956-7), pp. 233-4.

[89] *A Relation, or rather a True Account, of the Island of England*, ed. Charlotte A. Sneyd (Camden Soc., old ser., xxxvii, 1847), pp. 28-9, 42-3.

early twelfth century Henry of Huntingdon, explaining that England
acquired silver from her exports to Germany, added that there was
consequently as much silver in England as there was in Germany
itself.[90]   Historians agree with what both Henry of Huntingdon and
the Venetian diplomat say of the origin of medieval England's silver:
it came from the mines of Germany and was acquired through a
favourable balance of trade with northern Europe, latterly in
particular through supplying wool to the cloth industry of the Low
Countries.[91]   Relatively little silver was mined in England itself,
and in the late twelfth century production was declining.[92]   It follows
that if England was suddenly flooded with silver in the late twelfth
and early thirteenth centuries we must look to a massive increase in
her exports, especially of wool to Flanders.

There is nothing to make this impossible in what we know of the
history of the English wool trade or the Flemish cloth industry.[93]
On the contrary, the period of the inflation seems a likely enough time
for the development of the close interdependence that is so well
recorded in the late thirteenth and fourteenth centuries.   We know
that in the mid-twelfth century monasteries at least were developing
large-scale sheep-farming on the moors of northern England.[94]   The
end of the disturbances of the Anarchy and the more settled
conditions of Henry II's reign were a time when a dramatic increase
in trade might be expected.   It would take some years for the new
imports of silver to have any noticeable effect on prices and, as we
have seen, probably still longer for the price rises to appear on the
Pipe Rolls.   This is not to say, though, that exports to the Low
Countries and Germany now first became important.   Henry of
Huntingdon, after all, was writing before the reign of Henry II; he
mentions "very valuable wool" among England's products,[95] and we
know of Flemish merchants who came to England to buy wool in

---

[90] Henry of Huntingdon, *Historia Anglorum*, ed. T. Arnold (Rolls Series,
1879), pp. 5-6.
[91] As Cipolla, "Currrency Depreciation", p. 420.
[92] Poole, *Domesday Book to Magna Carta*, p. 82.
[93] I explore some of the implications of this suggestion for the history of the
English wool and cloth trade in "The English Trade in Wool and Cloth,
1150-1250: Some Problems and Suggestions", to be published by the Istituto
Internazionale di Storia Economica "Francesco Datini", Prato, in the
proceedings of its second *Settimana di Studio* held in April 1970.
[94] D. Knowles, *Monastic Order*, pp. 352-3, and *The Religious Orders in England*,
3 vols. (Cambridge, 1948-59), i, pp. 65-73; R. A. Donkin, "Cattle on the
Estates of Medieval Cistercian Monasteries in England and Wales", *Econ. Hist.
Rev.*, 2nd ser., xv (1962-3), p. 45.
[95] *Loc. cit.*

1113.[96] Recently, indeed, Professor P. H. Sawyer has convincingly argued that England's wealth in silver can be carried back to the end of the tenth century and was what attracted successive generations of raiders and invaders; he suggests that it may already have been exports of wool that brought the silver to England.[97] None of this contradicts the hypothesis proposed here: it is suggested only that this export trade vastly expanded in the second half of the twelfth century, not that it began then.[98] Nor need we look only to exports of wool. There is substantial evidence of exports of finished cloth from the towns of eastern England.[99] Production and export of tin were growing rapidly at just this period.[100] There is also evidence of export of corn on a large scale to the Low Countries, a sign of their growing urban markets and urban industries.[101] We may bear in mind the possibility that it was a decline in exports of cloth and corn (while the export of wool continued) that first slowed down and then ended the inflation in the course of the thirteenth century. Movements in the price of gold are in keeping with a connection between the inflation and the export trade. Gold was not in everyday currency at this period, though gold coins (*besants*) were used for certain formal or ceremonial payments and gold was in use along with silver as a medium for large-scale trade: in 1257 we find London merchants warning Henry III against the general circulation of gold in coinage, as this might reduce its value.[102] During the inflation the value of gold seems to have fallen, but not quite so much as the value of silver: in 1159 the Exchequer accepted twenty silver pence for one *besant* (a gold: silver ratio of 1:10), in 1186 twenty-four (a ratio of 1:12).[103] By 1265 the workable ratio seems again to have

[96] Eileen Power, *The Wool Trade in English Medieval History* (London, 1941), p. 52; P. H. Sawyer, "The Wealth of England in the Eleventh Century", *Trans. Roy. Hist. Soc.*, 5th ser., xv (1965), p. 162.   [97] *Op. cit.*, pp. 145-64.

[98] This hypothesis does, however, call in question Professor Sawyer's suggestion that there were at least as many sheep in England in the late eleventh century as in the late thirteenth (*op. cit.*, pp. 162-3); cf. the paper cited above, note 93.

[99] E. M. Carus-Wilson, "The English Cloth Industry in the late Twelfth and early Thirteenth Centuries", *Econ. Hist. Rev.*, 1st ser., xiv (1944-5), pp. 32-4, and in *Cambridge Economic History*, ii, pp. 374-5; Miller, "Fortunes of the English Textile Industry", p. 68.

[100] Poole, *Domesday Book to Magna Carta*, p. 83.

[101] Doris M. Stenton in introduction to *P.R. 10 Ric. I*, p. xiv; there is evidence also of export of corn to Norway (*P.R. 32 Hen. II*, p. xxi) and, probably, western France (*P.R. 29 Hen. II*, p. xxviii; *P.R. 30 Hen. II*, p. xxx).

[102] *De Antiquis Legibus Liber*, ed. T. Stapleton (Camden Soc., old ser., xxxiv, 1846), p. 30.

[103] *P.R. 5 Hen. II*, p. 42; *P.R. 32 Hen. II*, p. 149. The ratios assume that these *besants* were twice the weight of a silver penny, like the gold pennies of Aethelraed II (approximately) and Henry III (exactly): G. C. Brooke, *English Coins*, 3rd edn. (London, 1950), pp. 68, 107, 110.

been 1:12, but there may well have been fluctuations meanwhile.[104] Conservative tradition and international custom would tend to keep the ratio stable; the change recorded would be consistent with the import of both metals, but especially silver, in exchange for exported goods.

If excessive imports of silver really were at the root of the inflation there is a strange irony in the financial difficulties of Richard I and John. The policies of both kings led to great quantities of silver being sent abroad, especially in the decade between the payment of Richard's ransom and the final hopeless defence of Normandy. These exports of coin were on a scale to serve as a strong check to the rise in prices.[105] Yet nothing did more than this deflationary policy, which the kings pursued unwittingly, to bring about the Crown's serious financial embarrassments in John's reign. But whether or not this explanation of its origins is accepted, it is clear that 1180-1220 was a period of economic crisis or change in England. Its most spectacular manifestations were political, but its effects on the society and economy of the country were no less profound and long-lasting. It was the more devastating in that people at the time were probably completely unaware of what was happening. In 1927 Lord Beveridge suggested that the rise in prices from the mid-twelfth century to the late thirteenth "when fully examined, may prove to have been one of the most violent price revolutions in English history, comparable in speed to the revolution of the sixteenth century though not having equal social and economic consequences".[106] Professor Postan in 1944 wrote that "Historians and economists will easily find instances of social transformations brought about by additions to the mere volume of the circulating medium . . . . There was the well-known and much publicized increase in bullion in the sixteenth century, and a similar influx may also have occurred in the late twelfth and the thirteenth centuries".[107] Work over the last forty years has

---

[104] *Ibid.*, p. 110. In 1257 the London merchants told Henry III that the value of gold had recently been falling by 10 or 20%: *De Antiquis Legibus Liber*, p. 30.

[105] Powicke, *Loss of Normandy*, 2nd edn., pp. 233-5, 298; Doris M. Stenton, introduction to *P.R. 5 John*, p. xi; Poole, *Domesday Book to Magna Carta*, pp. 364-6, 373; Warren, *King John*, pp. 63, 91-2.

[106] Beveridge, "Yield and Price of Corn", p. 164.

[107] Postan, "Rise of a Money Economy", p. 128. If we compare the suggested size of the English coinage at the end of the tenth century, from 12 to 15 million pennies, with its known size of 168 million pennies, 20 million halfpennies and 20 million farthings at the end of the thirteenth century (D. M. Metcalf, "How Large was the Anglo-Saxon Currency?", *Econ. Hist. Rev.*, 2nd ser., xviii [1965], pp. 476, 481-2), and take into account both the reduction of its real value by two-thirds in the inflation and an estimated three-fold growth of population (J. C. Russell, *British Medieval Population*

increasingly confirmed these predictions. It is now time for 1180-1220 to take its place beside the sixteenth and the twentieth centuries as one of the three great inflationary periods of recorded English history. Historians and others attribute profound and dire consequences to the two later inflations of the currency. Need we still hesitate to attach a like importance to the first?

[Albuquerque, 1948], p. 280), we find that the purchasing power of the money owned by the average Englishman rose by not more than 69% between 1000 and 1300. This is a curious result, though not quite an impossible one; of the figures involved in the calculation the amount of depreciation by inflation is by no means the most vulnerable.

5. The Great Famine and Agrarian Crisis in England 1315-1322*

IAN KERSHAW

I

THE EXPANSION OF THE TWELFTH AND THIRTEENTH CENTURIES IS A commonplace of economic history. Substantial population growth brought rising land values, rising corn prices, and falling real wages. Pressure on the land led to a considerable extension of the area of cultivation as woodland, fen and waste were reclaimed for the plough. With a population of possibly more than five millions by the turn of the fourteenth century, the countryside of England may have been as full as at any time before the eighteenth century.[1] Equally commonplace is the contraction of the later middle ages as these trends were all reversed. In an era of falling population, wages rose as corn prices and land values dwindled. Arable dropped out of use, much of it never again to be tilled, tenements fell vacant, villages were deserted, and encroaching woodlands in some areas took partial revenge for the earlier victory of the plough.[2]

If all this seems clear, the reasons for the reversal of the population rise and economic expansion and the date of the crucial turning-point are anything but self-evident. It once seemed obvious: the Black Death of 1348-9 was the clear divider between expansion and contraction, a freak epidemic which cut the population by at least a third. But since the last war economic historians in Western Europe, notably in England Professor M. M. Postan, have come to argue that the seeds of the population decline and agrarian contraction are to be found in the very period of expansion, that this expansion had the makings of its own nemesis. The plough was forced to take over poor, marginal soils which after a while brought diminishing returns; and as the very limits of cultivation were reached, the colonization of new land more or less petered out. Yet all this while population had been growing and the poverty-stricken rural proletariat of landless and near-landless increasing its numbers. By the early

* I have benefited greatly from the comments and suggestions of Dr. J. R. Maddicott and Miss B. F. Harvey while preparing this paper. I am also most grateful to Dr. D. L. Farmer and to Dr. J. Z. Titow for allowing me to make use of their theses and other unpublished material.

[1] Cf. M. M. Postan in *The Cambridge Economic History of Europe*, vol. i, 2nd edn. (Cambridge, 1966), pp. 561-2, 570.

[2] Cf. esp. M. M. Postan, "Some Economic Evidence of Declining Population in the Later Middle Ages", *Econ. Hist. Rev.*, 2nd ser., ii (1949-50), pp. 221-46.

fourteenth century population had outgrown resources; England had too many mouths to feed. "In these conditions", wrote Postan, "a fortuitous combination of adverse events, such as the succession of bad seasons in the second decade of the fourteenth century, was sufficient to reverse the entire trend of agricultural production and to send the population figures tumbling down".[3] In other words, a Malthusian check has been substituted for a pestilential freak; the famine and agrarian crisis of 1315-22 replaces the Black Death, now reduced to an accelerant of existing trends, as the main turning-point.

This thesis has not gone unchallenged. Professor J. C. Russell argued recently that England was a prosperous country in all but the worst years of the early fourteenth century and that demographically the famine and concurrent epidemic disease were not sufficient to have made any significant impact on the population trend.[4] Another dissenting argument came about the same time from Miss Barbara Harvey, who based her case on land values and the topography of settlement. She argued that land values did not generally fall before the Black Death; that land was still coming into cultivation in the early fourteenth century; and, discarding the theory of soil exhaustion, that there were relatively few cases of land vacancies — and these occurring both on and off marginal land. She concluded that there is no evidence that the famine inaugurated a long-term decline in the population trend, which remained fairly stable in the decades before the great plague.[5]

In so far as her attack was levelled at the claim that the population figures were "tumbling down", Miss Harvey made her point. But the question of whether the famine years formed the turning-point in ending the previous economic expansion and population growth remains unanswered. Postan insisted that his case was no more than "a working hypothesis and a pretext for public debate",[6] yet in the midst of all this speculation about demographic and economic trends of the early fourteenth century, much of it centring on the agrarian crisis of the second decade, a surprising fact is that so little is known of the crisis itself — its scale, severity, and immediate effects. We know hardly anything other than what the chronicles tell us. This has encouraged me to look in some detail at the famine years themselves in the context of social and economic developments of the early

[3] M. M. Postan, "Histoire économique: Moyen Age", *IXe Congrès International des Sciences Historiques*, i, *Rapports* (Paris, 1950), p. 235.

[4] J. C. Russell, "The Pre-Plague Population of England", *Jl. of British Studies*, v (1966), pp. 1-21.

[5] B. F. Harvey, "The Population Trend in England between 1300 and 1348", *Trans. Roy. Hist. Soc.*, 5th ser., xvi (1966), pp. 23-42.

[6] Postan, *Rapports*, p. 241.

fourteenth century. How severe was the crisis? What were its immediate effects? Was it serious enough to provoke a long-term change in economic trends, to bring to an end the population rise or, still further, to begin a decline lasting to the precipitous fall of the Black Death? In sum, what *is* the evidence that the crisis of the second decade of the fourteenth century amounted to a turning-point of major significance in the social and economic trends of the middle ages?

This paper offers no more than a preliminary dip into the evidence and a summary of first findings. Much regional and local analysis of social and economic trends in the early fourteenth century needs to be undertaken before a more balanced appraisal of this complex question can be attempted. My paper is also confined to England, though the great famine and agrarian crisis certainly afflicted a wide area of northern Europe.[7] In one valuable regional study at least, of the Paris area, it was suggested that the turning-point in the economy did come in the famine period; it was from 1315 that a conjunction of crises "went to usher in an era of contraction".[8] However, little work has been done on the continent on the effects of the agrarian crisis and although it is now accepted orthodoxy that contraction in the agrarian economy set in well before the Black Death,[9] the varying chronology of this transition still awaits analysis.

In the early parts of the paper I shall describe the nature of the agrarian crisis, paying particular attention to its chronology and to price fluctuations — both of which were only superficially dealt with by H. S. Lucas.[10] Secondly, based on the evidence of manorial records, I shall discuss the scale of the crisis, followed by an assessment of its effects on landlords and on the peasantry. Finally, in a more speculative section, I intend to consider the rôle of the crisis in the early fourteenth-century economy and the question of whether it could have inaugurated a long-term contraction in the agrarian economy.

[7] Cf. H. S. Lucas, "The Great European Famine of 1315, 1316, and 1317" in E. M. Carus-Wilson (ed.), *Essays in Economic History*, vol. ii (London, 1962), pp. 49-72, repr. from *Speculum*, v (1930); and F. Curschmann, *Hungersnöte im Mittelalter* (Leipzig, 1900), pp. 33, 208-17. There is no evidence of a famine in southern Europe in 1315-17: M-J. Larenaudie, "Les famines en Languedoc aux XIVe et XVe siècles", *Annales du Midi*, lxiv (1952), p. 37.

[8] G. Fourquin, *Les Campagnes de la Région Parisienne à la Fin du Moyen Age* (Paris, 1964), p. 191.

[9] E.g. B. H. Slicher van Bath, *The Agrarian History of Western Europe A.D. 500-1850* (London, 1963), pp. 87-90, 137; G. Duby, *Rural Economy and Country Life in the Medieval West* (London, 1968), pp. 306-8, 318-20.

[10] Lucas, *op. cit.*: the chronology is not always clear and there is no real price analysis.

II

During the early years of the fourteenth century England experienced substantial price inflation. The prices of livestock, dairy produce, and most other foodstuffs rose considerably from about 1305, chiefly as a result of currency depreciation and the large influx of foreign silver coined into sterling.[11] By the end of the first decade of the fourteenth century many prices stood as much as 25 per cent higher than at the time of the last recoinage of 1299.[12] Grain prices, more affected by the quality of the harvest than by strictly monetary factors, followed a somewhat different pattern. After the high prices of the mid-1290s a series of favourable harvests brought relatively low prices for over a decade, though the harvests of 1308-10 were sufficiently poor to bring heavy price increases and a situation approaching a dearth in some parts of the country. In Scotland, coming on top of the warfare and general distress which faced the country, a dearth had already reached famine proportions by 1310.[13]

By 1315 the price situation was already serious. Reminting the coinage, which had proved a successful expedient in price control under Edward I, was not attempted.[14] But Parliament, sitting in the Lent of 1315, put pressure on the king to issue an ordinance fixing maximum prices for livestock and victuals.[15] The prices were fixed at levels only slightly lower than those prevailing, so the ordinance was apparently aimed at stabilizing rather than reducing prices.[16] No attempt was made to regulate corn prices, and clearly this would have been utterly impossible during the extreme scarcity of 1315 and after. In fact the harvest of 1314, only garnered with difficulty because of the wet conditions,[17] was proving deficient and grain

---

[11] J. E. Thorold Rogers, *A History of Agriculture and Prices in England*, i (Oxford, 1866), pp. 344-5, 352, 357-8, 431-2; D. L. Farmer, "An Examination of Price Fluctuations in Certain Articles in the Twelfth, Thirteenth, and early Fourteenth Centuries" (University of Oxford D.Phil. thesis, 1958), pp. 36, 84, 97, 135-7; and his "Some Livestock Price Movements in Thirteenth Century England", *Econ. Hist. Rev.*, 2nd ser., xxii (1969), pp. 12-14; M. Prestwich, "Edward I's Monetary Policies and their Consequences", *ibid.*, pp. 412-16.

[12] Farmer, thesis *op. cit.*, p. 203.

[13] *Scotichronicon Johannis de Fordun*, ed. T. Hearn (Oxford, 1722), iv, p. 1,005.

[14] Farmer, "Livestock Prices", pp. 12-13; thesis *op. cit.*, p. 203.

[15] *Rotuli Parliamentorum*, i, p. 295; *Johannis de Trokelowe et Henrici de Blaneforde Chronica et Annales*, ed. H. T. Riley (Rolls Series, 1866), pp. 88-90; *Vita Edwardi Secundi*, ed. N. Denholm-Young (London, 1957), p. 59.

[16] Farmer, thesis *op. cit.*, p. 204.

[17] *Vita Edw. Sec.*, p. 64. The Westminster version of the *Flores Historiarum*, ed. H. R. Luard (Rolls Ser., 1890), iii, pp. 160-1, refers to very heavy rainfall in 1314 but this almost certainly should refer to the following year. A number of chroniclers are very wayward in their chronology of the famine: e.g., the *Chronicon Henrici Knighton*, ed. J. R. Lumby (Rolls Ser., 1889), i, pp. 411-12,

prices rose sharply in the summer months of 1315, partly no doubt in anticipation of the prospects of the next harvest.[18]   Many people must already have been in serious straits before the full extent of the dearth was felt in the first famine year of 1315-16.   In the summer of 1315, in an atmosphere of impending gloom brought on by political troubles and the wretched weather which was destroying the crops, the archbishop of Canterbury ordered the clergy to perform solemn, barefooted processions bearing the Sacrament and relics, accompanied by the ringing of bells, chanting of the litany, and the celebration of mass.   This was in the hope of encouraging the people to atone for their sins and appease the wrath of God by prayer, fasting, alms-giving, and other charitable works.[19]

The harvest of 1315 was a disaster.   Chroniclers and manorial records concur in attributing the trouble to the torrential rain which poured down throughout the summer months of 1315, producing widespread flooding and the ruin of hay and corn crops alike.[20]   It has been suggested that underlying climatic changes, resulting in a long-term trend towards cooler and wetter weather, began about this time and help to explain not only the extremities of the famine years but also the general economic depression in western Europe during the later middle ages.[21]   Unpredictable and extreme weather conditions were certainly experienced in the decade 1315-25, but it is nevertheless difficult, from a comparison of harvest qualities in England during the thirteenth and fourteenth centuries, to agree with the assertion that the famine years marked the onset of a long-term deterioration in the weather.[22]

---

has the famine and dearth stretching from 1317 to 1319 and the *Eulogium Historiarum*, ed. F. S. Haydon (Rolls Ser., 1863), iii, p. 195, has 1319 to 1321.

[18] Rogers, *op. cit.*, i, pp. 196-7, 230; D. L. Farmer, "Some Grain Price Movements in Thirteenth-Century England", *Econ. Hist. Rev.*, 2nd ser., x (1957-8), p. 212; *Trokelowe*, p. 92.

[19] *Historical Manuscripts Commission: Appendix to 8th Report* (London, 1881), pt. 1, pp. 352-3: I owe this reference to Mr. P. S. Brown.   Cf. also, "Annales Paulini" in *Chronicles of the Reigns of Edward I and Edward II*, ed. W. Stubbs (Rolls Ser., 1882), i, p. 278.

[20] *Vita Edw. Sec.*, p. 64; *Trokelowe*, p. 93; *Chrons. of Edw. I and II*, i, p. 278; *Chronicon Abbatie de Parco Lude*, ed. E. Venables (Lincs. Rec. Soc., 1891), p. 24; *Chronica Monasterii de Melsa*, ed. E. A. Bond (Rolls Ser., 1867), ii, p. 332; J. Z. Titow, "Evidence of Weather in the Account Rolls of the Bishopric of Winchester, 1209-1350", *Econ. Hist. Rev.*, 2nd ser., xii (1959-60), pp. 385-6. H. J. Hewitt, *Medieval Cheshire* (Manchester, 1929), pp. 32-4 has references to flooded meadows and a wet harvest in Frodsham in 1315 (mistakenly given by Hewitt as 1316).

[21] G. Utterström, "Climatic Fluctuations and Population Problems in Early Modern History", *Scandinavian Econ. Hist. Rev.*, iii (1955), esp. pp. 15-21.

[22] This is the opinion of Mr. P. S. Brown, who is making a careful study of harvest qualities in this period.   After the very wet weather and unfavourable conditions of the famine years, there were long stretches of good harvests

Appallingly bad though the 1315 harvest was, the availability of new corn supplies mitigated the severity of the dearth in the autumn months. But Christmas 1315 could not have been a joyous season for the many suffering from the renewed, but even steeper, rise in prices which during the spring and summer of 1316 reached unprecedented heights.[23] The average price of a quarter of wheat in the first decade of the fourteenth century, according to Thorold Rogers's figures, was 5s. 7¼d.[24] But the modest 8s. a quarter which manorial lords were getting for their wheat in the autumn of 1315 had risen to as much as 26s. 8d. by the summer of 1316.[25] The scarcity was felt in every part of England and the price of all types of grain rose in sympathy with wheat (though oats, which cropped better than any other grain in 1315 and 1316, rose less vigorously than rye and barley).[26] In fact the price rise as demonstrated by the evidence of manorial accounts does not fully indicate the extent of the dearth. The chroniclers give a variety of exceedingly high, but not incredible, prices which presumably represent the retail value of corn in the markets of large towns. Trokelowe stated that wheat, which had sold for 20s. a quarter in the summer of 1315, rose to 30s. by June 1316, then climbed to 40s.[27] The *Annales Londonienses* record prices of 20s., 30s. and sometimes 40s. for a quarter of wheat.[28] The Bridlington chronicler noted that wheat sold commonly in England for 30s. a quarter, sometimes for 32s., and certainly not for less than 24s.[29] A Canterbury chronicle has a *summa* (equivalent to a quarter) of wheat selling at 26s. 8d. and a *summa* of barley at 16s.[30] In the market at Leicester as much as 44s. was paid for a quarter of wheat.[31] But in the west country prices remained at a more modest level. At Chepstow in 1316 wheat fetched only 16s. a quarter, servants' corn (presumably mixed grain) 12s., and oats 5s.[32]

---

between the famine and the Black Death and again in the late fourteenth century. Cf. also J. Z. Titow, *Winchester Yields: a Study in Medieval Agricultural Productivity* (Cambridge, 1972), p. 24; Slicher van Bath, *Agrarian Hist. of Western Europe*, p. 161; and the very sceptical criticism of Utterström's argument by E. Le Roy Ladurie, *Histoire du Climat depuis l'an mille* (Paris, 1967), pp. 14-17.

[23] *Trokelowe*, p. 94; *Vita Edw. Sec.*, p. 69; Rogers, *op. cit.*, i, p. 197; Farmer, thesis *op. cit.*, p. 75.

[24] Rogers, *op. cit.*, i, p. 245.

[25] Farmer, "Grain Prices", p. 215; Rogers, *op. cit.*, i, p. 197.

[26] Farmer, thesis *op. cit.*, pp. 64-71.

[27] *Trokelowe*, pp. 92, 94.

[28] *Chrons. of Edw. I and II*, i, p. 236.

[29] *Ibid.*, ii, p. 48.

[30] Trinity College, Cambridge, MS. R.5.41, *s.a.* 1316.

[31] *Knighton*, i, p. 411 (*s.a.* 1317, but should presumably be 1316).

[32] *Flores*, iii, p. 340.

Numerous grants of protection and safe-conduct to merchants and others during the winter and spring of 1316 illustrate the lure of high profits to be made out of long-distance grain trade. Merchants of Lincoln and servants of Kirkstead Abbey (Lincs.) went to Cambridgeshire and Huntingdonshire to acquire corn; burgesses of Ravenserodd and Hull travelled to various parts of the realm buying corn; and Richard atte Pole of Hull was given a safe-conduct to go overseas to purchase corn and bring it to England.[33] Merchants from Cornwall, which seems to have been little affected by the crop failures and famine, were also granted safe-conduct to take food to London.[34] And manorial lords who were accustomed to selling locally were persuaded to send their grain considerable distances in search of maximum profits.[35]

Corn prices were not the only ones to rise. Because of the lack of solar heat the price of salt quadrupled, soaring to levels as exorbitant as those of wheat prices. The mean price of salt in England in the decade before the famine, based on manorial sources, was just over 3s. a quarter; in 1315-16 the mean price over a wide area of England was over 13s. a quarter, dropping to just short of 11s. a quarter in 1316-17.[36] As with grain, the chroniclers give even higher prices and speak of a quarter of salt as fetching between 30s. and 40s. in 1315-16.[37] An increase also took place in the price of dairy produce.[38] In fact, according to the chroniclers there was a great dearth of all victuals, not just corn.[39] Trokelowe claimed that even horse-meat was too expensive, and he and other writers referred to the poor being forced to eat dogs, cats and other "unclean things".[40] Rumours of cannibalism — of people stealing children

[33] *Cal. Pat. Rolls, 1313-17*, pp. 380, 382-3, 390, 397, 399, 400. The chronicler John Hocsemius noted that although the granaries in the city of Liège were actually full in 1315, the grain was transported to the coastal regions where the dearth was greater (cited in Curschmann, *Hungersnöte im Mittelalter*, pp. 44, 41, 209).

[34] J. Hatcher, *Rural Economy and Society in the Duchy of Cornwall 1300-1500* (Cambridge, 1970), p. 85 and n. 2.

[35] Farmer, thesis *op. cit.*, pp. 91, 110-12.

[36] Dr. Farmer kindly provided me with a table of, as yet, unpublished salt prices which he has calculated on the basis of a wide range of manorial accounts. Cf. also Rogers, *op. cit.*, i, pp. 458, 480, 484. The high price of salt probably pushed up the price of fish by making it more expensive to preserve it: cf. Rogers, *op. cit.*, i, pp. 609, 612.

[37] *Trokelowe*, pp. 92, 94; *Chron. de Melsa*, ii, p. 332; *Chrons. of Edw. I and II*, i, pp. 238, 279; *ibid.*, ii, p. 48.

[38] Farmer, thesis *op. cit.*, pp. 92-3; "Livestock Prices", pp. 5, 14.

[39] *Chrons. of Edw. I and II*, i, pp. 237, 278-9; *ibid.*, ii, p. 48.

[40] *Trokelowe*, p. 95; *Vita Edw. Sec.*, p. 70; *The Brut or the Chronicles of England*, ed. F. W. D. Brie, pt. 1 (Early English Text Soc., 1906), p. 210; *Annales Monastici*, ed. H. R. Luard (Rolls Ser., 1866), iii, p. 470.

to eat them — may have been exaggerated but they testify to the stark horror which this period of extreme famine impressed upon the memories of contemporaries[41].

Dr. Farmer's conclusion, based on livestock prices recorded in manorial accounts, chiefly those of the bishop of Winchester's estates, was that little or no enhanced demand for meat resulted from the grain shortage.[42] His calculations demonstrate that animal prices did not all conform to the same pattern at this date. The price of oxen rose sharply in 1315-16 while the price of plough- and cart-horses fell drastically, as did the price of cows; though the data for sheep prices are less than satisfactory, the sale price of pigs, animals raised directly for consumption, appears to have risen very little during the famine years.[43] The rise in the price of oxen was not attributed by Dr. Farmer to growing demand for meat during a grain shortage but rather to increased investment in improvement of the plough-teams on the basis of the high profits attainable in corn production at the time.[44] Yet the chroniclers clearly state that there was a greatly accentuated demand for all types of victuals, including meat, in the wake of the grain shortage. The discrepancy between the chroniclers' reports and the conclusions based on manorial evidence may at least in part be explicable in terms of the contrast between the prices paid for livestock by the bishop of Winchester and other wealthy landlords, with resources and bargaining power on their side at a time when poverty was forcing many to sell off their livestock in return for cash in hand, and those charged for meat by butchers in the markets of large towns, where the situation must have been far more serious. Certainly the demand for meat was sufficient to bring about the recall, in February 1316, of the proclamation of eleven months earlier fixing livestock and meatstock prices. And the *Annales Londonienses* are quite precise about the reason: "they ordained that the ordinance regarding livestock, fowl, and eggs (*de bestiis et avibus et ovis*) should not stand, because few were found on account of the dearth and lack of victuals".[45]

There is no doubt that by the spring and early summer of 1316 England was in the throes of a famine of major dimensions.[46] And

[41] *Trokelowe*, p. 95; *Brut*, pp. 209-10; *Ann. Monast.*, iii, p. 470. Irish writers also state that "people used to eat one another, without doubt, throughout Erinn": *Annals of Loch Cé*, ed. W. M. Hennessy (Rolls Ser., 1871), i, p. 595, s.a. 1318; *Annals of Ulster*, ed. B. MacCarthy (Dublin, 1893), ii, p. 433.

[42] Farmer, thesis *op. cit.*, p. 160.

[43] *Ibid.*, pp. 86-93; Farmer, "Livestock Prices", p. 14.

[44] Farmer, thesis *op. cit.*, pp. 88, 94, 160.

[45] *Chrons. of Edw. I and II*, i, pp. 237-8; Rymer, *Foedera*, ii, p. 286.

[46] The dearth and famine certainly afflicted Scotland and Ireland at the same time. Cf. *Vita Edw. Sec.*, p. 60; *Annals of Loch Cé*, pp. 579, 595.

the famine was accompanied, during the course of 1316, by a virulent and widespread epidemic of an enteric type — perhaps typhoid — which greatly increased mortalities. The epidemic spread across social boundaries, for it affected the aristocracy as well as the poor.[47] Nevertheless, it seems a mistake to attempt to separate, as Professor Russell does, the mortalities of the famine from those of the epidemic. Contemporary chroniclers clearly related the two and expressly mentioned the great mortalities of the poor in this year.[48]

There is very little evidence on which to base an estimate of mortalities during the famine years. The rise in the number of heriots paid on a group of Winchester manors, particularly those paid by the near-landless, indicates a crude death-rate approaching 10 per cent in the famine years.[49] But in large towns and cities the mortalities must have been much greater. The bodies of paupers, dead of starvation, littered city streets; many were buried daily in every cemetery, and burial could not be delayed because of the foul stink; according to *The Brut*, "so miche and so faste folc deiden, that vnnethes men might ham bury".[50] No sources survive for an estimate of this mortality, such as occur in Flanders where the city of Ypres has left a remarkable burial register recording the burial of 2,794 inhabitants — probably about a tenth of the city's population — in only six months between May and October 1316.[51]

The social effects of the famine were worsened by reductions in seigneurial expenditure. Estate records corroborate Trokelowe's comment that during the famine magnates and religious cut down on their followings, withdrew their customary alms, and reduced the size of their households.[52] Alms in cash offered by the canons of Bolton Priory (Yorks.) were substantially reduced during the famine

[47] Cf. the figures from Inquisitions Post Mortem in Russell, "Pre-Plague Population", p. 8.

[48] *Ibid.*, pp. 8-9; *Trokelowe*, p. 94; *Flores*, iii, pp. 174, 341; *Chrons. of Edw. I and II*, i, pp. 236-7, 279.

[49] M. M. Postan and J. Z. Titow, "Heriots and Prices on Winchester Manors", *Econ. Hist. Rev.*, 2nd ser., xi (1958-9), pp. 399, 407.

[50] *Brut*, p. 209; *Trokelowe*, p. 94; *Knighton*, i, p. 412; *Chrons. of Edw. I and II*, ii, p. 48.

[51] Lucas, *op. cit.*, pp. 66-7; H. Van Werveke, "La famine de l'an 1316 en Flandre et dans les régions voisines", *Révue du Nord*, xli (1959), pp. 5-14. For chronicle reports of the miseries of towns in the Low Countries, see Curschmann, *Hungersnöte im Mittelalter*, pp. 209-11. Chroniclers also noted very heavy mortalities in German towns: cf. W. Abel, *Geschichte der deutschen Landwirtschaft* (Stuttgart, 1967), pp. 115-16 and W. Abel, *Agrarkrisen und Agrarkonjunktur*, 2nd edn. (Hamburg, 1966), pp. 45-6.

[52] *Trokelowe*, p. 93. Cf. also a reference in similar vein in Trinity College, Cambridge, MS. R.5.41, *s.a.* 1316: "such was the dearth in England that those who were accustomed to supporting themselves and their dependants in a suitable manner travelled along streets and through places as beggars".

years and the number of household servants and *famuli* employed by the priory was halved.[53] Despite the evident distress on the Winchester estates during the famine years, no alms of any sort were doled out — though this was no new venture here for alms-giving had practically ceased with the death of Bishop Peter des Roches in 1238.[54] On many manors of this vast estate agricultural workers were again the sufferers; grain liveries for *famuli* were suspended in 1316-17, the reason being frankly admitted as "on account of the dearness of corn".[55]

Trokelowe's assertion that those dismissed from aristocratic households, used to a delicate life, had to turn to crime to survive cannot be proven but may well have been true. The problem of lawlessness was, of course, already a serious one facing Edward II's government but the desperation of the famine years probably accentuated it. The commission to the Keepers of the Peace in Kent in 1316-17 refers to the danger presented by vagabonds, and robberies certainly account for the vast number of offences dealt with in these sessions.[56] Practically a third of all the thefts related to the stealing of foodstuffs — very largely grain and its products, such as bread and ale. About 40 per cent of the thefts involved the stealing of livestock, nearly half of these instances relating to sheep. Thefts of cash formed the bulk of the remainder. The proportionate number of cases involving theft of foodstuffs is strikingly large and much greater than in other peace session rolls for other years and other counties that I have seen, though admittedly comparison is not easy because of the particular fullness of the Kent proceedings.[57] For example, only eighteen out of a total of 269 instances of theft in the 1314 peace sessions in Berkshire, Buckinghamshire, Northamptonshire, Oxfordshire and Suffolk mention foodstuffs.[58] And the evidence of gaol delivery rolls points

[53] Cf. my *Bolton Priory: the Economy of a Northern Monastery* (Oxford, 1973), pp. 52, 77, 137, 141-3.

[54] J. Z. Titow, "Land and Population on the Bishop of Winchester's Estates 1209-1350" (University of Cambridge Ph.D. thesis, 1962), p. 126.

[55] Farmer, thesis *op. cit.*, p. 83; the phrase cited is taken from the account of the manor of Meon (Hants.). The Winchester estate managers practised the same policy in the late thirteenth century: cf. M. M. Postan, *The Famulus: the Estate Labourer in the XIIth and XIIIth Centuries* (Econ. Hist. Rev., suppl. no. 2, 1954), p. 37.

[56] *Kent Keepers of the Peace 1316-17*, ed. B. H. Putnam (Kent Records, xiii, 1933), pp. xxii-iii. I do not use any technical or legal definitions of stealing; these robberies embrace burglary, petty and grand larceny, etc.

[57] *Ibid.*, p. xiv, and B. H. Putnam, "Records of the Keepers of the Peace and their Supervisors, 1307-27", *Eng. Hist. Rev.*, xlv (1930), p. 436.

[58] *Rolls of Northamptonshire Sessions of the Peace, 1314-16, 1320*, ed. M. Gollancz (Northants. Rec. Soc., xi, 1940), pp. 8-55; Pub. Rec. Off. (hereafter P.R.O.), Just. Itin. 1/850, 1395.

in the same direction. Out of seventy-six cases dealt with by the Kent justices in 1316-17, twenty-six involved theft of foodstuffs, while in the Kent roll for 1308-9 there were only seven such cases out of 112.[59]

A greatly improved harvest was needed in 1316 if the sufferings of the past year were to be alleviated. But the summer of 1316 brought renewed downpours of rain and a harvest worse, if anything, than that of the previous year.[60] The highest prices of 1315-16 may not have been reached, but the price of wheat was more consistently exorbitant in 1316-17 and grain was possibly in even shorter supply this year.[61] Taken together, the two years 1315-16 and 1316-17 mark a rate of inflation in grain prices which is quite unparalleled in English history.[62] The chroniclers vary in their estimates of the duration of the famine,[63] but there can be no doubt that the severest hardships lasted throughout the accounting year 1316-17 until a better harvest in 1317 brought some relief and about a fifty per cent drop in grain prices.[64] The plentiful harvest of 1318 marked the real end of the scarcity and hardship, apart from those counties of northern England which were subjected to the terrors of Scottish raids.[65] In 1318 "god yer was agein i-come, and god chep of corn"[66] as prices fell to a lower level than any year since 1288, with dealers openly offering wheat at a price almost seven times lower than that demanded the previous year.[67]

H. S. Lucas treated 1318 as the end of the crisis and indeed the most grave and dramatic phase of the famine was over by that date.[68]

[59] Putnam, *Kent Keepers*; P.R.O., Just. Itin. 3/109. I did not analyse in full the Bedfordshire gaol delivery roll of 1316-17, but I did note that the first fifteen cases considered by the justices included seven that dealt with the theft of foodstuffs (P.R.O., Just. Itin. 3/1/2).

[60] Titow, "Weather", pp. 386-7.

[61] Farmer, thesis *op. cit.*, pp. 81, 83; Rogers, *op. cit.*, i, p. 198. The Tintern version of the *Flores* has higher prices for 1317 than for 1316: *Flores*, iii, pp. 340-1.

[62] Rogers, *op. cit.*, i, p. 198.

[63] *Knighton*, i, p. 411 has two years; *Brut*, p. 209 has two-and-a-half years; *Vita Edw. Sec.*, pp. 64, 90 has the dearth lasting from 1315 to 1318; and the *Chron. de Melsa*, ii, p. 332 also has three years; the Bridlington chronicler claimed the dearth lasted continuously for six years, though prices did not remain at the heights they reached in 1315-16: *Chrons. of Edw. I and II*, ii, p. 48.

[64] Farmer, thesis *op. cit.*, pp. 81-2.

[65] Cf. Jean Scammell, "Robert I and the North of England", *Eng. Hist. Rev.*, lxxiii (1958), pp. 385-403.

[66] *The Political Songs of England*, ed. T. Wright (Camden Soc., vi, 1839), p. 314.

[67] Farmer, thesis *op. cit.*, pp. 81-3; *Vita Edw. Sec.*, p. 90.

[68] Lucas, *op. cit.*, pp. 71-2.

But Lucas gave insufficient attention to another aspect of the agrarian crisis — the devastating series of livestock epidemics which afflicted most areas of Britain in this period.[69]   The famine years themselves were accompanied by a widespread sheep murrain.   Other livestock was not badly affected at this date, though disease or starvation did take some toll in lives.[70]   But although the depredations of the sheep murrain (the scale of which we will consider later)[71] had largely passed by 1317, a new epidemic afflicting only cattle and oxen and wiping out very large numbers of them, began its dreadful passage through Britain in the county of Essex at Easter 1319.[72]   It was probably imported from the continent where France, it was believed, was suffering from the disease at the same time.[73]   The Louth Park chronicler thought that it had raged through the whole of Christendom.[74]   The epidemic reached the north of England and Scotland later in 1319; in the north-east it was first heard of at the siege of Berwick in the late summer, when nearly all the oxen being led to the siege died suddenly.[75]   By 1321 the murrain was ravaging Scotland and Ireland, and the same "cow-destruction" returned again to Ireland in 1324-5.[76]   The reports of the chroniclers are substantiated by manorial evidence, which points to widespread destruction of cattle-herds on an unprecedented scale during the accounting years 1319-20 and 1320-1.[77]   Fully understandable were the sentiments of a contemporary, that the cattle murrain was the coming of:

> ... another sorwe that spradde over al the lond;
> A thusent winter ther bifore com nevere non so strong.
> To binde alle the mene men in mourning and in care,
> The orf deide al bidene (all the cattle died straightaway),
>   and maden the lond al bare,
>   so faste,
> Com nevere wrecche into Engelond that made men more agaste.[78]

[69] He passes over the subject in no more than a few lines: *op. cit.*, pp. 57, 59-60.
    [70] *Trokelowe*, p. 92; *Vita Edw. Sec.*, p. 64; *Chron. de Melsa*, ii, p. 333; and cf. below, n. 116.   [71] Cf. below, pp. 102-4.
    [72] *Trokelowe*, pp. 104-5.   The Westminster *Flores* places the epidemic in 1318, which is certainly an error; the Tintern version states that the epidemic began in Scotland, spread to England, and then finally to the Welsh Marches: *Flores*, iii, pp. 186-7, 343.   The incidence of the disease as gleaned from the manorial evidence, however (cf. below, pp. 106-8) seems better to fit Trokelowe's explanation, and the Lanercost chronicler also thought the murrain had spread northwards not southwards in 1319: *Chronicon de Lanercost, 1201-1346*, ed. J. Stevenson (Edinburgh, 1839), p. 240.
    [73] *Trokelowe*, p. 105.   [74] *Chron. de Parco Lude*, p. 27.
    [75] V. H. Galbraith, "Extracts from the Historia Aurea and a French 'Brut' (1317-47)", *Eng. Hist. Rev.*, xliii (1928), p. 210.   The Lanercost chronicler was mistaken in thinking that the cattle murrain had been raging for two years before 1319 in the south of England: *Chron. de Lanercost*, p. 240.
    [76] *Fordun*, iv, p. 1,010; *Ann. of Ulster*, ii, pp. 437, 439, 441.
    [77] Cf. below, pp. 110-11.   [78] *Polit. Songs*, p. 342.

Even now the seemingly interminable hardships of the protracted agrarian crisis were not at an end. Corn prices had remained quite low in 1319 but rose considerably in the year following the mediocre harvest of the wet autumn of 1320.[79] This was preparatory to another disastrous harvest in 1321 and a rise in corn prices to inflated levels approaching those of 1315-17.[80] Some manors were able to sell wheat at higher prices than in 1316 and again lords were willing to send their manorial produce long distances to gain maximum profits from the soaring prices.[81] The sale price of barley on the Merton College manor of Holywell in Oxford doubled within six months of the harvest, swung upwards at the end of April, and reached a peak price in June before falling slightly at the end of the month.[82] Only one chronicler mentions the scarcity of 1321-2 and none the bad weather which presumably conditioned the wretched harvest.[83] With Scottish depredations in the north of England and the downfall of Thomas of Lancaster, the chroniclers had other things on their minds. But it is also conceivable that the harvest failure of 1321 was occasioned not by heavy rainfall but by the less spectacular prolonged drought. A possible indicator of this is the fact that barley, a crop not suited to very dry conditions, appears to have failed more resoundingly in 1321 than in 1315 or 1316.[84]

The more settled agrarian conditions after 1322, with better harvests and lower grain prices, can be said to mark the real end of the crisis in rural economy for most of the country. But, for south-eastern England at least, a great drought in the summers of 1325 and 1326 coupled with serious inroads of the sea and another devastating livestock epidemic had grave consequences.[85] Christ Church Canterbury claimed in 1327 to have lost 1,212 acres to the sea in recent flooding, and 257 oxen, 511 cows and their issue, and 4,585 sheep — livestock in all to the value of over £790 — dead in the

[79] Rogers, *op. cit.*, i, p. 200; Farmer, thesis *op. cit.*, p. 83 and "Grain Prices", p. 212; Titow, "Weather", p. 388.

[80] Rogers, *op. cit.*, i, pp. 200, 230; Farmer, thesis *op. cit.*, p. 83 and "Grain Prices", p. 212.

[81] Farmer, thesis *op. cit.*, pp. 110, 119.

[82] *Ibid.*, p. 116.

[83] Walsingham describes the year 1321 as "like the rest not worth praising, wretched in issue of crops or fruit . . .": *Thomae Walsingham Historia Anglicana*, ed. H. T. Riley (Rolls Ser., 1863), i, p. 163.

[84] Farmer, thesis *op. cit.*, pp. 74, 83, 283-5. The Winchester estates offer little help this year, though such indications as there are point to a dry summer: Titow, "Weather", p. 388.

[85] C. E. Britton, *A Meteorological Chronology to A.D. 1450* (London, 1937), pp. 134-5; Titow, "Weather", p. 389; R. A. L. Smith, *Canterbury Cathedral Priory* (Cambridge, 1943), pp. 126, 156.

murrain.[86] For the men of Southampton, too, 1325-6 seems to have been a greater disaster than 1315-17. The tenants of Godshouse in Southampton had managed to pay off their rent arrears satisfactorily in the late thirteenth century and there are few signs of dislocation in the famine years. But in 1325-6 large rent arrears owed by these tenants had to be written off and the tenements taken into the lord's hand. Entries in the margin of the account such as "dead in poverty and so nothing", "died a pauper", or "fled from the town as a pauper" supply the reasons for the rent defects.[87]

The agrarian crisis was not a single entity. It must be seen as a succession of arable and livestock disasters,[88] and it is the cumulative effect of the devastations which has to be weighed in an assessment of whether these years did form a turning-point in the agrarian economy of England.

III

The granary returns entered on the dorse of most manorial accounts provide some idea of the scale of difficulties in arable production during the famine years. Of course we can only measure grain yields on demesne lands and have no direct figures at all for peasant production. Nevertheless, it is exceedingly unlikely that the peasants bettered their lords — a view confirmed by such indirect evidence as we have — and the figures therefore reflect the best we could expect from the lands of the peasantry.

All the major crops, with the exception of oats, failed dismally in the harvests of 1315 and 1316. From a fairly extensive sample of estates in the midlands and south of England, though weighted by the accounts of the Winchester manors, Dr. Farmer estimated that the overall net yields (that is gross produce less the seed required for the following year) of wheat and barley were little more than half of normal in 1315.[89] Wheat was hardly better the following year, though barley improved to answer for about three-quarters of its normal yield. Oats, the hardiest crop and that best able to withstand heavy rainfall, produced returns little different from normal, though even in good conditions the gross yield of oats was seldom more than two-and-a-half times its seed.

---

[86] *Literae Cantuarienses*, ed. J. B. Sheppard (Rolls Ser., 1887), i, pp. 243-6.
[87] Bodleian, Queen's College MS. D.D., Box xliii, R.283; Box xliv, R.338; *Hist. MSS. Comm., App. to 6th Rep.* (London, 1877), pp. 552-67.
[88] A point well brought out in the "Poem on the Evil Times of Edward II": *Polit. Songs*, pp. 341-2.
[89] Farmer, "Grain Prices", pp. 217-18 and thesis *op. cit.*, pp. 74, 81-2.

With the complete yield figures for the Winchester estates over a period of a century and a half now available, we can assess the defectiveness of the 1315 and 1316 harvests on some thirty-odd manors in southern England.   The mean gross yield[90] of wheat from the manors was about 60 per cent of average in 1315 and 53 per cent in 1316.   Barley answered for about 80 per cent in 1315, falling to 68 per cent the following year.   The returns for oats were approximately 89 and 71 per cent.[91]   And the figures available for rye, mancorn, and drage show that these crops were also seriously affected in the famine years.[92]   For the Winchester estates, therefore, the the harvest of 1316 was more extreme even than its predecessor, a fact further illustrated by the figures in Table I.

For the north of England yield figures are less easy to come by, but on a group of estates in the West Riding of Yorkshire, belonging to Bolton Priory, the yields were consistently worse than those in the south.[93]   In both 1315 and 1316 gross yields of wheat on individual demesnes fell as low as 19 per cent of their early fourteenth-century average.   On the extensive home farm at Bolton itself rye returned 28 per cent of normal in 1315, falling to only 11·5 per cent the following year.   Beans gave half the usual crop in 1315 but fell to only 12 per cent in 1316.   Barley provided better returns at 41 per cent in 1315, recovering to 71 per cent in 1316, while oats again suffered less than the other crops, averaging 64 per cent of normal in 1315 and some 80 per cent in 1316.   From tithe returns, which indirectly reflect largely peasant production, it looks as if the priory's parishioners fared even worse.   Tithe from Skipton parish in 1315-16 provided only 39 per cent for hard corn (all types of grain except oats) and 53 per cent of normal for oats itself; and from Kildwick parish the following year 26 per cent for hard corn and 46 per cent for oats.[94]   Though in famine years peasants were presumably even less willing than ever to pay tithe, this must have been at least partly compensated by the extra efforts in collection at such a time made by the tithe receivers.

Obviously there were widely differing yields returned in the famine years — variations which were, on the whole, local rather than

[90] Henceforth all figures are for *gross* yields.
[91] Titow, *Winchester Yields*, p. 145; it is difficult to be precise about the reading from the graph provided there.   Cf. also Titow, "Weather", pp. 385-6.
[92] Titow, *Winchester Yields*, pp. 78, 127-34.
[93] The yield figures are laid out in Table III of my *Bolton Priory*, p. 41: the normal yields for the early fourteenth century were in line with those of estates in other parts of the country.
[94] Based on Table VI in *ibid.*, p. 64.

TABLE I

GRAIN YIELDS ON THE ESTATES OF THE BISHOP OF WINCHESTER 1315 AND 1316

Number of manors on the estates of the bishop of Winchester with the following yields in 1315 and 1316, expressed as a percentage of their average yield 1209-1349 (=100).*

% of average yield:	Wheat		Barley		Oats	
	1315	1316	1315	1316	1315	1316
150–9	0	0	0	1	0	0
140–9	0	0	0	0	0	0
130–9	0	0	0	0	2	1
120–9	0	1	0	3	2	1
110–9	0	2	4	1	4	0
100–9	1	1	3	0	4	2
90–9	1	0	8	2	4	2
80–9	4	4	4	4	6	5
70–9	7	3	9	4	5	6
60–9	8	3	3	2	3	7
50–9	7	3	3	3	3	2
40–9	5	5	1	6	1	3
30–9	2	5	0	2	1	3
20–9	1	7	0	4	0	1
10–9	0	1	0	0	0	0
0–9	0	0	0	0	0	0
Totals						
100%+	1	4	7	5	12	4
50–99%	27	13	27	15	21	22
0–49%	8	18	1	12	2	7

Total Manors from which figures are available:

	36	35	35	32	35	33

Manors where 1315 yield was greater than 1316 yield:

Wheat	Barley	Oats
23	22	25

Manors where 1315 yield was less than 1316 yield:

Wheat	Barley	Oats
11	10	7

Total number of manors from which comparison is possible:

Wheat	Barley	Oats
34	32	32

* Based on Titow, *Winchester Yields*, pp. 49, 59, 69, 121-35.

regional.[95]   Soil types, relief, climatic conditions and other localized factors must all have contributed to the varying response of arable land.   Manors situated in valley-bottoms and other low-lying ground, especially on clays or other heavy soils, must have been far more prone to flooding, and therefore to unsatisfactory grain yields, than those, providing their soils were good, which lay on the uplands

[95] Cf. Farmer, thesis *op. cit.*, pp. 188-93.

in an elevated position with sloping lands and good drainage. On the Bolton Priory estates, for example, the demesne at Malham, some 800 feet above sea-level but situated on well-drained limestone soils, contrasted vividly with the other demesnes based on grits, shales and sandstones, in providing perfectly normal wheat and barley crops in 1315 and 1316 with oats returning a higher yield than on any other grange.[96] And although most manors on the Winchester estates produced much diminished returns in these years — often less than half their normal yield — the figures in Table I above show that some manors actually managed to better their average crop. The manor of Fareham in south-east Hampshire is the most notable example, yielding above-average crops of wheat, barley and oats in both 1315 and 1316.[97] Fareham lies in an area of low rainfall, high sunshine-level, and on very good, freely-drained soils.[98] On the other hand, a group of estates in the north of Hampshire (Burghclere, High Clere, Ecchinswell, Ashmansworth and Woodhay), based mainly on clays, sands and gravel soils, and in an area of heavier rainfall, produced abysmally low yields for almost all crops in the famine years.[99]

That a reduction in output of, say, fifty per cent should produce a price-inflation for grain of something like fourfold or more is itself suggestive of a normal state of affairs in which resources were barely sufficient to meet demand. And a failure in production on this scale in two successive years was quite enough to create the prolonged and severe famine conditions which England experienced between 1315 and 1317. The famine was only assuaged by a moderately successful harvest in 1317, when all crops apart from oats (which produced returns worse than those of 1315 and 1316) yielded tolerably well, and a very good harvest in 1318 in which everything cropped well.[100] Moderately satisfactory harvests in 1319 and 1320 were, however, followed by the third of the great harvest disasters, the failure of 1321. The grain yield figures for this year assembled by Dr. Farmer are fewer than those of 1315-17, mainly because the Winchester yields cannot be calculated for this year. Those figures which are available show greater fluctuation than in 1315-17 but, on average, suggest that wheat yields were similar to those of 1316-17 and that

---

[96] Cf. my *Bolton Priory*, Table III, p. 41.
[97] Titow, *Winchester Yields*, pp. 49, 59, 69, 121.
[98] L. D. Stamp (ed.), *The Land of Britain: the Report of the Land Utilisation Survey of Britain*, pt. 89 (London, 1940), pp. 313-15, 321-2, 325, 331, 367.
[99] Titow, *Winchester Yields*, pp. 49, 59, 69, 127-8; Stamp, *op. cit.*, pp. 314, 330-1, 353-5.
[100] Farmer, thesis *op. cit.*, pp. 74, 81-2.

rye, barley and oats failed even more miserably than at the earlier date.[101]   The few figures for the Bolton Priory estates in this year, however, suggest that the harvest there, while very poor, was nowhere near so disastrous as in 1315 or 1316.   On the home farm at Bolton wheat answered about threefold, better than both the previous famine years; rye was little more than half of its early fourteenth-century average, but still almost double the yield of 1315; barley was slightly better than 1315 but notably worse than 1316; beans failed to reproduce the seed, as they had done in 1316; and oats, at just over double the seed, were more or less on a par with 1315 and 1316.   Malham again belied the general appearance of harvest failure with above-average wheat and oats yields, though barley produced only about three-quarters of the early fourteenth-century average yield.[102]   Generally, from the fact that prices did not soar quite so high in 1321-2 as they had done in 1315-17,[103] it might be presumed that the harvest failure was not so absolute, though the price level could have been held down to some extent by the inability of people, after the deprivations of the preceding years, to pay.

IV

As we have seen, arable failure was only one feature of the agrarian crisis of 1315-22.   Estate records fully endorse the remarks of the chroniclers who speak of a great sheep murrain at this time, and the crisis was no less severe for pastoral economy than for arable cultivation.

The effects of the murrain, like the crop failure, varied greatly; sheep grazing heavy soils and flooded grasslands were especially vulnerable to diseases such as liver-fluke spread by wet pastures.[104] Nor did the worst effects occur at the same time all over the country. Even so, there is plentiful evidence that estates in many widely-scattered areas suffered heavy losses of sheep through disease between 1313 and 1317, with mortality among lambs and yearlings particularly high.

At Inkpen, a Berkshire manor of Titchfield Abbey (Hants.), the

---

[101] *Ibid.*, pp. 74, 283-5.
[102] The figures for seed and harvest returns are given in my "Bolton Priory, 1286-1325: an economic study" (University of Oxford D.Phil. thesis, 1969), pp. 424-35.
[103] Farmer, "Grain Prices", p. 212; Rogers, *op. cit.*, i, pp. 200, 230.
[104] R. Trow-Smith, *A History of British Livestock Husbandry to 1700* (London, 1957), p. 157; *Walter of Henley and Other Treatises on Estate Management and Accounting*, ed. D. Oschinsky (Oxford, 1971), pp. 186-7.

468 sheep grazing the pastures in 1313 had fallen to only 137 by 1317.[105] On the king's stock-farm at Clipstone in Sherwood Forest the heaviest losses came in 1316-17 with the death of almost half the entire flock, including some 72 per cent of lambs and yearlings. In addition, 159 out of 193 goats and kids died that year, and not surprisingly perhaps the remnants of the sheep-flock and goat-herd were sold off the following year. No sheep or goats were kept for the next few years and when next we meet the manor, in 1341-2, it was in the hands of a farmer.[106] Even on the chalk-lands of Crawley (Hants.), where the worst of the murrain was over by 1315, losses in the three previous years had amounted to close on a fifth of the entire flock and almost a half of the lambs.[107]

If the first symptoms of the disease were noticed in time, lords could take the advice of the contemporary treatises on husbandry and sell their stock quickly to cut their losses.[108] We see this at Teddington (Middlesex), where thirty out of seventy-four sheep died in 1315-16 and a note explains that, of the remaining forty-four, thirty-seven were sold "because almost in murrain".[109] Sale was an expedient adopted too on the king's wealthy manor of Sheen (Surrey). Following the loss of nearly half the flock (including sixty out of sixty-one lambs) in 1313-14, when the account states there was "common murrain in the area", large-scale restocking was carried out the following year. In 1315-16 the account records sixteen sheep dead before clipping and the residue of the flock, 418 sheep, sold — also before clipping. For the next five years there were no sheep at all on this manor, which before the crisis period had close on a thousand. Feeling the crisis over, the king's officials restocked the manor in 1321-2 with 829 sheep, mainly from Essex, but of these more than half the lambs, and 291 sheep in all, died that same year.[110]

All these figures are again drawn from seigneurial estates but there is no reason to presume that peasant flocks were dealt with less severely. And when we see the difficulties that some great land-owners were facing at this date, it takes little imagination to realize that, without the lords' resources for restocking, peasants could have suffered grievous and lasting consequences through such heavy

[105] D. C. Watts, "A Model for the Early Fourteenth Century", *Econ. Hist. Rev.*, 2nd ser., xx (1967), p. 544.
[106] P.R.O., SC6/953/7-11.
[107] N. S. B. Gras and E. C. Gras, *The Economic and Social History of an English Village* (Camb. Mass., 1930), pp. 400, 406, 412.
[108] *Walter of Henley*, p. 275 ("Seneschaucy", chaps. 32-4).
[109] P.R.O., SC6/918/14.
[110] P.R.O., SC6/1014/2-9.

livestock losses.   From the render of tithe-lambs we have an indication of how Bolton Priory's parishioners fared during the murrain.
The parishes of Kildwick and Long Preston had, in pre-famine years,
sent between them as many as 160 tithe-lambs to Bolton; in 1315-16
the number sent was twenty-eight, the following year thirty-eight.
The priory's own demesne flock had numbered over 3,000 head of
sheep before the famine.   In 1315-16 it was reduced by over two-
thirds to only 1,005 sheep, falling again the next year to 913.[111]
And among the most devastating losses suffered must have been those
on the estates of the great fenland abbey of Crowland; over 3,000
sheep, some 28 per cent of the flock, died in 1313-14 — in absolute if
not in proportionate terms by far the heaviest losses on the Crowland
estates since the first accounts in 1257-8 — and fewer than 2,000
sheep were left in 1321 where only eight years earlier there had been
almost 11,000.[112]

Though an imperfect source, the customs returns give some indication of the extent to which the agrarian crisis affected the export of
England's staple commodity.   With the sole exception of Southampton, all England's major ports experienced a substantial decline
in their export of wool during the decade of the crisis, as Table II(A)
demonstrates.   And in the following decade, 1325/6-1334/5, only the
far-northern ports of Newcastle and Hartlepool recovered to export
a greater quantity than their average in the 1305/6-1314/15 period.
England's wool exports as a whole declined by little short of a third
in the 1315/16-1324/5 period, and did not fully recover in the subsequent decade.   Reflecting this fall in exports, customs revenues fell
from £10,750 before the crisis to £7,100 in 1315-16, sheep murrain
adding to the difficulties with which the English government had to
contend at this time.[113]

Of course murrain was not the only factor in causing the decline.
The greatest drop occurs in the ports of Newcastle and Hartlepool,
whose exports were probably as greatly damaged by the devastations
of the Scots in the north as by the ravages of murrain.   Nor are the
figures necessarily true indicators in themselves of the drop in
exports.   Ipswich, for example, shows a steeper decline over the two
decades 1315/16-1334/5 than any other port, but it has been demonstrated by Mr. Baker that the customs officials were embezzling on

[111] Cf. my *Bolton Priory*, Table IX, p. 80.
[112] F. M. Page, "Bidentes Hoylandie: a medieval sheep farm", *Economic
History*, suppl. to *Economic Jl.*, i (1926-9), pp. 609-11.   The dates given by
Miss Page are inaccurate: see below n. 133.
[113] J. R. Maddicott, *Thomas of Lancaster 1307-22* (Oxford, 1970), p. 163.

TABLE II

EXPORT OF WOOL IN THE EARLY FOURTEENTH CENTURY
(average number of wool sacks per year exported).*

(A)

Port	1305/6-1314/15		1315/16-1324/5		1325/6-1334/5	
Newcastle	1,081	(100·0)	375	(34·6)	1,354	(125·3)
Hartlepool	289	(100·0)	106	(36·7)	343†	(118·7)
Hull	5,538	(100·0)	3,184	(57·5)	4,974	(89·8)
Boston	9,697	(100·0)	5,158	(53·1)	5,945	(61·3)
Lynn	681	(100·0)	329	(48·3)	635†	(93·2)
Yarmouth	623	(100·0)	540	(86·7)	614	(98·6)
Ipswich	856	(100·0)	323	(37·7)	191†	(22·3)
London	14,747	(100·0)	11,784	(80·0)	11,878	(80·6)
Sandwich	349	(100·0)	172	(49·3)	149†	(42·7)
Southampton	2,729	(100·0)	2,950	(108·1)	2,792	(102·3)
ENGLAND	36,154	(100·0)	25,176	(69·6)	28,988	(80·2)

(B)

Port	1312/13-1314/15		1315-16		1316-17	
Newcastle	687	(100·0)	478	(69·6)	202	(29·4)
Hartlepool	240	(100·0)	134	(55·8)	195	(81·3)
Hull	3,899	(100·0)	1,716	(44·0)	4,468	(114·6)
Boston	8,743	(100·0)	5,760	(65·9)	6,551	(74·8)
Lynn	321	(100·0)	200	(62·3)	271	(84·4)
Yarmouth	391	(100·0)	251	(64·2)	408	(104·3)
Ipswich	592	(100·0)	201	(34·0)	252	(42·6)
London	16,016	(100·0)	10,361	(64·5)	11,839	(73·9)
Sandwich	157	(100·0)	120	(76·4)	199	(126·8)
Southampton	2,283	(100·0)	1,256	(55·0)	2,917	(127·8)
ENGLAND	32,910	(100·0)	20,144	(61·2)	27,576	(83·8)

* Figures taken from E. M. Carus-Wilson and O. Coleman, *England's Export Trade 1275-1547* (Oxford, 1963), except for the figures for England as a whole, which are those of R. L. Baker, "The English Customs Service, 1307-43: a Study of Medieval Administration", *Trans. American Philosophical Society*, new ser., li, pt. 6 (1961), p. 59.

† Port closed 1333-4, averaged over nine accounts.

the grand scale in these years.[114]   As far as the figures can be related to murrain, it looks as if the north and east of England suffered worse than the south.   The fenlands, which must have provided much of the wool exported from Boston and Lynn, were probably, as might be expected and as the stock figures of Crowland Abbey suggest, badly affected by the murrain.   Hull also, taking much wool from the northern abbeys, suffered badly in the 1315/16-1324/5 decade.   But London was little affected and Southampton's exports actually rose

[114] R. L. Baker, "The English Customs Service, 1307-43: A Study of Medieval Administration", *Trans. American Philosophical Society*, new ser., li, pt. 6 (1961), p. 21.

slightly.   Much of Southampton's wool must have been drawn from the chalk downs, where the sheep losses were probably much lighter, as the figures from Crawley seem to demonstrate.

The first years of the fourteenth century saw England's wool exports at their height and the decennial averages in Table II(A) give no indication that exports were already declining before the famine years.   Table II(B), therefore, provides an average figure for the years 1312/13-1314/15, immediately prior to the famine, and compares this level with that in the first two crisis years, 1315-16 and 1316-17.   Even based on the lower 1312/13-1314/15 average, it is significant that every port witnessed a steep decline in 1315-16, though a number of ports, including Hull, recovered well in 1316-17.   The worst years for export after these dates were 1318-19 and 1321-2, although it is notable that the southern ports of London, Southampton, and Sandwich recorded even worse returns between 1324 and 1328 — presumably brought about at least in part by the severe murrain experienced in the south-east at this time.[115]

V

The livestock-farming catastrophes of 1315-17 were largely though not wholly confined to sheep.[116]   But although other livestock escaped lightly at this date, the most devastating and widespread cattle murrain of 1319-21, probably rinderpest,[117] not only accentuated the distress already created by the arable and sheep-flock difficulties but hit at the very root of arable production — the supply of draught animals on the land.

From every region of the country there are signs in manorial records of great destruction among cattle-herds between 1319 and 1321.   On three Huntingdonshire manors of Ramsey Abbey the heavy mortalities were recorded during the accounting year 1319-20. The figures are striking: at Broughton, forty-eight head of cattle dead, leaving six; at Upwood, forty-five dead, leaving two; and at Houghton, fifty-six dead, leaving nine.   In a letter to the king in September 1319, bemoaning the abbey's poverty, the abbot

---

[115] Cf. above, pp. 97-8.

[116] On the Westminster manor of Stevenage (Herts.), where relatively light sheep mortalities occurred in 1316-17, seven out of twenty-three horses died, and in the same year at Clipstone in Sherwood the serious sheep losses were accompanied by the destruction of the goat-herd mentioned earlier and the death of seven out of twenty-seven horses and ten out of sixty-one pigs.   Nearby Wheatley lost a third of its oxen the previous year: P.R.O., SC6/871/6; SC6/953/7; SC6/954/22.

[117] R. Trow-Smith deals with later outbreaks of rinderpest in his *A History of British Livestock Husbandry 1700-1900* (London, 1959), pp. 34-5, 186-7, 318.

complained that a "sudden pestilence" had wiped out so many animals and was still so severe in that area that the abbey no longer had the means of tilling its lands. It was twenty years before the stock totals approximated again to those of the pre-famine period.[118] The ill-fated royal manor of Clipstone (Notts.) lost 20 per cent of its cattle-herd in 1318-19 and almost 40 per cent the following year. In 1316-17 there had been a total of 186 head of cattle and oxen on this estate; in 1320 there remained only sixty-four, of which thirty-two were described as diseased (*morbosi*).[119] More than 60 per cent of the cattle at Sheen died the same year, 1319-20, including twenty-three out of twenty-five cows, and some 77 per cent of the small cattle-herd at Teddington. No cattle or oxen were retained there the following year, and at Sheen, where the herd had previously been on average over eighty head, the number fell to twenty-seven by 1321-2, which were all delivered that year to stock the manor of Isleworth, itself presumably badly hit by the murrain.[120]

On three scattered manors belonging to Merton College, Oxford, the worst year was 1320-1. At Cheddington (Bucks.), ten out of fourteen oxen and six out of nine cows perished, and a few other animals were sold through fear of the murrain. Thorncroft (Surrey) lost seven out of fifteen oxen "by sudden death" in the same year, along with four out of thirteen cows, four out of nine calves, and both bulls. At Cuxham (Oxon.), where the murrain, like the other effects of the agrarian crisis, seems to have been less severe, the losses amounted to four out of thirteen oxen, five out of nine cows, a bull, and three young bovines.[121] In the west country, the manor of Langwm (Mons.), belonging to the Clares, lost nine of its thirty-three oxen this same year, 1320-1.[122] This was also the year in which the cattle murrain took its heaviest toll on the great Winchester estates in the south and south-west of England. At the end of the 1319-20 accounting year the total number of oxen on the estate as a whole stood at 1,088; by the end of the following accounting year it had fallen to only 500, and that in spite of considerable purchases during the year.[123] In the north-west, on the Bolton Priory lands, Scottish raids were assisting in the depletion of livestock at this date. Even so, the dramatic decline between 1319 and 1321 was largely

[118] J. A. Raftis, *The Estates of Ramsey Abbey* (Toronto, 1957), pp. 137-40, 319.

[119] P.R.O., SC6/953/9-10.

[120] P.R.O., SC6/1014/7, 9; SC6/918/15-16.

[121] Figures kindly supplied to me by Mr. P. S. Brown from Merton College Rolls 5548-55, 5749-51, 5842-6.

[122] P.R.O., SC6/922/34.

[123] I am grateful to Dr. Titow for permission to quote these figures which he gave me.

caused by murrain. By 1321 only fifty-three oxen and thirty-one head of other cattle remained. Before the famine years, when straitened circumstances forced the canons of Bolton to sell off their stock and begin the run-down of their herds, there had been almost 500 head of cattle and some 250 oxen.[124]

Such was the shortage of oxen following the murrain, wrote the Lanercost chronicler, that men had to plough with horses.[125] Significantly, the only reference in the Bolton accounts to horses used for ploughwork occurs in 1320-1.[126] Ploughing was exclusively performed by horses from 1320 on the Winchester manor of West Wycombe (Bucks.), a decision again presumably occasioned by the loss of oxen in the murrain.[127] Merton College also resorted to the import of horses in 1320-1 to counterbalance the loss of oxen at Cheddington and Thorncroft but here, as on other estates, the horses were relieved of their duties as new oxen were purchased.[128] This unloading undoubtedly contributed greatly to the substantial fall in the price of plough-horses as compared with the high oxen prices of the early 1320s.[129] On the Winchester estates, too, the losses of oxen in the murrain prompted heavy purchases of plough-horses. The administration bought as many as 140 — an unprecedented number — in 1319-20, though it must be said that oxen were also purchased where possible, 111 being bought in 1319-20 and 170 in 1320-1.[130]

Like crop failure and famine, murrain was no newcomer to England. Between the Norman Conquest and the end of the thirteenth century, at least twelve famines and nine murrains were thought serious enough to warrant mention in chronicles.[131]   Three of the murrains

---

[124] Cf. my *Bolton Priory*, Tables XI and XII, pp. 96, 98.

[125] *Chron. de Lanercost*, p. 240. The Tintern version of the *Flores* states that "men had hardly any oxen or none at all for tilling their lands", resulting in a dearth of horses: *Flores*, iii, p. 343. Dr. Farmer's figures ("Livestock Prices", p. 5) seem to bear this out; they show a substantial rise in the price of plough-horses between 1319 and 1321.

[126] Chatsworth MS. 73A, fo. 442v.

[127] Titow, thesis *op. cit.*, p. 42.

[128] Merton College Rolls, 5551-5, 5751 (*ex inf.* P. S. Brown).

[129] Farmer, "Livestock Prices", p. 5.

[130] Farmer, thesis *op. cit.*, p. 88; the figure for oxen purchases in 1320-1 was given to me by Dr. Titow.

[131] *Ann. Monast.*, i, pp. 12-13, 15, 17, 20, 25-6, 34, 57, 166; ii, pp. 195, 230, 247, 255, 388-9; iii, pp. 305-6, 430-1, 434, 462; iv, pp. 9, 18, 25, 41-2, 48, 118, 120, 127, 374-5, 386, 420, 438, 473; *Matthaei Parisiensis Chronica Majora*, ed. H. R. Luard (Rolls Ser., 1880), v, p. 674.

(1086, 1103, 1111) were described merely as "mortality of animals", one (1131) as "mortality of domestic animals", and in five years (1201, 1225, 1258, 1277, 1283) the murrain largely affected sheep. The murrains in 1086, 1103, 1201 and 1258 accompanied crop failure but, these years apart, the famines mentioned by the chroniclers did not coincide with outbreaks of murrain. On a local scale there were, of course, many more livestock murrains, though over a long period losses were not so frequent nor as devastating as one might think from the spectacular mortalities which occurred in individual years.[132] And it is worth remembering that the heavy mortalities and recurrent murrains largely affected sheep-flocks, where recovery was often surprisingly quick.

Over a long period, in fact, average losses even for sheep were lower than might be expected. On the Crowland Abbey manor of Wellingborough (Northants.), figures from twenty-two accounts between 1270 and 1312 show no serious murrains and an average mortality (for a flock whose normal size was in the region of 350 ewes and lambs) of 10·5 per cent for ewes and 14·3 per cent for lambs.[133] Figures from the Winchester estate at Crawley (Hants.), taken from some 137 accounts over practically the whole of the thirteenth and fourteenth centuries, reveal even lower mortality rates for adult sheep (averaging 5·7 per cent for wethers and 5·1 per cent for ewes) though the losses among lambs averaged 22·2 per cent.[134] Apart from the continually heavy loss of young sheep, the dozen or so years of outstanding mortalities between 1208 and 1400 were compensated by frequent runs of good years in which very few sheep died.

The murrain which accompanied the 1315-17 famine must take its

[132] For examples of severe loss in sheep murrains, cf. Trow-Smith, *British Livestock Husb. to 1700*, pp. 153-4; N. Denholm-Young, *Seignorial Administration in England* (Oxford, 1937), pp. 60-2; H. W. Saunders, *An Introduction to the Obedientiary and Manor Rolls of Norwich Cathedral Priory* (Norwich, 1930), p. 52; Page, "Bid. Hoylandie", p. 609.

[133] Figures calculated by me, based on *Wellingborough Manorial Accounts A.D. 1258-1323*, ed. F. M. Page (Northants. Rec. Soc., viii, 1936), pp. 12-116. I have omitted 1257-8, when the sheep losses were exceptionally heavy (about 70 per cent mortalities), 1266-7 and 1321-2, when the flock largely consisted of hoggasters, and 1313-14, when no sheep at all were entered in the account. The mortality rate of 56·4 per cent given by Miss Page for losses at Wellingborough in "1296-7" i.e. 1294-5 ("Bid. Hoylandie", p. 609) seems inaccurate. On the returns in *Wellingborough Accts.*, pp. 69-70 the figure should be 19·4 per cent. Here and elsewhere I have used the revised dating of the accounts by T. H. Aston, in an additional note in the 1965 reprint of *Wellingborough Manorial Accounts*, pp. xxxix-xlii.

[134] Figures calculated by me, based on Gras, *Econ. and Social Hist. of an English Village*, pp. 398-414.

place as one of a number of sheep epidemics which affected England
in the thirteenth and fourteenth centuries. But, as the figures
above show, murrain was not the overwhelmingly destructive visitor
to flocks even on a localized scale that we tend to imagine. And on
a national scale it was even less frequent. Much of the seriousness of
the 1315-17 murrain was derived as much from the geographical extent
of the epidemic, spreading throughout the whole of the country, as
from the severity with which it ravaged particular flocks. On this
basis it was probably rivalled in the thirteenth century only by the
murrain of the late 1270s.[135]

When we turn from sheep to cattle, we find — perhaps surprisingly
— that serious epidemics seem to be few and far between. From
the Crowland accounts edited by Miss Page, the heaviest losses were
six out of twenty-five oxen at Baston, four out of thirty-six cows at
Langtoft, and twenty-one out of sixty-nine calves at Nomansland, all
in 1257-8; otherwise the losses were trivial. At Wellingborough,
apart from a few calves from time to time, there were hardly any
cattle losses. And at Crawley there was a bad year in 1286-7, with
nine out of fifty-one oxen, five out of sixteen cows, and six out of
eight calves dead, but otherwise very few losses during the whole of
the thirteenth and fourteenth centuries.[136] The scale of the
catastrophe of 1319-21 is, therefore, put into perspective. Especially
is this so when one remembers the nation-wide spread of the epidemic
and the well-documented shortage of cattle, especially plough-beasts,
in many regions of the country in the 1320s. On the Crowland
manors — Wellingborough (Northants.), Drayton, Oakington, and
Cottenham (Cambs.) — the numbers of oxen in the 1321-2 account
were lower than in any year since the first accounts of 1257-8.[137]
Several Ramsey Abbey manors recorded between 1318 and 1326 their
smallest numbers of oxen and cattle in a period stretching from the
mid-thirteenth century until the demesnes were leased in the
fifteenth century.[138] At Crawley, only four oxen remained at the
end of the 1320-1 account — by far the lowest figure recorded in
167 accounts running from 1208 to 1449.[139] These figures are
suggestive of a cattle-plague unparalleled in its dimensions, both in

[135] *Ann. Monast.*, ii, pp. 388-9; and cf. Denholm-Young, *Seign. Admin.*, pp. 60-1.
[136] F. M. Page, *The Estates of Crowland Abbey* (Cambridge, 1934), pp. 189, 206, 209; Page, *Wellingborough Accts.*; Gras, *op. cit.*, pp. 382-93.
[137] Page, *Wellingborough Accts.*, p. 133; Page, *Estates of Crowland Abbey*, pp. 243, 251, 258.
[138] Raftis, *Estates of Ramsey Abbey*, pp. 132-40.
[139] Gras, *op. cit.*, p. 384.

the degree and in the extent of devastation, during the thirteenth, fourteenth and fifteenth centuries.

Arguably, the grave combination, affecting most of the country, of arable, sheep and cattle disasters, lasting in all for some seven or eight years and followed in some areas by further losses of livestock in 1324-6, was the worst agrarian crisis faced by England as a whole since the aftermath of the Norman invasion. That it affected an overpopulated countryside and an imbalanced economy adds weight to this argument. Certainly it was the worst agrarian crisis since manorial records begin at the start of the thirteenth century. The most serious famine of that century, in 1258, though bearing many hallmarks of the 1315-17 catastrophe, can hardly have been as serious. Prices rose, but at most only to half the level reached in 1315-17.[140] The grain yields of 1257, on the Winchester estates at any rate, fell to nowhere near the abysmal depths of 1315 and 1316.[141] The chroniclers mention sheep murrain and this is confirmed by the heavy losses on the Crowland manors at this time.[142] But most important of all in the comparison, there is no evidence in 1258 of cattle-plague joining forces with famine and sheep murrain.[143] And in the cruel combination of adversities in 1315-22 it was, above all, the annihilation of the cattle-herds that made it so hard for men to recover, as their efforts were rendered vain by the destruction on all sides of their means of production and livelihood.

VI

The ways in which the agrarian crisis affected seigneurial economy naturally varied widely. Wealthy landlords with numerous estates, extensive resources, some control over labour supplies and marketing, and with a large surplus of marketable produce, proved resilient and had little difficulty in weathering the storm, though even here the crisis could leave its mark. But for the less wealthy, often struggling to make ends meet even in better times, and forced to buy grain and other produce to supplement their own meagre resources, the crisis years did bring great hardships. From lack of evidence, we cannot demonstrate the difficulties which undoubtedly faced many lords of small estates at this time. But their fate was probably not too different from that of many of the less prosperous monasteries, and here the problems were often considerable.

[140] Farmer, "Grain Prices", pp. 212, 214-15; *Matt. Paris.*, v, pp. 660-1, 673-4, 701-2.
[141] Titow, *Winchester Yields*, pp. 45, 55, 65, 145; Titow, "Weather", p. 372.
[142] *Matt. Paris.*, v, p. 674; Page, "Bid. Hoylandie", p. 609.
[143] Except for the mortalities just mentioned on a few Crowland manors.

The chronicler of Louth Park (Cistercian, Lincs.) bewailed the fact that the crop failures and livestock murrain had ruined all the substance of the house — "oxen, sheep, and all kinds of beasts of the field, corn and other necessaries" — and what was left was plundered by the king's officers at the time of the parliament of Lincoln (January and February 1316).[144]   During the time he was in Lincoln, in February 1316, the king appointed a keeper for the Cluniac priory of Prittlewell (Essex), which was taken into his protection on account of its "poverty, miserable state, and indebtedness".[145]   This was typical of the fate of many religious establishments at this date.   Over a hundred grants of protection to religious houses and hospitals are recorded on the Patent Rolls of 1315-16 compared with a mere handful in any normal year of the early fourteenth century, and the great number of these protections were granted in the spring and summer of 1316.   In 1318 the king made a grant of alms to the prioress and convent of Elstow (Benedictine, Beds.), "out of compassion for the state of their house which is so greatly impoverished by the scarcity of the past years and diverse other oppressions that the goods of the house do not suffice for the sustenance of the prioress and convent".[146] And at a visitation by the abbot of Westminster in 1319, the hospital of St. James at Westminster claimed that the numbers in the hospital could not be maintained "on account of the mortality of animals and the poverty of their resources".[147]   At Bolton Priory (Augustinian, Yorks, W.R.), the famine years prompted measures affecting all sides of the house's economy, resulting in a heavy reduction in the quantity and quality of the foodstuffs consumed at the priory and a real lowering of the standard of living there.[148]   Rocester Abbey (Augustinian, Staffs.) was reduced to such poverty through lack of corn and livestock mortalities that the canons were sent out to solicit sustenance from their friends, "almost as beggars (*quasi mendicantes*)".[149]   Seven years of sterility and livestock murrain left the monks of Pipewell Abbey (Cistercian, Northants.) so poor that "sometimes they sat down in the refectory for three or four days with only black bread and pottage and sometimes they bought their bread from market to market".[150]

---

[144] *Chron. de Parco Lude*, p. 24.
[145] *Cal. Pat. Rolls, 1313-17*, pp. 387-8.   [146] *Ibid.*, *1317-21*, p. 227.
[147] I am grateful to Miss Barbara Harvey for providing me with this reference from Westminster Abbey Muniments, 17118.
[148] Cf. my *Bolton Priory*, pp. 78, 149-50.
[149] *Extracts from the Plea Rolls, 1307-27*, ed. G. Wrottesley (William Salt Soc., x, 1889), p. 25.
[150] Cited in E. Power, *The Medieval English Wool Trade* (Oxford, 1941), pp. 43-4.

That the famine years did not only create difficulties for impecunious monasteries and struggling hospitals is shown by the reaction of Thomas of Lancaster, holder of the greatest seigneurial estate in England.   Lancaster's huge income generally failed to meet the extraordinarily high level of his expenditure and the famine years undoubtedly worsened his position.   Contrary to his estate policy of converting direct exploitation to demesne leasing, the earl was forced to take up abandoned land through lack of tenants as rents fell drastically on some manors.   And his attempts to maximize profits, before and after the famine years, led to high-handed and extortionate methods of raising cash from his tenants.[151]

On a number of great estates the agrarian crisis does appear to have marked a turning-point in demesne production and exploitation. On the Ramsey Abbey estates, where direct exploitation was already declining in the late thirteenth century, a notable revival in the early fourteenth century ended after about 1320.   A major factor was the abbey's inability, in straitened circumstances, to provide sufficient capital investment to replace livestock wiped out in the murrain of 1319-20.   The reeves were left to rebuild by their own available resources over the next fifteen to twenty years.[152]   This fits almost exactly with the tightening up of financial control on the estates of St. Swithun's Priory, Winchester, where greater financial burdens were imposed on reeves and sergeants in a ten-year burst of auditorial activity beginning about 1318.[153]   On the lands of Christ Church Canterbury, where wool production reached its peak in the years 1308-15, a sizeable fall in wool sales in 1315-16 was more or less made up by 1320 but the pre-famine level of wool production was never quite regained before the catastrophic mortalities of 1324-6 led to a continued decline in sheep-farming.[154]   An ordinance of Prior Eastry, dating from the post-murrain period of the early 1320s and assigning a variety of sources of manorial income to restoring the numbers of livestock on the manors, shows how seriously the priory was taking its livestock losses.[155]   In the West Riding the agrarian crisis supplemented by Scottish raids certainly marked the end of a twenty-year period of expansion in Bolton Priory's economy and the level of demesne exploitation achieved in the pre-famine era, once

---

[151] Maddicott, *Thomas of Lancaster*, pp. 31-5.
[152] Raftis, *op. cit.*, pp. 137, 239-41.
[153] J. S. Drew, "Manorial Accounts of St. Swithun's Priory, Winchester", in Carus-Wilson (ed.), *Essays in Econ. Hist.*, ii, pp. 21-4, repr. from *Eng. Hist. Rev.*, lxii (1947).
[154] Smith, *Cant. Cath. Priory*, pp. 155-6.
[155] Brit. Mus., Cott. MS. E. iv, fo. 177.   Smith, *op. cit.*, pp. 218-19 prints the ordinance and summarizes the sheep statistics on pp. 152-3.

lost, was never recovered.[156]   And on the Titchfield manor of Inkpen
in Berkshire the sheep-flock, decimated in the famine years, was not
restored to its earlier strength until the very eve of the Black Death.
Cereal production there never recovered its pre-famine level; by
1347-8 it had fallen to a mere half of its early fourteenth-century level
and the reduction had largely been brought about by allowing some
arable to revert to pasture and leaving some land fallow for two or
three years at a time.[157]

Demesne acreage reductions, sometimes temporary, sometimes
permanent, can be seen on several estates at this date and the land
going out of use was by no means always taken up in tenant leases
bringing in increased rents or pasture dues.   Probably at least 600
acres on Bolton Priory's home farm and two adjacent granges were
lying idle after 1320.[158]   The effect of the agrarian crisis and
Scottish raids on demesne cultivation was still to be seen in this area
in 1325-6.   At Skipton in that year, forty-eight acres three roods of
demesne land, which before the Scottish attacks had been worth 10d.
an acre, lay uncultivated through lack of tenants and, though valued
as pasture at 4d. an acre, in fact brought in nothing "through lack of
animals in the area".[159]   Similarly in nearby Silsden there were no
takers for some fifty-two acres of uncultivated demesne, nor any
income from the land as agistment because of the Scottish
destruction and livestock murrain.[160]   Demesne cultivation suffered,
too, in south Yorkshire.   Only four acres three roods of demesne at
Carlton could be let in 1322; nineteen acres were left fallow and the
remaining thirty-eight acres lay "waste and uncultivated (*frisce et
inculte*) . . . through lack of animals in those parts".   The demesne at
Cowick was even worse affected, with ninety out of 120 acres untilled
and the rest fallow.   At Campsall forty-five out of 140 acres had been
ploughed but were not sown with spring crops "because of the
dearness of seed in those parts", and no profit could be taken from it
as herbage, certainly owing to the shortage of animals after the
murrain.   On the same grounds thirty-five out of 120 acres at

[156] Cf. my *Bolton Priory*, pp. 13-18.
[157] Watts, "Model for the Early Fourteenth Century", p. 544, and his thesis,
"The Estates of Titchfield Abbey, *c.* 1245 to *c.* 1380" (University of Oxford
B.Litt. thesis, 1957), pp. 175, 182.
[158] My *Bolton Priory*, p. 17.
[159] There may have been a renewed outbreak of cattle-plague, for the account
mentions the loss of thirteen out of twenty-six oxen "in murrain through
common infirmity" and six of the carcasses were fit for nothing but throwing to
the dogs.
[160] P.R.O., SC6/1148/21.

Rothwell and twenty-one out of 169 acres at Seacroft were also left unsown that year.[161]

In other parts of the country we meet the same phenomenon. The accountant on the Leicestershire manor of Fleckney did not answer in 1322 for twenty acres of demesne, valued at 5s., because "he could find neither animals to till the land nor even animals in the area to agist it as pasture".[162] At Sheen (Surrey) there was a striking fall of over a hundred acres of demesne between 1316-17 and 1321-2. The whole of this reduction related to the two crops which grow on inferior soils — oats and rye — and it looks as if the worst land was being taken out of cultivation.[163] The same was taking place on some of the manors belonging to the abbey of Bec during the early fourteenth century, where there was a slackening in demesne cultivation but no long-term breakdown during the reign of Edward II.[164] And on the bishop of Winchester's estates demesne lands were going out of cultivation on a considerable scale in this period. Here the peak of demesne expansion had long passed and substantial reductions in the demesne acreage had already taken place in the latter half of the thirteenth century. Nevertheless yields on some demesnes continued to fall, a fall which would presumably have been more marked had not the poorer lands been dropping out of cultivation.[165] For the Winchester lands the early fourteenth century was a period when the arable acreage of the demesne declined much further. The total area under seed in the five years prior to the famine (1310-11 to 1314-15) averaged some 9,725 acres. In 1315-16 there was a drop to 9,375 acres and then in 1316-17 a resounding fall to 8,525 acres. There was a slight recovery the following year to 8,737 acres and much of the ground was, in fact, made up by 1320-1 when the area stood at 9,055 acres. But between 1321 and 1325 there was another sizeable fall of over 750 acres to a figure of 8,292 acres, a level which remained fairly stable over the subsequent decade.[166] The declining demesne was certainly not compensated for by a switch

---

[161] P.R.O., SC6/1145/21.   [162] P.R.O., SC6/1146/17.

[163] P.R.O., SC6/1014/5-8.

[164] M. Morgan, *The English Lands of the Abbey of Bec* (Oxford, 1946), pp. 98-105.

[165] Titow, thesis *op. cit.*, pp. 28-35 and his *English Rural Society 1200-1350* (London, 1969), pp. 52-3. The most substantial acreage reductions came in the land under oats. Titow's recently published *Winchester Yields* now supplies the evidence and full discussion of its problems.

[166] Titow, thesis *op. cit.*, pp. 21-2. The figures allow for the change from customary to standard acres which some demesnes were undergoing about this time: cf. Titow, *Winchester Yields*, pp. 9, 10 n.1, 150-1.

to stock-farming; nor, though some land was let out to tenants, was it part of a general policy of preference for rents as against arable profits. The letting of demesne land to tenants can only account for a portion of the decline in demesne acreage which, as Dr. Titow convincingly argues, is most plausibly explained by the shedding of unproductive lands.[167]

For great corn-producing estates with a large surplus for sale, the dearth of the famine years could prove far from unwelcome, as the production failure was more than compensated by the exceedingly high price of corn. Despite the dismal yields and contracting demesne arable, sale of the major grains on the Winchester manors brought in some 23 per cent more in 1315-16 than in the previous year.[168]   The next year, 1316-17, was in fact financially one of the best years in the thirteenth and fourteenth centuries for the bishop's estates. Total profits, at almost £6,406, were exceptionally high — the product of handsome returns from demesne exploitation, especially of course from grain sales, and also of increased receipts from tenants.[169]   The latter were boosted by the rise in revenues from fines of courts which, with the rapid turnover of tenements during the famine years, reached their highest level until the Black Death.[170] On the estates of Christ Church Canterbury, too, the " 'high farming' period *par excellence*" of peak manorial profits embraced the years of the agrarian crisis, and profits on the Ely estates were also extremely high between 1319 and 1323.   The great fall in agricultural profits on these estates began around 1325, the beginning of two decades of depression for arable farmers, with low corn prices and higher labour costs.[171]

As we have been seeing, the agrarian crisis did not affect all areas and all landlords in the same way.   For some it was no more than a disturbed, but passing, phase which had no lasting consequences for their economy and demesne exploitation.   Though it took the Ramsey manors two decades to make good the cattle wiped out in 1319-20, Merton College was able to replace its livestock losses within

---

[167] Titow, thesis *op. cit.*, pp. 22-8; Titow, *Winchester Yields*, pp. 1-2.

[168] Farmer, thesis *op. cit.*, p. 88.

[169] Titow, thesis *op. cit.*, pp. 10, 55-6, 67-68a.   Titow defines "profit" in this sense as "receipts corrected, in the case of manorial produce, for the value of produce sent out of the manor or received from outside other than as a cash transaction": *ibid.*, p. 9, n. 2.

[170] *Ibid.*, pp. 61-3, 113; Postan and Titow, "Heriots and Prices", p. 407, Table 1 and Graph 1.

[171] Smith, *op. cit.*, pp. 143-4; E. Miller, *The Abbey and Bishopric of Ely* (Cambridge, 1951), pp. 105-6.   The Winchester estates also experienced a substantial drop in profits in this period: Titow, thesis *op. cit.*, pp. 68-8a.

two years at Cheddington and Cuxham.[172]   Dr. Harvey's careful
study of Cuxham, a village situated on good light gravel and chalk
soils, has no mention of famine or murrain which, as we have noticed,
dealt fairly lightly with the Cuxham herds; on this "classical" manor,
the social and economic changes seem distinctly a consequence of the
Black Death.[173]   At Chertsey Abbey (Benedictine, Surrey), the first
half of the fourteenth century was the period in which the "high
farming" abbot, John of Rutherwick (1307-47), "was raising his
house . . . to a position of economic importance without parallel in
its history, before or after".[174]   Of major lay seigneurial estates, those
of the Clares, situated predominantly in East Anglia and Wales,
showed few notable signs of change in the early fourteenth century,
though this was a period of stability rather than expansion.   Again
the significant changes come at the Black Death and after.[175]   And
a very recent study of rural economy in the south-west points out that
the estates of the earl of Cornwall certainly show no adverse effects
over this period, though since they deal with revenues drawn largely
from rents and other tenant dues the direct effects of the crisis on
agricultural production cannot be measured.[176]

For some major landlords, therefore, the evidence suggests a
scarcely interrupted pattern of estate exploitation in the early
fourteenth century, though there are seldom signs of notable
expansion in demesne economy during the half-century before the
Black Death.   For others the agrarian crisis of 1315-22 was a
turning-point which, succeeded by a lengthy depression for corn-
growers and wool-producers alike, ended or hastened the end of an
expanding demesne economy.   On such estates recovery in direct
exploitation, where it was made, tended to be slow and partial.   At
best the crisis was a serious interruption of agrarian enterprise by these
landlords; at worst it killed it.

---

[172] Cf. above, pp. 106-7 for Ramsey; Merton information supplied by Mr.
P. S. Brown.
[173] P. D. A. Harvey, *A Medieval Oxfordshire Village — Cuxham 1240-1400*
(Oxford, 1965).   It is worth noting that the highest recorded profit of the manor
in the period from 1291 to 1355 was easily the £64 18s. od. of 1316-17: *ibid.*,
p. 95.
[174] D. Knowles, *The Religious Orders in England*, i (Cambridge, 1948), p. 47.
The famine probably brought a temporary interruption to Rutherwick's work;
in a list of his building achievements, covering thirty-two years in all, only
eight years pass without comment and these include 1314, 1316, 1317 and 1319:
E. Toms, "Chertsey Abbey and its Manors under Abbot John de Rutherwyk,
1307-47" (University of London Ph.D. thesis, 1935), pp. 23-4.
[175] G. A. Holmes, *The Estates of the Higher Nobility* (Cambridge, 1957),
pp. 88-92.
[176] Hatcher, *Rural Econ. and Soc. in the Duchy of Cornwall*, p. 85.

VII

If the agrarian crisis could create difficulties for great landlords, with their massive resources, it goes without saying that for the peasantry, especially for those substantial numbers with insufficient land to provide for themselves and their families even under normal conditions,[177] the famine years must have brought unimaginable hardships and suffering. The question is whether these years were sufficiently damaging to mark a turning-point in the fortunes of rural society as a whole and a long-term end to population growth.

Miss Harvey looked to rents and especially to the topography of settlement — notably evidence for land vacancies and desertions — as providing the best guide to the problem.[178] However we must remember that where vacancies do occur in the famine years or thereabouts, they are evidence of very grave trouble. Land was not something to be given up lightly, least of all at this date. As Dr. Titow says of the Winchester peasantry in the period before the Black Death, "the choice before a large section of the population must have been to cultivate, however poor the holding, or to starve".[179] If the pressure on the land in the more populous parts of the country was as great as we believe it to have been, the sizeable rural proletariat of landless and near-landless must have been only too ready to gobble up any land which came its way. Certainly this is what happened on some estates at the Black Death when exceedingly heavy mortalities sometimes left no immediate tenement vacancies as surviving members of the family, neighbouring tenants still alive, outsiders, and the near-landless jumped readily into dead men's shoes.[180] So where we find cases of substantial difficulty in finding tenants for holdings in the early fourteenth century we must regard the situation as serious. And we ought to look for the most extensive vacancies not in those areas which we know to have been overpopulated or at least very populous, but in the less wealthy, more thinly-settled areas where the hardship involved in making a living from the land might have left the peasantry most vulnerable of all in the agrarian crisis of the early fourteenth century.

[177] Cf. Postan in *Camb. Econ. Hist. of Europe*, i, p. 619.

[178] B. Harvey, "Population Trend", esp. p. 24.

[179] Titow, thesis *op. cit.*, p. 121.

[180] Cf. for instance, Miss A. E. Levett's works, *The Black Death on the Estates of the See of Winchester*, in P. Vinogradoff (ed.), *Oxford Studies in Social and Legal History*, v, and "The Black Death on the St. Albans Manors" in her *Studies in Manorial History* (Oxford, 1938), pp. 248-86. Cf. also J. A. Raftis, "Changes in an English Village after the Black Death", *Medieval Studies*, xxix (1967), pp. 158-77.

Incomplete though it is, demographic evidence indicates that population growth might have been past its peak in some areas by the end of the thirteenth century. The population had stopped growing by the 1280s in some villages in the Lincolnshire fens and had begun to decline in others by the early fourteenth century.[181] From an admittedly small sample, Professor Sylvia Thrupp showed that there was a significant downward drift in replacement rates between 1280 and 1350 on a number of East Anglian manors, a trend which she considered capable of bearing a Malthusian interpretation.[182] And Postan and Titow were able to illustrate, from the record of heriots received, a notable rise in death-rates and a sizeable degree of over-population on some of the Winchester estates. They demonstrated the "calamity-sensitive" nature of society there by pointing to the close relationship of bad harvests, high corn prices, and heavy mortalities — a connection particularly obvious among the poorer tenants. Though the number of heriots paid subsided from its famine level, it remained extremely high and did not again fall to its already high pre-famine rate.[183]

The court rolls which I have looked at do not present a similarly striking rise in the number of heriots. Compared with the Black Death years, when almost every entry mentions a death, the court rolls of the famine period often show nothing untoward unless closely examined. Since the very poor, the worst sufferers, were often sub-tenants or landless labourers, we should not expect court rolls to reveal anything like the whole picture. What they do indicate is a considerable amount of severe rural disturbance and a good number of holdings changing hands. For example, on the manor of Hindolveston (Norf.), belonging to Norwich Cathedral Priory, three times as many holdings changed hands in the famine years as in an average year of the early fourteenth century.[184] We get a microcosmic view of what must have been going on in many parts of the country in the Buckinghamshire village of Sherington. Here the smallholders, badly hit in the famine years, were having to sell out, to the modest advantage of those families better placed who were able to buy up many minute parcels of land to add to their own holdings.

[181] H. E. Hallam, "Population Density in the Medieval Fenland", *Econ. Hist. Rev.*, 2nd ser., xiv (1961-2), pp. 78-9; and his *Settlement and Society* (Cambridge, 1965), p. 221.

[182] S. L. Thrupp, "The Problem of Replacement-Rates in Late Medieval English Population", *Econ. Hist. Rev.*, 2nd ser., xviii (1965), pp. 106-7, 117.

[183] Postan and Titow, "Heriots and Prices", *ibid.*, xi (1958-9), pp. 392-417.

[184] From figures in Saunders, *Obedientiary and Manor Rolls of Norwich Cathedral Priory*, p. 40.

Table III

SURRENDER OF HOLDINGS*

Year†	Park (Herts.)	Codicote (Herts.)	Barnett‡ (Herts.)	Chesterton (Cambs.)
1307-8	5	7	6	51
1308-9	5	15	16	72
1309-10	3	6	8	76
1310-11	6	10	6	71
1311-12	4	6	10	36
1312-13	4	6	3	41
1313-14	4	7	13	60
1314-15	5	9	20	42
1315-16	30	29	31	64
1316-17	12	38	28	116
1317-18	9	13	9§	59
1318-19	6	10	5‖	70
1319-20	5	1‖	5	46
1320-21	4	7	10	49
1321-22	15	29	19	129
1322-23	11	18	13	64
1323-24	5	25	7	67
1324-25	15	22	5	58
1325-26	12	8	0‖	49

* Based on the Court Books of Park, Codicote, and Barnet (Brit. Mus., Add. MS. 40625, fos. 41-64; Stowe MS. 849, fos. 30-49; Add. MS. 40167, fos. 33v-53v); and the Court Book or Register of Gersums and Fines on the Manor of Chesterton, the "Registrum Prioratus de Barnewel" (Bodl. Lib., MS. Gough Camb. 1, fos. 60-132).

† Regnal years of Edward II (8 July-7 July).

‡ The scribe seems consistently to have attributed the summer court each year to the wrong regnal year of Edward II and I have therefore adjusted the figures to bring them into line with those of the other manors.

§ No winter court recorded.

‖ No spring/summer court recorded.

From Sherington and the two nearby villages of Weston Underwood and Olney there survive more than three times as many peasant charters dating from 1315-24 as from either the preceding or the subsequent decade.[185]

The figures given above in Table III, from three Hertfordshire manors of St. Albans Abbey and the large Cambridgeshire manor of Chesterton, belonging to Barnwell Priory, provide further illustration of the effect of the agrarian crisis on the land market.

In all four places the high figures for 1315-17 and 1321-2 stand out sharply, a veiled reflection of the disturbed state of rural society during the agrarian crisis. On the manor of Codicote only the year 1342-3 with twenty-five surrenders approximated, in the period

[185] A. C. Chibnall, *Sherington: Fiefs and Fields of a Buckinghamshire Village* (Cambridge, 1965), pp. 121, 131-3.

1300-49, to the thirty-eight surrenders of holdings in 1316-17 and the twenty-nine in 1315-16 and 1321-2.[186] In the fifteen years before the famine there were on average about eight surrenders a year; in the period 1326-48 there were about nine a year; while in the decade 1315/16-1324/5 the average was as high as nineteen a year (or twenty-one if we discount 1319-20 when no summer court was recorded). In some cases, naturally, it was a question of transferring property to other members of a family — an aged parent relinquishing his hold on a tenement in favour of an able-bodied son or the provision for a newly-married couple, which were normal occurrences in the medieval village. But "family" transactions accounted for only forty-four surrenders at Codicote between 1315/16 and 1324/5. The vast majority of the surrenders (144 out of 192) were taken up by tenants who had no apparent connection with the surrendering parties.[187]

Of these 192 surrenders in the decade 1315/6-1324/5 the largest entailed no more than a few acres and the vast majority under two acres. It would be wrong to suggest that it was simply a matter of the smallholders selling out to the big men in the village. Nor were the same tenants doing all the buying. Even so there were few if any who were both buying and selling at the same time — investing in purchasing land to re-sell it. On the whole it is a case of gains for some tenants and losses for others. An example of one smallholder probably forced to sell out in the agrarian crisis is Michael Gorman of Codicote. With his wife he surrendered five parcels in all — totalling a messuage, two pieces of land and one-and-a-half acres — between 1315/16 and 1316/17. By November 1321, the third famine year, Michael Gorman was dead. He died, as he had probably lived, in abject poverty. The court book has the stark entry: "no heriot because he had nothing" and his land, such as there was of it, was taken into the lord's hand.[188] At the other end of the scale there were certainly tenants able to consolidate and build up their own holdings on the misfortunes of others. Roger le Heldere, a free burgage tenant at Codicote, may have had other landholdings in the area to provide him with the capital for investing in property at Codicote. Whether or not this was the case, he was able to make no fewer than twenty-two separate purchases between 1315/16 and 1324/5, amounting to sixteen-

---

[186] Brit. Mus., Stowe MS. 849, fos. 24v-74v. Though I have not made a similarly detailed analysis of the land market at Park, Barnet, and Chesterton, the pattern of transactions at Codicote seems in no way unrepresentative of these other manors.

[187] Only one holding was taken into the lord's hand following a surrender and there are few other signs of vacant holdings in Codicote (cf. below, p. 122).

[188] Brit. Mus., Stowe MS. 849, fo. 43v.

and-a-half acres and a few plots of land.   These acquisitions account
for practically the whole of the holding of twenty acres, a cotland, two
messuages and three shops with which he was credited in an extent
of 1332.[189]

The rapid quickening of the land market at Codicote and other
St. Albans manors in 1315/16-1324/5 undoubtedly accelerated the
process of disintegration of the traditional tenemental structure which
was already well under way.   From this date if not before, half-virgate
and ferling holdings ceased to bear even a façade of reality as they
splintered into many pieces in the hands of different tenants.   By the
1330s tenants were willing to pay fines to have the rents and services
on their disintegrated tenements properly apportioned.[190]   The
complexity of the landholding pattern is fully indicated in an entry
in the 1332 extent, pointing out that Roger le Dryvere held a half-
virgate "except for 11½ acres which 11 tenants hold".[191]   This state
of affairs owed much to the agrarian crisis of 1315-25.

Though the pattern of landholding on the St. Albans estates was
affected by the crisis, there were no land vacancies on a large scale
or lasting more than a short time.   Nonetheless, the court books do
show that pressure was put upon tenants to take up holdings as they
fell vacant during this period.   There appear to have been no vacant
tenements at Cashio (Herts.) before 1317, but nine holdings were
taken into the lord's hand in 1317-18 and reluctant tenants were
elected by the homage to take them.   Four holdings (two ferlings and
two half-virgates) were vacant in 1321-2 and again the vacancies were
filled by elections the following year.[192]   Tenants at Park, too, were
ordered in 1316-17 and 1321-2 to take up the few tenements that fell
into the lord's hand.[193]   At Barnet there were orders to retain seven
holdings or parts of tenements in the lord's hand in 1323-4.[194]   And
at Codicote three holdings lay apparently unwanted in 1322-3.[195]
There were no signs of unwanted land in the 1332 extent, however,
apart from a few vacant plots in the market-place and seven shops in
a ruinous condition for lack of tenants.[196]

[189] Brit. Mus., Add. MS. 40734, fos. 12v.-13r.
[190] Brit. Mus., Stowe MS. 849, fos. 57r., 61r.
[191] Brit. Mus., Add. MS. 40734, fo. 5v.
[192] Brit. Mus., Add. MS. 40626, fos. 40r-45v.   For frequent cases of
"elections" to unwanted holdings on the Winchester estates, cf. Titow, thesis
op. cit., pp. 121-2 and Eng. Rural Soc., pp. 94-5. Cf. also B. Harvey,
"Population Trend", p. 35.
[193] Brit. Mus., Add. MS. 40625, fos. 52r, 58r.
[194] Brit. Mus., Add. MS. 40167, fo. 51v.
[195] Brit. Mus., Stowe MS. 849, fo. 45v.
[196] Brit. Mus., Add. MS. 40734, fo. 15r.

Elsewhere, however, the impact of the famine produced more extensive tenement vacancies. The Hampshire manors of Titchfield Abbey saw no sign of land going out of cultivation at this date. But vacancies at Inkpen, the abbey's outlying manor situated on poor soil in south Berkshire, left sufficient rent defects for the great famine there to be described as "a minor Black Death".[197] In Oxfordshire, too, marginal areas struggled in the famine years though their depopulation may well have been a gradual and slow process going back far into the thirteenth century. There had been eighteen holdings at Langley in Leafield in 1279; in 1316 the tax collectors noted that the village contained only four tenants. Heythrop was reduced to three tenants in 1316; Shelswell was described as "little and poor"; while Asterley, a twelfth-century clearing on the edge of Wychwood Forest, had its church united with the neighbouring parish of Kiddington in 1316 for reasons of poverty.[198] The twenty bovates of land lying uncultivated at Scawby in Lincolnshire in 1321 were probably only a small portion of the total amount of land which had gone out of cultivation in the county.[199] In a petition to parliament in 1321-2 the men of Lincolnshire pointed out that many had left their lands and houses. They asked the king and his council to have regard for the damage and losses they had suffered and were still suffering from the murrain of beasts, low-lying lands submerged under such a volume of water, and from crop failure.[200]

Some of the most clearcut evidence of vacancies caused by the agrarian crisis comes from the honour of Tutbury, belonging to the earl of Lancaster. On the Derbyshire manors of the honour, rents fell by 30 per cent between 1313-14 and 1321-2. On a sample of fifteen manors, fifty-five bovates and over 3,000 acres of land went out of use during this period. It was said that tenants had abandoned it through poverty, that it was too poor to be cultivated, and that no new tenants could be found to take it up, even as pasture, because of a severe stock shortage caused by murrain and through the recent political disturbances.[201]

[197] Watts, thesis *op. cit.*, pp. 175, 182.
[198] K. J. Allison, M. W. Beresford, and J. W. Hurst, *The Deserted Villages of Oxfordshire* (Dept. of English Local History, Occasional Papers, xvii, Leicester, 1965), pp. 5-6; W. G. Hoskins, *The Making of the English Landscape* (London, 1955), p. 93.
[199] *Cal. Inq. Post Mortem*, vi, p. 197.
[200] *Rot. Parl.*, i, p. 400b. Cf. W. Abel, *Die Wüstungen des ausgehenden Mittelalters*, 2nd edn. (Stuttgart, 1955), pp. 74-5, and his *Agrarkrisen und Agrarkonjunktur*, p. 46, for contemporary desertion of settlement in Germany.
[201] Maddicott, *Thomas of Lancaster*, p. 31 citing J. R. Birrell, "The Honour of Tutbury in the Fourteenth and Fifteenth Centuries" (University of Birmingham M.A. thesis, 1962), pp. 53-7.

Similar, if less spectacular, indications of rural poverty, vacant holdings, and shortage of tenants, often associated with the effects of livestock murrain, can be found for many other regions of England. Officials were finding it difficult to find tenants willing to take on the farm of holdings, especially capital messuages, in some twenty-eight Herefordshire villages during the winter of 1322, and in the summer of that year it was explained that pasture rents in at least thirteen villages in Devon and Cornwall were lower than usual "through lack of animals".[202] It was also hard to persuade tenants to rent pasture on some Wiltshire manors and the same complaint was heard on the bishop of Winchester's estates, the reason being that "almost all the cattle (*averia*) of the area are dead".[203] Nor, for lack of animals, could purchasers of agistment be found on the Leicestershire manor of Stapleford, and a few tenements there and at Newbold (Leics.) were in the lord's hand on account of the poverty of tenants or their inability (*impotencia*) to cultivate the holdings.[204] For the north of England, suffering at this time from political upheaval as well as from famine and murrain, the long roll of ministers' accounts, dealing for the most part with the confiscated possessions of Thomas of Lancaster, paints a melancholy picture of poverty in the countryside of south Yorkshire in 1322.[205] Almondbury, near Huddersfield, is one example from many where herbage brought in no income "because of lack of animals in those parts both through the common murrain and through the great depredation in the time of disturbance". Shortage of tenants was also a frequent complaint and though, proportionate to the rental income, the vacancies were seldom serious they could occasionally be fairly substantial. In Ackworth, for example, twenty-six bovates were in the king's hand because their tenants "had been destroyed on the arrival of the king in those parts last year and the land now lies uncultivated and not sown with spring seed on account of the inability (*impotencia*) of the tenants". At Stainforth there had been a few holdings vacant in Thomas of Lancaster's time but the loss of 38s. 2d. from nine acres of meadow there was new: the tenants had had to give up the meadow through destitution (*propter inopiam*) and no new takers could be found.

Such difficulties were not necessarily short-lived. Shortage of tenants still accounted for vacancies in numerous villages in

[202] P.R.O., SC6/1145/6; SC6/1146/21.
[203] P.R.O., SC6/1145/12; Titow, "Weather", p. 388.
[204] P.R.O., SC6/1146/17.
[205] The following examples are all taken from P.R.O., SC6/1145/21.

Lancashire and the Forest of Bowland in 1323-4. Though the total extent of the vacant land was only a small proportion of the total rented area, some untenanted holdings — such as one of twenty-four acres in Burnley, one of thirty-four acres in Tottington, and one of fifty-three acres in Briercliffe — were of substantial size.[206] Uncultivated land, lack of tenants, and shortage of livestock were still noted in the Skipton area of the West Riding in 1325-6, and in the same year in the North Riding we find lasting traces of tenements destroyed by the Scots in Easingwold and numerous holdings lying vacant, without takers "owing to the poverty of the area", in Goathland on the North York moors.[207]

Of course there were parts of England where assarting, a reflection of steady pressure on the land, continued after the famine years. Miss Harvey pointed to a number of such areas though, as she admitted, such reclamation was never on the heroic scale and amounted for the most part to "nibbling at the waste".[208] Her examples could be augmented by others, sometimes of quite extensive areas. In Gloucestershire an assart of sixty acres was being made in 1317 "at the Hoarstone"; one of ninety acres is registered at Littledean in 1319; and an assart of 60 acres at Abenhall occurs as late as 1347.[209] At Laughton, in the Weald of east Sussex, the last assault on the waste took place in 1324-5 when over 126 acres were cleared. The extension of the cultivated area had already reached its limits in some of Laughton's neighbouring areas but other parishes continued reclamation into the 1330s and 1340s.[210] And at the other end of the country, in Nidderdale in the West Riding, assarting was going on up to 1314 and again in the 1340s when the documentary sources recommence, though clearance was probably halted between these dates by Scottish raids as well as crop failures and livestock murrains.[211]

The mere presence of assarting, however, is not necessarily evidence of pressure on the land. Assarting and vacant land could be found on the same manor at the same date. The large manor of

[206] P.R.O., SC6/1148/6.
[207] P.R.O., SC6/1148/21 (cf. above, p. 114); SC6/1148/23.
[208] B. Harvey, "Population Trend", pp. 40-2.
[209] H. P. R. Finberg, *Gloucestershire: the History of the Landscape* (London, 1955), p. 69.
[210] J. S. Moore, *Laughton: a Study in the Evolution of the Wealden Landscape* (Dept. of English Local History, Occasional Papers, xix, Leicester, 1965), pp. 41, 43.
[211] B. Jennings (ed.), *A History of Nidderdale* (Huddersfield, 1967), pp. 50, 54; and his *A History of Harrogate and Knaresborough* (Huddersfield, 1970), pp. 64-7.

TABLE IV

NEW AND UNOCCUPIED LANDS ON THE MANOR OF WAKEFIELD 1312-31*

Years	New Lands Taken		Unoccupied Lands Taken	
	No. of Entries	No. of Acres	No. of Entries	No. of Acres
1312-17	202	308½	7	33
1317-22	No court rolls survive†			
1323-31	23	50½	57	119
1312-31	225	359	64	152

* Based on the *Court Rolls of the Manor of Wakefield*, vols. iii-iv, ed. J. Lister, vol. v, ed. J. W. Walker (Yorks. Archaeol. Soc. Rec. Ser., lvii, lxxviii, cix, 1917, 1930, 1944). There are numerous gaps in the rolls in the period 1312-31 other than the five-year span 1317-22.

† This was the period when the manor was in the hands of Thomas of Lancaster, who dispossessed John de Warenne in 1317 (Maddicott, *op. cit.*, pp. 208, 236).

Wakefield (Yorks, W.R.), for instance, was an area where new rents for new land continue to be mentioned after the famine period.[212] But the entries are accompanied by far more numerous references to unoccupied land. In 1326-7, for example, the Wakefield court rolls list new rents from about twenty acres of assarted land, reclaimed from wood and waste; but the same rolls record over sixty-one acres of unoccupied land the same year.[213] Of course the court rolls noted unoccupied land only when it was being taken up by a new tenant, but for every acre mentioned in the rolls there must have been many more still lying vacant and unwanted in the West Riding of the 1320s. In fact if the Wakefield rolls, despite their incompleteness, are carefully analysed, they point clearly to a distinct turning-point in the occupation of the land in that area between 1317 and 1322, as the figures in Table IV show.

Land values, as represented by entry fines, reflect the situation. In 1312-13 entry fines for new lands were low, often no more than 6d. an acre and seldom above 2s. There may well have been a tightening up on entry fines shortly after this date because the fines for new land from 1314 to 1317 were far higher, 3s. to 4s. an acre being commonplace and 5s. to 7s. an acre being fairly often encountered.[214] After 1323 these fines slumped and most entries

[212] As cited in B. Harvey, *op. cit.*, p. 40 for example.

[213] *Court Rolls of the Manor of Wakefield*, v, ed. J. W. Walker (Yorks. Archaeol. Soc. Record Ser., cix, 1944), pp. 79-134.

[214] An attempt made by the administration in 1316 to catch up on older assarts reveals very vigorous clearance in the previous ten years or so. Some 240 entries in all refer to payments for encroachments made in the main between six and ten years earlier: *ibid.*, iv, ed. J. Lister (Yorks. Archaeol. Soc. Record Ser., lxxviii, 1930), pp. 88-94, 115-23.

were at a rate of 1s. to 2s. an acre. Even this was higher than the entry fines charged for previously unoccupied land, usually between 6d. and 1s. per acre, which explains the attraction of vacant holdings compared with the pre-1317 period when tenants had sometimes to be forced into taking them up.[215] The fall in land values occurs strikingly in entries such as the one for Horbury in 1325, where William the son of Alexander of Wakefield gives 6d. to take a bovate of land formerly held by Robert of Look for 9s. a year, but now unoccupied, at a rent of 6d. a year until a fitting time when the old rent could be levied on the bovate.[216] Most cases of reoccupied tenements, however, involved very small amounts of land; closer analysis might again reveal the more substantial tenants taking advantage of the vacation of holdings by poorer peasants.

Assarting on the manor of Wakefield appears to have continued throughout the famine years of 1315 to 1317. Whether, in this pastoral area, the great cattle murrain of 1319-21, adding to the earlier disaster, proved the turning-point or whether it was predominantly the Scottish raids of 1318 and 1319 is hard to say. On Bolton Priory's estates in the West Riding the Scottish raids certainly caused extensive social upheaval. Rent defects, never rising above 7s. 6d. in any year between 1306-07 and 1314-15, increased to almost £53 between 1315-16 and 1322-3, diminishing the rental income of the priory by little short of a third.[217] The number of tenements falling vacant, which rose in the famine years, soared as men fled from the Scots and though recovery was beginning by the date of the last extant account, in 1324-5, extensive vacancies still remained. The Bolton estates, however, were in the direct path of the Scottish raiders as they passed up the valleys of the Aire and Wharfe. But there is no evidence that they reached anywhere close to the four townships of Holme, Sowerby, Hipperholme and Rastrick, where the great amount of unoccupied land on the manor of Wakefield was to be found. Fear of the raiders might well explain some vacancies but the likeliest cause is the acute shortage of livestock which, as we have already seen, was besetting so many areas of south Yorkshire at this very date.[218]

The evidence from Wakefield points towards the second decade of the fourteenth century being the turning-point there, as in some

[215] Fines based on *ibid.*, iii-v. For examples of tenants being compelled to take up tenements, cf. *ibid.*, iii, ed. J. Lister (Yorks. Archaeol. Soc. Record Ser., lvii, 1917), p. 46.
[216] *Ibid.*, v, p. 71.
[217] Cf. my *Bolton Priory*, pp. 23, 25.
[218] Cf. above, pp. 114-15. Sale of herbage brought in nothing in Sowerby in 1322 "because almost all the animals in that area were destroyed by murrain": P.R.O., SC6/1145/21.

other areas, for land settlement. The calamities of these years left
many of the most vulnerable members of society poverty-stricken,
landless, homeless, and starving. Smallholders scraping a meagre
living from their acre or two of land were turned into refugees, tramps,
vagrants living a mere shadow of an existence.

And although, as we have seen, some land was still coming into use
in the early fourteenth century, it hardly seems on such a scale as to
compensate for that land lost to cultivation, especially in the areas
considered above. By 1341 the returns of the *Nonarum Inquisitiones,*
a source which has often been discounted out of hand simply
because it is a taxation record, reveal abundant evidence of large
areas of land which had gone out of cultivation.[219] If the extensive
vacancies of the North Riding point largely to the legacy of Scottish
depredations, the contraction of some 16,000 acres of former ploughland in the counties of Buckinghamshire, Cambridgeshire and Sussex
(apart from 4,000 acres in Sussex lost to the inroads of the sea), and
the retreat of arable in a hundred or so villages in Shropshire and
Bedfordshire, seem to have been related in some instances to poor
soils, more often to shortage of seed corn, and above all to lack of
tenants who had abandoned their holdings through poverty. Areas
with lighter population densities tended to be particularly badly
affected. Entries like the one for Tugford in south Shropshire, where
"the tenants do not cultivate their lands because of poverty, and six
tenants are begging", are fairly common.[220] Of course, no direct line
can be drawn between the agrarian crisis of 1315-22 and the contracting arable of the 1341-2 enquiry; some of the difficulties in 1341 were
undoubtedly the product of very recent harvest failures and sheep
murrain.[221] Still, the explanations for contracting arable accord well
with the situation I have been able to describe, as it existed in many
parts of the country, particularly the poorer and less populous regions,
in the 1320s. It is not hard to believe that in many instances such
regions had never recovered from the agrarian crisis of 1315-22.

[219] A. R. H. Baker, "Evidence in the 'Nonarum Inquisitiones' of Contracting
Arable Lands in England during the Early Fourteenth Century", *Econ. Hist.
Rev.*, 2nd ser., xix (1966), pp. 518-32. Cf. also his fuller studies of Sussex and
Bedfordshire: "Some Evidence of a Reduction in the Acreage of Cultivated
Lands in Sussex during the Early Fourteenth Century", *Sussex Archaeol.
Collections*, civ (1966), pp. 1-5 and "Contracting Arable Lands in 1341", *Beds.
Hist. Rec. Soc.*, xlix (1970), pp. 7-17; and B. Waites, "Medieval Assessments and
Agricultural Prosperity in Northeast Yorkshire, 1292-1342", *Yorks. Archaeol.
Journ.*, xliv (1972), pp. 134-45.
[220] *Nonarum Inquisitiones in Curia Scaccarii, temp. Regis Edwardi III* (Record
Commission, 1807), p. 186.
[221] E.g. *ibid.*, pp. 183-7 for many references to storms, flooding of the Severn
in Shropshire, and "common sheep murrain this year". And cf. also Titow,
"Weather", pp. 396-8.

And entries in the *Nonarum Inquisitiones* such as the one for Battlesden (Beds.), where the lord of the manor had forty acres which had not been sown for thirty years, show that some of the arable contraction was of long standing.[222]

One claim made by many tenants in 1341 was that they had been impoverished through the weight of taxation and there is no doubt that the extra and heavy impositions on the peasantry's resources brought about by the increasing burden of royal taxation in the early fourteenth century could have prevented any hope of recovery from the agrarian crisis. The rapid expansion in the late thirteenth and early fourteenth centuries of the use of purveyance for supplying the king's army in Scotland, as well as lay subsidies and the need to furnish men and arms, fell heavily on the peasantry, especially on the very poor. For if the very poor were exempt from subsidies, they were not able to escape the prise, which was becoming a frequent imposition, when their corn, beasts, and foodstuff would be seized by the king's officials. The wealthy could buy themselves protection from the purveyors; the poor had to suffer their arbitrary and unjust demands. When we realize that in such a critical year as 1316 the king's men rode through the famine-stricken English countryside demanding over 12,000 quarters of corn and malt, and produce in all worth some £7,000, it needs no great powers of imagination to realize that such taxation could make all the difference between survival and destitution for many.[223] A growing body of literature, perhaps written and collected by friars or the poorer clergy, poignantly reflects the sense of grievance felt by the peasantry at this time over royal taxation and shows what effect it could have on their lives. "To seek silver for the king, I sold my seed", goes the so-called *Song of the Husbandman*, "wherefore my land lies fallow and learns to sleep. Since they fetched my fair cattle in my fold, when I think of my weal I very nearly weep. Thus breed many bold beggars, and our rye is rotted and ruined before we reap".[224] And the *Song against the King's Taxes*, dating from 1338-9, echoed with foreboding; "People are reduced to such ill-plight that they can give no more; I fear if they had a leader they would rebel".[225]

---

[222] *Non. Inq.*, pp. 12, 14.

[223] Dr. Maddicott, who is preparing a paper on the peasantry and royal taxation in the early fourteenth century (now *Past and Present Supplement I*), provided me with these figures, based on *Rotuli Scotiae*, i (1814), pp. 160-1. Cf. also the comments of E. B. Fryde on purveyance in "Parliament and the French War, 1336-40", in T. A. Sandquist and M. R. Powicke (eds.), *Essays in Medieval History presented to Bertie Wilkinson* (Toronto, 1969), p. 258.

[224] *Polit. Songs*, pp. 149-53.

[225] *Ibid.*, pp. 182-7. For the date, cf. Fryde, *op. cit.*, p. 263, n. 71.

VIII

The half-century before the Black Death was as a whole a disturbed period for rural economy and society in England. It was a period which saw the end of an expanding demesne economy; contracting arable cultivation and a drop in agricultural production; declining exports and great uncertainties in the wool trade; the end of the population rise and probably a fall in some areas; increasing distress and widespread poverty for large sections of the peasantry. Such were the trends of the early fourteenth century as a whole.

A monocausal explanation would be simplistic. Obviously a number of factors were at work in shaping this situation. In some areas Malthusian causes seem to have been in operation. The drying-up of all available sources of colonizable land, falling crop yields from exhausted soils, proliferation of smallholders on the verge of starvation, and declining opportunities resulting in a drop in marriage- and birth-rates could all have played their part in some places. Taunton, on the Winchester estates, seems to have been one such locality.[226] In the north, warfare and political upheaval, adding their weight to the famine and murrains, produced extensive poverty and social dislocation.[227] In the south-east, floods and live-stock epidemics in 1325 and 1326 did much grave damage, as we saw earlier.[228] And throughout the country, royal taxation for fruitless wars against the Scots and then the French added to all these manifold miseries.

The part played by the agrarian crisis in all this is not easy to isolate. It has certainly not been my intention to claim too much for it, nor to elevate it to a position of sole responsibility for the reversal of agricultural production and population trends. On the contrary, I have been anxious to emphasize the very varied effects of the crisis on different regions and localities, on different types of landlord, and on different sectors of the peasantry. But all the evidence does go to demonstrate the gravity of the crisis and the severity of the disruption to the agrarian economy during the famine years. The extensive and lasting rural poverty to be witnessed in many parts of England in the aftermath of the crisis is on a scale which, especially when taken in conjunction with that so clearly illustrated in the

---

[226] Postan and Titow, "Heriots and Prices"; Titow, "Some Differences between Manors and their Effects on the Condition of the Peasant in the Thirteenth Century", *Agric. Hist. Rev.*, x (1962), pp. 1-13.

[227] Scammell, "Robert I and the North of England"; E. Miller, *War in the North* (St. John's College, Cambridge, Lecture, 1959-60).

[228] Cf. above, pp. 97-8.

Nonarum Inquisitiones, is hard to reconcile with Professor Russell's considered opinion that "England was a prosperous country in all but the worst years" of the early fourteenth century.[229]

The evidence points irresistibly to the conclusion that for some areas of the country, and for the estates of some major landlords, the agrarian crisis did mark the turning-point in agricultural production, demesne exploitation and the occupation of the land. The areas worst affected were the less densely populated and poorer regions, where there seems to have been a sharp but protracted downturn in the fortunes of rural society at the time of the crisis. And the crisis brought severe problems even for major landlords, with consequential changes in the organization and exploitation of their estates. Here too the famine years often marked a turning-point. And where not themselves a turning-point, they accelerated developments already under way, as on the Winchester estates.

On the other hand, in many of the wealthier and more densely populated parts of the country there is no indication that the agrarian crisis initiated a lasting decline in production and occupation of the land. Clearly the famine and murrains had immediate consequences. The manorial economy and village society were disturbed and shaken in these years. But there is no evidence that in the long-term the crisis was a turning-point for such areas. Though even in well-populated, and especially in over-populated, localities, where the motto must often have been "cultivate or starve", too much should not be made of the fact that rents were paid and vacancies few as an argument for the general well-being and prosperity of rural society. If there are no clear signs of decline, the keynote is usually stagnation not buoyancy. Regions of expanding rural economy — such as Cornwall — are seldom to be found in the early fourteenth century.[230]

It is again hard to provide a satisfactory general answer to the question of whether the mortalities of the famine and its concomitant epidemic disease were serious enough to have triggered off a lasting fall in population. Certainly there was depopulation in some parts of the country during the agrarian crisis but one's impression is that this was more through mobility — peasants being forced by poverty to relinquish holdings and become vagrants — than through heavy famine mortalities (though naturally the two are not unrelated). The loss of, say, ten per cent (at a guess) of the population — and those the poorer and weaker members of society for the most part — ought to

[229] Russell, "Pre-Plague Population", p. 21.
[230] Hatcher, *Rural Econ. and Soc. in the Duchy of Cornwall*, pp. 80-101.

have been recoverable fairly quickly.[231]   Nevertheless, it is arguable
that the increasing poverty of early fourteenth-century rural society
was sufficient both to put an end to previous population growth and to
prevent any early recovery from famine mortalities being made.
The low grain prices of the 1330s and 1340s may not point to
population figures "tumbling down" but they *are* suggestive of an
impoverished society in which, certainly in the late 1330s, a shortage
of money checked the purchasing ability of the populace and heavy
taxation created a general deflationary situation.[232]   And the rise in
agricultural wages between the famine and the Black Death points to
either increased demand for labour (which would be odd at a time of
arable contraction and depressed prices) or a shortage of labour which
is all the more striking when we recall both the reduced scale of arable
cultivation and the many uprooted and landless peasants who must
have been desperate for work at this date.[233]

In the final analysis, it seems Postan's view[234] that the reversal of
agricultural production and population trends came some decades
before the Black Death has much to commend it, if one bears in mind
the need to modify the generalization in the light of local and regional
variations.   To look to the "succession of bad seasons in the second
decade of the fourteenth century" as a turning-point is also
acceptable, if one remembers that the agrarian crisis was far from the
sole agent of social, economic and demographic change at this date;
that its significance is as one element, though an important one, among
many involved in bringing about an end to previous expansion and the
beginnings of a recession in the rural economy of England.

---

[231] The famine might even have been followed by a temporarily sharp rise
in marriage and birth rates. Cf. Fourquin, *Campagnes de la Région
Parisienne*, p. 192 and n. 6 for a suggestion of this in the Paris area, where there
is no indication that the famines instigated a marked and lasting fall in
population.
[232] Fryde, *op. cit.*, pp. 264-5.
[233] Rogers, *op. cit.*, i, pp. 264, 269 and his *Six Centuries of Work and Wages*,
9th edn. (London, 1908), pp. 217-18; Lord Beveridge, "Westminster Wages in
the Manorial Era", *Econ. Hist. Rev.*, 2nd ser., viii (1955-6), pp. 20-2, 24;
Titow, *Eng. Rural Soc.*, p. 52, n. 28.   I am grateful to Dr. Farmer for allowing
me to see the figures which he has prepared, based on substantial information
from a wide area, for the forthcoming *Agrarian History of England and Wales*,
vol. ii.
[234] Postan, *Rapports*, p. 241, and cf. above, pp. 85-6.

6. *The Knight and the Knight's Fee in England* *

SALLY HARVEY

I

"MUCH LABOUR HAS BEEN VAINLY SPENT ON ATTEMPTS TO DETERMINE the true area of the knight's fee", J. H. Round thundered nearly eighty years ago.[1] Rightly historians continue to ignore the warning, the association between the knight and his fee being central to feudal England and to English feudalism; for it is on obtaining specialized service, essentially military, by granting support in land (known as the fee or fief) that the characterization of feudalism and feudal societies hinges. On the size of the knight's fee depends, too, the character of the knightly class and relations between the other tenures: the tenants-in-chief above, whose interest in the knights' service derives in part from the conditions of their own military tenure from the king; and the agricultural classes below, on whom the knights must ultimately rely for their landed revenues. As Vinogradoff wistfully said: "it would be exceedingly material to know what estate was considered as the minimum outfit for a fully equipped fighting knight. Typical estimates of knights' fees would allow us to draw certain boundaries between classes of society and to explain indirectly some of the processes which led to their formation". But the problem of the landed basis of the effective knight remains unsolved, hindering a clear practical picture of English feudalism. No one would seek a precise all-valid figure, yet it seems not overdemanding to ask what was reckoned an appropriate, approximate norm. Round himself believed that the knight's fee ranged in size between two and ten hides (the hide being a notional 120 acres); according to Poole it might extend up to twenty-seven; while Stenton concluded that the typical knight's fee proves "elusive".[2]

* I should like to thank Professor R. H. Hilton, whose research seminar inspired this study, and Mr. T. H. Aston for their help and encouragement, and Professor H. A. Cronne and Dr. R. C. Smail for commenting on a draft of this article, which is based on a paper read to the Cambridge Historical Society in December 1968.

[1] J. H. Round, *Feudal England*, 2nd edn. (London, 1964) (hereafter cited as Round), p. 231.

[2] P. Vinogradoff, *English Society in the Eleventh Century* (Oxford, 1908) (hereafter cited as Vinogradoff), p. 44; Round, pp. 231-2; A. L. Poole, *From Domesday Book to Magna Carta*, 2nd edn. (Oxford, 1954), p. 15; F. M. Stenton, *Anglo-Saxon England*, 2nd edn. (Oxford, 1955), p. 629; F. M. Stenton, *The First Century of English Feudalism*, 2nd edn. (Oxford, 1961) (hereafter cited as Stenton), p. 23.

One difficulty is that definition of the knights as a class is also elusive. So, at the same time as looking for their landed basis we need to find out how far the word *miles*, usually translated for the medieval period as "knight", is itself a precise term or whether its general use (and indeed its single translation) is partly responsible for some of the obscurity; how far it has particular connotations, military, tenurial or social, in the first century after the Norman Conquest, and how they change and develop. It will then be of importance to diagnose when and why. To do this effectively we need to abandon our hindsight view of the splendidly-equipped figure of chivalric gamesmanship afforded by the late medieval knight, or at least to balance it by two other views: one from the Anglo-Saxon beyond, of the unheralded serving retainer, or *cniht*, a term which was unhesitatingly applied by native writers to the military men William I brought with him, and from which the word "knight" derives; the other, of the men contemporaries called *solidarii* or *milites solidarii*, now usually translated "mercenaries", but whose nature may often be more aptly conveyed by the modern derivation, "soldiers".[3] (For the moment for convenience and to avoid pre-judgements we shall render *miles* consistently as "knight".) And so there is a central question as to whether knights in England were of the noble classes as in a few parts of Europe in the eleventh century, or whether peasant knighthood was prevalent, as in other regions.

The real difficulty is that the evidence is apparently discrepant. It points on the one hand to knights, perhaps of later "gentry" type, who had about five hides; on the other to knights, usually dismissed as "exceptional", who hold a hide or so, humble people, no better off than prosperous peasants. Two unresolved contentions on these lines appear at different points in Professor Hollister's recent detailed studies of military organization,[4] and also in Professor Galbraith's

[3] For the hindsight view see, for instance, Professor Boussard, who by-passes the problem and turns reasoning on its head by assuming that all the early knights were noble and so, after the Conquest, when "land was abundant", the knight's fee was not merely the minimum for "a knight to live nobly with his family, in many cases, it was very much larger": J. Boussard, *Le Gouvernement d'Henri II Plantagenêt* (Paris, 1956), p. 209. On the *cniht* see Stenton, pp. 133-7; on "soldiers" see H. Ellis, *Introduction to Domesday Book* (Record Commission, 1833), i, p. 62.

[4] C. W. Hollister, *The Military Organization of Norman England* (Oxford, 1965) (hereafter cited as Hollister), pp. 44, 235-6; "The five hides of the Anglo-Saxon soldier correspond to the five hides of the average knight's fee"; "the insignificance of many of the smaller knights' fees suggests that some knights were no better off than prosperous peasants", Hollister, pp. 67, 71. Possessors of five hides would not be peasants by Anglo-Saxon definition: "if a ceorl prospered so that he possessed fully five hides of land of his own . . . then he was henceforth entitled to the rights of a thegn": in an early eleventh-century compilation "On Status", *English Historical Documents*, i, ed. D. Whitelock (London, 1955), p. 432.

valuable discussion of a Herefordshire land-grant of 1085, an important text for this topic, showing that even a single district can produce seeming contradictions.[5]   Only Vinogradoff seems to have diagnosed the nature of the problem, to have recognized the two groups of evidence, and the necessity as well as the difficulty of their reconciliation.   He correlated them with the two groups of fighting men depicted in the Assize of Arms of 1181.[6]   It was a stimulating suggestion but it does not readily help with the plentiful evidence of much larger fiefs of that period, or with the dynamics during the century or so before.

Yet the evidence is reconcilable.   Investigation suggests that in the first decades after the Conquest the two types of evidence represent two completely different social and tenurial classes, the influential knightly sub-tenants and the professional knights, whose services can at first be obtained for a small amount of land.   Then, as the twelfth century progresses, the basic minimum needed to furnish those called knights increases, and, as a consequence, first the small professional, then the knight of merely local importance finds difficulty in fulfilling an active rôle as a knight.   But, to clarify matters, contemporary estimates of the knight's fee must be evaluated without pre-conceived notions; we must remember that testimony divided by a century or so cannot be expected to present the same picture; and, most important of all, a different picture of the feudal process emerges according to the tenurial level which furnishes the information.[7]   Much of this comes from levels of society which are more concerned with the tenurial and fiscal aspects than the military realities of feudal tenure and the prosperity of the knight himself.   It may help to distinguish these levels if we first rehearse some familiar developments.

Militarily, the king is concerned that he receives from his tenants-in-chief their support, and that this potential force is competent and loyal.   It is for the tenant-in-chief to organize and provide for his

[5] "There is ample evidence in Herefordshire of villages assessed at five hides, with a normal *valet* of 100 shillings, forming the enfeoffment of a knight (*militis*)".   In an earlier footnote: "it was presumably by these *milites* [i.e. fully equipped horsemen] that the bulk of the military service was actually performed.   They were comparatively humble people of a hide or so, and their names are rarely if ever given.   Examples of them have been found paying money rent for their land".   V. H. Galbraith, "An Episcopal Land-Grant of 1085", *Eng. Hist. Rev.*, xliv (1929) (hereafter cited as Galbraith), pp. 369, 362. Cf. H. G. Richardson and G. O. Sayles for whom the knights include "all grades from substantial landowners to men who had to be content with a small-holding that put them on a level with the English peasant": *The Governance of Medieval England* (Edinburgh, 1963), p. 60.

[6] The two groups to him consisted of large fiefs of 4-7 hides and small fiefs of 2-3 hides, which he correlated with the holders of 16 marks and 10 marks worth of land respectively in the Assize of Arms: Vinogradoff, pp. 51-8.

[7] See Round, pp. 197, 234; Vinogradoff, p. 46; Galbraith, p. 361.

commitment. Several ways are open to him. In the early days of conquest, he could, as the abbot of Abingdon did, provide permanent protection for himself at the same time by having knights at hand in his household.[8] Or he could employ mercenaries; but as these were often aliens from Flanders or Brittany,[9] it took time to arrange their hire, and provision had to be made for them as for the others. In fact, at Abingdon and elsewhere, mercenaries formed the initial nucleus of the abbot's household recruits.[10] When their presence became a patent embarrassment, as it did to many ecclesiastical institutions,[11] then the alternative of giving the knights land and an opportunity to settle was adopted. This could be effected directly; and such cases will reveal the landed basis of the individual fighting knight. However, the tenant-in-chief with large estates and a large responsibility to organize had an opportunity to kill several birds with one stone. He could depute some of this organization to influential contemporaries, who in return were enfeoffed with a few manors. These intermediaries were frequently the honorial barons, that is the powerful sub-tenants, though in the first decade or so after the Conquest we tend to learn most of the arrangement when one tenant-in-chief becomes the sub-tenant of another. For the tenant-in-chief of widespread power, these grants afforded the opportunity to gain bases in parts of the country where he himself held no lands in chief, as the count of Eu's tenure by knight-service from the arch-bishop of Canterbury gave him a manor in Kent.[12] For the regional magnate, it meant the chance to gain land in convenient juxtaposition to that he already held. Roger de Lacy, a tenant-in-chief powerful in the western marches, held from the bishop of Hereford two manors in return for providing two knights.[13] One holding, Onibury in Shropshire, was adjacent to two of Roger's own rich manors, Stanton Lacy and Stokesay.[14] Such influential feudal tenants then had open the same range of choice when deciding how to fulfil their commit-

---

[8] *Chronicon Monasterii de Abingdon,* ii, ed. J. Stevenson (Rolls Series, 1858), pp. 3-4; Hollister, p. 55.

[9] Both before and after the Norman Conquest: *The Anglo-Saxon Chronicle,* ed. D. Whitelock (London, 1961), p. 145; Henry of Huntingdon, *Historia Anglorum,* ed. T. Arnold (Rolls Series, 1879), pp. 217-8; Ordericus Vitalis, *Historia Ecclesiastica,* ed. A. le Prévost (Paris, 1840), iv, pp. 40, 45.

[10] *Chron. Mon. de Abingdon,* ii, p. 3.

[11] See Hollister, p. 173; e.g. *Liber Eliensis,* ed. E. O. Blake (Camden Soc., 3rd ser., xcii, 1962), p. 217.

[12] *Domesday Book,* i, fo. 4: references here to Domesday Book will be to the two volumes edited by A. Farley, issued without title pages in 1783, hereafter abbreviated *Dom. Bk.*; *The Domesday Monachorum of Christ Church Canterbury,* ed. D. C. Douglas (London, 1944), fo. 7r.

[13] Galbraith, pp. 371-2.   [14] *Dom. Bk.,* i, fo. 260b.

ment. But one thing we know; the land granted to them was not entirely shared out among the knights they employed.[15] Were that so, the whole process would have been without point. The feudal tenant had to be given sufficient land to provide for his knights and leave for himself manors enough to make the negotiation worthwhile. In fact so profitable were these arrangements that they were often sought out and sometimes the result of pressure, if not actual coercion. Roger de Lacy sought the grant from the bishop of Hereford "by means of friends and money"; and in return for one of the manors Roger agreed to pay the bishop £1 a year, further indicating that Roger anticipated commercial benefits from the arrangement.[16] One of the few manors that Domesday Book specifically tells us was "in fee" (*in feudo*) was held by a royal chamberlain "in fee for a set payment (*firma*) of £3 a year", when the rest of the entry indicates that the estate was producing between £6 and £12 during that period.[17] It may be suggestive, too, that among the list of those holding by military service from the archbishop of Canterbury, Odo of Bayeux's companions and sub-tenants feature prominently.[18] For one of the activities from which Odo's notoriety stemmed was the way in which he had appropriated much land rightfully belonging to the archbishopric. Even after the great land-suit which restored the stolen lands, some of Odo's associates in the crime were still military sub-tenants of Canterbury,[19] evidence that his candidates had forcefully maintained their profitable position in despite, not support, of their tenant-in-chief.

The tenant-in-chief, on the other hand, while he may have granted out more land than was strictly necessary to provide for the fighting knights stipulated, reaped other benefits besides that of deputing part of the organization of his contingent. He acquired in the feudal relationship, involving the homage and fealty of his often powerful sub-tenant, ties of personal and political influence. The fact that Roger Bigod, sometime sheriff of Norfolk and Suffolk, was enfeoffed with some of the abbey of Bury St. Edmunds' lands[20] had great political potential for the monastic house whose main estates lay in those two counties (even though such a situation made the ultimate return of the lands unlikely). Dr. Matthew has recently brought out

---

[15] See Vinogradoff, p. 46; Round, p. 188.
[16] Galbraith, p. 363.
[17] *Dom. Bk.*, i, fo. 129b.
[18] *Domesday Monachorum*, fo. 7r.
[19] *Ibid.*, pp. 31-3; Ordericus Vitalis, *Hist. Eccles.*, ii, pp. 222-3.
[20] *Feudal Documents from the Abbey of Bury St. Edmunds*, ed. D. C. Douglas (British Academy Records in Soc. and Econ. Hist., viii, 1932), pp. 11-14, 16, 55.

well the social and political importance of the feudal tie.   He quotes
Haimo Dapifer's tenure of an estate of St. Augustine's, Canterbury
where Haimo promises to give "counsel, aid and succour to the
church, to the abbot and his successors, concerning all pleas of the
shire or in the king's court, against all barons, except those whose
vassals he will have become by the giving of hands".[21]   And the
tenant-in-chief had really lost little: for one of the great problems,
indeed characteristics, of a feudal society is the lack of an educated
administrative class; this resulted through all sectors of society in the
"farming-out" of responsibility accompanied by a provision for
revenue.   The supervision of the scattered estates which made up
a sizeable proportion of the Anglo-Norman honour was often beset
with difficulties, and great could be the transport problems that the
estates posed.   True, the tenant-in-chief had granted out estates;
but these were not his largest and wealthiest, which were normally
retained as demesne.   In return, he had rid himself of part of his
military responsibility, and gained for himself political and personal
influence as well — often more useful to him than military support,
which he could only use personally as a final sanction.

Two already well-known classes of sub-tenants epitomize the
primarily political or social rôle of many enfeoffments: they are those
intruded by the king and the nepotic tenures.   If sub-enfeoffments
embodying political or personal favours were commonplace, it is only
natural that the relatives of tenants-in-chief, as well as the influential,
should be among the recipients.[22]   Nepotic enfeoffments, to be
expected on lay estates, were common on ecclesiastical fiefs also.
Round long ago drew attention to their important influence on sub-
infeudation, and produced examples from the archbishopric of York
and the abbeys of Ely, Abingdon, Tavistock, Evesham, Abbotsbury
and Glastonbury.[23]   To this list can be added instances at St.
Edmunds and Rochester, all incidents of the first half-century following
the Conquest.[24]   Some of these relatives may have been professional

---

[21] D. J. Matthew, *The Norman Conquest* (London, 1966), pp. 108 *et seq.*,
esp. p. 115; *The Register of St. Augustine's, Canterbury*, ed. G. J. Turner and
H. E. Salter (British Academy Records in Soc. and Econ. Hist., ii and iii, 1924),
ii, p. 462.

[22] This, of course, was a recurrent situation.   The element was there in
tenth-century appointments, too.   Among the thegns of St. Oswald, the tenth-
century reorganizer of the Worcester estates, were two brothers of the bishop and
a nephew: Stenton, pp. 127-8.

[23] Round, pp. 236-8; see also D. C. Douglas, "The Norman Conquest and
English Feudalism", *Econ. Hist. Rev.*, ix (1938-9), pp. 130-1.

[24] *Feudal Documents*, pp. 4-6; F. R. H. Du Boulay, *The Lordship of Canterbury*
(London, 1966), p. 95.

knights themselves, but they were not given land solely on that account and their enfeoffments are no true guide to the economic basis of a professional knight. This was also true of the times when the king interfered on a level that, in feudal theory, ought to have been beyond his concern. It may be just to supplement the income of the royal official: a writ directs that Eudo Dapifer be given an estate at Peterborough Abbey to be held as a fief,[25] and Domesday Book might protest that such enfeoffments were "on the king's order against the abbot's wish".[26] Or the king's word might be given as a justification for a nepotic enfeoffment: on the bishop of Salisbury's lands we read of a nephew of Bishop Herman who was a knight "by order of the king".[27] Or the king might display an inexpensive compassion in the case of one who, in fact, was a professional knight in the service of the abbot of Abingdon. The knight had been involved in an attack by pirates while returning from the continent and had been badly injured, having had his hands cut off. Unfortunately he had not yet received any land from the abbot and now, useless for his profession, it was obvious that he never would. Nevertheless he put his position to the king who "feeling pity, commanded the abbot that he should provide for the man enough land of this kind to support him as long as he lived".[28] So-called enfeoffments might indeed be so beneficial that military reasons were often used to justify grants otherwise unjustifiable. Instructive here is one of the qualities for which an abbot of Ely was to be commended: he enfeoffed knights, says his panegyrist, solely because of compulsion, and "not by intention or rather partiality for riches, nor by exerting himself for relatives".[29] The widespread tendency for factors such as these to motivate enfeoffment is evident in an archbishop of York's explanation for the excessive number of his knights. His predecessors, he said, "had enfeoffed many more than they owed to the king, not on account of the obligation of service which they owed, but because they wanted to make provision for their kinsmen and for those who served them".[30]

In practice magnates often provided for their military responsibility by a combination of all methods. This way they had the advantages

---

[25] *Chronicon Petroburgense* ed. T. Stapleton (Camden Soc., xlvii, 1849), p. 168; also the example of Picot, sheriff of Cambridgeshire, who was given an Ely estate, *Dom. Bk.*, i, fo. 200.

[26] *Dom. Bk.*, i, fos. 222, 191.

[27] *Dom. Bk.*, i, fol 66.

[28] *Chron. Mon. de Abingdon*, ii, p. 6.

[29] *Liber Eliensis*, p. 217; Abbot Turold of Peterborough "evilly gave lands to his relatives and to the knights who came with him": *Chronicle of Hugh Candidus*, trans. C. and W. T. Mellows (Peterborough, 1941), p. 43.

[30] *Red Book of the Exchequer*, ed. H. Hall (Rolls Series, 1896), i, p. 413.

accruing from each: that is, a nucleus of locally based knights, sometimes living within the household, sometimes given land or, as at Westminster and Bury, dwellings close by,[31] who could act as an armed escort; while the rest of the commitment was supplied either from directly, or indirectly enfeoffed knights. This last method of recruitment, offering substantial profits for the "middleman", enabled the tenant-in-chief to wield real political influence or to provide for dependants, officials and relatives.

The tenant-in-chief, in noting those who provided his military service, included all types of men with whom he made arrangements and they appear without differentiation: they all are from his point of view his "knights". The eleventh-century list of the "Knights of the Archbishop" of Canterbury in Domesday Monachorum furnishes an example. The heterogeneity of this list has puzzled its editor, Professor Douglas, who doubts whether its eleventh-century compilers could distinguish a knight accurately.[32] There is no need, however, to fall back on such reasoning; here, as elsewhere, its composition is explicable, but needs further analysis. The holders and their fiefs may be divided into two main categories: the influential and the professional. The "influential" class may be further subdivided. First, there were those sub-tenants of baronial character, often tenants-in-chief elsewhere, who were responsible for blocks of knights. At Canterbury these include the bishop of Rochester (10 knights), Haimo the sheriff (6), Gilbert fitz Richard (4); at Bury St. Edmund's Roger Bigod, Robert Blunt, Peter de Valoignes. The rest of this category were baronial contacts of all sorts who might be responsible for perhaps one to three knights (or even for less).[33] From Canterbury, Agelwin, son of Brihtmaer, an important man in contemporary London, held responsibility for one knight; he had retained his status over the Conquest and is only one of several London contacts attested in this list.[34] A few of this class are the type one expects to find as knights, active knights of good birth holding a manor or two, but they are often younger sons or brothers

[31] *Dom. Bk.*, i, fo. 128; *ibid.*, ii, fo. 372.
[32] "The Norman Conquest and English Feudalism", p. 133.
[33] *Domesday Monachorum*, fo. 7r; *Feudal Documents*, pp. lxxxii-lxxxiv.
[34] *Domesday Monachorum*, pp. 58-63. Cf. an important contract but very unmilitary enfeoffment of the twelfth century. A prominent Londoner of Stephen's time, Gervase of Cornhill, one-time justiciar and sheriff, developer of real estate, money-lender, was given a half knight's fee, the service being appropriately commuted to a cash payment in London: *Regesta Regum Anglo-Normannorum*, iii, ed. R. H. C. Davis and H. A. Cronne (Oxford, 1968), no. 244; H. G. Richardson, *The English Jewry under the Angevin Kings* (London, 1960), pp. 47-8, 59.

of important men, and as a type are in a minority. We may for convenience refer to them as "middling knights". In fact, the use of the word *miles* for many in this list (and others in a similar position elsewhere) is better interpreted as "vassal" rather than "knight", especially as it is known that *miles* supplanted the word *vassus* in this connotation from the tenth century onwards.[35] Very different in economic and tenurial position were those of the second category: those who were largely professional knights, some responsible for a whole knight, some for a fraction; in the eleventh century their fiefs were seldom whole vills or manors, but consisted of small portions of one or more. Usually nameless in Domesday Book itself, they are sometimes to be identified by a single name from the lists of tenants-in-chief and from ancillary texts. In Domesday Monachorum we meet five professionals on one demesne manor, all holding about a sulung each, though in Domesday Book they simply appear as "men" (*homines*);[36] all the characteristics of this situation, we will show, are normal for the early professional.

In view of the use that has been made of the Worcester evidence for five-hide fees, it is interesting to see that an analysis of the bishop's fees in the Red Book of Worcester produces just the same pattern. In the twelfth century the influential sub-tenants responsible for blocks of knights were William de Beauchamp (15), Bohun (7½), and the earl of Gloucester (7½). There were few "middling" knights, but a great many with small portions of land. The only neatness is indeed in the *results* of the bishop's arrangements, which are made up in all sorts of ways. The five-hide unit has no intrinsic military reality: when land is channelled down the tenurial hierarchy, it seldom passes proportionately with military responsibility and the amount indeed was rearranged according to the recipient. The only difference at Worcester is that it was more evenly arranged than elsewhere at the highest stage. Even there, the one general conclusion to be observed is that the identity of one professional knight, with responsibility for one knight and with a whole knight's fee or even a substantial manor or two, is a rarity.[37] Rather than being

---

[35] P. Guilhiermoz, *Essai sur l'origine de la noblesse en France au Moyen Age* (Paris, 1902), pp. 336-41.

[36] *Dom. Bk.*, i, fo. 3b; *Domesday Monachorum*, fo. 2v.

[37] That the bishop could rearrange the component parts of each knight's fee over which he had direct control is illustrated by various groupings at different times: one knight's fee was at one point made up by Richard de Vehim 1 hide, Gilbert Croc 1 virgate, Robert Young of Cleeve 1 virgate, Robert Franceys 1½ hides; at another time it consisted of Samson ½ knight's fee, Richard de Vehim 1 hide, Richard of Wye 1½ hides, Gilbert Croc 1 virgate, Robert of Hampton 1 virgate. By 1208-9, a list of the bishop of Worcester's knights, excluding those

those on which our ideas of the early knight should be based, early examples of this type seem to come about as a chance result merging some of the characteristics of each of two easily definable and contrasting types. It is the mixture of directly and indirectly enfeoffed knights in such lists that has caused the difficulties about the knight's fee. Just as one cannot divide the total estate of a tenant-in-chief by his military responsibility and call the result the size of the knight's fee, so one cannot do this with those sub-enfeoffments not made with serving and individual knights themselves. Yet this is the inference that historians have made.

The important vassals did not themselves perform the military service due to the tenant-in-chief. But their existence accounts for the sub-tenures of about five hides per knight for which they owe responsibility. There were several reasons why there should be so many five-hide fiefs. Traditional concepts and fiscal estimates of Anglo-Saxon derivation had lingering force: five hides formed a basis suitable for a person of status, and five hides was capable of providing from its surplus an armed man equipped with horse.[38] Also hides were used as fiscal ratings for public obligations (including military) and in many parts of the country were imposed in decimal units, so that an estate of four to six agricultural hides would tend to be rated at a round five hides.[39]

The military position of the men of influence is reflected precisely in phrases from Bury St. Edmunds's Feudal Book. They received their land that "they should be able to ride in the Saint's service" (*qui ire possent in servicium Sancti*); this is their theoretical position. A line or two later we learn that they are enfeoffed "that they should find knights for the Saint's service" (*ut . . . invenirent milites in servicium Sancti*); here the actuality.[40] It is only in Domesday's uniquely detailed description of Bury St. Edmunds, that the elusive professionals emerge. After the list of bakers, ale-brewers, tailors, washerwomen,

holding of the king also, shows 70 names of which 1 holds 3 knights' fees; 2 hold 2 knights' fees; 8 hold 1 knight's fee; 8 hold ½ knight's fee; some 50 hold lesser fractions, often described in terms of hides and virgates or small fractions of knights' fees. *Red Book of Worcester*, ed. M. Hollings, iv (Worcester Hist. Soc., 1939), pp. 414-418, 430-42. I owe this analysis to an unpublished paper by Professor Hilton.

[38] Vinogradoff, p. 83; M. Powicke, *Military Obligation in Medieval England* (Oxford, 1962), p. 19.

[39] *Dom. Bk.*, i, fos. 56b, 100, 64b; Round "Danegeld and the Finance of Domesday", *Domesday Studies*, i, ed. P. Dove (London, 1888), pp. 119-21; Round, pp. 44-9. In areas where duodecimal units of assessment were used, the corresponding unit would presumably be six carucates.

[40] *Feudal Documents*, p. 4.

shoemakers, robe-makers, cooks, porters, agents, "who all daily wait upon the abbot and the brethren", we learn that "besides these there are fourteen reeves over the land, who have their houses in the said town, and, under them, five bordars. Now there are thirty-four knights, French and English together, and under them twenty-two bordars".[41] Douglas rightly observes that one does not expect Roger Bigod to be permanently resident in Bury at the disposition of the abbot.[42] But just as there is no case for identifying these thirty-four with the nominal "Enfeoffed Men" (*Feudati Homines*), likewise there is no need to divorce them entirely as Douglas does. They are obviously their representatives, "provided", just as the Feudal Book stipulated they should be, "for the service of the Saint".[43] The large size of some sub-enfeoffments, and the obviously high political and social standing of their holders need no longer disturb us.[44] The crown itself was early aware that the process of sub-infeudation was not always immediate and direct, and that the position of the feudal middleman was particularly advantageous. Thus its insistence that all under-tenants of significance should take an oath of fealty direct to the king. To Salisbury in 1086 were summoned "all the people occupying land who were of any account all over England, no matter whose vassals they might be; and they all submitted to him and became his vassals and swore oaths of allegiance to him that they would be loyal to him against all other men".[45]

The magnates and the non-professional sub-tenants made their own advantageous arrangements with the professionals, and if they enfeoffed them, they gave them very small amounts of land. The process is recalled clearly in 1166 by Alexander de Alno. "My father gave to his brother, Hugh de Alno, a small amount of land from his

[41] *Dom. Bk.*, ii, fo. 372.   [42] *Op. cit.*, p. cvi.
[43] A later incident from Bury St. Edmunds shows a deputed responsibility and the size of the support depending on the status of the deputy. To a young claimant of the position of steward, who was not yet a knight, Abbot Samson made answer: "Henry's rights I neither deny, nor wish to deny. If he was able to serve me in person, I would give him all that is needful for the maintenance of ten men and eight horses .... If you should present to me as his substitute, a steward who knows how to perform the duties of stewardship, I would accept him on the same terms as my predecessor granted to his steward ... that is, four horses and their appurtenances". Eventually a deputy was presented: "a simple and ignorant steward, Gilbert by name". We are left not knowing how little was given. *The Chronicle of Jocelin of Brakelond*, ed. and trans. H. E. Butler (London, 1949), p. 27.
[44] E.g. "The term [*miles*] is used in Domesday Book to describe persons of every imaginable level of wealth, social status and military training": Hollister, p. 115.
[45] *The Anglo-Saxon Chronicle*, s.a. 1086, p. 161.

demesne, so that, if it became necessary, he could do the service of one knight to answer for the whole of my father's land. And that grant was made to him and his heirs in the time of King William".[46]   An active knight in a similar situation appears in another instance from the 1166 returns on the fief of Gilbert de Lanval, who holds by service of two knights and writes: "of this fief a certain knight holds from me a quarter part [of the land of] one knight".[47]

Disentangled from the nominal knights we are now free to follow up the position of the fighting professional to whom the sub-tenant farmed out the service together with some land. Domesday Book contains the largest amount of information about such knights in the eleventh century. Surprising though it may seem, this obvious source has not been fully utilized to elucidate this obvious problem.[48] Its use has been rather as a historian's lucky dip to provide extraordinary examples, and has never been systematic. The only serious objection to the usefulness of Domesday is Professor Hollister's suggestion that the landed basis of its knights (*milites*) is too small to allow us to think of them as the feudal knights, so they must be the remnants of the Anglo-Saxon fyrd. Apart from the preconceived notions which determine this argument, elsewhere the same historian himself supplies evidence that the Domesday *miles* is also the feudal *miles*. The Peterborough *Descriptio Militum* of the second decade of the twelfth century "discloses the exact assessment of the Peterborough knights' fees in hides, virgates, or carucates, and thereby enables us to deduce the number of hides supporting each knight". Then, instead of following up this idea, Hollister dismisses Peterborough's fiefs as "exceptionally small", just as he did those in Domesday. This happens even though he thinks the Peterborough evidence is "in certain respects our most important source relating to the nature and extent of military service on a great Anglo-Norman honour", even though he admits that "in some instances, the knights of the *Descriptio* are the very tenants of Domesday", and even though he stresses the distinction there between the knights themselves and the sokemen who serve "with the knights" (*cum militibus*).[49]   The detailed Abingdon and Canterbury texts also demonstrate the identity

---

[46] *Red Book of Exch.*, i, p. 230.   [47] *Ibid.*, p. 442.
[48] Domesday evidence has received very mixed receptions from historians, including the hopeless: "unfortunately D.B. says nothing about knights' fees", S. Painter, *Studies in the History of the English Feudal Barony* (Baltimore, 1943), p. 21; Mr. Richardson and Professor Sayles have some perceptive remarks on knights and Domesday Book, *The Governance of Medieval England*, p. 127.
[49] Hollister, pp. 235-6.

of the Domesday knight and the feudal knight.[50]   There is therefore
a good case, which has not been undermined, for taking a thorough
look at Domesday's neglected evidence.

The results are surprisingly consistent.   An analysis of the instances
in Domesday Book, nearly 500, which give details of the number of
hides or carucates each knight holds, reveals the normal landed basis
of the eleventh-century knight to be about $1\frac{1}{2}$ hides.   This puts him
only just above most well-to-do peasants.   The mean of the holdings
of the Domesday knight approaches $1\frac{2}{3}$ hides.   That this figure is not
the result of averaging very diverse amounts is demonstrated by the
histogram (below, p. 146).   The mode, that is the size which occurs
most frequently (broken down to $\frac{1}{8}$s of a hide) constitutes almost a
quarter of the total entries.   It gives the same figure, 1 hide, as the
median, the category in which occurs the central number of the range
of data.   Looked at another way, over a third of the Domesday knights
have between $\frac{3}{4}$ and $1\frac{1}{2}$ hides, and another quarter of the total have
less land than this.   There are very few instances of fiefs over $3\frac{1}{2}$ hides
in size, so the profit of the influential feudal "middleman" on the
arrangement of approximately 5 or 6 hides per knight service was
substantial.   There is some evidence of a slight regional difference,
though not a great disparity.   The large size and value of the Kentish
fiefs are the most prominent.   The Kentish sulungs, representing
probably the order of 200 notional acres rather than the 120 acres of
the hide and carucate, have been left out of the above calculations;[51]
their inclusion would bring the average up to $1\frac{3}{4}$ hides.   Their
average mean is about $1\frac{1}{4}$ sulungs, that is just over 2 hides, while the
hidated counties, twenty-four in number, tend to average $1\frac{2}{3}$ hides
and the carucated counties, seven in number, average nearly 2
carucates.   The values given for the knightly holdings in Kent are
large too, averaging nearly £3 per knight, while the fees of the
carucated areas tend to the reverse, a very low value.   This suggests
that the larger size of the Kentish fiefs reflects their greater value,
while the larger size of the carucated northern fees is an attempt to
compensate for their low value relative to acreage.

Just how valuable are the figures gleaned from Domesday Book in
this way?   Let us examine the possibility of bias to see if the above
conclusion as to the norm may be an underestimate.   First, unless
the knights are referred to twice in Domesday, once by name and
once by function, the instances collected exclude any professional

[50] E.g. Du Boulay, *The Lordship of Canterbury*, p. 79.
[51] P. Vinogradoff, "Sulung and Hide", *Eng. Hist. Rev.*, xix (1904), pp. 282-6.

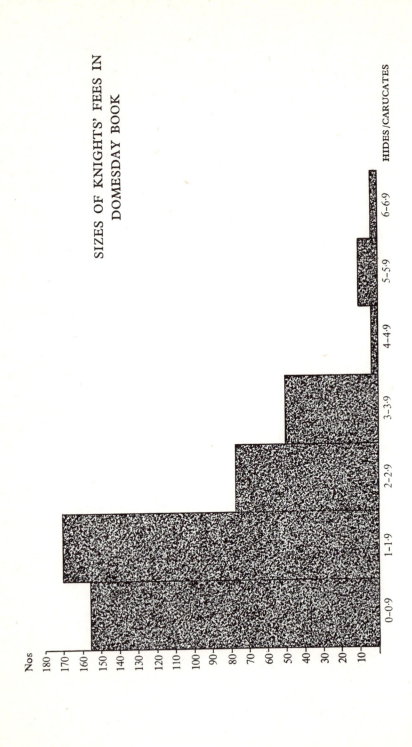

SIZES OF KNIGHTS' FEES IN
DOMESDAY BOOK

Nos

180
170
160
150
140
130
120
110
100
90
80
70
60
50
40
30
20
10

0–0·9 1–1·9 2–2·9 3–3·9 4–4·9 5–5·9 6–6·9

HIDES/CARUCATES

knight of sufficient importance to be mentioned by name rather than solely by function. This is unavoidable; yet it could mean that some such people might perform the professional duties themselves and we not know of it. However, their omission will not affect our findings as to the expected minimum for the professional; additional land was available to them because they were of consequence, not solely to provide the wherewithal for a fighting knight. Often those who performed military and all sorts of other service were able to take on extra lands at rent or lease from their lords, probably on beneficial terms.[52] That, on the whole, we have to confine ourselves to nameless knights is the source of a second possible bias: any one of these may hold more than one piece of land from the same or another lord. And there are indications that on one or two of the largest fiefs we may be duplicating knights and therefore under-assessing them: for example Girard, who holds half a hide, one hide, and a quarter of a hide of the count of Eu in Sussex. However, such entries usually concern only those who hold small portions of land.[53]

This tendency to underestimate size may be balanced by two features which pull the other way. One, the entries which tell us only that knights, number unspecified, hold: in these cases we have assumed there to be two knights, although there may well be more, as larger groups are quite usual (for example, the four knights on a manor of the count of Mortain).[54] The other is the number of knights whom we have had to ignore in our calculations, because they appear listed with other personnel of the manor, without a distinct holding attached to them. Such knights tend to be the less well provided. Amongst over thirty examples we find "ten villeins with one knight and four bordars" in Hertfordshire, and the "certain knight" with one

[52] E.g. "Robert de Vere holds a knight's fee and, besides this, one and a half hides for which he ought to pay rent", *Red Book of Exch.*, i, p. 212; see also B. Harvey, "Abbot Gervase de Blois and the Fee-Farms of Westminster Abbey", *Bull. Inst. Hist. Res.*, xl (1967), pp. 129-42.

[53] *Dom. Bk.*, i, fo. 18.

[54] *Dom. Bk.*, i, fo. 93. These four are given names as well: three hold 1 hide and one holds 1½ hides. I have limited these assumptions, however, to holdings under 10 hides, so that I have not counted the knights of the archbishop of York whose knights, no number given, hold 52 carucates in one entry, or the bishop of Lincoln's knights, no numbers given, who hold a total of 131¼ hides in Oxfordshire: *Dom. Bk.*, i, fos. 302b, 155. As the former was charged at 7 fees before 1166 and returned 43 fees, and the Lincoln fee was charged at 60 fees before 1166 and had in fact enfeoffed 102 knights, neither of the Domesday figures for land need imply that the norm ought to be greatly raised. See H. M. Chew, *The English Ecclesiastical Tenants in Chief and Knight Service* (Oxford, 1932), pp. 19, 32 for the figures. There are recorded instances of up to nine knights on one of the count of Eu's manors in Sussex, and ten knights on one of the archbishop of Canterbury's estates in Kent, *Dom. Bk.*, i, fos. 18, 4.

plough on the demesne of Geoffrey Alselin in Derbyshire.[55]   In addition, there are those apportioned only ploughs or values in Domesday, and for whom no hidage or carucage is given; of these there are at least thirty-four instances.   Such were two knights who held land worth three shillings in Hertfordshire from Count Eustace, and the two knights of Count Hugh in Northamptonshire, one of whom had one plough with two villeins and the other half a plough.[56]   The information given shows that their holdings cannot have been large. Omitted, too, are all the nameless Domesday "men" (*homines*), many of whom may have been their lords' men through homage and fealty for military purposes.   We know that some Domesday "men" do reappear in contemporary texts amongst the tenant-in-chief's own list of knights; we know this when they are named in both documents.[57]   But there are many "men" with sub-manorial holdings on the lands of the magnates whom we cannot trace.   Some of them are undoubtedly vassals or vavassors with military qualities; but we cannot assume them all to be, as others, equally undoubtedly, are those who serve in other ways, military and non-military: like the Peterborough sokemen who serve "with the knights" (*cum militibus*), and others who are simply huntsmen or cooks.   But the unnamed "men", who were military tenants, would again swell the numbers of the lesser knights.

For some areas, among the records of ecclesiastical tenants-in-chief, there exist independent checks, which corroborate Domesday findings. The additional knowledge these offer also reduces the number of tenants-in-chief, not very great to start with, who have sufficient numbers of knights of the same name holding in the same parts of the country to arouse the suspicion that there is more than the occasional duplicate among them.   The sixty-two Peterborough knights, who are enumerated in the feudal list, enable us to check the thirty-nine knights who appear on the Peterborough lands in Domesday Book, and the average holding of the Peterborough knights bears out our findings as to size as well as to personnel.   The sixty-two knights have between them about 120 hides and carucates.[58]   They include two

[55] *Dom. Bk.*, i, fos. 140, 276b; "Geoffrey Alselin had there 2 ploughs in demesne, and a certain knight of his, 1 plough; 32 villeins there", "20 villeins with 2 knights and 2 bordars": *Dom. Bk.*, i, f. 139.

[56] *Dom. Bk.*, i, fos. 137, 224b.

[57] E.g. above, p. 141 and note 36; below, p. 152 and note 74; *Chronicon Petroburgense*, pp. 168-75, cf. *Dom. Bk.*, i, fo. 221b.

[58] *Chronicon Petroburgense*, pp. 168-75. The identity of many of the Domesday and Peterborough knights is confirmed by the recent careful study of the Peterborough evidence by E. King, "The Peterborough 'Descriptio Militum' (Henry I)", *Eng. Hist. Rev.*, lxxxiv (1969), pp. 84-97.   Dr. King

military tenants who are responsible for as many as six knights, but the majority are responsible for two or three. Remembering some benefit is needed for the sub-tenant who takes on multiple commitments, the number of hides indicates enfeoffments which are very much in keeping with the Domesday evidence. And Peterborough's own tradition harmonizes: "Turold, in fact, gave the stipendiary knights sixty-two hides of land from the church of Peterborough's land".[59] Shaftesbury Abbey offered a similar minimum of landed support for its active knight and, much more unusually, shows it was a concept expressed in native English. A late version of an early list of knightly holdings includes, for instance, "one hide and one yard [$1\frac{1}{4}$ hides] and answers for one *knystesmetehome*".[60]

How effectively did land of 1-2 hides support a fighting knight? There is some indication that this amount would be just adequate during the eleventh century. The knight needed arms and one or two horses, and the resources to sustain them. Just what military service entailed at his period and for how many has not yet been worked out and some of the practical problems have hardly been posed. The practical implications of early fractions of fees will come up later, and it is not possible now to give the military logistics of the Anglo-Norman period the investigation they need. But we can say that there are strong indications that the first generation of knights was expected, potentially at least, to be "full-timers", that the lord often agreed to provide expenses during some or all of the service, and that in talking of service, we cannot stop at the royal service which the tenant-in-chief must supply for the king, but must take into account the aid and escort on all sorts of occasions which the tenant-in-chief might expect from his knights, service often larger in numbers than the contingent which, fiscally- and tenurially–speaking, he supplied to the king. Considering that most evidence derives from concern about relations between the tenant-in-chief and the king, the distinction between royal (*regale servitium* etc.) and other service is

concludes that "the amount of land supporting a Peterborough knight would be under 2 hides" and that complicated calculations were being made there "which revolved round the figure of two hides".

[59] There is no need to allow for the possible effects on the value of fees of the Northamptonshire reduction in hide ratings, as the hides were reduced to tally with lower land values consequent on ravaging; even if the hides of the Northamptonshire fees are more notional than usual, they still represent the same scale of income: cf. Hollister, "The Knights of Peterborough and the Anglo-Norman Fyrd", *Eng. Hist. Rev.*, lxxvii (1962), pp. 424 ff. where a different view is expressed; *Chronicon Angliae Petriburgense*, ed. J. A. Giles (London, 1845), p. 55.

[60] *Monasticon Anglicanum*, ed. W. Dugdale (London, 1819 edn.), ii, p. 477.

not infrequently observed therein. Of course, knights lodged in the household would probably be on similar terms to those at Ely; they received their food from the cellarer and also cash, and the abbot provided many of them with arms. The early and detailed charter of enfeoffment from Bury St. Edmunds seems to refer to four types and conditions of royal and abbatial service. The text is not clear, but on at least one type of occasion, when the abbot conducts the knights, he will provide their maintenance. One Peterborough knight who had been given just over half a hide in sergeanty was supposed to serve with two horses and his own arms in the army, with the abbot affording all other necessaries. Later, in 1166, the abbot of Evesham returns that his knights do the full service of a knight with horses and arms, but the abbot provides their expenses as long as they are in the king's army.[61]

In cost the equipment of the eleventh-century knight was probably comparable with that of the fully equipped Anglo-Saxon representative of five hides. For even if the latter did not fight on horseback he required a mount strong enough to carry him to battle, and the type and weight of the armour of the Norman and the Anglo-Saxon was not greatly different.[62] We know that the Anglo-Saxon was given 4s. from each of five hides, that is £1 (4d. a day), with which to support himself for customarily two months' service and maybe to provide for a replacement at home as well,[63] and the alternative for each *miles* owing from Oxford, Warwick and Malmesbury was the payment to the king of £1.[64] In the twelfth century the scutage levied was sometimes 13s. 4d. in the early years, often £1, and only once did it exceed that figure.[65] It is generally recognized that, other things being equal, a holding in Domesday Book is often worth approximately £1 per hide. The Domesday knightly holdings already analysed, where they afford separate values, have a mean value of £1 17s. 0d. per holding, or, excluding the valuable Kentish fees, of

---

[61] At Malmesbury, service due in homage, relief and aids amounted to 8¾ knights, whilst that due to the king was 3½: J. H. Round, "Knight Service of Malmesbury Abbey", *Eng. Hist. Rev.*, xxxii (1917), pp. 249-52. The surplus enfeoffments of 1166, esp. those on demesne, may often be connected with the baron's own requirements. Certainly the lay tenants-in-chief tended to retain more of them than did the ecclesiastical. J. Beeler, *Warfare in England, 1066-1189* (Ithaca, N.Y., 1966), p. 272; *Liber Eliensis*, p. 217; D. C. Douglas, "A Charter of Enfeoffment under William the Conqueror", *Eng. Hist. Rev.*, xlii (1927), p. 247; *Chronicon Petroburgense*, p. 175; *Red Book of Exch.*, i, pp. 301-2.
[62] R. Glover, "English Warfare in 1066", *Eng. Hist. Rev.*, lxvii (1952), pp. 1-18; cf. N. Denholm-Young, "Feudal Society in the Thirteenth Century: the Knights", *History*, xxix (1944), p. 108.
[63] Hollister, p. 16; *Dom. Bk.*, i, fo. 56b.
[64] *Dom. Bk.*, i, fos. 154, 238, 64b.
[65] *Red Book of Exch.*, i, p. 193; Richardson and Sayles, *op. cit.*, p. 87; Hollister, *op. cit.*, pp. 157-60, 211-13.

£1 13s. od. per holding. Hence the serving knight had an approximate yearly income of between 30s. and £2. This sort of sum, compared with the provision for the Anglo-Saxon fyrd delegate, might enable him to sustain the equipment of his profession, though it would leave no surplus for status-seeking.[66] On the other hand it makes nonsense of Boussard's assertion that "from the time of William the Conqueror a knight's fee was land with an annual revenue amounting to £20" and that "the fief charged with the service of a knight could never represent less than the grant essential in order to be able to live nobly".[67]

Besides the fact that these knights have not sufficient economic backing to pose as an élite, some distinctive and rather extraordinary characteristics emerge from an analysis of Domesday Book which may throw further light on their professional rôle and comparatively low status. One notable feature is that there is scarcely any instance of a knight holding the whole of a manor or main Domesday unit of tenure. On the one or two occasions this happens the knight ranks third rather than second in the tenurial scale. More often the knight is the holder of a small unit: a unit sometimes akin to an important manorial appurtenance — "there, four slaves, a church and three knights"; more frequently akin to berewick, that is an outlying holding within the structure of the manor but geographically distinct — "Ralf holds from William de Braose. Leofwine held it from King Edward. Then it answered for seventeen hides .... Of this land one knight holds one hide; he has in demesne one plough and two villeins, four bordars, a salt-pan bringing in 2 shillings, and two acres of meadow".[68] One of the earliest charters of enfeoffment shows the abbot of Westminster in the early 1080s giving a "berewick" of the township of Westminster to be held by the service of one knight.[69] Lanfranc himself speaks of the hamlets (*villulae*) with which he had enfeoffed some of his knights.[70] A charter of Henry I suggests a similar tenurial position: it gives to Eudo Dapifer seisin of all the appurtenances of certain manors "with the exception of those knights who serve with hauberks".[71] It is an interesting cross-reference that Stenton pointed out in another context that the

[66] The sum is not disproportionate with Henry I's contract with the count of Flanders to pay £500 as a retainer for the service of 1,000 knights when needed: *Regesta Regum Anglo-Normannorum,* ii, ed. C. Johnson and H. A. Cronne (Oxford, 1956), nos. 515, 941.

[67] Boussard, *Le Gouvernement d'Henri II Plantagenêt,* pp. 211-12.

[68] *Dom. Bk.,* i, fos. 57, 28b-29.

[69] J. Armitage Robinson, *Gilbert Crispin* (Cambridge, 1911), p. 38.

[70] *Cartulary of St. Gregory's Priory, Canterbury,* ed. A. Woodcock (Camden Soc., 3rd ser., lxxxviii, 1956), p. 2.

[71] *Colchester Cartulary,* i, ed. S. Moore (Roxburghe Club, 1897), p. 25.

"ecclesiastical dependence of nearly all the numerous [Anglo-Saxon place-names] Knighton suggests very strongly that they arose as settlements within pre-existing estates".[72]   Second, and a corollary to knights not being given whole manors, they were often given lands which were part of the demesne manors of their lords.   Professor Galbraith has discussed the possible interconnection, at first sight extraordinary, between land-grants for life, feudal grants, and demesne land *de vestitu* (for clothing) or *de victu* (for food).[73]   At Canterbury, knightly tenants of all types held lands worth £344 though the value of Canterbury lands under the specific title *Terra Militum* in Domesday was only £148, and consisted chiefly of the manors of the noble sub-tenants, the difference here being made up by the portions of demesne manors held by knights.   Following on from Stenton's point, it is also interesting that on the estates of the bishopric of Worcester, so often associated with the five-hide fee, there is a sub-holding of one hide called Knightwick which is specifically said in Domesday to be part of the monks' demesne for food (*de dominico victu monarchorum*) and in King Edward's time to have performed all the king's service for the main manor.   The Abingdon knight whose armless plight has been already mentioned was finally given land which was for the monks' sustenance (*possessionem victualia monachorum*).[74]   The very next stage from supplying the knights with food and cash within the household was to give them claims on specific pieces of demesne whose revenues anyway went to supply the conventual or other establishments.

In view of the number of Domesday knights holding portions of demesne manors, perhaps we ought to reconsider the most usual interpretation placed on two twelfth-century documents.   In 1181, the first clause of the Assize of Arms stipulates that whoever has fiefs on his demesne shall hold equipment in readiness for the fiefs' tenants.   In 1166 three main questions were put to the tenants-in-chief.   (1) What was the number of knights enfeoffed before 1135? (2) What was the number enfeoffed since that date?   (3) How many knights' fiefs are on the demesne of each?   Round admits that the obvious interpretation of (3) is that it "implied the existence of actual knights enfeoffed on the demesne"; then he dismisses it since "to those who realise the working of the system of knight service [this reading] is an absolute contradiction in terms".   So he contorts the question to

---

[72] Stenton, p. 136.
[73] Galbraith, pp. 364-8.
[74] Du Boulay, *Lordship of Canterbury*, pp. 55, 58; *Dom. Bk.*, i, fo. 173b; above p. 139.

read "how many, if any, remain to be enfeoffed to complete the service due from the fee"; and both Stenton and Galbraith follow this interpretation.[75] In both 1166 and 1181 the knights on demesne would seem better interpreted as referring to the immediate entourage of tenants-in-chief in and about the household, some of whom may have been given a small part of the land of the demesne manor. Certainly in 1166 these demesne knights were no suppositious phenomena; they appear by name in the replies of several of the barons.[76] It seems probable that the 1166 enfeoffments "on the demesne" were the remnants of the class similarly situated in the eleventh century.

Our knowledge of the knights' tenurial position is borne out and taken further by additional Domesday information that the lands many knights hold is villein land (*terra villanorum*), for example: "Of the monks' demesne, two knights hold three and a half hides of villein land". This detail is offered for one in six of the knights of Kent, Sussex, Wiltshire and Somerset, counties where the knights are most numerous and in possession of the more valuable lands. That these are not all is strongly indicated by the Abingdon cartulary. It shows that one of the wealthiest of Abingdon's knights holds five hides of villein land while Domesday is silent on this point, though the knight there appears in possession of a berewick-type five hides.[77] One of Turstin fitz Ralf's knights had "the land of four villeins" in Gloucestershire. From these and other instances of sub-holdings of villein land in Domesday Book a certain pattern emerges. Middlesex, albeit the shortest county in Domesday, contains several instructive examples. Besides knights, those who have such holdings are Rannulf Peverel (1 hide), a priest, groups of Frenchmen, and a burgess of London:[78] all people with good reason for not being personally involved in villein agriculture. A happy detail in one such entry shows we are successful in tracking the active knight: there the knights, several French and one English, are all called "proved

[75] Round, pp. 190–4; "The amount of knight-service for which the tenant-in-chief had made no provision by the creation of knights' fees", Stenton, p. 137; Galbraith, p. 370.

[76] E.g. *Red Book of Exch.*, i, pp. 192, 203, 219. Mr. T. H. Aston kindly pointed out their appearance to me.

[77] *Dom. Bk.*, i, fo. 67, 58b. Although at first sight extraordinary and meriting Round's comment on knights on demesne, there is on reflection little need to be worried about the identity of those tenures discussed here and in Galbraith's article, and normally considered to be the main contrasting types. For the identity is only temporary and only recorded to mark a recently changed situation which those concerned could not know might be permanent. But just such record is especially helpful in tracing the dynamics of change.

[78] *Dom. Bk.*, i, fos. 169b, 127–9.

knights" (*milites probati*).[79] Certain snippets of information are
peculiar to these entries: the various peasant personnel are said to be
"dwelling under them" (*manentes sub eis*) — an implied sense of
permanency in contrast to the burgess, the French and the knights
who receive their rents.

A record of an enfeoffment in the form of rents which in effect
supplied a non-resident stipend remains from the twelfth century:
a certain Robert de Turri was given, in return for service, land worth
£1 a year "on which to dwell" and four pounds of pence from rents
each year.[80] Initially, the knights had not the time, nor were they
the type, to be immersed personally in agriculture or its supervision.[81] Hence their first landed revenues were derived most
appropriately from rents, which combined the advantages of a money
fief, and a landed fief.   In fact, the *rente constituée*, a grant of assigned
rents, sometimes from land, is a well-recognized type of *fief-rente* or
money fief.[82] Professor Lyon, discussing the evolution of household
knights, supposed that they would be among the first to receive *fief-
rentes*.   Might not Domesday supply the deficiency which has caused
Lyon to lament that "not a record of this period, however, shows the
English barons granting *fief-rentes* to household knights"?[83]

For it seems that Domesday has caught the early active knight in
the first stage of becoming landed.[84] The knights allotted revenues
from villein holdings, (which may mean simply the non-home farm
sector) or in other words, rent-charges, represent a stage just a little
removed from complete dependence.   They needed to be ready, as
the Bury charter of enfeoffment has it, "beyond or within the
kingdom, wherever and whenever the abbot wants to have his own
knight".[85] Lyon has noted that everywhere, except England, the
fief-rente is especially important in supplying castle-guard.[86] Now

---

[79] *Dom. Bk.*, i, fo. 130.

[80] Stenton, p. 108; also "the aforesaid knights should have 15 shillings from
the villeins, cultivators and inhabitants of the land", *Recueil des actes du Prieuré
de Saint-Symphorien d'Autun*, ed. A. Déléage (Autun, 1936), p. 57.

[81] The effect of the presence or absence of the knight, though there is no clue
as to how this operated, may be the explanation of a curious Kentish entry
where the "villein land" of some knights is worth £9 "when there is peace in
the land": *Dom. Bk.*, i, fo. 12.

[82] B. Lyon, *From Fief to Indenture* (Cambridge, Mass., 1957), pp. 99-100.

[83] *Ibid.*, pp. 183, 187.

[84] Due to the structure of Domesday Book, household knights themselves
could only be enumerated by inclusion among demesne personnel.   This may
be the reason for the occasional instance of knights on the demesne portion
of demesne manors, e.g. *Dom. Bk.*, i, fos. 128, 276b.

[85] "A Charter of Enfeoffment", *Eng. Hist. Rev.*, xlii, pp. 245-7.

[86] *Op. cit.*, pp. 96, 189.

castle-guard was particularly suited to the lesser knight (as we will see below) and the distribution of Domesday knights may be indicative here. The largest numbers appear in the counties of Sussex (47), Kent (34) and Herefordshire (43). All are districts of great strategic importance, the first two of easy access to the continent also, and all have numerous early castles; tenants-in-chief who held land in several counties would find it useful to have their knights ready planted in these districts.

It is possible that the tenure of villein land may also have implied an original intention on behalf of the lord that his knights should hold their grants attached to service, as villeins held. That grants of land were initially dependent on active service we learnt from the near-disastrous position of the armless Abingdon knight. Certain phrases which occur in proximity on the lands of the knights of the bishop of Wells may be relevant here. On one manor three knights are said not to be able to take their lands from the church. The next entry says that the two knights there hold villein land.[87] Perhaps both details are statements of inalienability.[88] Certainly the original grants were not supposed to be hereditary. The early extant charters of enfeoffment of the bishop of Hereford and the abbots of Ramsey and Westminster stipulate that the lands they endow are to be held for life only.[89]

There is another aspect of the knights' tenure of villein land, that is the fiscal. For villein lands paid geld while the demesne portion of a manor often had a low or non-existent geld responsibility.[90] This could be because of royal concession, as was reported obtained during the reign of William I for the demesne lands of ecclesiastical tenants in-chief;[91] or it might simply be the result of the lord's apportioning out much of the geld due from the manor among the villein holdings.[92] Knightly lands received similar treatment, at least at

---

[87] *Dom. Bk.*, i, fo. 89.

[88] Galbraith discusses other phrases in *Dom. Bk.*, but not this, which may be due to the tenant-in-chief insisting on the "for life only" aspect of the grant: Galbraith, pp. 363-8.

[89] Galbraith, p. 363; Hollister, pp. 51-3. It is interesting to see that perpetual rent-charges were associated with tenure in fee simple in their prohibition to Jews in the thirteenth century: Richardson, *English Jewry*, pp. 104, 106.

[90] E.g. *Dom. Bk.*, i, fo. 203; R. S. Hoyt, *The Royal Demesne in English Constitutional History* (Ithaca, N.Y., 1950), pp. 28 *et seq.*, 52.

[91] *Die Gesetze der Angelsachsen*, ed. F. Liebermann, i (Halle, A.S., 1903), pp. 634-7. The author of the *Dialogus de Scaccario* says that barons of the Exchequer had their demesnes exempt from geld: ed. and trans. C. Johnson (London, 1950), p. 56.

[92] Round, "Danegeld and the Finance of Domesday", *Domesday Studies*, i, pp. 96, 126; for the mechanism of this process see E. Searle, "Hides and Virgates at Battle Abbey", *Econ. Hist. Rev.* 2nd ser., xvi (1963-4), pp. 290-300.

HPK

first.   In its *Notitia Terrarum*, St. Augustine declares "of those lands which shall be subject to the lord abbot, the monks' part never paid tax or cutomary dues, but the knights and other men of the honour answered for everything",[93] and this arrangement has echoes elsewhere.[94]   Whether the knights themselves paid geld or whether it was paid by the villeins whose rents were allotted to the knights, the ultimate effect was the same.   Such tax constituted a transfer of surplus from the villeins and prevented their being so profitable to their immediate tenurial overlord.   That contemporaries realized this is evident from the beneficial rating of demesne lands of favoured tenants-in-chief, and from the almost reverse mechanism of ancient demesne.   This last involved the king's right to tallage villeins on land once royal demesne and now alienated; to do this effectively, the king therefore defended the villeins from both seigneurial tallage and increased services.   Both institutions recognized that the less tenants are tallaged the more they represent a potential source of income.

This fiscal aspect harmonizes with the more familiar evidence of Henry I's Charter of Liberties, where the king's feudal concessions to the magnates are explicitly to be passed on to the under-tenants.[95] Interest in the position of under-tenants is patent in another clause concerning the professional knights:

> To the knights who do service with hauberks for their lands, I concede their demesne ploughs exempt of all taxes and all works by my grant, so that, being relieved of a great burden, they may furnish themselves so well with horses and arms that they may be properly equipped and prepared for my service and for the defence of the kingdom.[96]

This clause, explicitly confined to the serving knights, is wholly comprehensible in the light of our findings that many knights were granted small amounts of geldable land only.

Blatant here is Henry's oft-rehearsed interest, so annoying to the magnates, in supporting professional classes of low birth who could be of direct use to him.[97]   Events quickly justified his forethought and protection.   Florence of Worcester tells how, in 1101, bishops, Englishmen and *milites gregarii*, all remained loyal to Henry against the rebellious magnates.[98]   In a debate after the revolt of Robert of Bellême in 1102, the magnates put forward the view that it would be dangerous to draw up a peace which would give Henry an over-strong

[93] Pub. Rec. Off., MS. Exchequer (K.R.) Miscellaneous Books (E.164), vol. 27, fo. 16.
[94] *Chron. Mon. de Abingdon*, ii, p. 136; see note 92.
[95] W. Stubbs, *Select Charters*, 9th edn. (Oxford, 1921), p. 118, *caps.* 2, 4.
[96] *Ibid.*, p. 119, *cap.* 11; Hoyt, *op. cit.*, p. 53.
[97] Ordericus Vitalis, *Hist. Eccles.*, iv, p. 164.
[98] *Chronicon Florentii Wigorniensis*, ed. B. Thorpe, ii (London, 1849), p. 49.

position. On hearing this the "three thousand rustic knights" (*pagensium milites*) protested, and warned Henry against the lords' soft measures.[99] The adjectives indicate the knights' low status as the incidents do their active part in events.

The low social status of the knights themselves is another reason why there should be no surprise at their tenurial position in the eleventh century.[100] A recent study has complained of the English historical tradition which regards feudal society as aristocratic, remaining remote from landed practicalities.[101] Now it seems that the professional knight in England in the century following the Conquest is of a type similar to the knights of north-east France and counties bordering on the North Sea and the Channel.[102] Studies of the noble and military classes in these areas have found that knights of the eleventh and first half of the twelfth century are often of lowly or even unfree origin and in possession of minuscule fiefs and rents, until about 1150 when knighthood increases in grandeur.[103] Since the ruling military class in Norman England came from these parts, the only surprising aspect of our conclusion is that it has not been obvious from the first. A decade or so before the Conquest there were in Normandy types similar to the Domesday knights in a similar tenurial position. One charter concerns an estate with its appurtenances, that is, "a church, land for three plough-teams, twelve peasants, five free knights and a mill". Moreover, among the charter witnesses are several knights of the other sort, the great men.[104] Bloch's words on the Norman vavassors spring to mind here. The vavassors "were the lowest grade amongst the holders of military fiefs" and the type of grant they were given "was, in fact, half fief, half villein tenement". One knight, Ralf, in the decade after the

---

[99] Ordericus Vitalis, *op. cit.*, iv, pp. 173-4.

[100] E.g. Stenton, pp. 21-2.

[101] Du Boulay, *op. cit.*, p. 75; but the study itself did not change our point of view, see the review in *Econ. Hist. Rev.*, 2nd ser., xx (1967), pp. 161-3.

[102] G. Duby, "La noblesse dans la France médiévale", *Rev. Hist.*, ccxxvi (1961), p. 13; cf. the position in the Macon, and other more southerly areas of France, where the knights were drawn from noble families much earlier, *ibid.*, p. 16.

[103] Duby, *loc. cit.*; L. Genicot, "La noblesse au Moyen Age dans l'ancienne 'Francie' ", *Annales Écon, Soc., Civil.*, xvii (1962), p. 16; J. M. van Winter "The Ministerial and Knightly Classes in Guelders and Zutphen", *Acta Neerlandica*, i (1966), esp. p. 174; G. T. Beech, *A Rural Society in Medieval France* (Baltimore, 1964), p. 94; J. Dhont, "Les 'Solidarités' médiévales", *Annales. Écon., Soc., Civil.*, xii (1957), esp. p. 545.

[104] *Recueil des actes des ducs de Normandie*, ed. M. Faroux (Caen, 1961), no. 199; e.g. "in the same township are dwelling (*manentes*) three knights with their benefices", *Cart. de l'abbaye de Saint-Père de Chartres*, i, ed. B. Guérard (Paris, 1840), p. 108.

Conquest, gave the abbey of Préaux his land, "namely that of a vavassor"; this he did with the consent of both William I, and of his own lord in whose demesne the land lay.[105] It is also interesting that the early knight's situation has many features in common with that of the dreng in northern England. Professor Barrow recently summarized earlier work on the dreng, "who must be considered as part of the noble order yet clearly on its borderline", strongly "ministerial" in character; "his holding would be typically a single ploughgate, a small township, or an outlying dependency of a village", and he also often had lordship over villeins and bordars. Moreover in the twelfth century mercenary knights were granted, in knight's fee, land which had previously been held in thegnage or drengage. Finally, from 1179 onwards, thegns and drengs became subject to incidents of "feudal type" and the tendency to commutuation.[106]

We may remember the initial difficulty of sorting out the basic serving knight from the "middling" well-connected knight. Contemporaries as well as historians ran into likely misinterpretations by the use of the single word for all military men from the magnate who went on campaigns downwards, and so in prose they often use distinguishing adjectives to make themselves plain. William of Poitiers's account of the preparations for the Norman Conquest depicts Duke William giving instructions first to his compeers, then to "middling noble knights" (*milites mediae nobilitatis*), then to the "common knights" (*milites gregarios*), a classification which corresponds very happily with the categories we delineated earlier.[107] At least two writs of Henry I which concern military services and castle-guard, talk of the "barons" and "vavassors" of a tenant-in-chief.[108] The author of the *Gesta Stephani* usually manages to make himself clear. Many of the forces he describes consist of knights and archers, or knights and infantry. The close association of knights and crossbowmen is interesting in view of the appearance of archers amongst the archbishop of Canterbury's list of knights, and

---

[105] M. Bloch, *Feudal Society*, trans. L. Manyon (London, 1961), pp. 177, 332; *Calendar of Documents preserved in France*, ed. J. H. Round (London, 1899), i, pp. 108-9; also Guilhiermoz, *op. cit.*, pp. 184-6, where vavassors are equated with lesser knights; also, "L'Enquête de 1133 sur les Fiefs de l'Évêché de Bayeux", *Bull. Soc. Antiquaires Normandie*, xlii (1934), pp. 13-23.

[106] "Northern English Society", *Northern History*, iv (1969), pp. 10-11; Vinogradoff found that drengs usually had holdings of about 1 hide, p. 66.

[107] Guillaume de Poitiers, *Hist. de Guillaume le Conquérant*, ed. and trans. R. Foreville (Paris, 1952), p. 232. On the continent, the adjective *gregarii* was much used, in contrast to *nobilissimi* etc., to distinguish the ordinary knight from the influential: Guilhiermoz, *op. cit.*, pp. 145-7, 336-41.

[108] *Eng. Hist. Doc.*, ii, ed. D. C. Douglas (London, 1953), p. 923; *Regesta Regum Anglo-Normannorum*, ii, no. 33.

their appearance elsewhere in Domesday Book. (A crossbowman, however, was no casual performer. In Henry II's reign he cost 4d. a day to hire, whereas a knight then commanded 8d. a day, a sergeant at the same period being paid only 1d. a day).[109] Three times the author of the *Gesta Stephani* distinguishes the "common" or "rustic" knights (*gregarii* or *rustici*); sometimes they go into action alongside mercenaries or hired knights (*milites stipendarii*).[110] On the other hand, he feels the need when introducing a knight, Robert of Bampton, who had a castle and several manors in Devon, to add that he was a knight "not indeed of the lowest birth, nor of small landed estate". The chronicler describes the king giving his son, Eustace, the belt of knighthood, and elsewhere makes use of this honorific mark to distinguish the knights of importance, speaking of a group of "bishops and belted military men"; at other times he implies the distinction with the adjectives "finely-equipped" and "highly-equipped" and such knights are never coupled with archers or foot-soldiers.[111] It might make discussion of feudal England much easier for historians to borrow the distinction made by contemporaries between the two major types of knights, the "belted knight", and the "common or garden" or, more officially, the "vavassor knight".

In all, there seems little justification for distinguishing as sharply as is often the case between the early vavassor knights and mercenaries. There was a large identity of rôle and often of person between the so-called mercenaries and the so-called knights in the early period. The mercenaries were not so low nor the knights so high as is usually implied. We remember that those enfeoffed at Abingdon and Peterborough were in fact mercenaries, and it is only to be expected that when they or their descendants became associated with land or unsuitable for service others of a similar type were employed. Mercenaries too had links with their lord other than purely material gain. At the siege of Bridgenorth, the stipendiaries were anxious to remain loyal to their rebel lord; they were appalled when their co-besieged submitted and they retired with their horses muttering that the event had cast a slur on their character.[112] Mercenary troops had played a large part in the battle of Hastings. When outside London, William the Conqueror asked all his followers

[109] Richardson and Sayles, *op. cit.*, p. 74.
[110] Ed. and trans. K. R. Potter (London, 1955), pp. 4, 10, 85, 86, 108, 113, 135-6; cf. *milites gregarii* and *plebei* distinguished by the chroniclers of the Second Crusade: R. C. Smail, *Crusading Warfare 1097-1193* (Cambridge, 1956), pp. 110, also 130-1; also Ordericus Vitalis, *Hist. Eccles.*, ii, p. 181.
[111] *Gesta Stephani*, pp. 18, 83, 137, 143, 145.
[112] Ordericus Vitalis, *op. cit.*, iv, p. 175.

whether he should be crowned at once or wait until his wife could be crowned with him. Haimo of Thouars, the spokesman of the army, was obviously shocked; probably thinking of the "common" as well as the stipendiary, he said that knights were rarely or never asked an opinion on that sort of thing.[113]   In fact all William's most important campaigns needed mercenaries.[114]   And his anticipation of what was potentially the biggest test, that of Cnut's invasion, brought to England in 1085 "a larger force of mounted men and infantry than had ever come to this country". Though, when the threat subsided, the king "let some of the army go to their own country", yet "some he kept in this country". Perhaps one of the few under-developed pieces of central evidence in a much-discussed subject is the Anglo-Saxon Chronicler's information that "the king had all the army dispersed all over the country among his vassals, and they provisioned the army each in proportion to his land".[115] This major threat may have promoted a more complete merging of the two traditions than had hitherto been possible or necessary in the post-Conquest years: the allocation has hints of personalized vassal responsibility on the one hand and English local responsibility based on the number of hides of land on the other.   Mercenaries were also used, as were lesser knights and sergeants, for defending marcher and coastal counties and for garrisoning castles.[116]   In fact the gradations of difference between mercenaries, stipendiaries, household knights, professional knights given rents-charges, and professional knights given incipient fiefs were initially very small.[117]

II

The late twelfth-century feodaries that declare "five hides make a knight's fee" and the fashionable status and developed ethos of knighthood are all incompatible with the early evidence.   The next

[113] Guillaume de Poitiers, *op. cit.*, pp. 216 ff.
[114] Ordericus Vitalis, *op. cit.*, ii, p. 187; J. O. Prestwich, "War and Finance in the Anglo-Norman State", *Trans. Roy. Hist. Soc.*, 5th ser., iv (1954), esp. pp. 24-5.   [115] *Anglo-Saxon Chronicle*, p. 161.
[116] The Abingdon knights were associated with the garrisoning of Windsor castle and with the threatened invasion by the Danes: *Chron. Mon. de Abingdon*, pp. 3-4; *Pipe Roll 14 Henry II* (Pipe Roll Soc., xii, 1890), pp. 198-9.
[117] Cf. Roger Foliot, a twelfth-century knight, whose "father never had more than half a hide of land; he himself had only what he acquired by his service as a knight.   Till the present time he has served the lord Brian as a stipendiary (*ad donativum*) and now, despoiled of his horses and arms, he has lost everything he had all at once": quoted in H. A. Cronne, *The Reign of Stephen* (London, 1970), p. 151, from *Patrologia Latina*, ed. J. P. Migne, cxc, ed. J. A. Giles, no. lviii.

crucial question is therefore: how and when does this transformation come about?

It seems that a first watershed is reached by the early years of the reign of Henry II.[118] But evidence between the Domesday period and the detailed documentation of the last two decades of the twelfth century is by comparison fragmentary. Both the berewicks and villein land of Domesday often became manors in their own right. We may already be witnesses of this process in Domesday Surrey where on one manor there is a sub-holding of "villein land" which has a demesne of its own.[119] This development was aided, no doubt, by the twelfth-century extension of cultivation, as well as by the tendency towards hereditary tenure of land, which lessened the lord's jurisdictional hold.[120] Land developed in this way offered the opportunity of a profitable and independent base for the descendants of many eleventh-century professional knights. But shortage of officials meant that only magnates could hope to attract their services, and knights could not effectively supervise their small estates themselves and still remain professionals. On the other hand those knights who were still living solely off rents from a small amount of land would also suffer. Hence military commitment tended to assume the proportion of an alien burden, rather than a prime function.

Yet, on the other hand, the demands of service had to some extent grown by the mid-twelfth century. No longer were the problems of conquest pre-eminent, with their attendant revolts, Viking attacks, and Welsh and Scottish campaigns. Civil revolt and border campaigns were endemic throughout the medieval period, but now the main emphasis was on continental interests, associated with the Angevin and Aquitaine inheritance, and on Irish campaigns. These expeditions, being further afield, involved high transport costs, the possibility of long terms of absence, and the desirability of well-equipped, highly professional forces.[121]

---

[118] See also Génicot, *La Noblesse*, p. 16: "by 1100 or 1150 *milites* detach themselves from the rest of the *familia* to form an especially honourable group": Boussard suggests that progress in effectiveness of manpower and tactics is ascribable to the period 1156-8: "Les Mercenaires au xiie siècle: Henri II Plantagenêt et les origines de l'armée de métier", *Bibliothèque de l'école de chartes*, cvi (1946), pp. 189-224.

[119] *Dom. Bk.*, i, fo. 36b.

[120] E.g. Hoyt, *The Royal Demesne*, pp. 34, 53; S. E. Thorne, "English Feudalism and Estates in Land", *Cambridge Law Jl.*, 1959, pp. 193-209; compare above p. 25; Galbraith; and H. M. Colvin, "Holme Lacy: An Episcopal Manor and its tenants in the twelfth and thirteenth centuries", *Studies presented to Rose Graham*, ed. V. Ruffer and A. Taylor (London, 1950), pp. 15-38.

[121] Prestwich, *loc. cit.*, p. 21.

Faced with an increased range of activities, sooner or later the result of the knight's small economic basis was his acknowledgement of only a fraction of his former responsibility. The prevalence of fractions of fees has long been a disturbing feature of twelfth-century tenure. To Vinogradoff as to others "the parcelling of fees [into fractions] was the complicated result of divers causes": the division of land by lack of male heirs, and so its devolution to co-heiresses, and the effects of "sales", farming out, and family commitments.[122] However, two other origins of fractional fees deserve consideration. One possibility stems from the fact that some fractions were evident early, so early as to look deliberate: the Canterbury knights of the 1090s include thirty-three whose commitment is computed in amounts of halves and quarters. At Rochester at the same period twenty-eight persons hold part-responsibility for Rochester's knight-service, twenty-four of whom are responsible for only some fraction of a knight.[123] This may suggest the early practice of several knights contributing to provide one who is ready to serve. It seems that this arrangement, familiar to us from the royal records of the twelfth and thirteenth centuries, was already in use by tenants-in-chief and under-tenants as a practical answer to problems stemming from the divergent pulls of land and military service: so it may have been more or less forced on the crown from below. It may be here too, at the lowest levels of organization, that practical elements have evolved from Anglo-Saxon practices. The apparently aberrant evidence from Ramsey Abbey on military service and perhaps from Malmesbury Abbey, may simply be due to a greater preponderance of direct, one-stage arrangements resulting in vavassor knights, supported by freeholders who at Ramsey paid contributions according to the hides they held, as also at Chichester;[124] perhaps on these ecclesiastical estates responsibility for military service was not distorted through so many stages of personal and tenurial ties usually consequent on the Conquest and redistribution from above.

Certainly, a second factor, the vavassor knight's own insistence that his land, even if it stayed undivided, was too small to provide a

[122] Vinogradoff, p. 45.
[123] *Domesday Monachorum*, fo. 7r; *Textus Roffensis*, ed. P. Sawyer (Early English MSS. in Facsimile, xi, Copenhagen, 1962), fo. 217v; Vinogradoff, also, saw the possible importance of this aspect, pp. 45-6.
[124] Round, "Knight-Service of Malmesbury Abbey", pp. 250-1; *Cartularium Monasterii de Rameseia*, ed. W. Hart and P. Lyons, iii (Rolls Series, 1893), pp. 48-9, 210, 219-20; just as different numbers of virgates are said at Ramsey to make up a free hide and a hide of villeinage, so different units can be drawn together to provide a knight as at Worcester (above n. 37); at Ramsey too, the one- or two-hide unit for a knight's holding is usual, e.g. p. 210.

full knight, needs recognition as one cause of fractional fees. We can only guess at the long battles between tenant-in-chief and enfeoffed tenant which lie behind the 1171 list of knight-service at Canterbury. Most of those mentioned were descendants of those in the 1090s list. Many were holding, as the typical eleventh-century knight did, part of a manor: for instance, Barham was an outlying part of the Canterbury manor of Adisham, and holding there was "Lambert of Barham who owes one knight but acknowledges only a half". The reduction was eventually acknowledged by his lord in the thirteenth century. A smaller fraction is involved at Deane in Wingham. There by 1171, "the sons of William of Deane owe $\frac{1}{2}$ knight but they acknowledge only $\frac{1}{8}$".[125] In the eleventh century the Kentish fiefs had an average value a third higher than those of the rest of the country and were larger in size also. It may be deduced that the twelfth-century holders of knight's fees elsewhere were in a worse position. Even the tenants-in-chief themselves acknowledged that a bare minimum of land was necessary for service and that the size affected what demands were possible. The Bayeux Inquest of 1133 in Normandy expects service only from those vavassors who hold freely fifty to sixty acres or more. Some vavassors are expected to provide one knight's service; others a quarter or half a knight. The Inquest affords a parallel for the evolution suggested here during the partial documentary gap in England. Soon after the Inquest the less important vavassors disappear altogether and even the more important only survive by becoming quarters, halves or thirds of a knight.[126]

A fading class is more difficult to document than a rising one. But discernible is a marked attempt, for fiscal and economic reasons, by the once military to try to lose their tenurial distinction, and to become merged with the prevalent local tenure, for better or worse. The descendants of the eleventh-century Canterbury knight, Heringod, appear with very little land under the same name on the same manor in 1285 among the gavelkinders. And at Wrotham, the descendants of Fareman, probably a Domesday knight of substance, were holding by gavelkind. Hence the archbishop's request of King John in 1201 to convert into knight's fee the lands held of his bishopric in gavelkind, for the reverse process had lost the barony feudal incidents.[127] A

---

[125] H. M. Colvin, "A List of the Archbishop of Canterbury's Tenants by Knight-Service in the Reign of Henry II", *Medieval Kentish Society* (Kent Records, xviii, 1964), pp. 11, 15, 16, 27-8, 33.

[126] Navel, "L'Enquête de Bayeux", pp. 13-23, 51.

[127] F. R. H. Du Boulay, "Gavelkind and Knight's Fee in Medieval Kent", *Eng. Hist. Rev.*, lxxvii (1962), pp. 504-11.

similar development elsewhere is depicted in the 1166 returns: "those knights the bishop established were made into rent payers and they held thus in the time of my predecessor and their heirs still hold thus".[128]   Anyway, once military responsibility became either representational or commuted, it did not matter nearly so much that the land market or hereditary tenure began to operate and to sub-divide holdings into further fractions which could be held alongside other free tenures.   So by the late twelfth century it was quite usual to find grants like that of William de Turville who gave to William the fisherman "for a third of a fief of a hauberk", three yardlands, two acres, some assarts, and some fishing,[129] and instances of holders of small amounts of land paying both rent and scutage, as well as occasional cases in the 1279 Hundred Rolls of tenants in villeinage who pay scutage.[130]

It was the use of scutage and the employment of mercenaries which enabled the vavassor knights to drop out; this has long been recognized.   The crown's preference for the mobility and reliability of the paid professionals has been clearly demonstrated by Mr. Prestwich.[131]   This, plus the realization of the position of the small knight, may account for the crown's championship of his cause and its permission for him to fade from the scene.   By 1100, the economic position of the serving knight was such that Henry I felt compelled (for political or other reasons) to help his finances, as we have already noted.   In the late 1170s the attention that *The Dialogue of the Exchequer* gives to contingencies concerning knights in debt is worth quoting fully as significant in itself and for its echo of Henry I.   Its author, Richard fitz Nigel, tells of the distinction in cases of debt made between the belted knight (*cingulum*) and the active knight (*strenuus*) and the reasons for it.   For the belted knight,

> when the other chattels are sold, a horse will be left to him and it must be a trained horse, lest he who is entitled by his rank to ride, should be compelled to go on foot.

For the active knight,

> the whole of his personal armour, along with the horses necessary shall be exempt from distraint so that when need arises he can be employed on business for the king and realm, fully equipped with arms and horses . . . always supposing he is to serve not at his own cost but the crown's.

---

[128] *Red Book of Exch.*, i, p. 210.

[129] Stenton, p. 16.

[130] F. Pollock and F. W. Maitland, *The History of English Law* (Cambridge, 1895), i, pp. 256-7; N. Neilson, *Customary Rents and Services* (Oxford Studies in Social and Legal Hist., ii, 1910), p. 87, both of whom are concerned about the evolution of this situation.

[131] *Loc. cit.*

As well as Henry II's interest in scutage, the *Dialogue* tells us too of his intervention in the difficulties which faced knights economically and as a result of their tenurial association with villein land.

> If the tenant-in-chief who is responsible to the king, fails to pay scutage, not only his chattels but those of his knights and villeins are sold indiscriminately. For the principle on which scutage is raised mainly affects the knights, since it is only due to the king from knights and by reason of their service. Yet I myself, though not yet hoary-headed, have seen not only the lord's chattels lawfully sold for his personal debts, but also those of his knights and villeins. But the king's ordinance has restricted this practice to scutage alone . . . that if the knights have paid to their lord the scutage due from their fees, and can produce pledges to prove it, the law forbids the sale of their chattels for the lord's debts.

In 1159 Henry II had realized that knight service in Toulouse was not a burden he could impose on the vavassor knights with their small lands. "King Henry therefore, setting out on the aforesaid expedition and considering the length and difficulty of the journey, not wishing to distress the country knights (*agrarios milites*)", instead levied a sum on the knight's fee and "took with him his chief barons and a few others and countless paid knights (*solidarios milites*)".[132] The practice of asking several knights to group together to provide and finance one was, in fact, a measure part-way between scutage and personal service; it was certainly in frequent use by the crown by the second half of the twelfth century. For the 1157 campaign against the Welsh Henry II levied a force by providing that every two knights should furnish a third.[133] The Malmesbury evidence of the 1170s shows both a reduction in service secured, and grouping of the knights and also freeholders (*liberi tenentes*) to perform or contribute to it.[134] Only dying desperation, in the face of rebellion from the combined forces of sons and wife, made Henry appeal for the help of the erstwhile knights. From the continent he sent Rannulf Glanville, "so that he should assemble and convey over all the knights of England, even the poor and diminished".[135]

Though the institution of scutage and the crown's acceptance of the knights' economic position solved some practical problems, it disturbed further the nice balance between lord's support and vassal's service on which the successful operation of feudal relations depended

[132] *Dialogus de Scaccario*, pp. 112, 111; *The Chronicle of Robert of Torigni*, in *Chronicles of the Reigns of Stephen, Henry II and Richard I*, iv, ed. R. Howlett (Rolls Series, 1889), p. 202; Stubbs, *Charters*, p. 152.

[133] Also earlier, see "L'Enquête de Bayeux" where one knight in ten is due to serve the French king; in 1157, two out of three, *Robert de Torigni, loc. cit.*, p. 193; also in 1191, 1197, 1205, one knight in every ten was required: Chew, *op. cit.*, pp. 30-1.

[134] Round, "Malmesbury Abbey", pp. 250-1.

[135] *Gervase of Canterbury*, i, ed. W. Stubbs (Rolls Series, 1879), p. 447.

(disturbed anyway from inception by the tendency of lands to become hereditary). For, when scutage was taken, all three tenurial levels laid claim to the fiscal advantage to be derived from surplus enfeoffments and supernumerary knights.[136] The knights claimed that altogether they should contribute only the scutage due to the crown, thus lessening the burden on each of them.[137] The tenant-in-chief, who had presented the income to the supernumerary knights, and who was still committed to accompany his king on feudal service abroad, felt entitled to the surplus scutage as compensation. And both Henry I and Henry II inquired about, and levied impositions on, over-enfeoffment.[138]

Many are the traces of the evolving situation. Some knights received official recognition that the older type fiefs of 1-2 hides were much smaller than the newly accepted standard. The central government distinguished them by special terms, "petty fiefs" (*parva feoda*), "little fiefs" (*minuta feoda*), or Mortain fiefs, for instance: "these are of the type of the count of Mortain's fief, which are only two thirds of a knight because they are small".[139] It is not without significance that two vavassors and at least nine knights appear in Domesday Book on the Mortain honour.[140] Other vavassor knights still fulfilled a rôle similar indeed to the original intention, in local castle-guard or in service as sergeants.[141] In the mid-twelfth century, John of Lee was given one hide, its appurtenances, and a mill in Weston by Geoffrey de Turville, in return for keeping post in "the castle of Weston for forty days in time of war with a destrier and a rouncey and for three weeks in time of peace".[142] Some of the services were no longer even military in character. An instance from the 1166 returns shows the evolution from fractional

---

[136] For instance, at Canterbury in the closing decades of the eleventh century, the archbishop's military tenants were in theory responsible for 98¼ knights. In 1165 and 1168 the number is 84¾, while what we know of Canterbury's later commitment suggests that the service required from Canterbury was 60: *Domesday Monachorum*, fo. 7r; Round, pp. 224-5; Chew, *op. cit.*, p. 19.

[137] A claim made successfully by the knights of Malmesbury — though at Bury St. Edmunds, faced with their litigious abbot, the knights' claim was defeated: *Jocelin of Brakelond*, pp. 65-7.

[138] By the thirteenth century the writ *de scutagio habendo* was necessary before the tenant-in-chief was allowed to recoup himself; see also Hollister, p. 203.

[139] E.g. also "the small knights of the count of Mortain, three of whom only do the service of two knights to the king"; "my predecessors enfeoffed a certain knight, called Golonis, of the the old enfeoffment of a third of a knight": *Red Book of Exch.*, i, pp. 232, 443, also pp. 43, 64, 71, 82, 101, 125, 167, 169, 233.

[140] *Dom. Bk.*, i, fo. 93, 146b.

[141] *Regesta*, ii, no. 33; Navel, *op. cit.*, p. 54 for vavassors particularly associated with castle-guard.

[142] Stenton, p. 208.

fiefs to fiscal "aids" to sheer administration: "the bishop's sergeants held, as serving officials, fractions of fiefs from which the bishop once took money for the king's aid".[143]   Moreover, the equipment of the military sergeants of the thirteenth century seems not dissimilar from that of the eleventh-century knights: the essentials were hauberk, and horse.   Often in fact the same type was both still in demand and still the most easily available.   Hence the seeming paradox of the tenant-in-chief who, having by the thirteenth century obtained a reduced responsibility, then not infrequently sent two sergeants to replace one knight.[144]   Though no longer accorded the title "knight" (*miles*), these men were often known as "vavassors" (*vavassores*),[145] and vavassors were by that time looked down on by the chivalric classes proper, as those who took no part in tournaments and who did not fight abroad.[146]

On the obverse side, those who were accorded the title "knight" in the later twelfth century needed a larger revenue.   The important sub-tenants had originally been granted land on the basis of perhaps 5 to 7 hides in return for a fighting knight; they, in turn, had farmed out the service to lesser men granting them 1-2 hides.   When the vavassor knight was unable to take on an increased rôle and faded out, much of the responsibility devolved on to the important sub-tenants and their associates.   And as costs rose, it was no longer so very profitable to be a feudal "middleman".   The difficulty was most telling for the smallest men of these "middling" knights, those of merely local importance and very moderate estate.   William fitz

---

[143] *Red Book of Exch.*, i, p. 222.

[144] See below p. 172; also Vinogradoff, "it seems that in some counties the service of a knight in light armour was regarded as sergeanty and properly appreciated at half the service of an ordinary knight", p. 62; Chew, *op. cit.*, p. 91; J. E. Morris, *The Welsh Wars of Edward I* (Oxford, 1901), pp. 44-5; Richardson and Sayles, *op. cit.*, p. 127. See esp. G. Barrow, "The Beginnings of Feudalism in Scotland", *Bull. Inst. Hist. Res.*, xxix (1956), pp. 19-20 who quotes a grant of land by William I of Scotland to a clerk by the service of one mounted sergeant with hauberk; when this grant was confirmed by Alexander II or III, it was for ¼ knight's fee.   Smail, *op. cit.*, p. 107.

[145] "Vavassors with shield and lance", Robert de Torigni, *op. cit.*, p. 349; Stenton, pp. 17-19; above pp. 157-8 and 162.

[146] *L'histoire de Guillaume le Maréchal*, ed. and trans. into modern French by P. Meyer (Paris, 1901), iii, pp. 23-4.   I am indebted to Professor F. Barlow for this reference.   Professor Strayer has observed a similar evolution for Normandy, though he says that in England "the reasons for the change are obscure".   From the bishop of Bayeux's 100 knights' fees were raised 10 "best knights" (*optimos milites*).   And later Norman law distinguished between those vassals who actually did service and those who simply owed payment.   Eventually the net result there, as in England, was a return to the use of those they called "sergeants".   J. Strayer, *The Administration of Normandy under St. Louis* (Cambridge, Mass., 1932), pp. 60-7.

Robert was, in fact, a tenant-in-chief, but with just a single knight's fee his economic position was similar to that of the smaller of the "gentry" knights.   Rather pathetically, he wrote to his king in 1166: "know that I hold from you one very poor knight's fee; nor have I enfeoffed anyone else in it because it scarcely supports me; and thus held my father.   Farewell".[147]   Many influential sub-tenants with greater powers of resistence were now refusing to provide their agreed commitment.   One of the two knights' service that the Lacys owed to the bishop of Hereford, and quoted earlier, was refused by Hugh de Lacy in 1167-8.[148]   The 1171 list from Canterbury tells us "the earl of Clare owes 4 knights and acknowledges only 2" and "William of Eynsford owes $7\frac{1}{2}$ knights and he recognizes only $4\frac{3}{4}$ knights".   The most outstanding example of this refusal to fulfil service comes from the archbishop's largest tenant by knight-service, the bishop of Rochester.[149]   In the 1090s the bishop owed 10 knights.   To meet this commitment he had enfeoffed 28, mostly local men with a number of small fees totalling $12\frac{7}{8}$ out of his 66 sulungs, giving himself a profitable margin (and his brother a quite aberrant £10 fee for $\frac{1}{2}$ knight).   Already early in the twelfth century the bishop only accepted responsibility for $6\frac{1}{10}$ fees, and by 1171 we are told "he owes 10 knights and acknowledges only one".[150]   The service stayed disputed until a nominal commutation was settled in the thirteenth century.[151]

So, for a time in the later twelfth century, tenants-in-chief were trying to emphasize that 5 or 7 hides or whatever still made their influential tenants responsible for a knight as reckoned in the first place.[152]   And many of these assertions survive.   The now-familiar responsibility computed at Worcester "four virgates of land make one hide and five hides make a knight" is not a platitude; it is the bishop's contention in a dispute with the bishopric's greatest sub-tenant, William de Beauchamp, who is refusing to produce his commitment.[153]

[147] *Red Book of Exch.*, i, p. 363.
[148] Colvin, "Holme Lacy . . .", p. 21.
[149] *Loc. cit.*   See also *Red Book of Exch.*, i, p. 188: "The earl of Gloucester owes the service of two knights in Gloucestershire, which he performed for the furthest expedition in Wales, but later he defaulted"; also p. 250.
[150] *Textus Roffensis*, fo. 217v; Colvin, "Archbishop of Canterbury's Tenants by Knight Service", pp. 5, 11; Chew, *op. cit.*, pp. 184-5.
[151] Du Boulay, *The Lordship of Canterbury*, p. 85.
[152] In 1166 Richard de Haia's return laid out the two-tiered arrangement: "the knights of Richard de Haia serve for the king's service by carucates.   Five carucates make one knight, and the knights hold the five carucates, some more and some less".   *Red Book of Exch.*, i, p. 390.
[153] *Red Book of Worcester*, p. 445; M. Hollings, "The Survival of the Five-Hide Unit in the Western Midlands", *Eng. Hist. Rev.*, lxiii (1948), p. 454.

"Know that two sulungs make one knight's fee" thunders from Canterbury to the discontented.[154] When we recall that the eleventh-century northern fees were somewhat larger, but still very much poorer, than those of the hidated counties it is interesting to see that a very much larger scale obtained there in the twelfth century. In feodaries in the Danelaw some tenants-in-chief assert that there are 12 or 14 carucates to the fee; and as many as 24 are not uncommon in the north.[155] One or two tenants-in-chief had never held enough land to make much from their service arrangements. Lambert de Scoteni had to provide 10 knights from his 16 carucates and 2 bovates in Lincolnshire and it is not surprising to hear him ask the king's help to enforce service from one of his powerful sub-tenants, Richard de Haia, who also held in chief of his own right.[156] One attempt to prevent disputes gave rise to the increased use of a less economically ambiguous term than hide or carucate to measure grants.[157] The word was *librate* (the amount of land which brought a yearly income of £1). Stenton has noticed that there was a sudden rash of fiefs of about 10 librates in the twelfth century, that enfeoffments measured in librates tended to be larger, and that persons of high rank were keen on taking on fiefs of this value.[158] This was the sort of scale, that is about twice the Domesday level, on which tenants-in-chief were now having to offer in order to attract support of consequence.

They did not succeed fully or for long. For the expense of equipping and attending a knight was soaring. In the twelfth century increased costs as reflected in rates of pay show a rise approximately parallel to that of foodstuffs. The fragmentary evidence available from the mid-eleventh to the mid-twelfth century suggests that during that time rents and prices may have very approximately doubled over the century;[159] but they were to increase very much faster. We may remember the early evidence accounting for a knight at 4d. a day; in 1173 the wages of a knight for castle-guard rose from 8d. to 1s. per day; under John, the cost of finding a knight went up to 2s. a day; later, to 3s. and 4s.[160] From 1172 there is a very sharp rise in the price of cereals, which is not however sustained

[154] R. S. Hoyt, "A Pre-Domesday Kentish Assessment List", *Early Medieval Miscellany* (Pipe Roll Soc. lxxvi, new ser. xxxvi, 1962 for 1960), p. 199.
[155] E.g. "Archdeacon Osbert holds 11 carucates of land from which 14 carucates of land make a knight's fee": Vinogradoff, p. 56.
[156] *Red Book of Exch.*, i, p. 385.
[157] *Danelaw Charters* ed. F. M. Stenton (British Academy Records Soc. and Econ. Hist., vi, 1920), no. 471; other examples, Stenton, pp. 159-60.
[158] Stenton, p. 168.
[159] J. A. Raftis, *The Estates of Ramsey Abbey* (Toronto, 1957), pp. 56-65.
[160] Hollister, pp. 157, 212-5.

beyond 1176. A more steady general climb is characteristic of the period 1178-1204. This rise would have affected the cost of provisioning households. The price of oxen, often perhaps somewhat traditional, had certainly begun their climb by the 1180s, a demonstration of the premium on traction power of all sorts, which would be more sharply felt amongst the knightly classes in their demand for high quality horses. By the second decade of the thirteenth century the cost of grain had doubled and that of livestock more than doubled from an 1180 base, and was to continue to escalate.[161]

On top of generally increased prices was added expense owing to the elaboration in both the equipment of knighthood and its social accompaniments. From the last decade of the reign of Henry II both knight and mount became better protected. Complete coats of mail were assumed and a heavy helm replaced the light Norman headpiece. Equipment developed further in the thirteenth century to plate-armour.[162] And, as the costliness of armour increased, so did that of mounting a knight, for heavier horses were needed.[163] The sumpter horse of Domesday at the high price of £1 had to be changed for the somewhat larger animal costing at least £5 a hundred years later.[164] One hundred years later still, the animal performing the same rôle under plate armour was worth between £40 and £80.[165] Writing from the second decade of the thirteenth century William the Marshal's biographer felt he had to explain the paucity of the Marshal's retinue when equipped "as a man of gentility" in the 1150s: "the world was not then so proud as in our days. A king's son would ride with his cape bundled up, without any more equipage; now, there is hardly a squire who does not want to have a baggage horse".[166]

Much increased costs meant that reduction of commitment and substitution did not end at the early professional knight, but spread up the tenurial hierarchy. The changeover to the knight of local importance had taken place by the mid-twelfth century, but by the close of the century, as costs mounted, many of these lesser "gentry" types faced

[161] D. L. Farmer, "Some Price Fluctuations in Angevin England", *Econ. Hist. Rev.*, 2nd ser. ix (1956-7), pp. 24-43; A. L. Poole, "Livestock Prices in the Twelfth Century", *Eng. Hist. Rev.*, lv (1940), pp. 284-95.
[162] Chew, *op. cit.*, pp. 89-90; Denholm-Young, *op. cit.* pp. 114-5.
[163] Smail, pp. 106-7, where the change in the social standing of those called knights (*milites*) is succinctly expressed.
[164] *Dom. Bk.*, i, fos. 154b, 172; *Pipe Roll 3 Richard I* (Pipe Roll Soc., new ser. ii, 1926), p. 91.
[165] Chew, *op. cit.*; Denholm-Young, *op. cit.* These changes in prices include of course a certain amount of inflation: see D. L. Farmer "Some Livestock Prices in Thirteenth Century England" *Econ. Hist. Rev.*, 2nd ser., xxii (1969), pp. 1-16.
[166] *L'historie de Guillaume le Maréchal*, iii, p. 14.

the same dilemma that had meant the opting out of the early knight: they could not keep up their activities, now not simply military but also quite normally civil in assize work and taxation assessment,[167] and supervise their land effectively themselves, all at a time when costs were soaring. This led to a polarization of the class of military tenants and freeholders. Small wonder that many local knights emerge to light at this time in records of debt to Jews, and that the 1181 Assize of Arms is concerned about the armour that has come into the possession of Jews.[168] At the same time it is of interest that the Assize itself associates the equipment of a knight with a minimum revenue even while trying to increase the number with that equipment, stipulating that those laymen with income to the value of 16 marks should hold the equipment of a knight, those with 10 marks should have a hauberk.[169] On the other hand, the class of military tenants and freeholders had an obvious interest in not only keeping abreast of the market, but taking advantage of its buoyancy by producing themselves, as indeed some descendants of the early vavassor knights who had cast to oblivion their military tenure managed to do. All in all it was not surprising the Assize provoked the scathing comment that "unskilled rustics, accustomed to furrows and ditches, were thus unwillingly vaunted with knightly arms".[170]

By the late 1180s the crown was forced to give up all attempts to exact scutage on the new enfeoffments uncovered in 1166.[171] The increased costs and difficulty of knight-service are relevant to the interest in reserves of service displayed by the Assize of Arms. And the 1217 Charter sees the magnates again trying to assert control of their vassals' tenurial commitments.[172] Their difficulties with their vassals and mounting costs meant that, by the last decade of the

---

[167] See Poole, *From Domesday Book to Magna Carta*, pp. 406-12; F. M. Powicke, *King Henry III and the Lord Edward* (Oxford, 1947), pp. 33, 36 etc.

[168] Richardson, *English Jewry*, pp. 77-9, 95-105; Stubbs, *Charters*, p. 183, cap. 7.

[169] *Loc. cit.* By 1242 the government was attempting to get those with 15 librates of land or over to equip themselves with horse and hauberk: M. Powicke, "Distraint of Knighthood and Military Obligation under Henry III", *Speculum*, xxv (1950), p. 459.

[170] The half knight's fee held by Brutin from the bishop of Rochester at Gillingham had developed well by the thirteenth century. Then the reeve's total charge on the account amounted to over £66 one year: Du Boulay, "Gavelkind and Knight's Fee", pp. 510-11; see also M. M. Postan, "The Rise of a Money Economy", *Econ. Hist. Rev.*, xiv, (1944) p. 130: *Gervase of Canterbury*, ed. W. Stubbs (Rolls Series, 1879), i, p. 297.

[171] Painter, *Feudal Barony*, p. 36.

[172] Stubbs, *Select Charters*, p. 343, cap. 39: "No man shall grant or sell so much of his land that he cannot provide from the remainder the service due from the fee".

twelfth century, unwillingness to serve in person abroad had extended to the tenants-in-chief also. So the crown was forced to turn to the use of the money-fief on a much larger scale,[173] also to attempts at distraint of knighthood for military leadership as well as for administration.[174]

Eventually, the tenants-in-chief too managed to obtain reduction of their own military quota, though for scutage the larger assessments were retained. By the thirteenth century the bishop of Bath and Wells was financially responsible for 20 knights, but claimed to hold by the service of 2 knights only; similarly the bishop of Lincoln's 60 was cut to 5. In all, the ecclesiastical tenants-in-chief who had furnished about 750 knights for Henry II now consented to supply only 121½.[175] It might take a year's income to be an armed knight in Edward I's reign;[176] it probably did in Henry II's and William I's reigns too, measured by the price of a top-quality horse together with an average income. The great difference is that, even allowing for the depreciation in the value of money, it cost in each case a year's income from a fief of a very different size.

The rising cost of knighthood played a part in the final transformation of the knightly type into an aristocratic figure. By the early thirteenth century men of noble birth were proud to style themselves knight (*miles*) in their formal documents. When only the wealthy could be accoutred as a knight, knighthood appeared socially desirable, and the burden of the knightly rôle acceptable to some.[177] Other influences, however, were initially instrumental in this change: the promulgation of the Crusades by the Papacy in 1095, the foundation of the military-religious orders of the early twelfth century, and the development of both a political and a courtly literature which promoted ideals in a knightly context.[178] These features are familiar; so we have here confined our attention to some economic and tenurial aspects of the change in order to show why the descendant of the Norman vavassor knight was called only "vavassor" but not "knight" a century or so later, that is, not unless he boasted a truly remarkable prowess or had managed to augment his estate. Richard de Lucy

---

[173] Lyon, *Fief to Indenture*, p. 11.
[174] M. Powicke, *op. cit.*, pp. 457-65.
[175] Chew, *op. cit.*, pp. 32-5.
[176] Denholm-Young, *op. cit.*
[177] Though full knighthood became possible for even smaller numbers as costs continued to rise: see Denholm-Young, *op. cit.*
[178] For instance, Bernard of Clairvaux's, *De laude novae militiae*; *The Statesman's Book of John of Salisbury*, trans. J. Dickinson (New York, 1927), esp. pp. 199-208.

was well aware of the higher status of those called knights in the later twelfth century and was contemptuous of those who were not. "It was not the custom in the old days" he said "for every petty knight (*militulum*) you care to name to have a seal".[179] By the thirteenth century the word knight did not denote simply a military function; it had also become a title with attendant civil duties.

[179] *Chronicon Monasterii de Bello*, (Anglia Christiana Soc., London, 1846), p. 108. I am indebted to Professor Hilton for this reference.

7. Freedom and Villeinage in England

R. H. HILTON

AT AN EARLY STAGE IN OUR ATTEMPTS TO UNDERSTAND THE NATURE OF social relations in the past we are faced with the problem of the meaning of certain terms. How can we tell that a word whose meaning we think we know meant even approximately the same in another social context? In our own day, the meaning of the word "freedom" is disputed enough. How can we expect its meaning in the middle ages to be any less fluid and elusive? Yet for the student of medieval society, this is a problem which cannot be avoided for it was central to some important social and political conflicts of the time.

We are still far from certain what was a "free man", especially before the thirteenth century. If we look at the English evidence for the latter part of the thirteenth century, which is relatively abundant,[1] we find, as every historian knows, vast economic and social differences within the ranks of those who were regarded by the courts as free, ranging from the wealthy franklin who paid money rather than be dubbed a knight, to the poor cottar or landless labourer, with no ancestors or relatives to prove him other than free. But by 1280 the economic differentiation of the free tenants is a relatively straightforward topic. Problems in an earlier period seem to concern status rather than wealth, and are not so easy to understand let alone solve.

In England, we are accustomed to think of the problems connected with the demarcation of freedom in the middle ages as concerning only the lowest ranks of the free. Where, we ask, is the dividing line between free man and serf? And this is the problem with which this article will be mainly concerned. But we must draw attention to other inquiries which show that the problem of free status concerns a wider social spectrum, for they have shown that there is also ambiguity about the status of the upper ranks of the free. This ambiguity mainly arises in connection with evidence which has recently been produced by Léopold Génicot for the county of Namur in the eleventh and twelfth centuries. An examination of early chronicles and charters has led him to the conclusion that the term free man (*liber homo*) was equivalent to noble (*nobilis*). Other historians, such as P. Bonenfant and G. Despy for Brabant, P. Dollinger

---

[1] Partly because of the Hundred Rolls of 1279-80. See E. A. Kosminsky, *Studies in the Agrarian History of England in the Thirteenth Century* (Oxford, 1956) and B. Dodwell, "The Free Tenantry of the Hundred Rolls" *Econ. Hist. Rev.*, xiv (1944).

for Bavaria, L. Verriest for the Frankish lands in general and Hainault in particular, while not going as far as Génicot, produce other evidence to show that there was a fairly widespread equation between nobility and free status.[2] Even when the terms *liber homo* and *nobilis* were not equivalents, the *liberi homines* or *alodiarii* (that is owners of family lands which were not dependent tenures) of the post-Carolingian period in the Frankish dominions constituted, as M. Verriest puts it, "une véritable aristocratie".[3] Now it is generally agreed that at this time the class of true serfs (*servi*) was comparatively small. Hence there must have been a considerable body, perhaps the majority of the rural population, of dependent cultivators who were not officially counted as *liberi homines*, but who were not serfs.

F. W. Maitland noticed that the equation between nobility and freedom has some puzzling echoes in the early twelfth-century English law books. The thegn is sometimes described in Latin versions of old English laws as *liberalis homo*. Vassals (*vavassores*) who have pleas relating to wite and wer over their men are defined as those who hold "free lands" (*liberas terras*). The right to sit in judgment is to be enjoyed by barons of the county holding "free lands", but not by such low and indigent persons (*viles et inopes personae*) as villeins and cottars. Yet the same law books specifically include the villeins, that is the *villani*, Latin for Old English *twyhindmen*, among the free.[4] In Magna Carta the typical beneficiary of many clauses is the *liber homo*. Now if we consider this document in its social and political context, whatever this term may come to mean, in 1215 and in Magna Carta it could hardly have meant anything less than a "privileged man",[5] and possibly much more, a baron.

Yet the author of the treatise attributed to Ranulf Glanvill, written before 1215, when discussing the problems of freedom and servility, clearly assumes that the free men about whom he was writing were socially peasants. Bracton, writing about half a century later, under

[2] L. Génicot, *L'économie rurale namuroise au bas moyen âge. Les hommes — la noblesse* (Louvain, 1960); P. Bonenfant and G. Despy,"La noblesse en Brabant, XIIe - XIIIe siècles", *Le Moyen Age*, lxiv (1958); P. Dollinger, *L'évolution des classes rurales en Bavière depuis la fin de l'époque carolingienne jusqu'au milieu du XIIIe siècle* (Paris, 1949); L. Verriest, *Institutions Médiévales* (Mons, 1946). See also, G. Duby, "La noblesse dans la France médiévale", *Revue Historique*, ccxxvi (1961).
[3] *Op. cit.*, p. 14.
[4] F. W. Maitland, *Domesday Book and Beyond* (Cambridge, 1897), pp. 43, 106; *Leges Henrici Primi*, chaps. 27, 29, 70, 76.3a and *Institutiones Cnuti*, chaps. 31.1a, in F. Liebermann (ed.), *Die Gesetze der Angelsachsen* (Halle, 1903-16).
[5] Sidney Painter, *Feudalism and Liberty* (Baltimore, 1961), p. 247.

the title "De personis", places the *liberi homines* next to the *servi* at the bottom of the social hierarchy after the *potentes*, the *vavassores* and the *milites*. His famous notebook, based on cases settled in the king's court, deals with the problems of the free man in an entirely peasant social context.[6] This need not mean, of course, that the aristocratic connotation of the term *liber homo* had no significance. If medieval social terminology was often ambiguous, when would this be more likely than when it concerned a social and legal status that was constantly changing, constantly threatened, and much sought after ? To be "free" or (as Sydney Painter suggested[7]) "privileged" in the social context of Magna Carta, or of some of the clauses in the twelfth-century law books, would mean, if not noble, at least aristocratic. To be "free" in a peasant social context meant something quite different. The word could mean different things at the same date according to the circumstances in which it was employed. As Professor R. W. Southern has observed, "It was only when the quality of freedom was articulated by being attached to the status of knight, burgess or baron that it could be observed, analysed and measured".[8]

These ambiguities about the quality of freedom still confuse us somewhat when we confine ourselves purely to the peasant social context. Little that has been written about the subject much extends Vinogradoff's discussion in his first remarkable book in English, *Villainage in England*. He drew attention to the way in which, in the twelfth century, the development of royal administration and jurisdiction, in particular the writs concerning the ownership and possession of land, clarified and protected the position of tenants of free land, but surrendered the villeins to their lords. It might also be suggested that the same process may have helped to remove the earlier, aristocratic connotations of the term *liber homo*. He also made the highly significant suggestion, from which much of the argument in this article might be said to proceed, that "by the side of the freeholder recognised by later law there stands the villain as a customary freeholder who has lost legal protection".[9] But Vinogradoff rather saw this loss as a gradual process from the time of Domesday Book until the end of the thirteenth century. In this

[6] Glanvill, *De Legibus et Consuetudinibus Regni Angliae*, ed. G. G. Woodbine (New Haven, 1932), book v; H. Bracton, *De Legibus et Consuetudinibus Anglie*, ed. G. G. Woodbine (New Haven, 1915-42), iii; and *Bracton's Note Book*, ed. F. W. Maitland (Cambridge, 1887).
[7] *Loc. cit.*   [8] *The Making of the Middle Ages* (London, 1953), p. 108.
[9] P. Vinogradoff, *Villainage in England* (Oxford, 1892), p. 220.

article I propose to examine the evidence again to see whether the process of depression might not have been rather sudden, producing sharp reactions on the part of the villein tenants. If this is so, the suggestion that villeins only claimed freedom in royal courts as a device to initiate pleas of service, loses much of its force.[10]

Historians risk falling into the trap dug for the peasants by the lawyers, for most of our evidence about freedom and serfdom depends on evidence which is a by-product of legal or administrative process. But record evidence of this type has the deceptive appearance of objectivity, and is often compared favourably with literary evidence, the writings of poets or chroniclers. The reports of lawsuits, mainly of the thirteenth century, seem to constitute a solid body of proof that the man who was a villein and who was identifiable as such because he did labour services, owed merchet, heriot and similar customary payments, was unfree. Indeed, by the end of the thirteenth century this had become the case. Bearing this in mind, it was inevitable that when historians examined the thirteenth-century surveys, the most numerous class within them, the *villani*, should have been taken to be unfree. All the more reason for doing so apparently because in the same surveys a smaller separate category of men is referred to as the *liberi*, or *libere*, *tenentes*. Still further, in that massive official survey, the Hundred Rolls of 1279-80, groups of tenants who in one village would be put down as *villani* would in the next be described — by the scribe — as *servi*.[11] From this point, it is a natural, though risky assumption that the *villani* and analogous categories of men found in the twelfth-century surveys should be thought of as being as unfree as their thirteenth-century descendants. This assumption is made in spite of the general belief that the *villanus* of Domesday Book was free. However, there are some important differences between the twelfth- and the thirteenth-century surveys which may have some bearing on the subject under discussion.

If we examine the extant twelfth-century surveys without hindsight, there are few indications which would justify us in confidently classifying villein tenants as unfree. It is true that the term *liber tenens* or *libere tenens* seems to cut off a few from the rest. But if the continental, and some of the English, evidence cited above is to be

[10] J. C. Holt, "The Ballads of Robin Hood", *Past and Present*, No. 18 (Nov., 1960), reprinted as chapter 11 below, p. 236.
[11] The use of the term *servus* for *villanus* is frequent in the Warwickshire Hundred Rolls (P.R.O., E. 164, xv).

taken seriously, the term *liber* used as a tenurial or as a status description need not imply that men not so qualified should be taken as unfree, in the sense that thirteenth-century villeins were thought to be unfree. This is a point which Léopold Delisle emphasized as long ago as 1851.[12]

Let us take as examples the surveys made in the twelfth century which describe the estates of the following institutions: the Benedictine Abbeys of Peterborough, Burton-on-Trent, Ramsey, Evesham and Glastonbury; the Bishoprics of Durham and Worcester; the English Knights Templars; and the nunnery of the Holy Trinity, Caen (English lands). The dates of all the surveys are not certain but they seem to fall into three groups. Those of Peterborough, Burton and Ramsey were drawn up in the early part of the century. The three Caen surveys, and that of Evesham Abbey are of uncertain date but are not earlier than the middle of the century. Those of Worcester, Durham, the Knights Templar and Glastonbury were all drawn up in the 1180s. In many cases, of course, the descriptions refer back to situations at earlier dates, as we shall see.[13]

As far as social classification is concerned, it is noticeable that in these surveys there is no neat grouping of tenants into the three or four classes found in those of the thirteenth century.[14] In some surveys there are few status descriptions but each tenant's name is given (Ramsey, Caen, Worcester, Templars, Glastonbury). In others, the status descriptions do not normally indicate legal or social position. It is true that in a twelfth-century context, the word

[12] *Etudes sur la condition de la classe agricole en Normandie au moyen âge* (Paris, 1903 edn.), pp. 16 ff.
[13] *Chronicon Petroburgense*, ed. T. Stapleton (Camden Soc., 1st ser., xlvii, 1849). "Burton Abbey Surveys", ed. C. G. O. Bridgeman (*Collections for a History of Staffordshire: The William Salt Arch. Soc.*, 1916). *Cartularium Monasterii de Rameseia*, ed. W. H. Hart (Rolls Series, 1884–93) vol. iii. "Chartrier de l'Abbaye de la Saincte Trinité de Caen", Bibl. Nat., MS. Lat. 5650: this contains two surveys, for the dates of which see C. H. Haskins, *Norman Institutions* (Cambridge, Mass., 1918), p. 161 and R. Carabie, *La Propriété Foncière dans le Très Ancien Droit Normand* (Caen, 1943), pp. 149 ff. Another Caen survey, a fragment concerning part of the Gloucestershire property, is at the Worcester County Record Office, 705: 128/11 BA 1488. Evesham Abbey Cartulary, Brit. Mus., MS. Cotton, Vesp. B xxiv. *Boldon Buke*, ed. W. Greenwell (Surtees Society, xxv, 1852). *The Red Book of Worcester*, ed. M. Hollings (Worcestershire Hist. Soc., 1934–50). *Records of the Templars in England in the Twelfth Century*, ed. B. A. Lees (British Academy, Records of Social and Economic History, ix, 1935). *Liber Henrici de Soliaco . . .* , ed. J. E. Jackson (Roxburghe Club, 1882).
[14] Except for the Evesham Abbey surveys where the numbers of tenants in a particular category are usually given without names. There is also one manor (Withington) in the *c.* 1182 surveys of the bishopric of Worcester where the same arrangement is found.

homines, frequently used in the Peterborough, Burton, Caen, Durham and Templars surveys, could imply dependence, but not necessarily lack of freedom. The *minimi homines* of Ramsey are simply smallholders. Other terms are derived from the size or type of the holding (*virgarii*, "virgate holders", Glastonbury; *cotmanni, coterii, cotsetles*, "cottagers", Peterborough, Burton, Ramsey, Caen, Evesham, Durham; *bordarii*, "cottagers", Peterborough Caen, Evesham, Durham). Some derive from the occupation or service of the tenant (*operatores, operarii*, "workers", Caen, Evesham, Glastonbury, Durham, Worcester; *bovarii, bubulci*, "oxherds" or "ploughmen", Peterborough, Burton, Caen, Evesham, Worcester; *acremen*, "ploughmen", Ramsey; *avercmen*, "ploughmen", Worcester). Some indicate the payment of money rent (*malmen*, Worcester, Durham; *censarii*, Burton, Worcester). Others simply indicate the occupation of land (*landsetes*, Peterborough; *undersetes*, Peterborough, Worcester).

In addition to these more or less descriptive terms, there are those words whose original meaning was simply countryman or villager. In the surveys of Evesham and Worcester we find the terms *rusticus operarius* and *rusticus*, and *villanus* in those of Peterborough, Burton, Caen and Durham. In all cases, as far as freedom or the lack of it is concerned, these terms seem entirely neutral in meaning. There is in fact comparatively little all told about this question. All references to unfreedom are confined to those whom we may suppose to be the descendants of slaves. In the Ramsey material there are *nativi*, persons who, as the name implies, were unfree by birth. In the earliest Caen surveys there are also references to a small number of male and female slaves, *servi, ancille, mulieres serviles*. The Caen surveys for Minchinhampton (Glos.) however throw, indirectly, a little extra light on the question of the freedom of the customary virgaters. This class is certainly separated from the *francalani*,[15] for the *francalani*, like the *liberi feudati* of Ramsey, the *liberi homines* or *liberi tenentes* of Evesham, or the *radmen* of Worcester belonged to a small near-aristocratic group, socially close to the knights, and merging into them. It may be right to regard them as descendants of pre-Conquest thegns. They might also be compared with the unfeudalized *alodiarii* of the continent, where the racial element does not at this date confuse social distinctions. Nevertheless there are clear indications that the Minchinhampton customary virgaters were normally free, for after the recital of their normal labour services we are told that in addition "all males and females who are not free

---

[15] For instance in the obligation of wives to pay Peter's Pence: Bib. Nat., MS. Lat. 5650, f. 56.

(*omnes qui non sunt liberi masculi et femine*) must reap at three bedereaps".[16]

In view of the importance attached in the thirteenth century to certain tests of personal unfreedom, it is of some interest to see the importance they had in the twelfth-century surveys. Anyone acquainted with the mid and late thirteenth-century surveys will know that after the enumeration of labour services, there were usually added the "unassessed customs" (*consuetudines non taxatas*), to borrow a phrase from the Gloucester Abbey cartulary. The most important of these for our purpose were merchet (payment on the marriage of a daughter or son), heriot (death duty), the payment of a licence fee (*tolnetum*) for the sale of stock, and the annual aid or tallage. These were regarded as important financially as well as being tests of the unfree status of the payers, and are invariably mentioned in recitals of tenants' customs. What do we find in the twelfth-century surveys? First, there are none of these systematic lists of customs added to the lists of labour services. This is well illustrated by comparing twelfth- and thirteenth-century surveys of the same estates, especially those of Ramsey, Worcester and Glastonbury.[17] Next, the obligations later thought to be indicative of unfree status are hardly mentioned, except in the latest of the twelfth-century surveys. Merchet, perhaps the most frequent test of unfreedom in the thirteenth century, is only found in three of these documents. It is described by its name with respect to tenants in only four of the Templars' villages (mid-1180s). It is referred to in the latest of the Caen surveys, though not by name. The document tells us that free men at Minchinhampton have to get permission to marry off their daughters, but do not pay; by contrast the unfree must pay. Finally in a survey from the Ramsey Abbey estates, intermediate in time (*temp.* King John) between the two groups of surveys already mentioned, there is also a reference to merchet on the manor of Walsoken.[18] Heriot is found in two of the Templars' villages, one reference is made in an additional note to the latest of the Caen surveys, and in the survey of Ramsey abbey's Norfolk manor of Walsoken (*temp.* King John) it is also mentioned. But the only early

---

[16] *Ibid.*, f. 55.

[17] For thirteenth-century surveys, see *Cartularium . . . Rameseia*, vol. i, e.g. the Holywell survey of 1252, esp. p. 298; the 1299 surveys in the *Red Book of Worcester;* and the mid-century rentals and custumals of Glastonbury in *Rentalia et custumaria Michaelis de Ambresbury 1235–52, et Rogeri de Ford 1252–61 . . .*, ed. T. S. Holmes and E. Hobhouse (Somerset Rec. Soc., v, 1891).

[18] There are also two references to the allied custom of leyrwite (fine for a woman's incontinence) in the 1182 Worcester survey.

twelfth-century reference is in the Burton surveys, where heriot is owed, not by serfs but by sokemen at Winshill (Staffs.).[19] Payment of a licence to sell stock is found in the mid-century Caen surveys, and in two of the Templars' villages. Tallage or *donum* is found in one Glastonbury village (1189), in one Worcester village (*c.* 1182) and in the Walsoken survey of the time of King John.

It could be argued that the insistence of the thirteenth-century surveys on these incidents of unfreedom simply proves that existing customs were not until then written down, not that they did not exist earlier. This is a reasonable argument. I would not wish to insist that these incidents were inventions of the late twelfth century. Their appearance in the written record does however require some explanation. Merchet was the next most frequent single criterion for unfreedom after labour services in the early thirteenth-century villeinage cases in the *Curia Regis*, and it is not until after this period of intense legal pressure that we find merchet universally claimed as an incident of unfree villeinage in the later surveys.[20] It is tempting to think that incidents of personal unfreedom, such as merchet, were being generalized in the last two decades of the twelfth century. In this connection, it is worth remembering that it was also in the twelfth century that similar incidents, such as *formariage* and *mainmorte*, were being pinned on to the legally free *vileins* of the continent, and that aspects of their status and obligations were making their condition so like that of the serfs that historians as well as contemporaries tended to confuse them.[21] Perhaps it is not accidental that the estates whose owners had the most widespread foreign connections, the Templars, were those whose surveys show the most general early occurrence of merchet and heriot.[22]

[19] Sokemen of the abbey of Bury St. Edmunds were subject to merchet in Abbot Samson's time, but whether this was a pre-manorial obligation or not seems uncertain: *The Kalendar of Abbot Samson*, ed. R. H. C. Davis (Camden Soc., 3rd ser., lxxxiv, 1954).

[20] A rough count of tests of villeinage in the first fourteen volumes of the *Curia Regis Rolls* (London, 1922-61) gives the following results: labour services 19; merchet 17; unfree kin 14; described as *nativi* 5; toll for selling beasts 5; payment of aid 4; tallage at will 3; pannage payment 3; being sold as persons 2; no right to leave holding; reeve service; suit of court; ultimogeniture; payment of entry fine; leyrwite; — one case each. Note the absence of heriot as a test.

[21] Cf. Verriest's criticism of Marc Bloch in *Institutions Médiévales*, pp. 172 ff. G. Duby sums up the present position in *L'économie rurale et la vie des campagnes dans l'occident médiéval* (Paris, 1962), esp. p. 452.

[22] One of the most detailed examinations of merchet, referred to with approval by F. W. Maitland in F. Pollock and F. W. Maitland, *The History of English Law*, 2nd edn. (Cambridge, 1898), p. 373 n., was that of L. O. Pike, in his introduction to the *Year Book of 15 Edward III* (Rolls Series, 1891), pp. xv-xliii. All his examples are of the thirteenth century or later. He accepted a close connection between merchet and *formariage*.

On the whole, then, the extant twelfth-century surveys, even the late ones, whilst indicating that labour services figured largely in the tenurial obligations of peasants, give little ground for supposing that the majority of the rural population, the *villani*, the *rustici* were as yet unfree. Real serfs, *servi* or *nativi* there certainly still were, but they were in a small minority. Not that the concept of freedom was precise; it varied from one social context to another, and even within the peasant social context was a relative rather than an absolute condition. An inquiry (*c.* 1155) into conditions of tenure at Cirencester states that "no man is so free that he must not plough and carry" (*non est tam liber qui non debeat arare et cariare* . . .). A tenant of Glastonbury Abbey at Badbury (Wilts.), while doing services similar to those of other tenants of demesne land, pays less (or even no) aid "because he holds more freely than his predecessors used to hold" (*quia tenet liberius quam predecessores sui solebant tenere*). There are other, slightly later, examples of this relativity. A sokeman of the Abbey of Bury St. Edmunds "holds more freely than the others: he gives his daughters without fine" (*tenet liberius aliis: dat filias suas sine gersumio*). In a dispute about villeinage in Sussex in 1225, the plaintiffs, who are asserting their freedom, agree that by their custom the youngest son inherits. This is because "their land is socage and is not so free that the eldest son should have it" (*terra est socagium et non est ita libera quod promogenitus filius eam habere debeat*).[23] Now this relativity of peasant freedom in many twelfth-century contexts seems to depend on freedom *from* certain obligations. These obligations are most often labour services, and the more often money was paid instead of them, the freer was the tenant. There is, of course, nothing new about the equation of tenure by money rent with free tenure, though in the thirteenth century, when the doctrine of villeinage had hardened, lords took care to prevent the permanent or long-term commutation of services into money rent from becoming a way to personal freedom.[24] Not so in the twelfth century. The impression derived from the surveys is that while landlords might regret the gain to the tenant implied in the transition from labour rent to money rent, the point at issue was not personal freedom in a wider sense, but simply freedom *from* certain irksome obligations.

The annoyance felt by the estate administrators is well expressed

[23] *The Cartulary of Cirencester Abbey*, ed. C. D. Ross, vol. i (Oxford, 1964), no. 20. *Liber H. de Soliaco*, p. 121; *Kalendar of Abbot Samson*, p. 6; *Curia Regis Rolls*, xii, no. 361.
[24] See R. H. Hilton, "Gloucester Abbey Leases of the Thirteenth Century", *Birmingham Univ. Hist. Jl.*, iv (1953-4).

in the latest of the Minchinhampton surveys, referring back to earlier events. It also demonstrates the simple, but not (at that time) far reaching equation of the qualification "free" with the fact of money rent payment from the holding:

> Richard the son of Palmer holds one virgate for four shillings which owed works in the time of King Henry and King Stephen, but they do not know how it was made free, but he gave the abbess J. 4s. so that he could hold it as his father . . . .
> Roger the big holds a virgate for 5s. which owed works, but he made up so much to Simon of Felstead and afterwards to other people that he has held it for 5s. up to now . . . .[25]

There were similar complaints by the monks of Evesham against their abbots:

> Walter holds two virgates for 6s. and used to give 8s., and gives aid and boon ploughing and reaps, pays geld and scutage. Abbot Maurice gave his niece to Walter's predecessor and unjustly removed the labour services, and this is at the abbot's will . . . .
> Rondulf in the time of Kings William and Henry used to do labour services and all customs, but at the request of Eluric prior of Evesham he was made free and this unjustly . . . .[26]

A similar situation on the Ramsey abbey estates has been referred to by Professor Raftis,[27] where the "ancients" of the villages had complained about money rented lands either paying less than they should or not at all. At Damerham (Wilts.) on the Glastonbury estates we read: ". . . this half virgate should do works but is now free. But the virgate of Stapleham, after that exchange, should do works and was free before . . .". These possible alternatives are

---

[25] "Ricardus filius Palmer tenet i virgatam pro iiii.s. que operaria fuit tempore Henrici regis et in tempore Stephani regis sed nesciunt quomodo libera facta fuit, sed abbatisse J. dedit iiii.s.ut teneat eam sicut pater suus..." (Worc. County Rec. Office, MS. *cit.*)
"Rogerus magnus tenet i virgatam pro v.s. que fuit operaria sed ipse tantum fecit apud Symonem de Felstude et postea apud alios quod pro v.s. eam tenuit hucusque . . ." (*ibid.*).
Abbess Joan of Coulonges is probably referred to; she was abbess by 1173 and died 1181(?): *Gallia Christiana* (Paris, 1850-77), xi, pp. 431-8. Simon of Felstead appears as a substantial tenant in the earlier surveys. He may have been farmer or steward, and was accused of spoliation. (Bib. Nat., MS. *cit.*, ff. 38v - 39).
[26] "Walterus tenet ii virgas pro vi.s. et solebat dare viii.s. et dat auxilium et arat prece et metit et geldat et servicium regis Abbas Mauricius dedit neptem suam predecessori Walterii et abstulit opus terre iniuste et hoc est in voluntate abbatis . . ." (Brit. Mus., MS. *cit.*, f. 53v.)
"Rondulfus . . . in tempore regis Willelmi et Henrici solebat operari et omnes consuetudines facere sed precibus Elurici prioris Evesham factus fuit ille liber et iniuste . . ." (*ibid.*)
Maurice was abbot 1096-1122. Rondulf's services by this act were reduced to money rent, suit of county and hundred, and escort duty.
[27] J. A. Raftis, *The Estates of Ramsey Abbey* (Toronto, 1957), p. 50.

referred to explicitly in the *capitula* put to the village juries on the Glastonbury estates: ". . . whether any land was made free at the time of Bishop Henry or afterwards which ought to owe works, by what warrant this was and *how far it might be free* . . ." (my italics). This question echoes one put at a slightly earlier date many miles away on the estates of St. Paul's cathedral: ". . . which of the peasants enjoy freedom, which are burdened with works, which are rent payers and which are cottars . . .".[28] It must be remembered, of course, when reading these remarks, that what was at issue was the risk of the permanent escape of a holding from the burden of labour services, not the partial and temporary commutation under the lord's control which was implied, for instance, in the Evesham alternative "if the virgate owes money rent . . . if it owes labour services".

As far as peasant holdings were concerned, the word "free" seems to have had a concrete and specific reference to the absence of (freedom from) labour services. By the beginning of the thirteenth century, judging by the legal activity in the king's courts, this freedom from services was being applied as a touchstone for the freedom of the person. The absence of court records before the 1190s makes it difficult to know exactly what was happening, but in the light of the remarks in surveys drawn up as late as the 1180s, it seems as though these last two decades of the century were the crucial period for the depression of the majority of the rural population.

*   *   *   *

If the removal of the *villani* from the ranks of those with free status had been a gradual process during the late eleventh and twelfth centuries, one would hardly expect a sharp reaction from the victims. If, as has been suggested here, there was a sharpening of the attack from the last two decades or so of the twelfth century, we should expect to see some sort of immediate reaction. This would be all the more likely at this period, one of general social and political crisis for

---

[28] ". . . hec dimidia virgata operari solet nunc autem est libera. Virgata vero de Stapelham post illud excambium operari solet que ante hoc libera fuit . . ." (*Liber H. de Soliaco*, p. 21.)

". . . Si aliqua terra fuerit facta libera in tempore Henrici episcopi vel postea que debuit operari quo garanto hoc fuit et in quantum sit libera" (*ibid.*, p. 130). Henry of Blois, bishop of Winchester (1129-71), was abbot of Glastonbury (1126-71).

". . . qui colonorum libertate gauderent: quive gravarentur operibus qui censuales quive cottarii . . ." (*The Domesday of St. Paul's*, ed. W. H. Hale [Camden Soc., 1st ser., lxix, 1858], p. 112).

all classes, when men were particularly conscious of their rights and quick in defence of encroachments on them. We are now beginning to appreciate the economic factors behind the political and social unrest of John's reign, the rising prices, the intense fiscal pressure. But so far it is only its effect on the barons and the lesser lords that has been examined. What could be more natural than that in a feudal agrarian society rising costs should be passed on to the basic producer, what more natural in the conditions of the time than that this must involve a worsening of his legal and social status ? All this is perhaps obvious. What needs to be appreciated is that freedom of personal status, about the year 1200, if much compromised for the mass of the peasantry, was something that was only just being lost. Only the feeling of immediate loss can explain the widespread and intense insistence on freedom of condition which filters through the records of the courts, almost our only evidence.

It is from the printed records of the *Curia Regis* that we can best obtain something approaching a quantitative evaluation of the disputes over the freedom of villeins. These survive only from the last decade of the twelfth century. How do we know that the pressure on the tenants which they reveal was just beginning ? We cannot know this. All we can say is that the trend in the interpretation of villeinage which is shown in them seems to go well beyond what we learn from the twelfth-century surveys, but is embodied in the middle and late thirteenth-century surveys.[29] Such later evidence as is easy of access, or published, consists of samples from the records of particular estates, the calendars of chancery rolls, and such published extracts from the plea rolls as are contained in the *Placitorum Abbreviatio*.[30] The evidence from the early thirteenth-century *Curia Regis Rolls* gives a fair impression of the range of litigation. The later evidence shows that the matter of free status was still an issue for the peasants long after the unfreedom of villeinage had become established doctrine in the courts. This peasant enthusiasm for freedom is shown as late as 1381. It is remarkable that the demand for it should be first on the list of rebel demands when villeinage was economically and socially a good deal less irksome than it had been in the thirteenth century.

[29] *Rotuli Curiae Regis*, i-ii (London, 1835); *Three Rolls of the King's Court* (Pipe Roll Soc., xiv, 1891); *Curia Regis Rolls*, i-xiv (London, 1922-1961). Vinogradoff thought that the manorial records and the records of the king's court reflected two ways of looking at the situation: *op. cit.*, p. 212. This does not take into account the differences between the surveys at the different dates.
[30] Record Commission (London, 1811).

In the first thirty years or so of the thirteenth century there are some eighty detailed records of villeinage cases in the *Curia Regis Rolls*, as well as additional references to many more cases for which there is little or no detail. Most of the fully reported cases (sixty-three) involve a head-on clash between lord and tenant, the one asserting that the other is a villein, the other asserting his freedom. In forty out of these sixty-three cases the plaintiff was the tenant.[31] The fact that in the majority of cases the tenants took the initiative is of considerable significance when we remember their socially inferior position, the physical risk they took in opposing their lords and the expense of litigation. It implies a genuine sense of grievance. It is also likely, of course, that many of these grievances never came to court.

Contests in the courts were seldom solely about whether a man was or was not free. This issue normally followed some other cause of conflict and the course of the conflict often illuminates what in concrete terms was understood by freedom.

Some cases initiated by tenants started with writs for possessory assizes, usually novel disseisin and mort d'ancestor. The defendant is the lord, who justifies his entry on the tenement on the ground that it is not held freely but in villeinage. An example comes from Lincolnshire in the roll of 1200. Ailric the son of Agge impleaded Conan of Holbeach and others for unjust disseisin of his free tenement. Conan said there could be no assize as Ailric was his villein. Both produced relatives of Ailric, those on Conan's side declaring that Ailric owed works, aid and merchet. Ailric produced two free relatives, nephews. Conan then demanded a jury and offered ten marks for it — a large sum probably beyond the capacity of most peasants. The jury of ten knights, whose inclinations can be guessed at, gave the case to the lord.[32] In this case, though not stated, it may be that the entry on the tenement followed a refusal by the tenant to do some of the services. This in fact was frequently and explicitly a point at issue, for free tenure and "freedom" usually meant security and a fixed money rent.

The root of the insecurity of the tenant at this time was that his holding was customary. In the future, custom was to give security; but now what the tenant wanted to do was not protected by custom against the contrary will of the lord: buying and selling land and

---

[31] If one were to enumerate the cases which are barely mentioned, and for which no detail is given (e.g. a number of dower cases) the proportion of cases initiated by tenants would be increased.

[32] *Cur. Reg. Rolls*, i, pp. 187, 262, 278 (1200).

avoiding irksome personal services. A case in Buckinghamshire in 1225 illustrates this and also brings in other aspects of the contemporary situation. Richard the son of Hudard impleaded Robert of Broughton on the grounds that Robert had come to his house at Chesham with an armed band, had beaten him and his wife and had taken their goods. Richard raised the hue and cry, and the bailiffs of Berkhampstead arrived on the scene to find them still fighting off Robert and his following. During the course of the fight, two of Richard's defenders were wounded by Robert and his men. However, Robert denied that he had committed a felony on the grounds that Richard had been a villein of his father. He claimed that Richard's father Hudard had acknowledged his villeinage in a cyrograph in court during King John's reign, and that Richard, like Hudard, had held in villeinage until that year. Then Robert heard that Richard had made himself free (*fecit se liberum*). The aspect of this freedom which Robert noted is significant — it was that Richard wanted to sell land. The disturbance arose because Robert and his wife came to hold a court at Richard's house. In the king's court the cyrograph admitting villeinage was produced, wounds on both sides were examined and a day given for judgment — of which there is no record.[33]

This attempt by Richard to sell land must not be read as if there were established and accepted restrictions on villein or customary land sales. Professor Postan has shown that even in the late thirteenth century these restrictions were by no means as absolute as the custumals seem to indicate, and has plausibly suggested that "at the end of the twelfth and in the early thirteenth centuries land was frequently bought, sold and leased by villeins without any recorded licence from the lord".[34] But the evidence of the *Curia Regis* cases, which he is right to use for the free buying and selling of land by villeins, also shows that lords were now reacting against this freedom as they were reacting against other freedoms.

There is evidence of considerable violence in not a few cases. An episode in Suffolk reported in the 1220 roll is not unique, but typical. Roger of Kyrkele complained that Henry de Ver came to his house in Mutford and attacked his daughter, chasing her about the place until she escaped through one of the windows. Henry, thinking she was hiding in a barn full of barley, set fire to it, as the woman's husband, who was keeping a chest of clothes there, testified. Henry denied the

---

[33] *Cur. Reg. Rolls*, xii, no. 1579 (1225).
[34] *Carte Nativorum*, ed. C. N. L. Brooke and M. M. Postan (Northants. Rec. Soc., xx, 1960), p. xli.

HPK

story, stated that the fire was accidental and that Roger, his villein, had made up the story out of malice (*de odio et atia*) because he (Henry) would not allow him his freedom or give permission for the marriage of a daughter. He counter-appealed Roger of another burning and Roger's initial appeal fell through. A jury was named to decide whether the accusation had indeed been made out of hatred, but their verdict is not recorded.[35] The violence and malice were no doubt present on both sides; there was much of this about at the time. In a number of cases it was an inevitable by-product of the recognized process of the lord's sanctions against tenants. When tenants who considered themselves free and owing nothing other than money rent (however recently established by commutation) were faced with a demand for what their lords asserted were customary services, the sanction was distraint of chattels. In the Cambridge sessions of 1225 a process of law by Roger of Huntingfield against his tenant Robert the son of Saledi was ended. Robert had initiated the process by complaining that Roger had unjustly taken away his beasts (*averia*) to oblige him to do services that he did not owe. Roger said that Robert was his villein but had made himself free (*fecit se liberum*), and in the end Robert was obliged to accept villein status.[36] Many tenants however found themselves in prison, this being a more frequent sanction in these cases than distraint, though the two sanctions were sometimes employed together. So, in Essex in 1205 John the Tanner, coming to market, found he was set on by three men and robbed of £10 in cash, a surcoat (7s. value), 5 rings (1s. 6d.), and a belt (12d.). He was then flung into the abbot of Waltham's jail. The three men were, of course, the abbot's servants; they denied the robbery and claimed that John was the abbot's villein. John in turn denied this. As often happened when the day came for an appointed jury to give its verdict, the plaintiff did not appear.[37] This is not surprising. It was not only in the days of the statutes of livery and maintenance that local potentates controlled the verdicts of the public courts.

Lords did not always win in their action against tenants, especially when tenants produced written evidence. For example, in 1207, William de Pinkeney impleaded a priest named Ralph for giving twenty acres of villein land in Tattersett (Norfolk) to a religious house. Ralph claimed it was free land and produced charters from William and his father. William accepted the charters but said that

[35] *Cur. Reg. Rolls*, ix, pp. 336-7 (1220).
[36] *Cur. Reg. Rolls*, xii, no. 996 (1225).
[37] *Cur. Reg. Rolls*, iii, pp. 324-5 (1205); iv, p. 37 (1205).

Ralph had not availed himself of them, but had done villein services and had paid merchet for his sister. The case went to Ralph because of the charters.[38] Similarly, in 1230, a tenant of Richard Angot in Norfolk complained that his lord had distrained him in his cash and beasts to do services other than those specified in a cyrograph made in 1199. Richard claimed the tenant as a villein, and got his brother (who had been the tenant's original lord) to support him. But the cyrograph was accepted as guaranteeing the tenant's right, and in addition the court instructed the brother to confirm it by charter. However, in a case in 1201 between William de Longchamp and his tenant Hubert son of Reginald, whom he claimed as a villein, the tenant's case, though appearing stronger, failed, in spite of a charter from the previous lord. This charter had given the land for a term, and, if the grantor did not return from Jerusalem, in fee and heredity for a fixed money rent instead of services. A day was given to the litigants for decision, but the tenant did not turn up and the case went by default to Longchamp.[39]

The fact that decisions sometimes went to the tenants does not entitle us to assume that the courts were impartial, and that therefore judgement for the lords was normally based on right. Coercion, bribery and the social sympathies of the court helped the lords. But it was not only that. The courts were apparently accepting tests which excluded once free men from their old condition and in spite of challenge after challenge were consistent in their reinterpretation of villeinage as if it were serfdom. It may also be suspected that in a way, tenants were hoist with their own petard. In the economic conditions of the twelfth century,[40] they had preferred to pay a money rent rather than to do labour services. They regarded money rent tenure as "more free" than tenure by customary services, even though customary tenure was not thought of as servile. But when the onslaught came, they accepted the lords' battleground. They did not argue that the doing of labour services did not imply unfreedom, although later surveys often show free tenants performing services (never, however, very heavy ones). A Norfolk case of 1225 is a rare example of an admission by tenants that they owed such services but were nevertheless free. It arose, as in so many cases, from a complaint by a tenant, Geoffrey Thweit, and other tenants of Norwich cathedral priory that the prior had distrained their beasts in

[38] *Cur. Reg. Rolls*, v, pp. 94-5 (1207).
[39] *Cur. Reg. Rolls*, ii, pp. 13-14 (1201).
[40] M. M. Postan, "The Chronology of Labour Services", *Trans. Roy. Hist. Soc.*, 4th ser., xx (1937).

order to exact extra services.   They did admit ploughing and harvest boons in addition to money rent.   The court supported the prior in his claim for extra service, and in his assertion that they were villeins, not free tenants.[41]

There is no way of judging whether the villeins fought court actions for freedom at the same rate throughout the century without an extensive study of all the royal court records as well as those of manorial courts.   Some samples from the later thirteenth and fourteenth centuries have already been cited, and give the impression that conflict continued, more intensely at times (for instance the 1270s) than at others.   But however vigorously tenants might resist attempts to worsen conditions of tenure or assert their right to buy and sell land without licence, the battle had, in a sense, been lost by the middle of the thirteenth century.   That is, villeinage was now generally accepted as virtually equivalent to serfdom or naifty.   It may be that this is partly the explanation for the apparently novel appearance of many cases whereby tenants sought to claim the privileges, analogous to those of free tenure, of the ancient demesne of the crown.   These were rarely successful, for ancient demesne privileges were by no means elaborated for the benefit of tenants.   In face of villein rebels, whether claiming freedom or the privilege of ancient demesne, the law had by now been solidly built from many precedents, as the canon of Leicester Abbey commented in the 1270s on a recent failure:

> He shall be pure serf, deprived of freedom.
> The law's judgement and the king's court prove this.
> In the king's court usage still leads the law.[42]

NOTE, 1976

J. Scammell, in "Freedom and marriage in medieval England", *Econ. Hist. Rev.*, 2nd ser., xxvii (1974), p. 531, quotes examples of merchet in Domesday Book.   In this article, the author is attempting to throw doubt on my argument that hitherto free villeinage was being defined as servile from the late twelfth century, by arguing that marriage

---

[41] *Cur. Reg. Rolls*, xii, nos. 457, 1020 (1225).

[42] R. H. Hilton, "Peasant Movements before 1381", *Econ. Hist. Rev.*, 2nd ser., ii (1949-50); *Leger Book of Stoneleigh Abbey* (Dugdale Soc., xxiv, 1960), pp. xxiv-xxviii.   The concluding quotation is translated from my article "A Thirteenth-Century Poem on Disputed Villein Services", *Eng. Hist. Rev.*, lvi (1941), pp. 90-97, and is at p. 97; in the original it runs:

> Purus servus erit et libertate carebit.
> Judicium legis probat hoc et curia regis.
> Uncore a la curt le rey, usum menie la ley.

fines (merchet) were a dignified replacement for the degrading leyrwites imposed on slaves in the pre-conquest period. Apart from the apparent difficulty of finding references to leyrwite in pre-conquest documents, the author seems unaware of the significance of leyrwite in the thirteenth century manor. P. Vinogradoff was right in seeing the payments as alternatives (*Villainage in England* (Oxford, 1892), p. 154) but had no idea how widespread and lacking in social stigma pregnancy out of wedlock could be. For example, there were 117 leyrwite payments for pregnancy out of wedlock to 220 merchet payments on the large Worcestershire manor of Halesowen between 1270 and 1348 (Z. Razi, *The Population of Halesowen 1270-1400*, University of Birmingham Ph.D. thesis, 1976). The solution to the problem of leyrwite will be found at the intersection of demographic history with that of lord-peasant relationships and this requires a good deal more evidence than Mrs. Scammell has been able to find.

8. *A Redistribution of Incomes in Fifteenth-Century England?*[1]

CHRISTOPHER DYER

THIS CONTRIBUTION TO THE DEBATE ON THE LATE MEDIEVAL ECONOMY is concerned with the relationship between a lord and his tenants, and will suggest, in a tentative way, one of the factors that led to social and agrarian changes in the fifteenth century. Recent additions to the controversy have continued to base their arguments on studies of fluctuations in urban development and international trade.[2] This is understandable, because series of municipal and government archives lend themselves to statistical treatment. But the economy of western Europe throughout the middle ages was predominantly rural, based not on large scale commodity production, but on peasant agriculture, of which only part of the produce would be sold, and then mainly in local markets. The importance of trade and industry, particularly in the Low Countries and northern Italy, cannot be discounted, but for much of Europe, including England, growth and recession of trade indicates changes in only a small and unrepresentative sector of the economy. A. R. Bridbury's refreshing revision of the English evidence can be criticized on the same grounds, but he does admit the omission, pleading a lack of sources for the activities of the productive element in late medieval rural society, the peasants and the demesne farmers.[3] The same lack of documentation restricts our knowledge of the peasants before the leasing of the demesnes, and the result has been that English work on medieval agrarian history has been bedevilled by an uncritical use of the abundant archives of the great landed estates. As Edward Miller has shown, this obsession with seigneurial agriculture and revenues resulted in a fundamental misreading of economic and social development in the thirteenth century.[4] The crude equation between the level of seigneurial incomes and economic "growth" and "decline" has now been discounted. The documents of the great ecclesiastical estates are still a valuable source, and it is surprising that studies of them tend to stop

---

[1] I am indebted to Professor R. H. Hilton, who encouraged the writing of this article.
[2] E.g. R. S. Lopez and H. A. Mimiskin, "The Economic Depression of the Renaissance", *Econ. Hist. Rev.*, 2nd ser., xiv (1961-2), pp. 408-26.
[3] A. R. Bridbury, *Economic Growth. England in the Later Middle Ages* (London, 1962), especially ch. vi.
[4] Edward Miller, "The English Economy in the Thirteenth Century", *Past and Present*, no. 28 (July, 1964), pp. 21-40.

short with the leasing of the demesnes, normally in the late fourteenth century.[5] After leasing, the basic source material, manorial accounts, become less informative and "fossilized", with some sections being copied from year to year, sometimes for a century or more.[6] It will be seen, however, that some information can be obtained from fifteenth-century manorial accounts, particularly when they are used in conjunction with central administrative documents, and that they contain evidence of movements among the peasantry, as well as material for an examination of the lord's income.

Recent research into the late thirteenth century has revealed a crisis situation among the peasantry — population pressure was so great that the size of holdings was severely restricted, preventing the balanced relationship between arable and pasture that would allow a measure of agricultural efficiency.[7] The result was that bad harvests were usually followed by an increased death-rate, especially among the middling and lesser peasants.[8] It is difficult to exaggerate the important rôle played by rents, taxes, and other exactions in precipitating and exacerbating this crisis, and estimates of the budget of thirteenth-century peasants show that seigneurial rent, levied in many varied forms, combined with royal taxes and ecclesiastical dues, absorbed most of the peasant's meagre surplus.[9] This applies in particular to the majority, those with holdings of fifteen acres (half-yardland) or less.

The declining population of the fourteenth century relaxed the demographic tensions which restricted the size of holdings, but rent and other seigneurial exactions remained, and continued to divert at least part of surplus production from the hands of the tenants. By 1400 rents were paid almost entirely in cash, but the low cereal prices of the period made it difficult for the peasantry to obtain large amounts of money on the market. The chronic problem of all peasant societies

[5] A notable recent exception is F. R. H. Du Boulay, *The Lordship of Canterbury* (London, 1966).

[6] For strong criticism of these accounts, see E. M. Carus-Wilson, "Evidences of Industrial Growth on some Fifteenth-Century Manors", *Econ. Hist. Rev.*, 2nd ser., xii (1959-60), pp. 196-7.

[7] J. Z. Titow, "Some Evidence of the Thirteenth Century Population Increase", *Econ. Hist. Rev.*, 2nd ser., xiv (1961-2), pp. 218-23; H. E. Hallam, "Population Density in the Medieval Fenland", *ibid.*, pp. 71-81; M. M. Postan, "Village Livestock in the Thirteenth Century", *Econ. Hist. Rev.*, 2nd ser., xv (1962-3), pp. 219-49.

[8] M. M. Postan and J. Z. Titow, "Heriots and Prices on Winchester Manors", *Econ. Hist. Rev.*, 2nd ser., xi (1958-9), pp. 392-411.

[9] E. A. Kosminsky, *Studies in the Agrarian History of England in the Thirteenth Century* (Oxford, 1956), pp. 230-42; R. H. Hilton, *A Medieval Society* (London, 1966), pp. 122-3.

is the shortage of capital, and a prerequisite for the development of large holdings and efficient agriculture is the growth of facilities for capital accumulation.[10] Seen in this light, any change in the level of rent must be a matter of profound significance in the social and economic history of the later middle ages.[11]

What factors determined the level of rent? It is often implied that the laws of supply and demand operated in the middle ages, and that just as rents were high during the population growth of the thirteenth century, so they fell as the population declined. The level of rent was determined by the lord's powers of non-economic compulsion, as well as the supply and demand situation. The bargaining position of the peasants was greatly improved by the low population of the later middle ages, and reductions in rent were partly the result of peasant resistance which successfully countered the coercive power of the lords. Thus the peasantry did not passively wait for the lord to reduce rents when he realized that the demographic situation made a low rent necessary — the events of 1381 show that passivity was not the predominant characteristic of the peasants. There is evidence that the tenants of some estates actively resisted payment of certain rents, and by means of rent-strikes were able to prevent the appropriation of part of their surplus.[12]

* * * *

As is so often the case, we must rely on the archives of an ecclesiastical estate to provide such evidence, and the estate of the bishopric of Worcester is particularly well provided with fifteenth-century documents.[13] No estate is "typical", but there are many similarities between this estate and those of the other great ecclesiastics, both bishops and the regular clergy, particularly in southern England, in terms of administration and social structure. The lands of the bishop of Worcester had been acquired in the seventh and eighth centuries, and from the tenth to the sixteenth century the bishop drew most of his revenues from seventeen manors, all of which were

---

[10] R. H. Hilton, "Rent and Capital Formation in Feudal Society", *Second International Conference of Economic History 1962* (Paris, 1965), pp. 33-68.

[11] E. A. Kosminsky, "The Evolution of Feudal Rent in England", *Past and Present*, no. 7 (Apr., 1955), pp. 12-34; and E. A. Kosminsky, *op. cit.*, ch. vii.

[12] This suggestion was first made in R. H. Hilton, "Kibworth Harcourt", in W. G. Hoskins (ed.), *Studies in Leicestershire Agrarian History* (Leicester, 1949), pp. 39-40.

[13] The collection is now at the Worcester County Record Office. All references below to these will be to W.R.O.

situated in the three west midland counties of Worcestershire, Gloucestershire, and Warwickshire.[14]   Thus the estate belonged to a region which had some social and geographical coherence, but the manors were widely scattered over different terrains, from the wooded clay plain of north Worcestershire, through the fertile river valleys of the Avon and Severn, to the limestone uplands of the Cotswold Hills.[15]   The thirteenth-century surveys incorporated in the *Red Book of Worcester* show that, in spite of local differences, the manors belonged to the type normally found on large estates; most had demesnes with between 200 and 500 acres of arable, with large numbers of rent-paying tenants, of which there were about 1,800 listed for the whole estate in 1299.[16]   The characteristic Worcester tenant of the late thirteenth century was a half-yardlander who owed high rents, including heavy labour services.   It is impossible to make a precise estimate of the bishop's revenue at the end of the thirteenth century.   At the end of the vacancy of 1302-3 the royal escheator owed £903, but this seems too low a figure for annual revenue in view of the total in the Valor of 1299 — £1,192.[17]

Rent always figured prominently in the bishop's finances, even at the height of demesne cultivation, for during the vacancy of 1302-3 more than a third of the money accounted for came from assize rents alone, and if all forms of rent, including commuted labour services and perquisites of courts are added, the proportion is nearer to two thirds.[18]   In the late fourteenth century the bishop abandoned direct cultivation of his demesnes, leasing them at first for short terms, but during the fifteenth century the leases lengthened, often to forty years or more.[19]   Until the 1450s sheep were retained under the control of a sheep-reeve, and even after this date hay was mown on some manors to supply the household, but in the fifteenth century the bishop's income was derived overwhelmingly from rents and farms.

The documents associated with the collection of rents on the bishopric estate are formidable in their bulk.   The central administra-

---

[14] Hemingus, *Chartularium Ecclesiae Wigorniensis*, ed. T. Hearne (Oxford, 1723), *passim*.

[15] Hilton, *A Medieval Society*, ch. i.

[16] *The Red Book of Worcester*, i-iv, ed. M. Hollings (Worcestershire Hist. Soc., 1934-50); hereafter referred to as *R.B.W.*

[17] *R.B.W.*, iv, pp. 546, 401.   All figures are given to the nearest pound, unless more detail is necessary.

[18] *Ibid.*, iv, pp. 498-547.

[19] A similar situation is described in E. M. Halcrow, "The Decline of Demesne Farming on the Estates of Durham Cathedral Priory", *Econ. Hist. Rev.*, 2nd ser., vii (1954-5), *passim*.

tive material, receiver's accounts, valors, and arrears rolls, all drew information from the accounts of individual manors, which survive in hundreds.   The form of the manorial account was established in the thirteenth century, and the accounting system has been described in many works on medieval administration and agriculture.[20]   It will be sufficient to recall here that the main object was to establish the liability of the estate officials, rather than to calculate profit and loss. If the form of the account was standardized in the thirteenth century, the contents were stereotyped in the fifteenth — they record the names of long-dead lessees, and calculate with elaborate detail theoretical totals of rent in the receipts section, only to subtract them as expenses.[21]   However, some parts of the accounts are not "fossilized".   Each year a total is given for cash delivered to the receiver (*liberationes denariorum*) and this was not copied from one account to another.   These totals were extracted and used to compile the receiver's account for the whole estate, which thus includes all cash payments to the receiver.

The manorial account includes arrears of previous years in the receipts section and cash payments to the receiver in the expenses, so that the balance represents the total owing to the lord from his officials.   The first figure of money owing was subject to various alterations, "allowances" and "respites", and after these deductions, a final figure of debt was established.   A good example is the account for the manor of Bredon of 1455-6.[22]   In that year the receipts and arrears totalled £164 9s. 5d. and expenses and cash liveries £75 6s. 2d., leaving a balance of £89 3s. 3d.   A few shillings were allowed "*per considerationem*" of the auditor, reducing the figure to £88 10s. 11d. The respites (*respecta*), uncollectable rents that had lapsed since the compilation of the last rental, were also deducted, leaving £86 14s. 1d. This final figure of debt, made up of arrears of the previous twelve years, was broken up into fourteen separate items, most of them representing the individual debts of former reeves, two of whom owed more than £20.   The items of debt were copied into arrears rolls for the whole estate, just as cash liveries were incorporated in the receiver's accounts.   The figures quoted above illustrate the scale of

[20] A. E. Levett, "The Financial Organisation of the Manor", *Studies in Manorial History* (Oxford, 1938); N. Denholm-Young, *Seignorial Administration in England* (Oxford, 1937), ch. iv.   A new aspect of accounting procedure is revealed by E. Stone, "Profit and Loss Accountancy at Norwich Cathedral Priory", *Trans. Roy. Hist. Soc.*, 5th ser., xii (1962), *passim*.

[21] For a critique of fifteenth-century accounts, *Ministers' Accounts of the Warwickshire Estates of the Duke of Clarence 1479-80*, ed. R. H. Hilton (Dugdale Soc., xxi, 1952) introduction.

[22] W.R.O. ref. 009: 1. B.A. 2636/157. no. 92012.7/8.

the arrears problem on one manor. What then was the total of arrears for the whole estate, and how did they affect the bishop's income ?

The accounts of the receiver, which begin in 1433, are not usually a reliable guide to the total income of the bishopric, although most, perhaps 90%, of the revenues passed through his hands as the bishop's chief financial official. Part of each year's income was delivered direct to the "lord's own hands", or to his creditors, and some allowance must be made for hay and other produce sent to the household. The only sources which include these "concealed" payments are the valors, of which five survive from the period 1454-66, and they suggest that the annual income was between £950 and £1,000.[23] However, the receiver's accounts of the early sixteenth century are a guide to total revenue, even in the absence of valors. Between 1497 and 1535 the bishops were Italians, notably Silvestro de' Gigli (1498-1521), who spent most of their time abroad, leaving the receiver to collect all revenues.[24] Total revenue in the period 1498-1510 varied between £948 and £1,017, suggesting that the income of the bishopric was fairly static between the mid-fifteenth and early sixteenth centuries.[25]

It was quite normal in the middle ages to pay large sums in instalments, so that it is not surprising to find that only part of each year's revenue came from rents and farms paid during that year.[26] The valors distinguish between payments made "this year" and those made "from arrears", so that in 1466, when the bishop's income was £990, the valor shows that £664 came from the year 1465-6, but £326 was paid from the arrears of previous years — the other valors confirm that in the mid-fifteenth century about one third of payments came from former years.[27] An analysis of the receiver's account for 1467-8 shows that more than £200 was paid from arrears, but most of this sum consisted of delayed payments from the year previous to that covered by the account, and only £20 came in the form of many small sums derived from the income of the period 1449-66.[28] This implies that, although it was a common habit of manorial officials and farmers

[23] W.R.O. ref. 009: 1. B.A. 2636/175. no. 92477 (1454);/175. nos. 92479, 92481 (1457);/174. nos. 92472, 92470.1/6; /191. no. 92625.4/12 (1465);/176. no. 92486 (1466).

[24] For the activities of Gigli, which possibly included the poisoning of Cardinal Bainbridge, see D. S. Chambers, *Cardinal Bainbridge in the Court of Rome* (Oxford, 1965), pp. 7-10, 42-3, 134-40, 145-50.

[25] W.R.O. ref. 009: 1. B.A. 2636/191, 192.

[26] M. M. Postan, "Credit in Medieval Trade", *Econ. Hist. Rev.* i (1928), *passim.*

[27] W.R.O. ref. 009: 1. B.A. 2636/176. no. 92486.

[28] W.R.O. ref. 009: 1. B.A. 2636/176. no. 92487.

to spread cash liveries over two years, after that time had elapsed payment was sporadic and the bishop was unlikely to receive any more money from them. Thus a distinction must be made between "temporary" arrears, or money in transit from the local officials to the central administration, and "permanent" arrears — sums due to the lord which, after a delay of two or three years, were often never paid.

The valors show that each year the manorial officials were owing arrears for a sum that varied between £286 and £441; total arrears, from the current and previous years, reached impressive heights in the mid-fifteenth century, the highest recorded being £1,499 in 1460.[29] These figures include both temporary and permanent arrears, but it is difficult to be certain of the exact proportion of each. The individual debts were reduced in various ways. They could, of course, be paid off, but this does not seem to have happened with the backlog of permanent arrears. On the death or translation of each bishop, arrears were in effect written off, as they were deemed to belong to the former bishop, and it seems unlikely that the executors of the dead bishop, or a bishop operating from another diocese, would be any more successful in collecting debts than the permanent estate administration. Some officials fled, like James Knolles, bailiff of Oswaldslow hundred, who "left the area" (recessit extra patriam) owing £6 12s. 4d. in 1465.[30] Debts that were "despaired of" would be allowed or pardoned, and if they were thus written off they must represent hard core arrears for which there was no hope of recovery. In the five valors a total of £388 was pardoned, particularly during the later years of the long episcopate of John Carpenter (1444-76), when arrears mounted and it became normal to pardon £60-£150 each year.

The arrears problem seems to have been a development of the fifteenth century. J. S. Drew, in a valuable study of accounting procedure at St. Swithun's Priory, Winchester, has shown that throughout the fourteenth century debts were not allowed to accumulate, either because the priory remitted arrears, or, more often, because reeves and other officials paid off the sum owing.[31] A comparable situation seems to have existed on the Worcester estate in the late fourteenth century, for individual debts rarely exceeded £20. The episcopate of Henry Wakefield (1375-95) was long enough for large amounts of debt to build up, but the arrears total for 1389, his fourteenth year, was £465; this should be compared with

[29] W.R.O. ref. 009: 1. B.A. 2636/191. no. 92625.2/12.
[30] W.R.O. ref. 009: 1. B.A. 2636/191. no. 92625.4/12.
[31] J. S. Drew, "Manorial Accounts of St. Swithun's Priory, Winchester", Eng. Hist. Rev., lxii (1947), passim.

the total for the tenth year of Carpenter (1454) which was £1,194.[32] On the Duchy of Lancaster estate, though arrears were apparently causing concern in the fourteenth century, they were treated as a serious problem during the reigns of Henry VI and Edward IV.[33]

Arrears were not the result of a loss of rent from vacant tenements or "official" reductions in rent. There was a serious decline in the number of tenants on the estate in the later middle ages, culminating in the total desertion of a number of villages, and rents were also reduced; but these changes would be allowed for in the manorial accounts. Arrears represent a blockage in the flow of money from the tenants to the lord, and this might occur either at the level of the rent-paying tenants, or while the money was passing through the hands of the estate officials. The position of the reeves, rent-collectors and beadles was highly ambivalent, for they were ordinary tenants for most of their lives, but were expected to look after the interests of the lord when elected or appointed. It can be argued that little of the lord's revenues stuck to the fingers of his officials, because some tenants showed themselves reluctant to shoulder the burdens of office, like Thomas Hedley of Hanbury, who took a holding in April 1429, agreeing to hold it "according to the custom of the manor" except that "the steward granted that he will not be rent-collector".[34] The administrative personnel usually changed from year to year, so that on the manor of Stoke Bishop, fourteen different reeves served in the seventeen years between 1443 and 1460.[35] This could mean that collection of rents was so difficult and exacting that no-one was willing to serve for more than a year or two, or that there was some kind of agreement within the village to share the office on a rota system so that no individual could keep the profits for himself for a long period.[36] Legal sanctions had been devised and used from the thirteenth century for claiming debts from recalcitrant officials, but there is no evidence for their use on the bishop of Worcester's estate.[37]

Failure to collect money by either manorial or estate officials could be blamed on laxity or incompetence, but the mass of surviving

---

[32] W.R.O. ref. 009: 1. B.A. 2636/193. no. 92628.4/9; /175. no. 92477.

[33] R. Somerville, *History of the Duchy of Lancaster*, 2 vols. (London, 1953), i, pp. 109-10, 216-7, 248-9.

[34] W.R.O. ref. 009: 1. B.A. 2636/166. no. 92269.

[35] W.R.O. ref. 009: 1. B.A. 2636/171.

[36] H. S. Bennett, "The Reeve and the Manor in the Fourteenth Century", *Eng. Hist. Rev.*, xli (1926) suggests that some reeves kept the post for many years, presumably because it was profitable; but some reeves may have been compelled to remain in office by either the lord or the electors.

[37] N. Denholm-Young, *op. cit.*, pp. 151-61.

documents, representing a mere fraction of the total output of the estate bureaucracy, suggests an excess of administrative zeal.[38]

The high totals of arrears in the fifteenth century cannot be attributed to any single cause. Some of the total resulted from corruption or carelessness, but a proportion of these sums stemmed from a refusal to pay rent at the base of the whole administrative edifice — the peasants and demesne farmers.

*   *   *   *

During the vacancy of the see of Worcester between August, 1433 and April, 1435, the temporalities escheated to the crown in the normal way, and the estates were administered by five keepers, all of them local gentry. These men had between them legal training, administrative experience of the bishopric estate, and personal knowledge of the problems of agriculture and rent payment on their own local lands.[39] They were unable to pay to the Exchequer the full amount that was due, and at the end of the vacancy they drew up a list of petitions so that they could be released from their "burden".[40] The items include administrative costs, such as the keepers' own pay "for diligent labour", and the loss of some revenues that had been squandered by the previous bishop, Thomas Polton.[41]

The first item in the petition was a large sum of £38 4s. od., for the recognition (*recognitio*) that was due to each new lord of the estate, whether bishop or king, at his first arrival (*in primo adventu*). A slightly greater amount, £40 3s. 8d., had been levied during the vacancy of 1302-3.[42] This sum was assessed, not on individuals, but on the customary tenants of each manor collectively, rather in the way that subsidies were levied in 1334 and after. The round sum due from each manor varied approximately with population, most manors paying £1 or more, increasing to £10 for the populous manor of Henbury and Stoke Bishop. The recognition was not a negligible burden, for if each tenant paid equally, his contribution would be at

---

[38] Arrears are attributed to carelessness in J. Rosenthal, "The Estates and Finances of Richard, Duke of York (1411-1460)", *Studies in Medieval and Renaissance History*, ii (1965), p. 145.

[39] The keepers were William Pillesdon, John Throckmorton, John Wode, William Wollashull, and John Vampage. All served as M.P.s, justices, etc.; Wode was *custos rotulorum*, and Vampage served as Attorney-General. All were steward, receiver or auditor at some time on the bishopric estate. All except Pillesdon held land in south or west Worcestershire.

[40] W.R.O. ref. 009: I. B.A. 2636/174. nos. 92465, 92471.

[41] Expenses of this type totalled £116 9s. 3d. — the largest sum involved.

[42] *R.B.W.*, iv, pp. 498-547.

least a shilling.[43]   However, not a single tenant paid so much as a penny.

The keepers prepared two versions of the list of petitions, and in these they offered three explanations for non-payment.   The first version, perhaps the most accurate, provided a simple excuse:—

"... the customary tenants ... would surrender their holdings into the hands of the same king if the said recognition or any part of the same was levied from the same customary tenants ...".[44]

But this explanation was crossed out, and a subtly different one substituted:—

"... the customary tenants of the aforesaid manors were at the time of the vacancy ... in such great poverty that if these recognitions were levied from them they would leave the lands, holdings and tenures of the aforesaid lordships vacant, to the great prejudice of the lord king and the final destruction of the aforesaid manors".[45]

The introduction of poverty was evidently insufficiently convincing, because another alteration appears in the final version:—

"... there were many plagues in the aforesaid lordships ... so that the greater part of the aforesaid tenants died ... and there is such great poverty that if the recognition was raised from them they would leave the lands, holdings and tenures of the lordships vacant ...".[46]

All three versions agree on one point — the population of the area was sufficiently reduced by the 1430s to make effective the threat of a mass exodus of tenants in the event of unpopular exactions by the lord.   It was considered preferable to have a depleted tenant population paying part of their rents, than to have no tenants at all.

How much trust can be put in these complaints?   The fifteenth century produced many wails of poverty and promises of disaster, and this example could be dismissed as a mere excuse for administrative

[43] This figure is based on an estimate of the total of customary tenants in the early fifteenth century, *c.* 800.

[44] "... quod dicti custumarii tenentes ... predicta tenementa in manu eiusdem regis dicti custodia sursum reddere voluissent si dicta recognitio aut aliqua parcella eiusdem de eisdem custumariis aut de aliquis eorum levata fuisset". (W.R.O. ref. 009: I. B.A. 2636/174. no. 92471.)

[45] "... quod tenentes maneriorum predictorum custumarii fuerunt tempore vacationis temporalium episcopatus predicti in tali grandi paupertate quod si he recognitiones de eis levari debuissent terras tenementa et tenuras dominiorum predictorum vacuas amisisse voluissent in magnum prejudicium domini Regis et finalem destructionem maneriorum predictorum". (*ibid.*)

[46] "... quod plures pestilentia fuerunt infra dominia predicta ita quod maior pars tenentium predictorum moriebatur et ita grandi paupertate existentes quod si haec recognitio de eis levari debuisset terras tenementa et tenuras dominiorum vacuas amisisse voluissent in magnum prejudicium domini Regis". (W.R.O. ref. 009: I. B.A. 2636/174. no. 92465.)

failure. However, the keepers were insistent on the dangers of peasant migration, a social phenomenon of the later middle ages for which there is considerable evidence. The reality of the danger of "final destruction" for some manors is attested by the number of deserted villages, particularly in the west midlands.[47] Poverty and disease were introduced as additional factors, presumably because reports of a rent-strike would not satisfy the Exchequer, but they are worth considering as explanations.

It is not yet possible to state any but the most cautious conclusions about the standard of living of fifteenth-century peasants. Many of the Worcester tenants were poor, and it is common to find in the court rolls cases of a peasant surrendering a holding and paying no heriot "because he is poor". On the other hand, at least a minority of the peasant population were not in such difficulties. A good example is Thomas Harryes, a villein of Lincombe near Hartlebury, whose death was recorded in the court roll of April 1429; he had held a messuage, a toft, two yardlands, and a parcel of meadow, implying a total area of more than 60 acres, and his heriots were a horse and two oxen.[48] It could be argued that "poverty", in the context of rent payment, means a shortage of cash rather than land or agricultural produce, but pleas of debt entered in the court rolls indicate a considerable volume of money circulating in the form of loans within the peasant community. Normally only small sums were involved, a few shillings or even pence, but inter-peasant debts of 15s., 16s. 8d. and 23s. 4d. are recorded at Kempsey in the 1440s.[49] We can be certain that among those who refused to pay the recognition of 1433 there were tenants with more than adequate material resources, in terms of land, stock, and money.

Chroniclers confirm the keepers of the Worcester temporalities in reporting plague in the year 1434, but the absence of court rolls during the vacancy prevents us from checking for a high death rate during that year. It seems inherently unlikely that the epidemic was so severe as to prevent payment of rents by the survivors.[50]

In the same document an even larger sum, £46 9s. 4¾d., was not levied, and this is important because it consists of the arrears of

[47] For deserted villages in Gloucestershire and Warwickshire see M. W. Beresford, *The Lost Villages of England* (London, 1963), pp. 351, 388; and for a deserted village on the bishopric estate R. H. Hilton and P. A. Rahtz, "Upton, Gloucestershire, 1959-1964", *Trans. Bristol and Glouc. Arch. Soc.*, lxxxv (1966).

[48] W.R.O. ref. 009: 1. B.A. 2636/169. no. 92372.

[49] W.R.O. ref. 705: 4. B.A. 54. October 1440 and January 1446.

[50] J. M. W. Bean, "Plague, Population, and Economic Decline in the Later Middle Ages", *Econ. Hist. Rev.*, 2nd ser., xv (1962-3), pp. 435-6.

various manorial officials, the reeves, beadles, rent-collectors, and bailiffs of a number of manors. The keepers explained the situation on the manors of Blockley and Wick Episcopi:

". . . nor can they be levied at present for all the tenants of the said manors from which the said arrears ought to be levied would leave the aforesaid manors immediately after such a decision".[51]

Here is direct evidence that some of the arrears of manorial officials included rents that had never been collected from the tenants, for attempts to levy the arrears would have the same effect as the collection of the recognition, and would involve "all the tenants", not just the officials themselves.

The petitions of 1435 thus illustrate two different manifestations of the peasant rent-strike: the concerted non-payment of selected dues, such as the recognition, and the less easily noticed refusal of other rents, which appear as arrears charged to manorial officials. Having dealt with these extraordinary documents, with their full and direct explanations, we must pass to the evidence of the more normal products of estate administration, manorial accounts, arrears rolls, and valors.

$$* \quad * \quad * \quad *$$

"Selective" refusals, usually involving a whole village or manorial community, were not very numerous, but were often treated separately in lists of debts. The recognition that was due on the accession of John Carpenter in 1444, met with the same opposition as that of 1433. It was still unpaid in 1460, and all hope of levying it was abandoned soon afterwards.[52] Common fines (known in English as head money) were associated with the lord's judicial franchise — his right to hold the view of frank-pledge — and they were entered on the court rolls.[53] Like the recognition, the fine was a round figure, usually a few shillings, assessed collectively on each tithing, and could be quite lucrative, for the fines of the whole estate totalled £17 in 1302-3.[54] The formula used in the lists of arrears is unequivocal: "because the tenants refuse to pay" (*quia tenentes negant solvere*). The villages that refused these fines were Bredon (9s. 4d.), Bibury (6s.), Throckmorton in Fladbury (3s.) and Southam and Brockhampton in Bishop's Cleeve (4s.), and all of them were consistent

[51] W.R.O. ref. 009: 1. B.A. 2636/174. no. 92465.
[52] The recognition appears in the arrears roll of 1460, W.R.O. ref. 009: 1. B.A. 2636/191. no. 92625.2/12, but not in that of 1462, *ibid.* /176. no. 92488.
[53] N. Neilson, *Customary Rents* (Oxford Studies in Social and Legal History, ii, Oxford, 1910), pp. 166-72.
[54] *R.B.W.*, iv, pp. 498-547.

opponents of paying fines in the third quarter of the fifteenth century.[55] The last two cases were the result of local lords, the Throckmortons of Throckmorton and the Botelers of Southam and Brockhampton, interfering with payments to the bishop by their tenants, who owed suit at the bishop's view of frank-pledge.[56] Conflicts between lords were certainly not a development of the later middle ages, but such quarrels may have intensified as seigneurial revenues declined.[57] At the manor of Withington the tenants refused to pay an annual tallage of 26s. 8d. from 1444 onwards, and at Tredington another collective charge, woodsilver, worth 5s. 4½d. *per annum* was also unpaid.[58] Some of these dues were very ancient: churchscot is first mentioned in charters of the ninth century, but the vills of Winson in Bibury (1s. 8d.) and Tidmington in Tredington (2s. 6d.) refused to pay. There can be no question in this example, as there could be in the case of recognition or tallage, of the long village memory perpetuating for generations a grievance against new impositions.[59]

We can discern something of the rationale behind the tenants' obvious dislike of these dues, for none of them were rents paid directly in return for land. Recognition and tallage were paid as an acknowledgement of the bishop's "lordship", the common fine was an admission of the lord's right to exercise franchisal jurisdiction, churchscot was an archaic ecclesiastical tax, and woodsilver was a payment for the use of the lord's timber, which the tenants probably considered to be part of their common rights.

The attitude of the tenants can be seen more clearly in a document of about 1450, the record of an enquiry conducted by, or at the behest of, the lord's council, into means of improving the revenues of the bishopric.[60] It is a remarkable testimony to the differences between the situation "of old" (*ex antiquo*) (the halcyon days of the thirteenth-century surveys when the bishop's income was high and the peasants knew their place), and "today" (*de modernis*). The struggles between the bishop and the lords of neighbouring manors figure prominently, but much of the inquisition was devoted to the problems of enforcing

---

[55] W.R.O. ref. 009: 1. B.A. 2636/176. no. 92488, *et al.*

[56] Throckmorton *infra*; Southam, W.R.O. ref. 009: 1. B.A. 2636/174. no. 92470.6/6.

[57] M. M. Postan, "The Fifteenth Century", *Econ. Hist. Rev.*, ix (1938-9), pp. 166-7.

[58] W.R.O. ref. 009: 1. B.A. 2636/193. no. 92627.10/12. For woodsilver see Neilson, *op. cit.*, pp. 51-3.

[59] W.R.O. ref. 009: 1. B.A. 2636/176. no. 92488. See also Neilson, *op. cit.*, pp. 193-6.

[60] W.R.O. ref. 009: 1. B.A. 2636/193. no. 92627.10/12.

rent payment. At Withington, for example, the tenants excused their failure to pay tallage "because they claim that they were released from the same by the lord's predecessors". The enquiry revealed a rather different attitude at Bredon. There the council recalled that in 1389 a declaration of custom had been made. It stated that the tenants of Bredon, Norton, and Hardwick should perform some light labour services, or pay commutation of them; these consisted of a few haymaking works, bedrips, ploughing and carrying services, and, for the tenants of Norton only, a service known earthily as "Shyttingeshep", but by 1450 "they do not now do the service". When the tenants were consulted, they gave a forthright reply — "they refuse the customs" (*negant consuetudines*). The commuted works which the bishop lost were worth 19s. 7d. per annum. This is the best example of refusals to pay commuted labour services, but there were other cases, notably at Bibury, where they were valued at 3s. 4d.[61]

The same inquisition indicates a similarity of aims between the village communities and some individuals. Labour services and tallage were directly associated with servile status, and were used as evidence to determine cases "*de villenagio*" that appeared before the royal courts in the thirteenth and early fourteenth centuries.[62] It is not generally realized that long after 1381, when the abolition of villeinage was included in the peasant demands, some villeins continued to protest against the social stigma and economic disabilities of unfree tenure. On the manors of Northwick and Wick Episcopi we find that:—

". . . tenants remain within the said lordship who say that they are free, who are villeins by blood, and this was legally proved in court before the steward by twelve villeins elected and sworn for this . . . naming and affirming the villeins of both lordships".[63]

The old tests for villeinage were still used in another case, involving William Boys of Wick Episcopi, who left the manor and denied "his villeinage" (*nativitatem suam*). The lord was able to demonstrate that Boys had served as reeve and beadle of the manor (both offices being occupied by villeins) "without any protest". His brother, who continued to live on the same manor, admitted his own servile status. The evidence used in this case could have come from Bracton's *Notebook* or other legal documents of the thirteenth century.

[61] W.R.O. ref. 009: 1. B.A. 2636/176. no. 92488 *et al.*
[62] R. H. Hilton, "Peasant Movements in England before 1381", *Econ. Hist. Rev.*, 2nd ser., ii (1949-50), p. 124.
[63] W.R.O. ref. 009: 1. B.A. 2636/193. no. 92627.10/12.

Customary holdings carried a higher burden of rent, and some tenants refused to pay such rents, in addition to those who claimed personal freedom. A tenant of Hampton Lucy, Richard Smyth, held land "which William Faber and Robert Faber once held in the Red Book for certain services, works, and customs". The rent was 10s. 3d. in 1299. "Now Richard Smyth claims to hold it freely for a rent of 4s. 10½d.".

"Pleas and perquisites of courts" were a valuable source of income to the bishop, the mid fifteenth-century valors giving figures that fluctuate between £38 and £64 *per annum*. The sums paid by the tenants to the court can be regarded as a form of rent, which was levied in various ways, from amercements imposed on erring tenants, and penalties to ensure that the orders of the court were obeyed, to taxes on land transfers, such as heriots, entry fines, and reliefs. Most court rolls have each amercement, penalty and due recorded faithfully, but often in the fifteenth century there is a blank where the total of perquisites should be entered. Our suspicion is aroused by the blatant refusal of some tenants to obey the orders of the court, as in the case of Richard Rook of Kempsey, who agreed to build a house of three bays on his holding in 1426. The case was brought up in 1432, and again in 1440, but even after fourteen years the house had not been built.[64]

Arrears rolls contain occasional references to amercements which a reeve or beadle should have collected, but had not paid to the lord "because it cannot be levied" (*quia levari non potest*), and the late fifteenth-century account rolls often include among their expenses "unleviable amercements" (*amerciamenta illevabile*). These are usually small sums, only three or four shillings at Henbury-in-Salt-Marsh, where court revenues often exceeded ten pounds, and they would lead us to suppose that only a small proportion of court revenue was uncollectable, and that, as the normal amercement was 4d., only a dozen or less tenants refused to pay.

These figures are misleading, as they probably represent those amercements which the steward realized at once would never be collected, as when magnates like the earl of Warwick, who held land on some of the bishopric manors, were "in mercy" for failing to attend the court. The chance survival of some pieces of parchment attached to the head of the Bredon account for 1455-6 clarifies the situation.[65] They are representative of the many ephemeral

[64] W.R.O. ref. 705: 4. B.A. 54. 1432 and April 1440.
[65] W.R.O. ref. 009:1. B.A. 2636/157. no. 92012.7/8.

documents that passed among the officials of the estate, but were not of sufficient long-term administrative interest to be filed away for future reference. They show that the Bredon reeves petitioned the auditor for an "allowance" to be made on their arrears for revenues that were "impossible to collect"; they include the common fine and commuted labour services mentioned above, as well as other rents, but the items described in most detail are amercements, broken penalties, and a heriot, all deriving from the manor court. The list of amercements include those for all the usual offences, defaults, breaking the assize of ale, assault, and poaching, as well as an amercement of 6d. imposed on one John Scotarde, who "insulted the steward in open court". Penalties demanded from the tenants because they failed to repair their buildings were ignored by them, and also a cash heriot of a shilling. One of these lists refers to the court revenue of the year of the account, 1455-6, and the total of uncollected dues was £1 6s. 10d.; the perquisites of court total, in the same year, was £1 10s. 9d., so that only 3s. 11d., or little more than one eighth of the supposed court revenue, actually materialized from the pockets of the tenants. We lack concrete evidence of the typicality of this single year at Bredon, but the impression gained from many Worcester court rolls is that the lord's orders to mend houses, clean ditches, and to recall villeins who had fled were consistently ignored, and the logical assumption must be that the peasantry were equally reluctant to pay even nominal sums to the court or to its officers.

Collective refusals of recognitions, tallage, commuted labour services and similar dues, together with individual denials of servility and a general lack of respect for the demands of the manor court are valuable pointers towards peasant attitudes to rent. The court evidence is perhaps the most important, both in terms of the large amount of money involved, and in illuminating the radical change in the position of tenants in the fifteenth century, for the court was much more than a source of revenue — it was the instrument through which the lord made his power effective. In the days of land hunger, the lord's ultimate sanction was the threat of eviction, which would frighten most tenants into submission, but the plentiful supply of land in the fifteenth century made the threats of bailiffs less terrifying to men who moved too freely and abandoned their holdings too readily for the continued health of the lord's rent-roll.

The bulk of the bishop's revenues came not from the dues already mentioned, but from the fixed money rent of the tenants, the assized rents, and also from farms of demesne lands, mills, and fisheries.

These were not immune from tenant action. One unusual example deserves special attention. Throckmorton was an outlying village of the manor of Fladbury, and in the early fifteenth century was worth about £10 *per annum*, but the emergence of a prosperous and active gentry family, bearing the surname of Throckmorton, created serious problems. In 1415 John Throckmorton, who wielded considerable influence as an ally of the Beauchamp family, obtained the whole manor at fee-farm for an annual payment of £10.[66] This did not satisfy Throckmorton's independent spirit, and he arranged, probably in the mid-1430s, to exchange the fee-farm for rents of comparable value in the Gloucestershire villages of Ablington and Ampney St. Mary.[67] In fact, the exchange was unequal, and the Throckmortons had to make up a third of the £10 sum. However, neither the bishop's new Gloucestershire tenants, nor the Throckmortons, paid any rent at all after a few desultory attempts in the first few years. The arrears mounted, and by 1473 had reached a total of £261.[68] A tradition current in Worcestershire in the sixteenth century records Bishop Carpenter's anger at the loss of the Throckmorton revenues, and in 1466 he attempted to regularize the transaction by obtaining papal permission for an exchange that had supposedly existed for thirty years.[69] The affair shows that tenants would refuse payment of all their rents only in very special circumstances. The exchange was probably ineptly organized, and a failure by the bishop's officials to collect rents immediately gave the Gloucestershire tenants an opportunity to evade payment; they may have resented the change of landlords.

Rent strikes against assized rents often took the form of individual refusals of small amounts of money, which were rarely recorded separately in the arrears lists, but, like unpaid court dues, are concealed in the arrears of bailiffs, reeves, and rent-collectors. Occasionally non-payment of these rents are mentioned in order to explain the large debt of an official, as in the arrears roll of 1473, in which a rent-collector at Wichenford, who had owed £3 12s. od. since 1462, blamed a free tenant who had not paid a rent of £1 3s. od. *per annum* during the collector's three-year term of office.[70] The unco-operative attitude of free and gentry tenants accounted for a number of debts, one example being such a substantial gentleman as

[66] *Cal. Pat. Rolls*, Henry V, i (1413-6), p. 340; *Cal. Pap. Reg.* (Papal Letters), vi (1404-15), p. 457.
[67] W.R.O. ref. 009: 1. B.A. 2636/172. no. 92428.4/5.
[68] W.R.O. ref. 009: 1. B.A. 2636/176. no. 92490.
[69] *Cal. Pap. Reg.* (Papal Letters), xii (1458-71), pp. 531-2.
[70] W.R.O. ref. 009: 1. B.A. 2636/176. no. 92490.

John Vampage, who had a number of manors in south Worcestershire, but did not pay a rent of 16s. 9d. for lands that he held in Ripple.[71] In order to investigate peasant activities we must return to the enquiry of 1450, which lists many individual refusals, as at Northwick:—

". . . various tenants of the same refuse to pay their rents and customs as listed in the new rental . . . and as paid by their predecessors in the said tenures, namely John Freman, 12d., Richard Fulford, 8d., John Alford, 16d., William Hall 4d. . . .".

Each sum was small, but their formidable numbers produced large totals from some manors — £2 12s. 4½d. at Northwick, or £1 18s. 6d. at Stratford. The wording of the enquiry does not always make clear the distinction between rents that had lapsed and those that were refused, but a total of at least £9 was recorded as lost to the bishop's annual revenue because of individual refusals by both free and customary tenants.

The bishop's urban tenants in Bristol, Warwick and Worcester figure prominently in lists of debts. A memorandum of the mid-fifteenth century records unpaid rents at Worcester (which were only partly urban because the bishop's property in the Foregate suburb included gardens and barns). The forty-six holdings in the list withheld payment of rents worth £4.[72] Here the position of the tenants must have been strengthened by the difficulty of collecting rents in a town where sales and leases could be very complex.

Demesne farmers were not bound to the lord by traditional ties, but by a contract, the terms of which were recorded in an indenture. The apparent modernity of this form of tenure should not conceal the fact that leases and farms had ancient roots in early medieval society. The farmers themselves were drawn from a broad section of society, with gentry, clergy, merchants, and graziers, but including many peasants, acting as individuals or in groups, whose relationship with the lord cannot have differed very greatly from that between the lord and the many tenants who held land "at will" or for terms of years. Those who see the demesne farmers as a "new" emergent group, heralding important social changes, are stressing only one aspect of the social and economic position of the fifteenth-century lessee.[73] The indentures were clearly composed with an eye to the problem of debt and arrears, for they include a long passage allowing the lord to distrain the property of the farmer if payment of rent was delayed for

[71] *Ibid.*
[72] W.R.O. ref. 009: 1. B.A. 2636/9. no. 43696, fos. 113 r.-115 v.
[73] F. R. H. Du Boulay, "Who were farming the English Demesnes at the end of the Middle Ages?", *Econ. Hist. Rev.*, 2nd ser., xvii (1964-5), *passim.*

as little as a month.[74]   The leases also contain clauses that the farmer should "repair, sustain and maintain" manorial buildings at his own expense, but the lord often had to foot the bill.   It is no surprise, then, to find that farmers rarely paid at the stipulated times, and that the delay could be very long.   In 1473 the demesne farmer of Old Stratford, William Harewell, had owed the large sum of £12 10s. od. for three years.[75]   He may have paid some of this at a later date, but such debts as the £10 3s. 6½d. recorded in 1462 as owed by the farmer of the Withington demesne for seventeen years were virtually irrecoverable.[76]   The same sluggishness in the payment of farms can be seen in the debts of the farmers of other assets, like the tithe corn of Blockley, the Droitwich salt-works, and the fishery at Fladbury, but our most flagrant example concerns a lease of demesne land.

The demesne at Stoke Bishop, a manor that lay only two miles from the centre of Bristol, was leased in 1447 to Richard Baylly for a term of sixty years, at an annual farm of £6 13s. 4d.[77]   He added to this the farm of the park and other lands, making the total due from him more than £8.   Baylly was a Bristol merchant, so that his financial resources extended beyond the profits of the Stoke demesne, which in themselves cannot have been inconsiderable in view of the proximity of a large urban market.[78]   In 1456 the arrears of the reeves of Stoke were £70, but they blamed £54 of this sum on the debts of Richard Baylly, who had not paid any of his farm since 1451, and very little after 1448.[79]   Two years later the steward attempted to cut the bishop's losses on this unprofitable lease, and pardoned £34 of Baylly's arrears in return for a cash payment of £10.[80]   Perhaps chastened by his interview with the steward, and the reduction of his term from sixty to forty years, Baylly seems to have paid a little more in the following years, but his debt still stood at more than £17 in the 1470s.[81]

The majority of demesne farmers paid up comparatively promptly, but in the case of the Stoke lease the bishop showed himself impotent when opposed by a determined debtor.

Having dealt with the various refusals of rents in detail, we must now attempt to assess the scale and implications of the rent-strikes.

[74] Register of John Carpenter, W.R.O. B.A. 2648/6 (ii), (iii).
[75] W.R.O. ref. 009: 1. B.A. 2636/176. no. 92490.
[76] *Ibid.* no. 92488.
[77] W.R.O. ref. 009: 1. B.A. 2636/171. no. 92414.3/6.
[78] He is described as a merchant (and also a debtor!) in *Cal. Pat. Rolls,* Henry VI, vi (1452-61), p. 269.
[79] W.R.O. ref. 009: 1. B.A. 2636/171. no. 92415.7/8.
[80] W.R.O. ref. 009: 1. B.A. 2636/171. no. 92421.
[81] W.R.O. ref. 009: 1. B.A. 2636/176. no. 92490.

In 1473 the arrears roll listed debts amounting to £896, and of this £366 can be definitely attributed to refusal to pay rent.[82] This is misleading because some debts, such as the arrears that resulted from the Throckmorton exchange, were allowed to accumulate over a period of twenty years, whereas the arrears of some reeves would be promptly pardoned. It is very difficult to calculate the proportion of a year's income that would have been retained by the tenants, because of the scattered nature of the evidence. A year in the 1450s would be well documented, and it would be reasonable to suggest an estimate of £4 for collective refusals, £40 for non-payment of court revenue, £10 for the tenants of Ablington and Ampney St. Mary and the Throckmortons, perhaps £10 for the assized rents of free tenants and also those listed in the survey of 1450, including urban rents, and at least £15 for withdrawals of rent by demesne farmers. Does the resulting figure of £79 have any real meaning? The refusal of court revenue may be exaggerated if the Bredon evidence is not typical, but the figures for assized rents and demesne farmers could equally be gross under-estimates. Only refusals of rent that were consistently pursued for a number of years appear in the surviving documents, but some tenants may have varied the amount of rent that they paid each year. Thus accurate calculation is impossible, but our figure of £79 gives an unexaggerated impression of the scale of the problem, and represents about one twelfth of the expected annual income of the see.

The probability remains that at least part of the uncollectable arrears of the estate were kept by manorial officials after rents had been paid by the tenants. It must be remembered that all reeves and beadles were also tenants of the bishop, and the lord would have the same difficulties in collecting the "issues of office" from them as he encountered in collecting unpopular rents from the same tenants.

The actual quantity of rent that was not paid to the lord because of peasant action is not so important as the light that refusals shed on the nature of the lord-tenant relationship. Rent-strikes must have been instrumental in securing "official" reductions, for they formed the tenants' most effective sanction in any bargaining that took place over the level of rent.

Thus refusals of rents, combined with the reluctance of officials to pay off their arrears, helped to transfer revenue, that would at an earlier date have passed to the lord, back into the hands of his tenants.

* * * *

[82] *Ibid.*

Most of the evidence that has so far been presented has been taken from the middle years of the fifteenth century, because of the abundant documentation for that period. But it is important to establish the chronology of these movements among the west-midland peasantry.

There are signs of difficulties in the fourteenth century. A communal refusal of services was organized at Henbury-in-Salt-Marsh in 1352, but seems to have been suppressed.[83] The manorial accounts of the late fourteenth century refer to rents that were unpaid "because it is not possible to levy them", and there were some specific cases, like the refusal, at Bishop's Cleeve in 1393-4, by the family of a fugitive villein to pay a penalty imposed on them in the manor court.[84] Land transfers recorded in court rolls of the same period include provisions for the payment of entry fines in instalments, and new tenants often had to find pledges who would guarantee rent-payment. However, the arrears of reeves often resulted from mistakes or misfortunes in the management of the demesnes, and not from refusals of rents. The total of arrears in 1389 was comparatively low, and even in 1412, the fifth year of the episcopate of Thomas Peverell, only £252 was in arrears.[85]

The recognition due on the accession of Tideman of Winchcomb in 1395 was paid on at least three manors, in full at Bredon and Henbury, though the tenants of Bibury contributed only 6s. 8d. out of 10s.[86] The early fifteenth-century material is deficient, but a list of tenants at Henbury, headed "*Recognitio tenentium*" that had been drawn up on the accession of Philip Morgan in 1419, suggests that at least part of the recognition was paid in that year.[87] Thus the first mass refusal of the recognition must have taken place in either 1426 or 1433, the latter being the date of the petitions of the keepers. Denials of common fines and tallage were all mentioned for the first time in the 1440s and 1450s; for example, the payment of the common fine by the hamlets of Southam and Brockhampton in Cleeve was first refused in 1441.[88] There is, however, some truth in the argument that rent-strikes were not recorded until the mid-fifteenth century because of changes in administrative technique and scribal fashion, in that administrators and scribes began to record strikes when they became a serious problem.

[83] *Cal. Pat. Rolls*, Edward III, ix (1350-4), p. 275.
[84] W.R.O. ref. 009: 1. B.A. 2636/193. no. 92627.11/12.
[85] W.R.O. ref. 009: 1. B.A. 2636/192. no. 92627.8/12.
[86] W.R.O. ref. 009: 1. B.A. 2636/158. no. 92020 (Bredon); /166 no. 92262. (Henbury) 160. no. 92063 (Bibury).
[87] W.R.O. ref. 009: 1. B.A. 2636/185. no. 92574.B.
[88] W.R.O. ref. 009: 1. B.A. 2636/174. no. 92470.6/6.

Opposition among the tenants resulted in the permanent removal of some unpopular exactions. No recognition was demanded after 1444, and some common fines and other collective dues also lapsed in the later years of the fifteenth century. But by the 1490s an increasing population deprived the tenants of their ultimate sanction, easy migration, and rising prices gave the lord a new incentive to maintain and increase his revenue. The receiver's accounts of the early sixteenth century show that arrears were paid much more promptly than before, and that more than 90% of each year's receipts came from the income of the same year. This particular movement was thus short lived, acting as a perceptible factor in the estate economy of the bishop of Worcester for little more than half a century, and soon giving way to a period of rising rents, notably entry fines.

Popular movements must be organized. One of the unsolved problems of late medieval social history is the extent to which the old cohesion and solidarity of the village community was disrupted by the social polarization of the peasantry. It is notable that refusals of collective dues are found in the old-established nucleated villages of the Avon and Severn valleys, and the Cotswolds, which had a high proportion of customary tenants among whom traditional communal loyalties may have lingered. The first mass refusal of the recognition on a large and scattered estate was clearly planned, and required close inter-village communication. Links may have been established by chance meetings of peasants on carrying jobs at the bishop's household, but the best opportunity would have been provided by the auditing sessions at the Worcester exchequer, when reeves, beadles and rent-collectors from all the manors would be able to meet and plan action.

The peasants of the west midlands took a limited part in risings and rebellions. There was a revolt on the estates of Worcester Cathedral Priory in 1381, and the Diggers of Warwickshire in 1607 made a contribution to the movements that were widespread in England in the sixteenth and seventeenth centuries.[89] Local revolts also took place, as on the estates of Halesowen Abbey, and lollardy was prevalent in the area, as may be seen from the west midland contingents that joined the rebellion of 1414.[90] Social unrest on the bishop of

[89] *Chapters of the English Black Monks 1215-1540*, ed. W. A. Pantin, iii (Camden Soc., 3rd ser., liv, 1937), pp. 204-5; R. H. Tawney, *The Agrarian Problem in the Sixteenth Century* (London, 1912), p. 338.

[90] Hilton, *A Medieval Society*, pp. 159-61; M. E. Aston, "Lollardy and Sedition, 1381-1431", *Past and Present*, no. 17 (Apr., 1960), pp. 14-15; below, pp. 284-5. Cases of lollardy also appear in the Register of John Carpenter: M. J. Morgan, "John Carpenter, Bishop of Worcester, 1444-1476" (Birmingham Univ. M.A. thesis, 1960), pp. 31-3; see also J. A. F. Thomson, *The Later Lollards, 1414-1520* (Oxford, 1965), chapters ii and iv.

Worcester's estate took the form of withholding rent, which may seem unspectacular, but shares common ground with more violent protests; just as the peasants of 1381 demanded a rent of 4d. per acre, the bishop's tenants had a clear idea of a "fair" rent. They were not intent on an anarchic denial of all rents, but resented and refused those rents that were too high, dues which were associated with servility, and acknowledgements of the bishop's judicial rights and lordship.

The "struggle for rent" in the thirteenth and fourteenth centuries was usually won by the lords, but in the fifteenth century social realities prevented such a victory. The lord's income was still high, but tenants were able to resist at least some rent payments with a measure of success; violent revolts were unnecessary when the peasants could negotiate from a comparatively strong position. So much of the lord's former income was diverted from its original source, because of strikes and the resulting lowering of rents, that capital accumulation was possible within the ranks of the peasantry. The peasants and demesne farmers seized the economic initiative, so that on the Worcester estate we find some tenants accumulating large holdings, purchasing stock, and consolidating and enclosing their lands.

A writer of the sixteenth century, describing the attitude of landlords in his own day, probably reflects accurately opinions that had been current for a century or more:—

"The peasant knaves be too wealthy . . . they know no obedience, they regard no laws, they would have no gentlemen. . . . They will appoint us what rent we shall take for our grounds".[91]

NOTE, 1976

Subsequent research indicates that refusals to pay dues did continue into the sixteenth century. In 1533 the bishop of Worcester's receiver, John Hornyhold, complained that the steward of the Gloucestershire manors of the estate, Nicholas Poyntz, was exceeding his duties by letting lands and taking fines "at his pleasure". In consequence, the tenants were "much annoyed" and refused to pay their rents, so that £60 had been lost from the revenues due in the spring of 1533. (*Letters and Papers of Henry VIII*, 6, nos. 533, 1274) The main issue seems to have been the level of entry fines at Henbury-in-Salt-Marsh, which rose from about £1 for a yardland in the mid-fifteenth century to an

[91] R. H. Tawney and E. Power, *Tudor Economic Documents*, 3 vols. (London, 1924), iii, p. 58: spelling modernized.

average of about £3 in 1530.   Some individual fines could be very high, as when a tenant paid £13 6s. 8d. for a half-yardland, equivalent to eight years' annual rent.   The main difference between this dispute and earlier refusals is that in the fifteenth century the issue was the payment of *old* rents, whereas in the sixteenth century the tenants were resisting *new* exactions.

9. *Landlords and Tenants in England in the Later Middle Ages: the Buckingham Estates*

BARBARA J. HARRIS

IN HIS RECENT ARTICLE IN *PAST AND PRESENT*, MR. CHRISTOPHER DYER examined peasant resistance to rent payments on the estates of the bishopric of Worcester in the fifteenth century.[1] Mr. Dyer suggested that collective resistance was a significant factor in the high arrears characteristic of the period and that this phenomenon was relatively short lived since "by the 1490s an increasing population deprived the tenants of their ultimate sanction, easy migration, and rising prices gave the lord a new incentive to maintain and increase his revenue" (p. 213).

The accounts of Edward Stafford, third duke of Buckingham, however, suggest that general economic trends in the 1490s did not necessarily alleviate the problem of arrears. Buckingham's lands, sprawled across twenty-four English counties and the marches of Wales, were valued at £5,061 18s. after deducting operating costs, routine repairs, and salaries.[2] They were divided into ten administrative units called receiverships. When the duke came of age in 1498, the arrears in Brecon alone were over £600, more than 10 per cent of his total estimated income. In 1502 they were still £491 3s. in that lordship.[3] Two years later arrears in Newport were £577 14s.[4] and in the Gloucester receivership £419 3s.[5] In 1506 unpaid income amounted to £482 11s. in Kent and Surrey.[6] In York arrears were £298 9s. for 1508 and 1509,[7] while in the Stafford receivership, they were £527 8s. in 1512.[8] By the latter year, they had risen to the phenomenal figure of £1,460 12s. in Newport, five times the estimated annual income of the lordship.[9] In the nearby

---

[1] "A Redistribution of Incomes in Fifteenth-Century England?", *Past and Present*, no. 39 (April, 1968), reprinted as chapter 8 above. Page numbers in brackets in the text refer to that chapter.
[2] Brit. Mus. (hereafter B.M.), Add. MS. 25, f. 294; Pub. Rec. Off. (hereafter P.R.O.), E36/150 and E36/181.
[3] B.M., Egerton Rolls 2193, m. 4 (1496).
[4] P.R.O., SC6/Henry VII/1665, m. 10.
[5] Stafford Rec. Off. (hereafter S.R.O.), D641/1/2/294, m. 1.
[6] P.R.O., SC6/Henry VII/1076, m. 14.
[7] P.R.O., SC6/Henry VIII/4224.
[8] S.R.O., D641/1/2/88.
[9] B.M., Egerton Rolls 2207.

Welsh lordships of Brecon, Hay, Huntingdon, Cantrecelly and Penkelley, they amounted to £766 14s. in 1516.[10]   Arrears due in the lordship of Caurs were £374 19s. in 1517.[11]   At Buckingham's death in 1521, they were £385 14s. in the general circuit, which included eleven English counties and London.[12]   While these figures are impressionistic, they come from all of Buckingham's receiverships and illustrate the huge sums which accumulated as arrears.

The difficulty was certainly not due to neglect on Stafford's part. As Mr. Dyer noted in connection with the bishop of Worcester's estates, there was, if anything, an "excess of administrative zeal" (p. 200). Buckingham put personal pressure on both his tenants and officials by visiting his estates and by sending his brother, the earl of Wiltshire, to check up on local affairs.   He constantly badgered his officials about keeping duplicate copies of court rolls, rentals, surveys, recognizances and leases.   Periodically he sent groups of trusted servants on inspection tours throughout his estates.   On these occasions he issued detailed instructions or articles which explained his policy on every aspect of estate management and asked questions about specific problems.

In spite of all this activity, the arrears persisted.   Why?   There is some evidence that the kind of collective peasant action Mr. Dyer observed on the bishop of Worcester's estates existed on Buckingham's. When the duke tried to convert customary tenures into copyholds in connection with a rent increase in 1517-18, for example, his representative John Pykeryng reported from Navisby, Northampton, "they wyll not consent therto; they had lever to departe the lordshipp, for they say they wyll pay the rent from yere to yere acordyng to their old custom and other wayes they wyll not".[13]   In another lordship, many of the tenants replied "they had lever dy"[14] than convert their tenures. Another example finds the tenants of Caurs joining in 1503 to petition unsuccessfully for relief from an obscure customary duty known as "Porthean Bagle".[15]

There was also resistance to payment of entry fines.   Pykeryng reported that the inhabitants "have no joye to offer no fyne, by reason that they stand 2 or 3 yers and nott fynysshed".[16]   Frequently he had

[10] S.R.O., D641/1/2/248.
[11] B.M., Egerton Rolls 2200.
[12] P.R.O., SC6/Henry VIII/5853, m. 5.
[13] Westminster Abbey, MS. 5470, f. 44.
[14] *Ibid.*, f. 48.
[15] Thomas B. Pugh, *The Marcher Lordships of South Wales, Select Documents* (Cardiff, 1963), pp. 286-7.
[16] Westminster Abbey, MS. 5470, fos. 56d-57.

to seize their lands to secure payment. In the Welsh lordship of
Newport, fines were due on 280 acres in 1500. Although the duke
tried to collect the traditional fine of a noble (that is 6s. 8d.) per acre,
the tenants "aunserd that they in no wise can be of power to make
their fynes of old tyme accustomed . . . but they offer to pay 2 shillings
for the fyne of every acre, or 2d. of the encrece for an acre, and not
above".[17] Buckingham's officials followed his orders and informed
the tenants they would have to pay at the old rate or vacate their lands
by Michaelmas. In private, however, they reminded their master of
all the dues and services his customary tenants owed and recommended a reduction.

Whatever the pressure of·population on land, the duke's tenants
displayed a hardy independence. In 1500 no one in Brecon offered
increased rents on empty tenements[18] or fines for new leases in
Newport.[19] In 1503 Jankyn Selby surrendered 17 acres rather than
pay more rent.[20] Over a decade later, the miller at Navisby,
Northampton went "owt off the towne and hathe toke another
farm".[21] By 1520 Buckingham was very concerned about unoccupied
lands in Stafford, Shropshire, Cheshire, York, and the lordship of
Caurs in Wales.[22] When he was executed the following year, lands
worth £219 9s. 9½d. were uninhabited.[23]

Peasant resistance was most widespread in Wales where Buckingham's claims as landlord were closely connected to his judicial rights
as Lord Marcher. His supreme legal authority was exercised in the
Great Sessions, a special commission which superseded the regular
courts and, in theory, provided swift and effective justice. In fact
little business was conducted at the Sessions. The inhabitants,
however, were compelled to attend on pain of forfeiting recognizances
and could only obtain permission to leave by paying fines that
amounted to over £2,000 for dissolving the Sessions.[24] The duke's
efforts to levy these fines frequently drove the inhabitants to the brink
of rebellion. In 1516-17 the receipts of the Great Sessions in
Cantrecelly, Penkelley and Alexaunderstone were £7,195. The fines
for redeeming the Sessions in these lordships were only £100 1s.
The rest of the debt represented fines for crimes or recognizances
forfeited by inhabitants who failed to appear.[25] In Hay the tenants
responded with force when the duke's officers tried to collect his

[17] Pugh, op. cit., p. 264.   [18] Ibid., p. 270.
[19] Ibid., p. 268.   [20] Ibid., p. 253 and note 2.
[21] Westminster Abbey, MS. 5470, f. 44.
[22] S.R.O., D641/1/4A/27, m. 9.
[23] P.R.O., E36/181, passim.
[24] Ibid., m. 54-6, 59-60.   [25] B.M., Egerton Rolls 2195.

arrears, boycotted the Sessions, and actively interfered with the execution of decisions made by the courts.[26] In Brecon the inhabitants forfeited recognizances totalling £15,858 15s. for boycotting the Sessions.[27] In 1518 collections of rent and other dues in that lordship were so poor that arrears of £27,574 14s. were carried over until the next year.[28] The movement was only broken when the crown, acting in Star Chamber, intervened and forced the duke to make substantial concessions.[29]

Peasant resistance and disorder in Wales was extreme. In other areas it took the form of threats to vacate in the event of rent increases, failure to take up vacant tenements and claims of inability to make customary payments.

Whatever its form, however, peasant resistance was not the only factor in the accumulation of arrears. The failure of officials to turn over money they had collected, sometimes for years, was at least as serious a problem. Kade Bampton, receiver of Newport in 1497, still owed £70 2s. 10½d. in 1504.[30] In 1512 Robert Whitgreve owed £307 3s. 3½d. from his tenure as receiver of Stafford, Shropshire, and Cheshire the previous year; other officials in that receivership owed £220 4s. 4¾d.[31] These debts equalled almost two years' expected revenue.[32] In 1519 Roland Bridges owed £848 19s. from his tenure as receiver of Brecon in 1507-8.[33]

Buckingham never solved the problem of forcing officials to account for all the money they had collected because two conflicting goals determined his behaviour as landlord. On the one hand he wanted to raise his income as high as possible. On the other he viewed his estates as a means of extending his political and social influence. Hence he sought the friendship and loyalty of the men he employed, many of whom were prominent in their own right. For example, his receivers included such gentlemen as John Corbet of Legh, John Skylling of Wiltshire and Hampshire, Walter Vaughan of Hereford, and Robert Whitgreve of Stafford. His bailiffs, park keepers, feodaries and other minor officials were frequently drawn from families important on a local, if not a national, scale.[34] Stafford

[26] This is deduced from the prohibition of these practices in P.R.O., Sta Cha 2/35/21 printed in Pugh, *Marcher Lordships*, pp. 135-8.
[27] P.R.O., SC6/Henry VIII/4775, m. 9d.
[28] *Ibid.*, m. 1.   [29] P.R.O., Sta Cha 2/35/21.
[30] P.R.O., SC6/Henry VII/1665.   [31] S.R.O. D641/1/2/88.
[32] The annual income of the Stafford receivership was slightly over £300. B.M., Add. MS. 25, f. 294; P.R.O., E36/150 and E36/181.
[33] P.R.O., SC6/Henry VIII/4775, m. 9.
[34] B. J. Harris, "Edward Stafford, Third Duke of Buckingham" (Harvard University, Ph.D. Thesis, June 1968), pp. 193-7, 277-81.

probably expected them to appropriate a portion of their revenues. Certainly there is no indication that he resorted to the law to recover arrears even though he frequently engaged in lawsuits in connection with other matters.

There were, then, many similarities in the behavioural patterns of peasants and officials on the bishop of Worcester's estates in the fifteenth century and the duke of Buckingham's in the first quarter of the sixteenth, indicating that there was no dramatic change in the conditions that produced arrears in the 1490s. Whether Buckingham's estates were typical of the early sixteenth century is, however, a question that can only be answered after further research.

10. *The Origins of Robin Hood*

R. H. HILTON

THOMAS BECKET, HENRY II'S CHANCELLOR AND LATER ARCHBISHOP of Canterbury, was an officially canonised saint, the most celebrated object of medieval English pilgrimages. Simon de Montfort, Earl of Leicester, a transplanted baron from the Île de France, was popularly and unofficially canonised for his part in the political upheaval and civil war of 1258-65. Another temporary, unofficial saint was Thomas, Earl of Lancaster, celebrated because of his rebellion against the government of his cousin, Edward II. But in spite of their official or unofficial sanctity, none of these, nor any other Englishman of the middle ages, ever became such a popular hero as Robin Hood. His popularity has never waned since we first hear of tales about his exploits in a version of Langland's Piers Plowman, probably composed towards the end of the seventies of the fourteenth century.

But Thomas Becket and the others really existed. Did Robin Hood ever live or was he a figment of popular imagination, or even the individual invention of a clever ballad maker? In this article I shall argue that probably there was no such individual, but that his historical significance does not depend on whether he was a real person or not. I shall suggest that what matters is that one of England's most popular literary heroes is a man whose most endearing activities to his public were the robbery and killing of landowners, in particular church landowners, and the maintenance of guerilla warfare against established authority represented by the sheriff. A man who would now, of course, be described as a terrorist. Perhaps a social historian can help to solve some Robin Hood problems which have so far mainly been considered by the literary historians.

On the face of it, the very scanty medieval evidence gives little grounds for supposing that Robin Hood was anything more than a literary creation. The reference made by William Langland occurs in his description of the allegorical character Sloth.[1] In his famous dream the author sees Reason preach a sermon to the people, after which persons representing the seven deadly sins are led to repent. Sloth is a priest who has been a parson (that is, a parochial rector) for thirty years. He is ignorant of Latin and of the things of religion,

[1] *The Vision of Piers the Ploughman*, I, ed. W. W. Skeat, 1886, p. 166. (A. V, 11. 401-2).

but he is a skilled hunter of hares.   He does not know his paternoster, but he knows rimes of Robin Hood and Randulf, Earl of Chester. The last Randulf (or Ranulf), Earl of Chester, died in 1232, so that while we need not conclude that the tales of the two heroes first began to be popular at the same time, the beginning of the Robin Hood legend may well be contemporary with the emergence of the ballad as a literary form in England, in the thirteenth century.   Other medieval references to Robin Hood are later than that of Langland.   They are in the Scottish chronicles of John Fordun and John Major.[2]   The references are vague and it seems likely that their source material was, in fact, ballads that already existed.   This is as we would expect, for the north of England and Scotland were the homes *par excellence* of the ballads, as any reader of Child's collection will have noticed, and the only identifiable location of Robin Hood's exploits is the West Riding of Yorkshire.

Another aspect of the Robin Hood legend, long known to literary historians, has been their association with the May Games of villages and towns in the sixteenth century.[3]   Troupes of May Day revellers dressed themselves up as Robin Hood and his outlaws, just as Morris Dancers included some grotesque or heroic character for the mime in their performance.   The perfectly natural appearance of these popular personalities on May Day has, unfortunately, provoked over-enthusiastic folklorists into supposing that Robin Hood and his men have their roots in popular paganism, even in the witch cult.[4] No doubt the May celebrations had a pre-Christian origin in the fertility rites of an agricultural people, and if Robin was known to us only in connection with these celebrations we might suppose, as Joseph Wright did in 1850,[5] that he was no more than a woodland sprite.   But when we come to analyse the earliest ballads themselves, we shall find abundant reference to the hard realities of thirteenth- and fourteenth-century secular existence, and only the most conventional references to religion.   I do not propose to go further into this aspect of the matter, but to deal with a more important

[2] Early English historians (such as Grafton and Stowe) took John Major's *History of Greater Britain* (1521) as their main source.   See the edition by A. Constable, Scottish History Society, vol. 10, 1892, p. 156.   Major refers Robin Hood's activities to Richard I's time.   The earlier writers, Fordun or his continuators, associate the outlaws with the disinherited followers of Simon de Montfort: Johannis de Fordun, *Scotichronicon*, III, ed. T. Hearne, 1722, pp. 773-4 note.   It is this account which suggests that the ballads themselves were the source of what knowledge there was of Robin Hood.

[3] E. K. Chambers, *The Medieval Stage*, I, 174-81.

[4] Margaret Murray, *The God of the Witches*, n.d., pp. 35-41.

[5] *Essays on the Literature . . . of England in the Middle Ages*, II, 1846, pp. 207-11.

problem, the recurring effort to manufacture an authentic, documented, individual called Robin Hood.

Two sixteenth-century historians, Richard Grafton and John Stowe, copying the Scottish chroniclers, introduced the idea, originally derived from the ballads, that Robin Hood had a real existence.[6] Grafton even suggested that he was a nobleman fallen on evil times, and this was taken up by two court playwrights of the latter part of the century.[7] Munday and Chettle's *Downfall and Death of Robert Earl of Huntingdon* (1601) started off a theory about Robin Hood which still goes the rounds of children's story books and films to-day. No doubt it was an attempt (probably unconscious) to make the popular hero acceptable to the snobbish and pedigree-conscious upper class of Tudor and Stuart England. The eighteenth-century antiquary, William Stukeley, fabricated a preposterous pedigree showing the descent of Robin (supposedly a contemporary of Richard I) from the baronage of the Conquest period. Despite its dismissal by Percy, the great ballad collector, it was reproduced by an important early ballad editor, Joseph Ritson.[8] But although no one seriously accepts the pedigree now, a curious by-product of the fabrication lives on in the assumption, by scholars and film producers alike, that the era of Robin Hood was that of Richard I (King of England, 1189-99). Sir Walter Scott, through *Ivanhoe*, is largely responsible for the popularity of this story, though it has support neither from contemporary sources nor from those ballads whose origin can safely be assumed to be medieval. Furthermore, none of the political or social upheavals of Richard's reign provide the same background of outlawry in the Midlands and the north which has been more plausibly associated with the Robin Hood legend in the reigns of Henry III and Edward II.

The development of accurate historical scholarship in the nineteenth century resulted in a number of rational attempts to account for Robin Hood, based on the study of authentic documents. The theory of fallen nobility was soon abandoned as some sort of chronological sequence of the ballads was established. Robin Hood's peasant origin was established. Some writers (such as the French historian Augustin Thierry) thought he was a champion of Saxons against Normans, like Hereward the Wake.[9] Unfortunately

[6] Richard Grafton, *Abridgement of Chronicles*, 1572, p. 54; John Stowe, *Annales*, 1615, p. 159.   [7] *Cambridge History of English Literature*, V, p. 35.
[8] T. Percy, *Reliques of Ancient English Poetry*, I, 1847, p. 85; J. Ritson, *Robin Hood*, I, 1795 pp. xxi-xxii. Both cite W. Stukeley, *Palaeographia Britannica*, II, 1746.
[9] A. Thierry, *History of the Conquest of England*, II, pp. 223-9, trans. W. Hazlitt, 1847.

the ballads show no trace of this animosity. But such general notions were not satisfying, so historians tried to find events which were known to have resulted in large scale outlawries. Since the ballads seemed to have become popular in the fourteenth century (the latest date, as we have seen, being fixed by Langland's *Vision of Piers Plowman*), it seemed reasonable to examine the political history of the thirteenth and early fourteenth centuries. This examination produced the two principal theories held by those who think Robin Hood was a real man.

J. M. Gutch's 1847 edition of the *Lytell Geste of Robin Hood and other Robin Hood Ballads* was prefaced by a discussion of the problems of identification. Gutch rejected the theory of aristocratic origin, following Thierry — and also the idea that Robin Hood was contemporary with Richard I. Following an article in the *London and Westminster Review* for March 1840, Gutch suggested that Robin Hood was one of the disinherited supporters of Simon de Montfort who went into hiding after their defeat at Evesham in 1265. His evidence, apart from guesswork, was from Fordun, who associates Robin Hood and Little John with the disinherited. Fordun mentions that the people in his time celebrated the outlaws in tragedy and comedy, and as we have suggested, these were in fact his source of knowledge of the Robin Hood band. The association with the disinherited has been lately revived — cautiously, of course— by Sir Maurice Powicke in his *King Henry III and the Lord Edward*.[10] There is, however, no positive evidence which links Robin Hood with the Disinherited, who were in any case members of the landowning nobility. They may have had followers of lower social status, but Robin Hood gives no appearance either of being any nobleman's follower or of being concerned with the political issues of the Barons' Wars.

More interesting and more convincing than Gutch's essay was Joseph Hunter's *Critical and Historical Tract no. IV* of 1852, entitled "The Ballad Hero, Robin Hood". Hunter was a historian and editor of records of some skill. He rejected the mythological explanation of Robin Hood, considered that he was not simply an abstraction of a number of outlaws, and suggested the reign of Edward II (1307-27) as the period of his activity. Hunter's merit is to have analysed with care the events described in those ballads which he considered to be of fourteenth-century origin, in relation to events for which there was documentary evidence. He came to the conclusion that Robin Hood and his friends were lesser

---

[10] Vol. II, p. 530 n.

members of the army which supported the rebel Earl of Lancaster, Thomas the king's cousin, who was defeated at Boroughbridge, Yorkshire, in 1322. The king confiscated the property of most of Thomas's supporters, referred to as the "contrariants". Among those mentioned in official records was a certain Godfrey of Stainton. This man, he suggested, was a relative of Elizabeth of Stainton, Prioress of Kirklees, traditionally supposed to have been the relative and murderess of Robin. The visit of the King to Robin in his greenwood home, described in the ballads, recounts in poetic form the itinerary of Edward II in the north in 1323. To cap all, Hunter finds evidence in the accounts of the King's wardrobe wage payments to a porter called Robert Hood. This fits in with the sojourn of Robin at the king's court which is mentioned in the ballads.

This very circumstantial identification of Robin Hood with the contrariants has been repeated with some additions by Mr. J. W. Walker, in the *Yorkshire Archæological Journal* for 1944. The principal new feature brought forward is the frequent mention in the Wakefield court rolls of a Hood family, one of whom was called Robert. And yet the whole reconstruction of Robin Hood as a fourteenth-century contrariant is based not simply on the evidence of the Wakefield court records, the royal wardrobe accounts and other public records, but on attempts to connect these evidences together by unjustifiable links of reasoning. The reasoning is based entirely on the assumption that various persons bearing the common name Robert Hood (Hade, Hod, Hodde or Hode) are in fact one person, and the same person as the ballad hero. It seems in fact to have been a common Yorkshire name, for another attempt to identify Robin Hood has been based on an entry in the Pipe Roll for 1230.[11] This entry shows that the sheriff of Yorkshire was accountable to the royal exchequer for the value of the chattels of Robert Hood, a fugitive from justice. There are, however, important elements in the theory which lack verisimilitude. The ballads themselves contain no reference to Thomas of Lancaster, who, though a thoroughly unpleasant personality, did enjoy in the north a posthumous popular canonisation like Simon de Montfort — probably simply because he was a rebel against authority. Further, any genuine supporter of Lancaster would not have easily been reconciled to Edward II, who was widely hated and despised. Thirdly, the argument that Robin or Robert Hood would naturally be a follower of Lancaster as Lord of the Manor of Wakefield, falls to the ground since Lancaster had only two or three years earlier

---

[11] Professor L. D. V. Owen, cited by J. W. Walker in *art. cit.*, pp. 11-12.

obtained Wakefield as a result of a private war waged against the Earl of Warenne, in whose family the manor had been for two hundred years.[12]   However, if the identification of the ballad hero with any one person is conceivable, it must be admitted that Joseph Hunter and his followers have so far produced the most likely case.   The case, is, of course greatly strengthened by the fact that the earliest ballads refer to Barnesdale, between Wakefield and Doncaster, as the main scene of Robin Hood's exploits.

In view of the uncertain and elusive references to an individual "Robin Hood" in medieval records, it may be the best policy to leave for the moment the task of finding a precise setting in which to fit him and his outlaw band.   The character of the hero and his associates has become so much of our tradition that it has been taken for granted.   Closer attention to the internal evidence of the earliest ballads may give us a line on the external circumstances of their creation.

What can we say of the social milieu from which the legend emerged?   It is, of course, generally accepted that the ballad audience was for the most part plebeian.   Professor Entwistle contrasts this audience with that of the epics of the preceding period, which, he says, was aristocratic.   We cannot follow him in supposing that the ballad audience was "the whole people organised under its natural leaders", for the period of the European emergence of the genre, the thirteenth and fourteenth centuries, was one when we cannot talk of "the whole people" or of a "homogeneous folk".[13] This, as we shall emphasise, was an era when society was the reverse of homogeneous, when peasants and landowners faced each other with mutual antagonism, when townspeople were regarded with suspicion by both, and when the peasantry itself was socially divided. However, the chasm which divided the landowners from the peasants and artisans was much deeper than those which were appearing amongst the people, and we must exclude the lords of manors from "the ballad people".

The "ballad people" lived in hard times, and if we are to recapture the authentic atmosphere of the first Robin Hood we must shed the common illusion that Robin and his fellows were simply a merry band of men who meant nobody any serious harm.   "Apart from the particular history of his feud with the sheriff and abbot", says Professor Entwistle, "the episodes tend to repeat the tableau of good-humoured cudgellings".[14]   For Mr. A. L. Poole, in *From*

[12] *Court Rolls of the Manor of Wakefield* (Yorkshire Archaeological Society Record Series), IV, 1930, p. vii.   [13] *European Balladry*, pp. 30-32.
[14] *op. cit.*, p. 235.

Domesday Book to Magna Carta, Robin Hood is an "elusive and irresponsible sportsman" who "represents the cheerful side of the life of the forest, where merry and carefree men consorted in defiance of the law".[15] For Professor Child the Robin of the *Gest* "yeoman as he is . . . has a kind of royal dignity, a princely grace and a gentlemanlike refinement of humour . . for courtesy and good temper he is a popular Gawain".[16] This bland and fundamentally harmless character given to Robin and his men is probably derived from the numerous post-medieval broadsheet ballads, with their emphasis on one of the more harmless of the original themes — the way Robin dealt with his own class of people. These show him as a bold fighter with casual passers-by, usually artisans, such as the potter, the butcher and the tanner. In these ballads Robin usually loses, but with good temper, and invites the victor to join him in the greenwood. These ballads are on the whole later than the *Gest* and with their emphasis on artisan prowess may well be associated with the spirit of the May Games, which were as much urban as rural. But the *Gest* itself, and other indubitably early ballads show that Robin and his men are capable of a primitive ferocity against their enemies which ill fits the conception of good-humoured cudgelling and irresponsible sportsmanship. This physical cruelty is typically medieval. It occurs naturally in a society where any cross road might be furnished with a well-loaded gallows, where the heads and quartered bodies of traitors were nailed to city gates, and where quarrels over trifles amongst peasants, townsmen and nobles alike led to bloodshed and killing. Violence and cruelty were intensified when occuring as part of social conflict. If lords thought themselves justified in beating and hanging rebellious peasants, peasants replied when opportunity arose with similar cruelty.

And so at the beginning of the *Gest* Robin Hood's advice to Little John, should he meet bishop, archbishop or sheriff, is to "beat and bind". In the sixth "fytte" of the *Gest* Robin pierces the sheriff of Nottingham with an arrow and then cuts off his head with his sword. After the fight to the death between Robin and Guy of Gisborne, described in the ballad of that name, Robin cuts off the head of the dead Guy and sticks it on his bow's end so that he can mutilate the face beyond recognition with his knife. In *Robin Hood and the Monk*, Little John intercepts the monk who has betrayed Robin to the sheriff. He cuts off not only the monk's head but that of "the little page", so as to ensure against betrayal. And the manner of Robin's own death at the hands of the wanton Prioress of Kirklees is as fierce and macabre as the tales of Robin's own doings.   The woman bleeds him.

> "And first it bled the thick, thick blood
> And afterwards the thin.
> And well then wist good Robin Hood
> Treason there was within"

and her lover, stabbing him as he tries to escape, is himself slain and left for the dogs to eat.

Now we must see if we can, on the basis of the evidence of the ballads themselves, put Robin and the outlaws in their place in society.   Robin is described frequently as a "yeoman" and in his own words shows that it is the yeomen who are his social equals whom he will cherish and protect above all.   The word "yeoman" is one which has meant different things at different times.   As it was commonly used in the sixteenth and seventeenth centuries it meant a wealthy peasant farmer, an employer of labour, holding most of his land freehold.   He ranked socially above the mass of small copyholders and below the gentleman or squire.   Two centuries earlier the word was not as clear in its meaning.   Chaucer's yeomen in the Canterbury Tales are both serving men, the one attached to the knight and squire, the other to the canon.   "Yeoman" in one of its meanings undoubtedly had the implication of service.   But the knight's yeoman was also a forester, "yeomanly" accoutred.   The fourteenth-century yeoman was not therefore necessarily in service, however honourable the service might be.   The word as used in the ballads is almost certainly meant to imply neither a serving man (except in one place) nor a rich peasant, but simply a peasant of free personal status.   And of course the first stanza of the *Gest* is addressed to an audience of free men:

> "Lythe and listin, gentilmen
> That be of free bore blode;
> I shall you tel of a gode yeoman,
> His name was Robyn Hode".

The reference to gentility and free birth in the audience, and the emphasis on the yeoman class does not mean that the ballads were not in fact addressed to, and sung by, men whom the lords and the lawyers would consider servile.   It is a persistent trait of thirteenth-century villeinage cases in royal courts that peasants (probably most often without success) considered themselves to be free men.   Their heroes, consequently, will be as free as they themselves aspired to be. And so, although Sir Edmund Chambers makes a shrewd guess when he calls the Robin Hood and similar ballads the product of a "yeoman minstrelsy", we must not suppose with him that it was only the rich peasant lessees of manorial demesnes who enjoyed the tales of Robin Hood.[17]

Social attitudes are better understood by attention to the relations between persons than by etymology. Let us consider the relations between Robin Hood and his men, and persons outside the woodland company, not as personal individual relations but as social relations, expressing the attitude of the outlaws to the various strata in society whom these persons represent. The Robin Hood band in a sense stood outside society since they were outlaws. Outlawry in Anglo-Saxon and Norman times had been the terrible lot of felons put outside the law. Their property was confiscated and any man could slay them with impunity. It was said of them that they "bore the wolf's head", they were to be treated as wolves by those within the law. By the thirteenth century outlawry was becoming less serious. An accused person who neglected to appear at four successive county courts for trial was automatically outlawed. Outlawry was becoming a sanction to compel attendance at court. But though it might no longer involve the lawful killing of the outlaw (except for resisting capture) it did involve the forfeiture of land and goods. Many a man who was not confident that law was the same as justice might prefer outlawry. At the Gloucester assizes in 1221 there were 330 homicide cases, but while only fourteen men were hanged, a hundred suspects had to be proclaimed outlaws in their absence.[18]

The outlaws were not necessarily guilty homicides. They were often victims of oppression, especially when legal processes were subject to the pressure of powerful interests. An early fourteenth-century poem, written in the Anglo-Norman that was common in all literate circles and was used in the law courts, expresses this very vividly.[19] The poem is about the way in which false accusers and interested persons could have a guiltless enemy flung into prison to await the travelling justices of "Trailbaston". The only remedy for the innocent was felt to be not to wait for the trial but to go to the woods:

> ". . . suz le jolyf umbray
> La n'y a fauceté ne nulle mal lay
> En le bois de Belregard, ou vol le jay
> E chaunte russinole touz jours santz delay".

[17] *English Literature at the Close of the Middle Ages*, 1945, p. 129.
[18] F. Pollock and F. W. Maitland, *History of English Law*, II, 557.
[19] This poem was printed by Thomas Wright in *Political Songs*, Camden Society, 1839, p. 231. I quote from Miss I. S. T. Aspin's edition and translation, *Anglo-Norman Political Songs*, 1953, pp. 67-78.

> [. . . in the beautiful shade
> There is no deceit there, nor any bad law.
> In the wood of Belregard where the jay flies
> And the nightingale always sings without ceasing.]

The poem is no lyric, however; life as an outlaw in the woods was not really merry or carefree.   The outlaw wants to go home:

> "Je pri tote bone gent qe pur moi vueillent prier
> Qe je pus a mon païs aler e chyvaucher".
> [I beg all good people they pray for me
> That I may go riding to my own country.]

Naturally the outlaw in the wood remembers those who are the oppressors and who are his friends.   In the Robin Hood ballads these are classified with the greatest clarity — and treated accordingly.

The stories told in the older ballads very largely turn on the social attitude of the outlaws.   Professor Child wrote that Robin Hood "has no sort of political character",[20] and truly he takes no position with regard to the feudal faction fights which made up so much of medieval politics.   We shall deduce this attitude from those ballads which are recognised as the oldest, that is mostly written down and even printed before 1500, and therefore probably derived from an oral tradition that goes back to the fourteenth century and beyond.   These are the composite *Gest of Robyn Hode; Robin Hood and the Monk; Robin Hood and Guy of Gisborne; Robin Hood and the Potter*.[21]

The *Gest* begins by Little John asking for instructions from Robin about how he and the others should treat various sorts of people.

> ". . . . .
> Where we shall robbe, where we shall reve,
> Where we shal bete and bynde?"

The answer is

> ". . . . .
> But loke ye do no husbonde harme
> That tilleth with his ploughe".
> No more ye shall no gode yeman
> that walketh by grenë-wode shawe
> Ne no knyght ne no sqyer
> That wol be a gode felawe.
>
> These bisshopes and these archebisshoppes
> Ye shall them bete and bynde;
> The hyë sherif of Notyngham
> Hym holde ye in your mynde".

Little John, Much the miller's son and William Scarlok then proceed to Watling Street somewhere in the Doncaster area and wait for a

[20] *op. cit.*, p. 43.   [21] Printed by Child, *op. cit.*

guest to take to dinner, preferably a rich guest who can be made to pay heavily for the privilege. In the event, the guest is poor, but the tale he tells is typical of the predicament of many a small landowner of the times.

Sir Richard at the Lee, to whom Robin plays host, has had to borrow money to get his son out of the consequences of a homicide. He borrowed the money from the Abbot of St. Mary's, York, and offered all his lands as security. The day for repayment has come and he has no money. Robin lends him more than enough, refits him with clothes, and sends Little John with him as attendant (as "knave" or "yeoman"). They arrive in the abbot's dining hall where the abbot is accompanied by his wealthy or subservient friends, including the high justice of England, retained by the abbot by fee and livery. The knight, concealing his money, asks for respite, is refused, and then, to the chagrin of the abbot, who coveted Sir Richard's land, throws the money on the table and leaves. Eventually, of course, Sir Richard comes again to the woodland home of Robin and repays the loan. The outlawed yeoman is shown to be possessed of Christian charity where the professed monk has none.

The sheriff of Nottingham figures on a number of occasions in the early ballads. In another of the stories in the *Gest*, Little John, disguised as Reynold Grenelefe from Holderness, is so successful in an archery competition in Nottingham that the sheriff takes him into his service. Reynold is an unruly servant, lies in bed when the sheriff is out and demands food and drink in such a way that after laying out the steward and the butler, he becomes involved in a fight with the cook. As so often in these stories, the fighters become friends and decamp with the sheriff's cash and silver. Still in his rôle as Reynold Grenelefe, Little John lures the sheriff to Robin's hiding place, where he is stripped to his breeches and shirt and made to lie out all night. Robin extracts from him a promise of immunity in return for his release. But the sheriff, of course, breaks the promise. This leads us to another section of the *Gest* (after a characteristic interlude involving the robbing of the high cellarer of St. Mary's Abbey). Robin and his men go to compete at archery at Nottingham, take all the prizes but are attacked by the sheriff's men. Little John is wounded and asks that his friends behead him rather than leave him alive in the sheriff's power. But they all escape and are sheltered by Sir Richard at the Lee in his castle. The knight defies the sheriff to inform the king of his protection of outlaws and the sheriff raises the siege. Robin and his fellows get away, back to the woods, but the sheriff surprises the knight out hawking and imprisons him.   At the appeal of the knight's wife, Robin and seven score followers storm Nottingham, slay the sheriff and rescue the knight.

The sheriff has to die more than one death.   In the ballad *Robin Hood and Guy of Gisborne* Robin dreams he is beaten and bound by two yeomen.   On waking he determines to find them.   He and Little John search the woods and eventually come on the sinister Guy of Gisborne, clad from head to foot in horse hide.   Little John and Robin quarrel about who is to deal with Guy, and John departs to find some of the other outlaws killed in an encounter with the sheriff.   John is taken by the sheriff after the failure of one of his arrows.   Meanwhile Robin and Guy, as yet unknown to each other, compete at archery.   Robin wins, and reveals his identity, for Guy has already said that he is searching for the outlaw.   They fight and Robin kills and mutilates Guy of Gisborne.   But since Guy is the sheriff's emissary, Robin puts on Guy's garment of horse hide and blows Guy's horn.   The sheriff understands this to mean that Guy has killed Robin.   The two meet and the sheriff offers the false Guy any reward he asks.   Robin asks to be allowed to kill the captive Little John, but of course cuts John free with his "Irysh kniffe" The sheriff runs for his life, but Little John, with Guy of Gisborne's bow and rusty arrows

"Did cleave his heart in twinn".

Apart from any documentary or linguistic proof of medieval dating for these stories, the references to persons and situations imply a thirteenth or at the latest fourteenth-century origin.   Such evidence as we have of peasant life in the century and a half before the rising of 1381 suggests that agrarian discontent was endemic throughout the country.[22]   Although economic conditions changed considerably during the period, the peasants at all times found themselves at odds either with the landlord or the state official, or with both.   Villagers' grievances up to the middle of the fourteenth century were focussed on landlords' demands for rents and services.   Quarrels about these matters — crucial for the countryman's standard of living — led to issues of personal freedom.   In a litigious age, the stage that was reached before riot broke out, was normally dispute in the courts.   This, in numerous cases, touched on whether the peasants involved were free men or serfs, for if they were serfs they were legally liable for increased rents and services at demand.   After the middle of the fourteenth century, though these issues were still

---

[22] R. H. Hilton, "Peasant Movements before 1381", *Economic History Review*, 2nd series, II, ii.

alive, an additional bitter cause of complaint was the attempted wage-freeze of 1349 and 1351. This history of intertwined economic and social grievances, affecting rich and poor peasants, the servile, the would-be free and the free, seems more likely to have generated the Robin Hood ballads than the short-lived outbreaks of civil war, mainly affecting the upper classes, that have been quoted by Gutch and Hunter.

The sheriff, as the principal enemy, fits well into this context. In the thirteenth and early fourteenth centuries, before the Justices of Labourers and of the Peace come into prominence, the sheriff was the omnipresent representative of the power of the government. He was in the first place the principal local financial agent of the Crown and notorious as a past master in the art of extortion. It was he or his agents who performed all the administrative functions which led up to the appearance of litigants in court — delivery of writs, attachment of accused persons, distraint on property, empanelling of juries. He, furthermore, was the official whom the government instructed, on receipt of complaint from aggrieved landowners, to mobilise forces to compel tenants to pay rent, to perform services or to dispel and arrest rioters.[23]

It could, on the other hand, be argued that the landlord does not seem to play a big enough part to support a theory of Robin Hood as a by-product of the agrarian social struggle. But this, of course, is the rôle of the Abbot of St. Mary's, York. The monks are not hated for their religion or for their lack of it. They are the exemplars of unrelenting landlordism, much more, one imagines, than the baron who, however extortionate, did not establish his presence in the shire as did the religious. St. Mary's, a Benedictine abbey, was the wealthiest religious house in Yorkshire, and indeed one of the first half dozen or so in the country.[24] Abbots of such houses were among the greatest men of the kingdom, very apt to have a chief justice as an intimate (even on the pay-roll, as the ballad suggests)

[23] For the activities of a midland sheriff, see G. Templeman, *The Sheriffs of Warwickshire in the Thirteenth Century*, Dugdale Society Occasional Paper, No. 7. [It may be worth mentioning that, *pace* Professor Holt, sheriffs were involved in pursuing recalcitrant bondmen, often in enforcing judgements by justice of oyer and terminer in support of lords of manors. Cf. *Calendar of Patent Rolls*, 1272-81, p. 290, concerning villeins of Harmondsworth. It was the sheriff who was ordered to pursue the ringleaders of the Romsley rebellion in 1386, referred to in my *English Peasantry in the Later Middle Ages* (Oxford, 1975), p. 63.]

[24] A convenient source for *comparative* income figures of English monasteries is the Appendix to A. Savine's *English Monasteries on the Eve of the Dissolution*, though it must be remembered that monastic landed incomes tended to fall in the late fourteenth and fifteenth centuries.

Furthermore it was the religious landowners who tended to be the most tenacious of their rights and the least sympathetic in face of social demands from below. The abbot of St. Mary's, in other words, is well cast, with the sheriff, as a target for peasant satire.

The attitude of the outlaws to authority as represented by the sheriff and the abbot is unmistakable. But it conflicts curiously with their attitude to the source of authority, the greatest landowner of them all, the King. In the *Gest* the King responds to the sheriff's appeal to come to punish Sir Richard at the Lee for sheltering the outlaw. The knight's lands are declared forfeit to the crown and offered to any man who could bring the king his severed head, for the king's wrath was further excited, as he travelled north, by the looting of the deer in his deer parks. But the king is warned that as long as Sir Richard is protected by Robin, any man sent to capture him will lose his own head first. The king's next move, on advice from one of his intimates, is to go to the wood disguised as a monk, in the hope of tempting the outlaws well-known greed for the riches of the church. The stratagem works, but after a competition in shooting and buffeting, the king is revealed. But Robin and the knight win the king's pardon, the king takes Robin's livery of Lincoln green, and Robin goes in the king's service for fifteen months to the king's court.

The king throughout is "our comely king" and shows himself in his visit to the wood as brave, strong, merciful and generous. Why the contrast between the king and his agents? In reality the king would have strengthened his officials' actions against peasant law-breakers, especially poachers of deer in his parks and forests. But the medieval peasants did not see the king as one of the landlords, protecting landlord power and privilege. They thought of him as the fount of justice, and justice in their minds meant protection against those who oppressed them (their landlords) and those local officials who protected and helped the oppressor (chiefly the sheriff). Of course, the king and central government agents very often acted against over-mighty subjects, not to protect the serfs of the over-mighty, but to protect the interests of the crown. The people were confused, they had no powerful protectors, so they invented one. Their faith in the king led to their downfall in 1381.

The illusions of the medieval English peasant that the king was really on their side, reflected in the Robin Hood ballads, shows that their rebellious outlook was one of protest against immediately felt hardship. It was not critical of the established order. There was no conscious attempt to envisage a different England until the brief moment of their power and glory in the summer of 1381.   And yet, while lacking political and social consciousness of a more modern type, they were not without aspirations.   Perhaps it would not be exaggerated to suggest that the carefree merriment of the outlaws in the greenwood, so unlike the starved and hunted existence of real outlaws, was an unconscious invention in poetic form of the life that those who enjoyed the ballads would have liked to live.   As we have seen, it was a life of peril at the hands of the sheriff and his open or secret emissaries.   But it was also a life where the fat abbot or cellarer always comes off worse and has to disgorge his wealth to the representatives of the class from whom the wealth was taken in the first place.   More important still, it was a life of abundance, of sportsmanship and without degrading toil.   It was a life spent among friends and equals, under the direction of a leader chosen for his bravery, not imposed because of his wealth and power.

11. *The Origins and Audience of the Ballads of Robin Hood*

J. C. HOLT

THIS PAPER IS CONCERNED WITH PRECISE BUT DIFFICULT QUESTIONS. When and why did the Robin Hood legend emerge? Who listened to the ballads about this famous outlaw and why? What, if any, were the literary sources of the story? Who, if anybody, was Robin Hood himself? — or, at least, who and what is he likely to have been?

One possible answer to some of these questions was presented by Dr. R. H. Hilton in a paper published in *Past and Present*, No. 14 [chapter 10 above]. Here he contended that the earliest versions of the Robin Hood legend were "a by-product of the agrarian social struggle" over rents, services and social status which culminated, after a century and a half, in the rising of 1381. These views were novel, for although these ballads have generally been regarded as "popular" or "yeoman" literature, no authority had associated them with immediate peasant discontents so emphatically as Dr. Hilton, except perhaps William Morris:

> Was it not sooth that I said, brother, that Robin Hood should bring us John Ball?[1]

My answer differs radically from Dr. Hilton's. First, I do not consider that the ballads expressed exclusive class interests, attitudes or ambitions. Secondly, I can find no evidence that the ballads were concerned to any significant or important degree with the agrarian discontents of the thirteenth and fourteenth centuries. In an illuminating paper on the Danish ballads, published in 1908, W. P. Ker wrote: "The Danish Ballads do not belong to 'the people' in the ordinary meaning of the term. They have come down to the common people, in those Jutland homes where so many of the old poems have been found surviving, but originally they belonged to the gentry — a gentry not absolutely cut off nor far removed from the

---

[1] *Dream of John Ball*, c. 2. Among critical authorities G. H. Gerould probably comes closest to Dr. Hilton: "The songs about Robin Hood give us no assurance that such a hero ever existed in the flesh, but they are a trustworthy index to the restiveness of the common people under political, economic and social abuses", but he adds, "together with their ability to view even their wrongs with tolerant humour". (*The Ballad of Tradition*, Oxford, 1932, p. 134). Similar views to Dr. Hilton's were advanced simultaneously by Maurice Keen in "Robin Hood: a Peasant hero", in *History Today*, October 1958.

simpler yeoman".[2] Ker, of course, recognized that the Danish ballads are more aristocratic in choice of subject than the English. Nevertheless, his conclusions on the Robin Hood ballads were closely similar: "Robin Hood . . . is put forward in so many words as the representative of the yeomen. 'Yeomanry' is an idea, like chivalry; it is the same thing essentially . . . The virtues of Robin Hood are courteous; he has the same virtues as Sir Gawain himself. But he belongs to a different order".[3] These views scarcely agree with Dr. Hilton's, suggesting as they do that the Robin Hood ballads were originally the literature, not of a discontented peasantry, but of the gentry. That this was indeed the case is the thesis of the following pages.

Dr. Hilton himself reveals, and to some extent discusses, some of the weaknesses of his position. First, as he states, "the north of England and Scotland were the homes *par excellence* of the ballads", and, indeed, it might be added that this is true of many of the surviving examples of the genre as a whole.[4] The Robin Hood ballads were before all else northern; the peasant movements of the fourteenth century were not. It cannot be argued that peasant discontent ceased at the Trent — Scarborough, Beverley and York were all the scene of movements in 1381; nevertheless, active agrarian discontent came chiefly from the south and especially in 1381, from Kent and East Anglia.[5] Now a Robin Hood based on the Weald, or the forest of Essex, or even the New Forest, might meet Dr. Hilton's bill very well, but one based on Sherwood or Barnsdale presents an important difficulty. The proper backcloth to these ballads is not that of John Ball, Tyler and Jack Straw, but one compounded of the problem of the north; at first of maintenance and misgovernment at their worst, of border and baronial warfare; later of medieval survivals, of the Pilgrimage of Grace, of the white-coated tenantry of the Duke of Newcastle, of the expensive largesse and nostalgic reconstructions of Lady Anne Clifford.

There is a second and much greater weakness in Dr. Hilton's argument, which is illustrated in the opening stanza of the earliest surviving version of the story, the *Gest of Robyn Hode*. This stanza

---

[2] "On the Danish Ballads", *Scottish Historical Review*, v (1908), pp. 385-401, especially pp. 396-9. See also *ibid.*, i (1904), pp. 357-8.
[3] "Spanish and English Ballads", *Collected Essays* (London, 1925), ii, p. 20. Compare M. J. C. Hodgart's opinion: "The Robin Hood Ballads are Yeoman minstrelsy and not aristocratic as the Danish ballads are, yet they express much the same code" (*The Ballads*, London, 1950, p. 133).
[4] W. J. Entwistle, *European Balladry* (Oxford, 1939), pp. 229, 230.
[5] The geographic distribution of the movement is shown on the map in A. Réville, *Le Soulèvement des Travailleurs d'Angleterre en 1381* (Paris, 1898).

was probably the work of the compiler of the *Gest* and therefore represents a late fourteenth-century or early fifteenth-century attitude towards Robin:

> Lythe and listin, gentilmen,
> That be of frebore blode;
> I shall you tel of a gode yeman,
> His name was Robyn Hode[6].

Robin is a free man, indeed a "prude" and "curteyse" outlaw, and his audience is gentle and free-born. It may be argued that the views of the compiler of the *Gest* are not evidence of the original content and social atmosphere of the ballads. But there is no strong evidence for such an argument and much against it. Nowhere in the whole cycle, as we have it, is there any hint that either Robin, his men, or his audience were unfree or at all interested in the problems to which villeinage gave rise. This fact cannot be evaded by suggesting, as Dr. Hilton does, that the heroes of the peasantry were "as free as they themselves aspired to be". Nor is it relevant to instance the cases in the royal courts in which villeins claimed free birth in an attempt to initiate pleas of service. A villein could only bring such a case before the justices by denying his status. There was no such technicality, legal or otherwise, to prevent a villein appearing in literature as exactly what he was. No matter how far we go in accepting Dr. Hilton's suggestion that the ballads represent peasant aspirations rather than the realities in which they lived, it is difficult to imagine that a peasant audience would readily accept the word "churlish" as a term of abuse synonymous with "boorish". Yet Little John abuses the monk twice in this manner in the *Gest*.[7] This was not sung or recited, still less written, for villeins.[8]

Dr. Hilton's views on this point form part of a more important

---

[6] W. H. Clawson, *The Gest of Robin Hood* (Toronto, 1909), pp. 48-9.

[7] Stanzas 219, 227; F. J. Child, *The English and Scottish Popular Ballads* (New York, 1957), iii, p. 67, in which edition nearly all the ballads mentioned below are printed. Compare *Robin Hood rescuing Will Stutly*, surviving from the seventeenth century, where Will addresses the sheriff as "Thou faint-heart pesant slave" (stanza 24).

[8] Great emphasis was given to Robin's freedom by Louise Pound (*Poetic Origins and the Ballads*, New York, 1921, pp. 97 ff.), who concluded that "the social atmosphere of the ballads is the atmosphere of the upper classes" (p. 99). This formed part of her advocacy of the "individualist" against the "communalist" thesis of ballad origins. For the history of this controversy see the excellent account by M. J. C. Hodgart, *op. cit.* pp. 151 ff., especially p. 156. Sir Edmund Chambers' comment on the opening stanza suggests an approach which differs from both Miss Pound and Dr. Hilton: "There is courtesy here, for some at least of the audience must have been of villein descent" (*English Literature at the Close of The Middle Ages*, Oxford, 1947, p. 137).

misapprehension, namely that the Robin of the ballads was a man whose "most endearing activities to his public were the robbery and killing of landowners, in particular church landowners". This view is widely held: Robin is presented as "the archetype of the social bandit";[9] "what he takes from the rich he gives to the poor";[10] F. J. Child himself, the editor of the ballads, described him as "friendly to poor men generally, imparting to them what he takes from the rich".[11] But it is based on a very minor part of the ballad cycle and gives a false impression of its total content. For example, not one of the extant ballads presents the outlaws robbing a secular landlord, and not one is concerned with robbing the rich, whether clerk or lay, *in order to* give to the poor.

This view of Robin is chiefly derived from Martin Parker's *True Tale of Robin Hood* of 1632. The following is typical:

> Poore men might safely passe by him,
> And some that way would chuse,
> For well they knew that to helpe them
> He evermore did use.

> But where he knew a miser rich,
> That did the poore oppresse,
> To feele his coyne his hand did itch;
> Hee'de have it, more or lesse.[12]

The *True Tale*, however, is a late compilation which presents Robin as the outlawed and bankrupt Earl of Huntingdon. Robin's gifts to the poor are here made to illustrate his Christian charity rather than any deliberately conceived social policy. Parker was not inclined to the unorthodox:

> We that live in these latter dayes
> Of civill government,
> If neede be, have a hundred wayes
> Such outlawes to prevent.

> In those dayes men more barbarous were,
> And lived lesse in awe;
> Now, God be thanked! people feare
> More to offend the law.[13]

[9] E. J. Hobsbawm, *Primitive Rebels* (Manchester, 1959), p. 13.

[10] J. W. Walker, *The True History of Robin Hood* (West Yorkshire Printing Co., 1952), p. xi. Compare his earlier expressions of the same view in *Robin Hood* (Wakefield Historical Society, 1943), introduction; and "Robin Hood Identified"; *Yorks. Archaeological Journal*, xxxvi (1944), pp. 4-46.

[11] Child, *op. cit.*, iii, p. 43.

[12] Stanzas 51-52. Compare stanzas 19-22, especially 21:

> The widdow and the fatherlesse,
> He would send meanes unto,
> And those whom famine did oppresse
> Found him a friendly foe.

[13] Stanzas 109, 110.

He was an ardent Royalist, best remembered for his banale *When the King enjoys his own again*.   He provides a warning that a bandit who robs the rich and helps the poor need not be a social revolutionary or appeal solely to those with such instincts.   He may simply provide material for a good yarn.   The ballad of Jesse James apparently won strong approval from no less a person than President Theodore Roosevelt, and yet:

> Jesse was a man, a friend to the poor,
> He would never see a man suffer pain;
> And with his brother Frank he robbed the Chicago bank,
> And stopped the Glendale train.[14]

Parker's views on Robin find only slight support in the other ballads of the cycle.   The concluding lines of the *Gest* run:

> For he was a good outlawe,
> And dyde pore men moch god.

In the *Noble Fisherman*, of the seventeenth century, Robin gives half the value of his captured French prize to the widow who owns the ship in which he sails, and devotes the £12,000 it contained to the founding of an alms-house.   In *Robin Hood and the Bishop*, also of the seventeenth century, but probably much closer than the *Fisherman* to the main stream of Robin Hood literature, Robin gets the collusion of an old woman because of past kindnesses:

> For I well remember, one Saturday night
> Thou bought me both shoos and hose.[15]

Even so, Robin does not give the old lady any part of the £500 which her help enabled him to extract from the Bishop.

Other ballads present an entirely different picture of Robin.   In *Robin Hood and Queen Catherine*, again of the seventeenth century, the beneficiary of his activities is far from poor, for it is the Queen herself.   In some of the group of ballads which deal with Robin's defeat in combat by a rustic, the fight is provoked by an attempt to demand money from, or rob, the opponent.   Robin demands "pavage" from the Potter and tries to inspect the Shepherd's bag and bottle; Little John tries to rob the Bold Pedlar of his wares; in another encounter with pedlars Robin tries to search their packs; in *Robin Hood and the Beggar II* he plans to take any money the Beggar may have.   The last three of these are late versions, first recorded, as we have them, in the eighteenth and nineteenth centuries; *Robin Hood and the Shepherd* is of the seventeenth century; *Robin Hood and the Potter* exists in a manuscript of *c.* 1500.   The tradition they embody is medieval in origin.

[14] Robert Graves, *The English Ballad* (London, 1927), p. 133.
[15] Stanza 9.

There is thus more than a hint of Robin as a simple robber, who preyed on rich and poor alike. In the fourteenth century, indeed, rogues and thieves were sometimes colloquially described as "Robert's men". In 1331 the phrase was incorporated in an Act of Parliament which referred to the "robberies, homicides and felonies done in these times by people called Roberdesmen, Wastours and Draghlacche".[16] It was repeated when this statute was confirmed in 7 Richard II, cap. 5;[17] Robert's knaves appear as robbers in *Piers Plowman*,[18] and so indeed does Robert the Robber himself.[19] It is perhaps worth recalling a famous letter in which John Ball addressed some of the rebels of 1381:

> Iohon Schep . . . greteth wel Iohan Nameles, and Iohan the Mullere, and Iohon Cartere, and biddeth hem that thei bee war of gyle in borugh, and stondeth togidre in Godes name, and biddeth Peres Plouyman go to his werk, and *chastise wel Hobbe the Robbere*, and taketh with yow Iohan Trewman and alle hiis felawes . . .[20]

The Hobbe the Robber of this passage has been identified as the Treasurer, Robert Hales,[21] but there is no compelling reason for making such an identification. The passage is better read as a warning against wanton and irresponsible plunder; in a companion letter of Jakke Carter the instruction is:

> lokke that Hobbe robbyoure be wele chastysed for lesyng of youre grace, for ye have gret nede to take God with yowe in all youre dedes.[22]

The names of the addressees in John Ball's letter are probably fictitious,[23] and it contains several allusions to *Piers Plowman*.[24]

---

[16] 5 Edward III, cap. 14 (*Statutes of the Realm*, i, p. 268).

[17] *Statutes of the Realm*, ii, p. 32.   [18] Text C, passus i, line 45.

[19] Text C, passus vii, pp. 316, 322; Text B, passus v, line 469.   I am indebted to Dr. R. I. Page for drawing my attention to this information, much of which is summarized in *N.E.D.*

[20] K. Sisam, *Fourteenth-Century Verse and Prose* (Oxford, 1955), pp. 160-1. For various versions of the letter see Walsingham, *Historia Anglicana*, ed. H. T. Riley (Rolls Series, 1864), ii, pp. 33-4.

[21] See H. Fagan in R. H. Hilton and H. Fagan, *The English Rising of 1381* (London, 1950), p. 101.   If an actual person was intended it could equally well be Sir Robert Belknap, Chief Justice of the King's Bench, who was sent to punish the outbreaks against the poll tax commissioners in Essex and was seized by the rebels.   See May McKisack, *The Fourteenth Century* (Oxford, 1959), p. 407.

[22] *Chronicon Henrici Knighton*, ed. J. R. Lumby (Rolls Series, 1895), ii, p. 139, where other letters are also given.

[23] See C. Petit-Dutaillis in Réville, *op. cit.*, pp. lxxvi n. 2, lxxvii; although a John Miller and a John Carter appear among the London and Norfolk rebels respectively (*ibid.*, pp. 224, 93).

[24] See the comments in the edition of W. W. Skeat (Oxford, 1886), ii, pp. xliv-xlv.   In addition to Skeat's arguments it is worth noting that the only fourteenth-century parallels to Ball's phrase "go to work" which are mentioned in *N.E.D.* are drawn from Piers Plowman and that no fifteenth-century examples of such a usage are given.   I am indebted to Dr. R. I. Page for bringing this to my notice.

The juxtaposition of Piers and Hobbe the Robber suggests that Ball was making a literary allusion in both cases, and there can be no doubt that he, like Langland, was setting up Hobbe, or Robert, as a target for scorn and disapproval.   Sir Edward Coke later considered that Robert the Robber and Robin Hood were one and the same person.[25] Certainly by the fifteenth century Robin was accepted as an archetypal robber, for a petition to Parliament of 1439 complained of one Piers Venables of Derbyshire, who had collected a company of misdoers "and, in manere of Insurrection, wente into the wodes in that Contre, like as it hadde be Robynhode and his meyne".[26] There is nothing to prove that Robert the Robber and Robin Hood were always identified in men's minds, but it is highly likely that the traditions of the two were intermingled.

The strongest support for Parker comes not so much from the other ballads as from the *Historia Maioris Britanniae* of John Major, published in 1521.   Here Major states that Robin and Little John took the goods of the rich, and killed only those who tried to resist or attack them.   "He permitted no harm to women, nor seized the goods of the poor, but in fact supported them generously with what he took from abbots".[27] Abbots may have been rich, but not all the rich were abbots.   Even so, some lost ballad in which Robin robbed a rich man, clerk or lay, and gave the proceeds to the poor, may lie behind Major's story.

There is, however, a much more probable explanation, namely that both Parker's and Major's views are of common stock with the famous passage in the *Gest* in which Robin declares his objectives to his men:[28]

> But loke ye do no **husbonde** harme,
> That tilleth with his ploughe.
>
> No more ye shall no gode yeman
> That walketh by grenë-wode shawe;
> Ne no knyght ne no squyer
> That wol be gode felawe.
>
> These bisshoppes and these archebisshoppes,
> Ye shall them bete and bynde;
> The hyë sherif of Notyingham
> Hym holde ye in your mynde.[29]

[25] *Institutes*, iii, p. 197.
[26] *Rot. Parl.*, v, p. 16; quoted in Child, *op. cit.*, iii, p. 41.
[27] p. 55 b.
[28] The connection is not inherently unlikely. The *King's Disguise and Friendship with Robin Hood*, surviving from the eighteenth century, clearly drew on the *Gest* or some common original.
[29] Stanzas 13-15.

Now it is immediately apparent that there are marked differences between this and Parker. Here there is no positive plan to help the poor. Here, too, the dividing line is not between rich and poor. Robin's enemies are bishops, archbishops and the sheriff of Nottingham. His friends include knights and squires, "if they will be good fellows"; indeed, a great part of the *Gest* is concerned with the doings of a knight who was a "good fellow".[30]   Robin makes no mention at all of barons.

Like bishops, knights were landowners, and often oppressive ones too, who were in large measure responsible for the enactment and enforcement of the Statute of Labourers and for the poll taxes which provoked the rising of 1381. Any attack on landlords in the fourteenth century would have to embrace the landed gentry. It is therefore certain that Robin's distinctions have nothing at all to do with the rift between landlord and peasant. Even apart from this, I can find no justification for Dr. Hilton's view that the Abbot of St. Mary's is cast in the *Gest* in the role of the landlord, or that the monks are "exemplars" of unrelenting landlordism. The Abbot plays the role of the creditor and mortgagee, the hard-hearted and eternal Shylock, here assuming monkish form. His fault lies not in his estate management, but in his greed and love of lucre, in characteristics which are presented as fundamentally unchristian. Indeed, nowhere in the whole cycle is a clerk given the role of a harsh and grasping landlord. In *Robin Hood and the Monk* Robin's devoutness is contrasted with the monk's irreligious treachery. In *Robin Hood and the Golden Prize* the outlaws compel the monks to take oaths of honesty, chastity and charity. In *Robin Hood and the Bishop* and *Robin Hood and the Bishop of Hereford* the target is the wealth, power and worldliness of the bishops. In several instances Robin's devotion to the Virgin and chivalry towards women are contrasted with clerical debauchery. Finally, clerks are always made to appear dishonest, for they are robbed not so much because they carry riches as because they will not openly admit it.

All this stemmed from a widespread and varied anti-clerical feeling, of which the ballads are only one expression among many. Hostility to the clergy was a crucial element in them; a treacherous

---

[30] Dr. Hilton considers that "this leniency to the knights is probably a consequence of the peculiar situation which was characteristic of England at the end of the middle ages — a blurring of the division between the richer yeomen and the lesser gentry" (Hilton and Fagan, *op. cit.*, p. 86). It is necessary to point out that knights were not lesser gentry, that this "blurring" was a marked feature of English society at least from the late-twelfth century, and that it is only necessary to explain this "leniency" thus because of the assumptions which form Dr. Hilton's starting point.

monk and a worldly prioress are respectively made the instruments of Robin's death;[31] but this has nothing at all to do with estate management.   In the *Gest*, especially, the problems presented are those of the knighthood and gentry, for the story revolves round the knight's debt to the Abbot of St. Mary's and its repayment, and the consequent loan from Robin and its repayment.   These related topics make up nearly half the whole poem and can have been of little concern to the peasantry.   Monastic investors were hunting bigger game; in any case, villeins had no security to offer.   Thus the evidence of the chief topic of the *Gest*, which is the earliest surviving version of the legend, is that it was primarily the literature of the county landowners, of the knights and gentry.   Its other themes also point to this conclusion.

However, the other main topics of the poem are not so socially distinctive.   These were, first, the royal forests and joys of hunting the royal game, and, secondly, the royal sheriffs and their. harshness and iniquity.   These were topics of general appeal; all men infringed the forest laws, from baron, bishop and abbot downwards, and all social ranks readily attacked shrieval administration.   They appear as themes in a wide range of ballad literature.   The forest theme, for example, occurs in the *Tale of Gamelyn;* in *Robin and Gandelyn*, an early fragment distinct both from *Gamelyn* and *Robin Hood;* and as the main element in *Johnnie Cock*, where the theme is centred on the Border, and in *Adam Bell, Clim of the Clough and William of Cloudesly*, which is centred on Inglewood in Cumberland.   The last, especially, was closely connected with the Robin Hood ballads.[32]   In all these works the forest is not simply the jolly greenwood in which outlaws lead an idyllic life and where it never seems to rain.   It is an object of attack, the target being the forest law, the royal foresters and the royal game itself.   The condition of the forest of Plumpton Park which the *Gest* describes was little different from the actual state of several northern forests in the thirteenth century:

> There our kynge was wont to se
> Herdës many one,
> He could vnneth fynde one dere,
> That bare ony good horne.[33]

This   resulted   from   Robin's   activities   which   are   described enthusiastically:

---

[31] For the monk see *Robin Hood and the Valiant Knight;* for the prioress see the *Gest*, stanzas 451-455 and *Robin Hood's Death*.

[32] Child, *op. cit.*, iii, p. 214; Chambers, *op. cit.*, pp. 157-9.

[33] *Gest*, stanza 358.

> But alway went good Robyn
> By halke and eke by hyll,
> And alway slewe the kyngës dere,
> And welt them at his wyll.[34]

These topics are near the heart of the Robin Hood legend, for they occur, in one form or another, in the *Gest*, in *Robin Hood and the Beggar I* and *Robin Hood's Delight*, both of the seventeenth century, and in the later *Robin Hood and the Three Squires*, in which Robin rescues three squires about to be executed for killing deer, *Robin Hood and the Ranger*, *Robin Hood's Progress* and *Robin Hood and the Bishop of Hereford*.

The theme of the sheriff is not perhaps so widespread, but the Robin Hood ballads share it with the *Tale of Gamelyn* and *Adam Bell*. Moreover, it appears in so many of the ballads of the Robin Hood cycle[35] that some authorities have viewed this as the dominating theme of the whole group.[36]

Although both the forest and sheriff themes had an almost universal appeal, there are strong reasons for thinking that they were not developed here primarily for peasant ears. In dealing with the forests, for example, the criticism of the ballads is directed against the royal forests, not against the private forests which steadily increased in number and size, nor against the rights of warren which manorial lords frequently enjoyed and which must have been at least as burdensome to the peasantry as the rights of the Crown. In brief, the poaching is of a lordly kind and its methods are well bred. The quarry is always the deer, which are always shot, never trapped or hunted down with dogs. It is a sport; the object is not simply sustenance; it is frequently a feast. In contrast, when the peasants poached, any method and any game were fair. The enraged reaction of the landowner is fairly represented by a statute of 1390:

Forasmuch as divers Artificers, Labourers, and Servants, and Grooms, keep Greyhounds and other Dogs, and on the Holydays, when good Christian People be at Church, hearing Divine Service, they go hunting in Parks, Warrens and Connigries of Lords and others, to the very great Destruction of the same, and sometimes under such Colour they make their Assemblies, Conferences, and Conspiracies for to rise and disobey their Allegiance; It is ordained and assented, that no Manner of Artificer, Labourer, nor any other Layman, which hath not Lands or Tenements to the value of xls. by Year, nor any Priest nor other Clerk, if he be not advanced to the Value of £10 by Year, shall have or keep from henceforth any Greyhound, Hound, nor other Dog to hunt; nor shall they use Fyrets, Heys, Nets, Harepipes, nor Cords, nor other Engines for to take or destroy Deer, Hares, nor Conies, nor other

---

[34] *Ibid.*, stanza 366.
[35] *Robin Hood and the Potter, Robin Hood and the Butcher, Robin Hood and the Beggar I, Robin Hood and Will Stutly, Robin Hood and the Three Squires, Robin Hood and the Golden Arrow.*   [36] Chambers, *op. cit.*, p. 134.

Gentlemen's Game, upon Pain of One Year's imprisonment; and that the Justices of the Peace have Power to enquire, and shall enquire, of the Offenders in this Behalf, and punish them by the Pain aforesaid.[37]

Robin's activities were clearly far removed from this. All he was doing in the ballads was what many landowners were doing in practice — zestfully and persistently attacking the forest rights of the Crown by gentlemanly techniques.

A similar social bias informs the treatment of the sheriff theme. As Dr. Hilton points out, sheriffs were sometimes called in to reinforce the authority of manorial bailiffs, but sheriffs were not immediately concerned with the maintenance of manorial discipline. Neither the *Gest* nor any other ballad in the cycle contains anything about the officials who were. Where justices appear, they are not Justices of the Labourers or Justices of the Peace, against whom the peasantry felt and showed great indignation, but Justices of the Forest or of the common law. The attack is directed against the highest ranks of the local administration with whom the knights and gentry were in regular contact and frequent conflict, not against those whom we might expect the peasantry to choose as their chief targets.

Many subsidiary and incidental features of the story in the *Gest* strengthen the knightly atmosphere evoked by its main themes. Robin wonders whether the knight is one by distraint. The sad material condition of the knight is emphasized; he rides "in simple array" and Robin remarks that his "clothynge is so thinne"; before his first departure from the outlaws it is necessary to clothe and accoutre him properly, with a "grey coursor" for his steed and Little John for his knave. Robin's extravagant generosity is itself related to the knightly code, especially perhaps the wasting of his funds and the loss of his following when he finally went to live at the King's court. And he preserves the forms:

It was neuer the maner, by dere worthi God,
A yoman to pay for a knyhht.[38]

Moreover, yeoman though he is, he fights, his famous bow apart, with knightly weapons. All the hand-to-hand conflicts in the *Gest* are with the sword. In *Robin Hood and the Potter* Robin's opponent, for the first time, uses the staff, but in the extant versions Robin himself does not stoop to this weapon until in *Robin Hood and Little John*, surviving from the seventeenth century, both he and Little John set to work on each other with staffs:

As if they had been threshing of corn.[39]

---

[37] 13 Richard II, I, cap. 13. Cp. *Rot. Parl.*, iii, p. 273. I owe this reference and that in note 62 to the kindness of Mr. W. H. Liddell.
[38] *Gest*, stanza 37.   [39] *Robin Hood and Little John*, stanza 16.

The evidence of the subject matter of the *Gest* is supported both by its construction and by the early references to the Robin Hood legend. It is not a single ballad, but a number of ballads strung together to form a poem of epic length. The compiler brought the different elements together by adding material of his own, much of which is knightly or "gentle" in character, dealing for example, with the mutual support of Sir Richard of the Lee and Robin in the fight against the sheriff.[40] The *Gest* was printed after 1500, but was composed earlier, possibly as early as 1400.[41] Even before this time Robin was already firmly rooted in the literary inheritance of the landowning class. The famous reference to him in *Piers Plowman* associates him with the *Geste* of Ranulf, Earl of Chester, an unquestionably knightly subject. Another early allusion occurs in *Troilus and Criseyde*, where Chaucer refers to those who:

> Defamen love, as no-thing of him knowe;
> They speken, but they bente never his bowe.

Here he was alluding to the proverb which appears in the *Reply of Friar Daw Topias:*

> And many men speken of Robyn Hood
> And shotte nevere in his bowe.[42]

Chaucer, indeed, constructed his knight's Yeoman in the unmistakable image of Robin Hood:

> And he was clad in cote and hood of grene;
> A sheef of pecock-arwes brighte and kene
> Under his belt he bar ful thriftily;
> (Wel coude he dresse his takel yemanly:
> His arwes drouped noght with fetheres lowe),
> And in his hand he bar a mighty bowe.[43]

Within a century of this there is clear evidence, in a letter of 1473, that Sir John Paston retained a servant who played St. George, Robin Hood and the sheriff of Nottingham.[44]

The Robin Hood ballads seem to have been part of a well developed and varied type of literature. The obvious parallels are *Adam Bell* and the *Tale of Gamelyn*. In *Adam* the heroes are, like Robin,

[40] Clawson, *op. cit.*, pp. 96-7.

[41] *Ibid.*, pp. 2-6. The chief argument for this date is the survival in the *Gest* of the ME final -e and -es as regular inflexional endings.

[42] *Troilus and Criseyde*, book ii, lines 860-1; *Political Poems and Songs*, ed. T. Wright (Rolls Series, 1861), ii, p. 59. The passage is discussed by R. M. Wilson in *The Lost Literature of Medieval England* (London, 1952), p. 139 and in the edition of *Troilus* by R. K. Root, (Princeton, 1926), p. 449. I am indebted to Dr. Kenneth Cameron for these references.

[43] *The Canterbury Tales*, Prologue, ll. 103-8. Skeat noted the significant analogue of the peacock feathers, which also tipped the arrows included in the knight's gift to Robin Hood. (*Works of Chaucer*, v, p. 11; *Gest*, stanza 132). Goose feathers were more effective and were normally used.

[44] *Paston Letters*, ed. J. Gairdner (London, 1910), iii, p. 89.

yeomen, but their leader, William of Cloudesly, becomes the King's "chief rider of the north country" and is made "gentleman of clothing and of fee"; his wife is made the chief gentlewoman of the Queen and governess of the royal children; Adam and Clim become yeomen of the Chamber.[45]

In *Gamelyn* the hero is the younger son of a knight. He expresses many of the attitudes of Robin Hood. He is hostile to wealthy clerics:

> Cursed mot he worthe bothe fleisch and blood,
> That ever do priour or abbot ony good.[46]

He flees to the greenwood and becomes king of the outlaws. He fights with the justice and the sheriff, who is his elder brother, and eventually:

> The Iustice and the scherreve bothe honged hye,
> To weyven with the ropes and with the winde drye.[47]

Finally he makes his peace with the King and is appointed Chief Justice of the Forest. But while in *The Gest of Robin Hood* similar topics are interwoven with the debts and subsequent mortgages of a knight, here the companion themes are concerned with the division of a knight's inheritance, the wardship of the younger brother, Gamelyn, and the wasting of his estates by his evil elder brother. The *Tale of Gamelyn* was preserved by Chaucer, probably as potential material for the Canterbury Tales. It also contributed indirectly to *As You Like It*. It is clearly far removed from John Ball and the grievances of the peasantry in the fourteenth century.

If the Robin Hood stories were designed primarily for a gentle audience, they were not confined to this audience. By the seventeenth century an aristocratic strain had developed. Robin had become Robert, Earl of Huntingdon, and Marion the Fair Maid of Dunmow, King John's famous legendary victim. Even before this Robin was fitting entertainment for Henry VIII and the ladies of his court.[48] At the other extreme, a much more plebeian tradition developed, which bore fruit in the association of Robin with the May Games and in the large number of ballads in which he or one of his men come to blows with a rustic of some kind, who usually proves himself equal if not superior to the outlaws. This must have been an early development for it is present in *Robin Hood and the Potter* of *c.* 1500, and there can be no doubt that peasants were part of the Robin Hood

---

[45] The ballad is most readily accessible in Child, *op. cit.*, iii.

[46] ll. 491-2. *The Tale of Gamelyn* is most readily accessible in W. W. Skeat's edition of the *Canterbury Tales*, pp. 645-667.

[47] ll. 879-80.

[48] E. K. Chambers, *The Medieval Stage* (Oxford, 1903), i, p. 180.

audience well before this. Bower, writing in the 1440s, described the audience of the "tragedies" and "comedies" of Robin Hood as the *stolidum vulgus*, "the stupid multitude".[49]   The fifteenth-century *How the Plowman learned his Paternoster* tells of ploughmen who:

> Eche had two busshelles of whete that was gode,
> They songe goynge home warde a Gest of Robyn Hode.[50]

This widespread appeal of the ballads is not to be explained solely by the overlapping interests of different classes in some of the topics they contained.   There must have been some central point of dissemination, and this most probably lay in the households of the gentry, not in the chamber but in the hall, where the entertainment was aimed not only at the master but also at the members and the staff.   From the hall the stories could easily spread to the kitchen, the scullery and out beyond the walls to the local tavern and the surrounding cottages.   But the original audience was not concerned with alleged or actual class conflicts, of which the ballads are remarkably free, but with hospitality and its formalities, and with the precedence which arose from service and status.   These are recurrent topics in the ballads, especially in the *Gest*.   Moreover, Robin himself is cast as a yeoman, as a member of such a household hierarchy, which ascended in order from yeoman to squire and from squire to knight.   A yeoman was as yet in an official status not a social rank.   He was not yet distinguished from a gentleman and equated with the 40 shilling freeholder, as he was by Sir Thomas Smith,[51] nor was he equated with a fee-farmer or a leaseholder of some few pounds income as he was by Sir John Fortescue[52] and later by Bishop Latimer.[53]   The earliest indication of some such distinction which I have found occurred in 1445 when it was laid down that knights of the shire were to be drawn from knights, "noteable Squires" and "Gentilmen of birth", and not from those who stood in the "degree of Yoman and bynethe".[54]   Long after this, gentlemen and yeomen could still be associated, as they were in 34 and 35 Henry VIII cap. 26, which arranged that two substantial gentlemen or yeomen should act as chief constables of the hundred.[55]   In the fourteenth and early fifteenth century there was even greater variety and fluidity.   Yeomen

---

[49] Child, *op. cit.*, iii, p. 41.
[50] Chambers, *English Literature at the close of the Middle Ages*, p. 131.
[51] *De Republica Anglorum*, ed. L. Alston (Cambridge, 1906), p. 42.
[52] *The Governance of England*, ed. C. Plummer (Oxford, 1885), p. 151.
[53] *Sermons*, ed. H. C. Beeching (London, 1906), p. 85.
[54] *Rot. Parl.*, v. p. 116; compare 23 Henry VI, c.14 (*Statutes of the Realm* ii. p. 342).   I owe this reference to the kindness of Professor J. S. Roskell.
[55] *Statutes of the Realm*, iii. p. 931.

appear as "gentlemen yeomen".[56]   In the settlement in 1411
between William, Lord Ros, and Robert Tirwhit, Justice of the King's
Bench, attendance was required from all the "Knyghtes and Esquiers
and Yomen that had ledynge of men" in Ros' party.[57]   In *Guy of
Gisborne*, one of the earliest ballads of the Robin Hood series, Guy
appears first as a yeoman and then as Sir Guy twice in consecutive
stanzas,[58] and he might have expected a knight's fee as his reward for
slaying Robin.[59]   The succession of yeoman, squire, knight, seems
to have been commonly accepted at this time,[60] and is indeed implied
by Chaucer's Prologue.   But Chaucer's yeoman was a special kind of
household officer.   He was skilled in woodcraft:

> A forster was he, soothly, as I gesse.

Indeed, one of the earliest sources for the word yeoman occurs in the
twelfth-century *Pseudo-Cnut de Foresta* where the "yongermen"
appear as foresters drawn from the *mediocres homines* or "laessthegenes".[61]   Robin's most famous weapons, his bow and arrows,
were at once the tools and insignia of the local foresters which
distinguished them from other bailiffs,[62] and which appeared as their
characteristic accoutrement on their tombs.   It is highly probable
that Robin's earliest audience thought of him as an outlawed forester,
who had been an established and in no way menial member of a lord's
or gentleman's household.   As such, he was on the landlord's side,
not the peasant's, and indeed when he was later compelled to do
battle with rustics in order to meet the tastes of a rustic audience, it
is significant that the rustic always held his own and sometimes,
indeed, won.

For such a convivial and socially mixed audience as a household
the ballads brought together a number of attractive and well-worn
themes: a roughly enforced and crudely conceived idea of justice and
morality; a code of honesty; a good fight, an adventurous chase; the
joke of trickery by disguise, the King *incognito*.   These formed a
common denominator, independent of class, which made up the
basic Robin Hood.

The ballads also showed a zest for lawlessness which was bound to

[56] *Monumenta Franciscana*, ed. J. S. Brewer, (Rolls Series, 1858), i. p. 583.
[57] *Rot. Parl.*, iii. p. 650.
[58] Stanzas 48, 49; 22, 23.
[59] Stanza 51.
[60] Higden, *Polychronicon*, ed. C. Babington (Rolls Series, 1869) ii. p. 171.
[61] F. Liebermann, *Die Gesetze der Angelsachsen*, (Halle, 1903), i. p. 620:
"Sintque sub quolibet horum (primariorum) quatuor ex mediocribus hominibus
quos Angli laessthegenes nuncupant, Dani uero yongermen uocant".
[62] *Close Rolls* 1234-1237, pp. 521-2.

appeal to the truculent, unbuttoned element in any class. In *Pierce the Ploughman's Crede*, of the late fourteenth century, the "Robertes Men":

> . . . raken aboute
> At feires and at ful ales and fyllen the cuppe.[63]

The atmosphere of the ballads sometimes comes close, as one suspects the audience sometimes did, to Falstaff and his cronies. Shakespeare made the point implicitly when he had Justice Silence trying to sing of "Robin Hood, Scarlet and John" after a drunken feast with the fat knight.[64] These general themes, the fighting and the buffeting, the excitement and the trickery, seem to constitute such appeal as the ballads had for the peasantry, for these were the elements developed in the more rustic versions of the story. Certainly, too, the peasantry would be on Robin's side against the clergy and the sheriff. But it is difficult to go beyond this. There is nothing in the ballads of the great economic issues of the fourteenth century, nothing of rents, or wages, or the attempt to maintain manorial discipline, or the fight against villein status, or even the dramatic "ballad-worthy" episodes of the rising of 1381 itself. All this is missing, too, in a literary form which is raw and down to earth.

Such is the evidence of the surviving ballads. It may be that the knightly versions of Robin Hood survived more easily than the peasant versions, and that part of the peasant tradition of the outlaw has not come down to us. It could be argued that the *Gest* presents us with a distorted "gentle" Robin, a relatively respectable version of some primitive social rebel. Of this there is no evidence. Indeed, any effort to penetrate behind the *Gest* leads us, not to rustic figures, but to the knightly heroes of the thirteenth-century romances and *gestes*.

In 1909 W. H. Clawson published a detailed analysis of the *Gest* in his *Gest of Robin Hood*.[65] In this he broke up the poem into its components, distinguishing between the sections which were the work of the compiler and those which were derived from, or repeated, earlier stories. He distinguished twelve of these earlier stories and then demonstrated that they had even earlier analogues, especially in the romances of Eustace the Monk, a Flemish knight and pirate, who served both King John and Prince Louis of France and was killed in the battle of Sandwich of 1217, and of Fulk fitz Warin, a marcher lord, whom King John outlawed for a time. The ballads, therefore,

[63] ll. 72-3; ed. W. W. Skeat (Early English Text Society, 1867), p. 3.
[64] Henry IV part 2, act v, scene 3.
[65] Published Toronto, 1909.

drew directly on these romances, or on some derivative of the romances, or on some common source.[66]

The *Roman d'Eustache li Moine* is a Norman-French poem, apparently of the thirteenth century.[67]   Like Robin, Eustace is an outlaw.   He has violently resisted an act of injustice.   He takes refuge in the forest where he gathers a band of followers.   He is skilled in disguise, and indeed flits from one disguise to another in a series of bewildering stratagems.   In addition to this general similarity of atmosphere, the *Roman* provides four close analogues with the *Gest* and the early Robin Hood ballads.   One of Eustace's disguises is that of a Potter, as is one of Robin's;[68] just as the sheriff is decoyed into the woods, captured and later released by Robin, so is the Count of Boulogne lured into the woods, captured and released by Eustace;[69] Eustace, like Robin, lets those who tell the truth about the money they carry retain it, in Eustace's case a merchant, in Robin's case a knight;[70] like Robin again, he robs those who fail to tell the truth, and both his victims and Robin's are monks.[71]

There are also close similarities between Robin Hood and Fulk fitz Warin.   The romance of Fulk survives as a late thirteenth- or early fourteenth-century prose paraphrase, in Anglo-Norman, of an earlier poem.[72]   Just as Little John takes service with the sheriff in the *Gest of Robin Hood*, so in this story one of Fulk's men gains admission as a minstrel to the castle and service of his enemy Maurice fitz Roger.[73]   Like the sheriff in *Robin Hood* and the Count in *Eustache*, King John is lured into an ambush by Fulk, who, disguised as a charcoal burner, promises to show him a fine stag. The King is captured, he swears to restore Fulk to estate and favour, and is then allowed to go.[74]

These two romances do not stand alone in providing analogues to the Robin Hood ballads.   The *Gesta Herewardi*, for example, was also used or was indebted to a source shared with the ballads, and the dramatic story of a King in disguise or *incognito* was the basis of a famous twelfth-century legend of King Alfred and was told again of Henry II.[75]   All this reinforces the conclusions of modern scholars

---

[66] Clawson's conclusions are conveniently summarized in tabular form on pp. 125-7.

[67] ed. F. Michel (London, 1834).   The story is summarized by T. Wright in *Essays on the Literature, Popular Superstitions and History of England in the Middle Ages* (London, 1846), ii. pp. 121-146.

[68] ll. 1072 ff.   [69] ll. 775 ff.

[70] ll. 928 ff.   [71] ll. 1744 ff.

[72] Most readily accessible in *Chronicon Anglicanum Radulphi de Coggeshall*, ed. J. Stevenson (Rolls Series, 1875).   [73] *Ibid.*, pp. 347 ff.

[74] *Ibid.*, pp. 387-9

[75] Clawson, *op. cit.*, pp. 104-6.

on the general origins of the ballads, namely that they were related in their origins to both the romances and the French *caroles*,[76] to literary and artistic forms which were alien to the English peasantry and which can only have been imported and initially developed by their masters. W. P. Ker's conclusion on the Danish ballad was that: "As in England and Scotland, it is a foreign importation, truly and entirely French".[77] The social implications of this are obvious.

If the foregoing arguments are valid, they establish an important corollary. The topics of the *Gest*, the sheriffs, the royal forests and ecclesiastical usury, are essentially problems of the thirteenth rather than the fourteenth century. The main attack on shrieval administration came in the period between Magna Carta and the reign of Edward I; by the fourteenth century the office had largely come into the hands of the county gentry. In the same period the extent and administration of the royal forest was another hotly argued political issue; by the fourteenth century many royal forests were in private hands, and, where they still survived, it is probable that their administration was less burdensome and effective. Finally, monastic acquisition of land, by foreclosure on mortgages or any other method, was made more difficult as the thirteenth century advanced by increasingly serious crises in monastic finances and by the successive measures against alienation in mortmain, especially by the statute of 1279; at the same time other sources of credit were becoming available to the indebted landlord. Thus it seems likely that the origins of the stories of Robin Hood, perhaps not at first in ballad form, lay in the hundred years or so before 1300. There are a number of incidental signs pointing in the same direction. When we first hear of Robin in *Piers Plowman* he is associated with Ranulf de Blundeville, Earl of Chester, who died in 1232. In Robin's first meeting with the knight, the outlaw wonders whether his guest may not have been "made a knyght of force". This reference to distraint of knighthood leads us most obviously to the time of Henry III or Edward I. Finally, if any historical figure lay behind the sheriff of the ballads, it was probably a sheriff who had a close interest in forest administration, a branch of government normally separate from the shrievalties. There are two obvious men to meet this bill; Philip Mark, sheriff of Nottinghamshire and Derbyshire from 1209 to 1224, who had custody of Sherwood from 1212 to 1217 and was still intervening in forest matters as late as 1220;[78] and Brian de Lisle,

---

[76] Hodgart, *The Ballads*, pp. 75 ff.
[77] *Scottish Historical Review*, i (1904), p. 364.
[78] On Philip's career see J. C. Holt, "Philip Mark and the Shrievalty of Nottinghamshire and Derbyshire in the early thirteenth century", *Transactions of the Thoroton Society*, lvi (1952), pp. 8 ff.

an important administrator in Yorkshire in King John's time, who was the chief forester of Nottinghamshire and Derbyshire from 1209 to 1217, Chief Justice of the Forest from 1221 to 1224 and sheriff of Yorkshire in 1233-4.

The arguments advanced above redirect us to the one historical Robert Hood we know of as an outlaw.   This is the Robert Hood to whom L. V. D. Owen first drew attention in 1936.[79]   In the pipe roll of 1226 the Yorkshire account includes a charge for the chattels of Robert Hod, fugitive.   The entry appears again on the roll of 1227 where there is a significantly familiar variation in the name: *Hobbehod*. There is no need to manufacture a historical outlaw with the right name.   We already have one, just where other evidence leads us to expect him.

Whether this was the man or not, the thesis I have advanced probably, but not certainly, involves the rejection of the claims of later Robert Hoods.   Two have been put forward, but it cannot be shown that either of them were outlaws.   One was in prison in 1354, awaiting trial for trespass of vert and venison in the forest of Rockingham in Northamptonshire.[80]   Here we have the right crime, but not the appropriate success in its pursuit; the end is imprisonment, not outlawry.   Further, as Professor May McKisack has recently pointed out, this Robin appears so late as to allow very little time for the development of the legend.[81]   The other is the Robert Hood who was a tenant of the manor of Wakefield in the reign of Edward II, and who could possibly have been, or is alleged to have been, an outlawed contrariant following the battle of Boroughbridge in 1322. This thesis was tentatively advanced by Joseph Hunter in 1852,[82] and was developed with conviction by J. W. Walker in several papers published between 1943 and 1952,[83] and by P. Valentine Harris in *The Truth about Robin Hood*.[84]   Dr. Hilton has pointed to some of the fallacies in the argument: one point is worth adding here to what he has said.   Walker's argument that the Robert Hood of Wakefield was a contrariant depends on identifying a house, newly built on

[79] "Robin Hood in the light of research" in *The Times, Trade and Engineering*, xxxviii, no. 864 (new ser.), February, 1936, p. xxix. The argument was later expanded in a contribution to *Chambers Encyclopaedia*, 1950. I am obliged to Mr. C. A. F. Meekings for correcting some of the detail in Owen's account and in the first version of this paper. It should be noted that the debt was due from the Liberty of St. Peter's, York, of which this Robert Hod must therefore have been a tenant.

[80] Chambers, *English Literature at the Close of the Middle Ages*, p. 130.
[81] *Op. cit.*, p. 209n.
[82] *Critical and Historical Tracts* no. 4.   [83] See note 10 above.
[84] Published London, 1951, new edn. 1973.

Bickhill, the Wakefield market place, and belonging in 1322 to an unnamed contrariant, as being built on a plot of waste land on Bickhill, measuring 30 ft. by 20 ft. and lying between two booths, which was bought for an unspecified purpose by a Robert Hood and his wife in 1316.[85] There is no apparent basis at all for this identification, and therefore no evidence that this Robert Hood was ever anything but a peaceful member of the community. Nor is there any reason to identify him with the Robert or Robin Hood who was serving in the King's household in 1324, well though this might fit the story of the *Gest*. Hood was a common name. Once the legend had been established many Hoods would be called Robert or Robin.

Hobbehod may sound a rustic hero for the knighthood and gentry, and it may be felt that these classes would reject the lawlessness, brigandage and brutality which the ballads express. But this was not so. The romances of Eustace the Monk and Fulk contain incidents with which the ballads, even Robin's mutilation of the dead Guy of Gisborne, can scarcely stand comparison. Eustace cuts off the feet of four of the Count's servants in revenge for the blinding of two of his own men; Fulk forces a rival outlaw, who had been operating under his name, to pinion and then behead all the members of his captured band; when this was done, Fulk himself beheaded the leader. In practice, too, the knighthood and gentry could easily match Robin's achievements. The followers of Piers Venables, who took to the woods in Derbyshire in 1439 "like as it hadde be Robynhode", were described as yeomen. But Piers himself was described by the petitioner, scarcely a favourable witness, as "of the Towne of Aston Gentilman", even though he was said to have "no liflode ne sufficeante of goodes".[86] And, if one is to believe the petitioner, Piers bullied and murdered his way through southern Derbyshire and northern Staffordshire until the effective administration of the area was made impossible. This was not in any way atypical. Professor Plucknett has drawn attention to the behaviour of several men who were knights of the shire in the first decade of the reign of Edward III. Of those who represented Bedfordshire in the parliaments of these years, one was imprisoned for killing a coroner, another accused of theft and maintaining false charges in the King's Bench, another was accused of housebreaking, and another was charged with penalties of £2,000 for various acts of

---

[85] Walker, *Robin Hood* (1943), p. 5; *The True History of Robin Hood* (1952), p. 11.

[86] *Rot. Parl.*, v, p. 16. For an excellent discussion of the early history of the word "gentleman" see F. R. H. Du Boulay, "The First English Gentlemen", *The Listener*, Oct. 30th, 1958.

violence.[87]   More recently, Professor E. L. G. Stones has presented a classic example of the type in the Folvilles of Leicestershire.   Here the oldest of a family of seven brothers seems to have lived a peaceful law-abiding existence.   The other six were criminals, whose record included complicity in the murder of a Baron of the Exchequer, the capture and ransoming of a Justice of the King's Bench, and several homicides.   Eustace de Folville, the oldest of these six, who was described as the "chief of the band" (*capitalis de societate*), died unpunished after a criminal career of at least twenty-one years, which included several murders, and which was interspersed with periods of military service in Scotland or on the continent, which won him pardons.[88]   To some, as Professor Stones shows, the Folvilles were daring, perhaps even "ballad-worthy" figures, who approached in real life the legendary deeds of a Robin Hood or a Fulk fitz Warin.

This kind of behaviour was not new in the fourteenth century. In the winter of 1231-2 there were risings and demonstrations against foreign clergy who enjoyed English benefices as a result of papal provisions.   These movements were near to the origin of that anti-clericalism which was later expressed in the ballads.   Papal messengers were attacked and their bulls destroyed; one was killed. Some Roman clergy went into hiding; others were captured and ransomed.   Armed bands attacked and pillaged the foreigners' estates and disposed of their corn.[89]   The official view was that this was the work of the company (*familia*) of one William Wither, which moved from county to county.[90]   This probably exaggerated the organization of the insurgents, but William Wither did indeed exist. He was a knight, Sir Robert Thwing, a member of a class which strongly resented papal infringment of secular rights of advowson. Robert had personal wrongs, for he claimed that he had been deprived of one of his benefices "without judgement" as a result of a provision.[91] One at least of these marauding bands which operated for a time in Kent went about *capitibus velatis*, that is "masked" or "*hooded*". Wherever the insurgents appeared they seized the barns of the foreigners and then sold the grain at low prices "for the benefit of

[87] *English Government at Work* 1327-1336, ed. J. F. Willard and W. A. Morris (Cambridge, Mass., 1940), i, pp. 102-3.
[88] "The Folvilles of Ashby-Folville, Leicestershire, and their associates in crime", *Trans. of the Royal Historical Society*, 5th ser., vii (1957), pp. 117-136.
[89] See Hugh MacKenzie, "The Anti-Foreign Movement in England 1231-1232", *Anniversary Essays in Medieval History by Students of C. H. Haskins* (New York, 1929), pp. 183-203.
[90] *Close Rolls* 1231-4, pp. 138-9.
[91] This was, in fact, the advowson of Kirk Leatham, in which his right was later admitted by the Pope.

many" or even gave it away to the poor.[92]   Their activities rivalled those of Robin at his best.   Sir Robert Thwing came from Yorkshire.[93]   One may well wonder whether Hobbehod, the Yorkshire outlaw of four years earlier, was a member of his company.

It is easy, of course, to invent Robin Hoods.   The name is the sole essential component and is common enough.   It is equally easy, if not indeed easier, to regard any attempt to identify a historical Robin as utterly invalid, for there must have been many Robin Hoods who never left their name in record.   This enforces caution.   Even so, there were other robbers, like Robber Dun of Dunstaple, whose fame, if permanent, was slight,[94] or Warin of Walcote, who died an ignominious death in the pillory in the early years of Henry II's reign and who is only known to us by his chance survival in legal records.[95] In contrast with these Robin achieved a widespread and growing reputation, and it is not easy to envisage this simply as a literary tradition conjured up from nothing.   If the romances of Eustace the Monk and Fulk fitz Warin, or for that matter the life of William Marshal, are any guide, they suggest that the ballads would be derived from a combination of fact and fiction.   We must, in short, look for a real Robin, and the Hobbehod of 1226 has this to be said of him:

He was an outlaw.   He lived at a time to which several incidental features of the *Gest* point and in which the main topics of the *Gest* were major problems for the lesser landowning class.   Within six years of the first reference to Hobbe and in areas which included the very county from which he is known to have come, there was an active outburst of Robin Hood-like activities led by men of this class. If we are to point at all to a historical Robin, Hobbehod's claims are at present supreme.

---

[92] Matthew Paris, *Chronica Majora*, ed. H. R. Luard (Rolls Series, 1876), iii, pp. 211, 217, 218-9.

[93] His chief estates lay in the east riding in and around Thwing and in Cleveland in the north riding. He also held lands in Lindsey.

[94] *Tractatus de Dunstaple* (Publications of the Bedford Historical Record Society, xix, 1937), p. 13; *V. C. H. Bedford*, iii, p. 350; *Place Names of Bedfordshire* (English Place Name Society, iii), p. 120.   I am indebted to Mr. F. B. Stitt, for bringing Robber Dun to my notice.

[95] *Rolls of the Justices in Eyre for Warwickshire* 1221-1222, (Selden Society, lix, 1940), case no. 390.

12. *Robin Hood – Peasant or Gentleman?*

MAURICE KEEN

IN A MOST INTERESTING ARTICLE IN THE LAST NUMBER OF *Past and Present* Mr. J. C. Holt has advanced a new theory about the origins of the Robin Hood myth. In this, he suggests that Robin Hood originally was not, as has been traditionally supposed, a hero of the common people, but a hero of the gentry, and in particular he criticises the views of Dr. Hilton,[1] who has associated the popularity of the Robin Hood myth with the social unrest of the period which led up to the Peasants' Revolt. Mr. Holt's case is argued with force and scholarship; there are nevertheless questions which must occur in the minds of those who, like Dr. Hilton and myself, have favoured the traditional belief that Robin Hood was the hero of a class inferior to the gentry. Among other things, his statements about the subject matter and social appeal of the ballads and about their dating, appear open to doubt.

Turning to the first of these subjects, Mr. Holt says that the ballads are concerned with questions of "service and status" which were of interest chiefly to the gentry. It is true, certainly, that the ballad writers were sensitive on such matters, but, one may ask, is this any more than one would expect from any writer of the medieval period? Medieval social thought accepted the idea of a stratified society: indeed it is doubtful if it could have contemplated any other. One may therefore expect Robin Hood in the ballads to be portrayed as respectful to his social superiors,[2] but the respect in question does not identify Robin necessarily with the outlook of the knightly class. In ballads written in an age when society was taken to be hierarchical, questions of status and the respect due to it inevitably crop up. But they are surely not the real theme of the Robin Hood ballads. The dominant theme appears to me to be rather the righting of wrong done and the downfall of those who control the law by bribery and the abuse of office; and the triumph of justice whose forces are, by an irony of fate, represented by those who are outside the law. The main question is therefore this; what kind of tyranny and injustice

---

[1] *Past and Present*, No. 14 (Nov. 1958). See chapters 10 and 11 above.
[2] Eg. *Gest of Robyn Hode*, stanzas 37, 75. This, and all other references to ballads are to the versions in F. J. Child, *The English and Scottish Popular Ballads* (New York, 1956).

was it that the outlaws were fighting against? Herein must lie the
clue to the appeal of the ballads for their audience.

The wrongs in question are certainly not the economic wrongs of
the peasantry, but I doubt if this can be used as an argument for
denying the ballads an appeal to rustic listeners. If, for instance,
the ballads do not (as Mr. Holt points out) reveal any animosity
towards secular landlords as such, no more did the peasants even in
1381. The persons who suffered in the revolt of that year were for
the most part either churchmen (and the ballads, as the peasants, do
reveal an animus against the richer cleric), or individuals personally
associated with misgovernment or the abuse of office (the sheriff of
Nottingham's chief crime was clearly abuse of his official position).
The men who were attacked in 1381 were persons such as Sudbury
and Hales and Legge, whose names were linked with the imposition
of the Poll Tax; John of Gaunt, who was suspected of designs on the
throne, and his affinity: and the lawyers, from justices like Bealknap
and Cavendish down to the apprentices of the Temple — the men,
that is, who would have been individually responsible for resisting
the peasants' claims at law, when they attempted to establish their
free status by exemplifications out of Domesday,[3] or were charged
with breaking the Statute of Labourers. In other words the brunt
of the attack in 1381 fell on those who were, either professionally or
personally, directly associated with political mismanagement or legal
oppression. It was the same at the time of Cade's Revolt, when
lesser gentry fought side by side with the peasant: their attack was
on the politicians and the corrupt Lancastrian officials, James Fiennes
and his affinity, and the sheriffs and under-sheriffs of counties.[4]
Rumours of plans for the wholesale slaughter of the aristocracy in
1381, and of the clergy in 1450, were clearly exaggerated. Men of
the period, both humble and gentle, accepted a stratified society:
what they resented was the abuse of official or social position, and this
is precisely the attitude which the ballads echo, with their detailed
catalogue of the crimes of men like the sheriff of Nottingham and
the Abbot of St. Mary's. One should not expect popular literature
to concentrate its attack on the manorial system or the inconvenience
of villein status, because the peasants themselves did not see their
grievances in economic or systematic terms: they saw them rather
in terms of the personal viciousness of individual lords. The men
they were after were Hobbe the Robber and the lawyers who had

---

[3] Cf. *Rot. Parl.*, iii. pp. 21-2.
[4] Cf. the Complaint of the men of Kent in Stow's *Annals* (1631 edn., p. 389).
Among those mentioned, Cromer and Slegg were closely connected with
Fiennes, and held the offices of sheriff and under-sheriff.

set "Trewthe under a lokke" and would not unfasten it for any "but he sing dedero".[5]

There are however other reasons, Mr. Holt declares, why the ballads should not appeal to a peasant audience. For instance, the crucial events centre round the county courts, where the sheriff and the knights were the dominant figures; and there is no mention in them of the justices of the peace, with whom the humble criminal would surely have had more to do. The reason for this seems, however, to be elementary: the justices of the peace could not declare outlawry, which had to be proclaimed by the sheriff in the county court. That peasants would be unconcerned about this would hardly seem a tenable view in the light of Wat Tyler's demand at Smithfield in 1381 "that sentence of outlawry be not pronounced henceforth in any process at law".[6] Again, Mr. Holt asserts that the methods and manner of poaching in the ballads are aristocratic, and its object sport, not food. What then of the outlaws' claim in the *Gest of Robyn Hode:*

> We lyve by our kyngës dere,
> Other shyft have not wee.[7]

Here surely food is the implied object of poaching. That the ballads make no mention of the trapping of rabbits and other lesser game is hardly germane, for the ballads are certainly intended to be heroic and this is not a heroic topic. Peasant poaching was by no means confined to humble quarry: another of Wat Tyler's demands in 1381 was that all warrens, parks and chases should be free, "so that throughout the realm, in . . . the woods and forests, poor as well as rich might take wild beasts and hunt the hare in the field".[8] Moreover the manner of poaching in the ballads surely stamps it as humble. The rich man hunted with dogs, as the example of Abbot Clowne of Leicester, whose success in breeding hounds earned him the respect of the highest in the realm, reminds us.[9] The outlaws shot their deer with the bow, which was not the weapon of the aristocrat. The great schools of English archery were the village butts, and it was from among the men who had learned their skill there that Edward III recruited his longbowmen. The military importance of the archer led Edward to make archery contests compulsory on feast days,[10] but it never earned the archer social

[5] Letter in *Chronicon Henrici Knighton,* ed. J. R. Lumby, (R[olls] S[eries] 1895), ii. p. 139.

[6] *Anonimalle Chronicle,* ed. V. H. Galbraith, (Manchester, 1927) p. 147.

[7] *Gest,* stanza 377; compare ballad of *Robyn and Gandeleyn,* stanza 2, "He wentyn to wode to getyn hem fleych".

[8] *Chronicon Henrici Knighton,* ii. p. 137.   [9] *Ibid.,* p. 127.

[10] Rymer, *Foedera,* vol. iii, pt. 2, pp. 79, 96 (Hague edn.).

status. The poachers of Sherwood, whose skill proved so useful at Halidon Hill in 1333, were not sporting gentry, but men arrayed from among those humble people whom the Statute of Winchester had commanded to keep "bows and arrows out of the forest, and in the forest bows and bolts".[11] Edward I had clearly realised to what use men who had less than twenty marks in goods and who lived in the forest would put their arrows, and protected his venison accordingly.

The arguments which are said to preclude the ballads from appealing primarily to a peasant audience seem therefore to be weak ones. What then of the positive arguments for their being composed for gentle ears? Mr. Holt says that the knightly class is consistently treated with favour in them. It is true that in the *Gest* Sir Richard atte Lee is on the side of light and that Gamelyn was a knight's son. What, however, are we to make of the county knights in the *Tale of Gamelyn*, who were ready to a man to conspire with Gamelyn's villainous elder brother to cheat the boy of his inheritance?[12] What are we to say of Alan a'Dale, who but for Robin Hood would have died broken-hearted, because his love was chosen "to be an old knight's delight?"[13] And from what class were the sheriffs and justices of the ballads chosen, if not from among the knights? The fact is that the knights as a class are not treated consistently in the ballads, which in my submission is what we should expect. The commons had no animus against social rank as such: what they resented was the lordship of unjust men and their corrupt practices. Their political horizons were limited and local: their grievances were specific. Their appeal in 1381 was to specified rights of ancient standing, to charters of Cnut[14] and Offa[15] and to Domesday Book:[16] in 1450 they drew up their complaints in a list, setting them out one by one.[17] And on both occasions they limited their governmental demands to the removal of evil councillors and officials. So in the outlaw stories the final resolution is the substitution of just men for corrupt officials: the way to set the world to rights is not to reform the system, but to kill the sheriff of Nottingham and to make Gamelyn Chief Justice of the Forest. Hero and villain are differentiated in

---

[11] W. Stubbs, *Select Charters*, 9th edn., (Oxford, 1913), p. 468.
[12] *The Tale of Gamelyn*, ll. 41-4, (ed. W. W. Skeat, 1884, pp. 2-3).
[13] *Robin Hood and Allen a Dale*, stanza 10.
[14] *Chronicon Angliae*, ed. E. M. Thompson, (R.S., 1874), p. 303.
[15] Walsingham *Gesta Abbatum*, ed. H. T. Riley, (R.S., 1867-9), iii. p. 365.
[16] With Mr. J. O. Prestwich, I take their reference to the "law of Winchester" (*Anonimalle Chronicle*, p. 147) to mean a claim by the peasants to the same rights as sokemen of ancient demesne.
[17] Stow's *Annals, loc. cit.*

the manner which a medieval audience would have understood, by distinction of personal character rather than social class. The knights are not all good or all bad: Gamelyn, the Outlaw King, is the hero, and his brother, the sheriff, is the villain, but both are born of the same father and are of the same social standing.

Neither the attitude expressed in the ballads towards persons of high social status nor their attitude towards social problems seem necessarily to associate them with the views of the knightly class. Mr. Holt claims that their appeal to this section of the community is also revealed by the background of the stories, which he describes as that of "maintenance and misgovernment at their worst, of baronial and border warfare", subjects of primary interest to the gentry and to the northern gentry at that. I have failed to find a single reference to border warfare in any of the genuinely early Robin Hood ballads. This is the more surprising, since certain incidents recounted of Robin Hood in the ballads are also told of border heroes. The Outlaw Murray of Ettrick Forest warred on the "Southrons"[18] at the head of a band clad in Lincoln green, and William Wallace, according to Blind Harry, adopted the classical outlaw's disguise of a potter to spy on his enemies.[19] This disguise was used by Eustace the Monk, the central figure of a thirteenth-century romance, and by Robin Hood. Incidents in another French romance of the same period, that of Fulk Fitzwarin, also resemble stories told of Robin Hood, as do some of the incidents in the story of Hereward the Wake. Since a great deal of the matter common to these stories (for instance the chivalrous episodes, the fights with giants and dragons, and the scenes of courtly love) are clearly intended for an aristocratic audience, Mr. Holt argues that the Robin Hood ballads were meant for the same ears. What seems to me significant, however, is that while the romances share these common themes with the story of William Wallace, which concerns knightly struggles in Scotland and on the Border, courtly and chivalrous material are entirely lacking from the story of Robin Hood. In other words, it looks as if the matter common to these knightly tales and to the outlaw ballads is not in the latter case derivative, but is the result of borrowing from the same source. Moreover, the omission from the ballads of chivalrous material and of references, for instance, to the border wars, surely suggests that they were aimed not at the same audience as the longer romances, but at a different one which was less interested in these subjects.

[18] Ballad of *The Outlaw Murray*, stanza 4.
[19] *Schir William Wallace*, Bk. vi, ll. 436-87, (Scottish Texts Soc., 1889, ed. Moir, p. 124).

That this was the case is confirmed both by the testimony of the earliest references to Robin Hood in the chronicles,[20] and by the consistently favourable attitude of the outlaws of story towards the poorer classes. The outlaws were not always poor men, but the poor man did not demand that. He demanded kindness, good lordship to engage his fidelity, and this is what the outlaw gave. It is the theme of Robin Hood's famous advice:

> But loke ye do no husbonde harm,
> That tilleth with his ploughe.[21]

It is the theme, too, of his final epitaph in the *Gest:*

> For he was a good outlawe,
> And dyde pore men moch god.[22]

How the outlaw was rewarded is told in the *Tale of Gamelyn:* the knights of the county might conspire to cheat him, but his villeins were faithful even in the hour of extreme misfortune:

> Tho were his bonde-men sory and nothing glad
> When Gamelyn her lord wolves heed was cryed and maad.[23]

It was to protect them against the oppressions of their new master that Gamelyn came to the Moot Hall, where he was arrested and bound by the sheriff. Whether he is like Gamelyn a knight or like Robin Hood a yeoman, the outlaw hero of the fourteenth- and fifteenth-century stories is the friend of the poor: he is not consistently the friend of the knight.

The word "poor", as I have used it here, does require a gloss. The poor men of the outlaw ballads are not, certainly, thirteenth-century villeins, bound down by ancestral thraldom and working three days a week on their lord's land. They are mostly yeomen, bound to one another by the ties of "good yeomanry", proud, independent and free. Because this independence of spirit is a striking feature of the outlaw ballads, Mr. Holt has drawn a sharp distinction between the yeoman and the peasant. He defines the word yeoman as meaning a special kind of household servant, in rank only a little inferior to the squire and quite possibly of gentle breeding. I doubt very much whether the word can be limited to this meaning in fourteenth- or fifteenth-century usage, and this is after all the period in which the ballads as we know them were composed. I do not see how such a meaning can be squared with the reference to "genz de mestre et d'artifice appellez yomen" in the Parliament Roll of 1363,[24] or with Barbour's description of yeomen who fight "apon fut"[25] — a most unknightly situation. In

---

[20] See Mr. Holt's article, note 49.   [21] *Gest*, stanza 13.   [22] *Ibid.*, stanza 456.
[23] *Tale of Gamelyn*, ll. 699-700, (ed. Skeat, p. 26).   [24] *Rot. Parl.*, ii. p. 278b.
[25] Barbour, *Bruce*, Bk. xi, l. 101, (ed. Jamieson, 1820, p. 365).

the fifteenth century Mr. Holt's meaning cannot be applied exclusively: Fortescue declared that rent was a fair living for a yeoman,[26] and Bishop Latimer described his father, a prosperous farmer who rented his land and was alive at the turn of the fifteenth and sixteenth centuries, as of yeoman stock.[27] Mr. Holt quotes Chaucer's Prologue to the Canterbury Tales, and points out that his yeoman was a household servant and has been placed next in rank after the squire: but this evidence is thoroughly inconclusive, as the Reeve's miller, a well-to-do countryman, is also described as a yeoman later on.[28] Trevisa, writing at about the same time, speaks sharply of the yeoman who "araieth him as a squyer",[29] implying inferior status. His criticism at once calls to mind Froissart's remark that it was the "grant aisse et craisse" of the "menu peuple" of England that led to the Peasants' Revolt.[30] This is an important observation. It is clear that in the fourteenth and fifteenth centuries demesne farming became much less profitable, and that among those who took up lands which were consequently put out to rent, or even purchased freeholds, there were a good many who by purely genealogical standards were peasants. Some of these men were quite wealthy and accumulated substantial holdings (Latimer's father, though he had no freehold, could still send his sons to school and distribute largesse to the poor). There was not a great deal to distinguish such a man from the less prosperous of the knightly or "gentle" class. Even the question of his gentility was an open one, because the word "gentleman",[31] like the word "yeoman", was in this period vague in its connotations, as references to such enigmatic categories as "gentlemen yeomen"[32] and "parish gentry"[33] attest. The co-operation of the less influential among the gentry with persons of much lower status in Cade's revolt confirms the view that in this period their interests and outlook could be similar. This same problem of distinction is brought out vividly in the words of the

---

[26] Sir John Fortescue, *The Governance of England*, ed. C. Plummer, (Oxford, 1885), p. 151.

[27] See Stubbs, *Constitutional History*, (1878 edn.), iii. p. 554.

[28] *The Reves Tale*, l. 29.

[29] *Polychronicon Ranulphi Higden*, ed. C. Babington, (R.S., 1869), ii. p. 171.

[30] Froissart, *Chroniques*, ed. S. Luce and G. Raynaud, (Soc. de l'Hist. de France, 1897), x. p. 94.

[31] Cf., for example, the remark made to the deputy of Clarenceux King of Arms in 1534 by Sir John Townley, knight, that "ther was no more Gentilmen in Lancashire but my lord of Derbye and Mountegle." (quoted in A. Wagner, *Heralds and Heraldry*, 2nd edn., Oxford, 1956, p. 104).

[32] See Mr. Holt's article, note 56.

[33] A. M. Everitt, *The County Committee of Kent in the Civil War*, (Leicester, 1957), pp. 8, 29. I owe this reference to Mr. R. M. Jeffs.

East Anglian peasants in 1381 to Sir Robert Salle: "Robert, you are a knight and a man of great weight in this country . . . but notwithstanding this, we know who you are: you are not a gentleman, but the son of a poor mason, just such as ourselves. Do you come with us and be our commander".[34]

What all this suggests is that with regard to the period in which the ballads were composed, we cannot take words such as yeoman or gentleman or even poor man as implying sharp definitions of social status. The poor man of the ballads is not a member of one specific social class: the phrase seems to refer rather to those generally whom lack of wealth, office, or powerful friends put at the mercy of influence and corruption. The poor man is he who, in an age when venality was the rule, not the exception, could not expect justice from the King's servants who "sold the laws like cows".[35] It did not greatly matter whether one was concerned with justices of Trailbaston, or of Labourers, or simply of Assize: the rule "lawe goys as lordship biddeth him" still applied. It was this situation which gave men such as Eustace de Folville, the Leicester bandit of Edward III's time, and Lionel, "king of the rout of raveners"[36] (a historical figure who stands close enough to the romantic King of the Outlaws in the *Tale of Gamelyn*), a place in popular esteem as the champions of a justice which could not be found within the framework of the legal system. In this context, moreover, the interests of peasant, unprosperous knight and yeoman were at one.

This brings out the final point on which I disagree with Mr. Holt. He has associated the Robin Hood ballads with the thirteenth century, when social distinctions were on the whole more rigid than they later became, and a yeoman, the "laess-thegn" of *Pseudo-Cnut de Foresta*, meant something quite different from a peasant, the villein of unnumbered manorial records. But this is not really the period with which the ballads, in the form in which we have them, appear naturally associated. The whole theme of archery and of long-distance shooting is for that period inappropriate, as the outlaw's long-distance weapon, the longbow, had not been developed. Nor is it true to suggest, as Mr. Holt does, that the central role of the sheriff dates the ballads to the thirteenth century: if Henry III's sheriffs were disliked, so were Henry VI's, as the events of Cade's revolt showed. The forest background is equally appropriate to both periods: Hobbehod, the fugitive of the 1228 Pipe Roll, may or

---

[34] Froissart, *op. cit.*, x. p. 115. Salle's correct Christian name was Ralph.
[35] Said of Richard Willoughby, Justice. See E. L. G. Stones, "The Folvilles of Ashby-Folville", *Trans. of the Royal Hist. Soc.*, 5th ser., vii (1957), p. 133.
[36] Both these men are discussed by Stones, *op. cit.*

may not be the original of Robin Hood, but there is no doubt that Richard Stafford, alias "Frere Tuk", who in Henry V's time was robbing the King's lieges, poaching the venison and burning the foresters' houses in the woods of Surrey and Sussex, was a forest bandit of just his stamp.[37] The attempt to dissociate the matter of the outlaw ballads from the period of the revolts of Cade and Tyler cannot be sustained. The ballads in fact mirror accurately the attitude and the grievances of the socially oppressed in this later period. Since it was then that they were composed, it seems natural to see a connection between their literary bias against the establishment, and these contemporary protests of the uninfluential against oppression.

[37] *Cal. Pat. Rolls*, 1416-22, pp. 84, 141.

NOTE, 1976

I no longer hold the views expressed in this article, and am convinced that, in broad outline, those expressed by Professor J. C. Holt in his article in *Past and Present* No. 18 (chapter 11 above) and his communication in No. 19 (chapter 13 below) are much closer to the truth. I do not believe that my attempts to relate the Robin Hood story to the social pressures of the period of the Peasants' Revolt will stand up to scrutiny.

13. *Robin Hood: Some Comments*

J. C. HOLT

THE *GEST OF ROBYN HODE*, WHICH WAS A SINGLE COMPOSITION, MUST not be confused with its component ballads, each of which matured over a period. Hence Mr. Keen's conclusions about archery, would, if correct, suggest a *terminus a quo* for the tales of shooting prowess, but not for the rest of the cycle. However, are they correct? Legal records show that the bow was a common household article in the early thirteenth century, and one regularly used by robbers and in cases of assault. It appears as a prescribed weapon in the Assize of Arms of 1252; Welsh archers were famous as soldiers in the twelfth century, as were the archers of the Weald in the civil wars of 1216-7 and 1264-5; Matthew Paris included archers, with characteristic "long-bow" actions different from the style shown in the Bayeux tapestry, in his drawings of the battles of Bouvines (1214) and Sandwich (1217). By 1200 the bow was already a highly penetrative long-range weapon. According to Gerald of Wales an arrow could pin a mailed knight to his mount through both mail and saddle or penetrate an oak door as thick as the width of the palm of the hand.[1]

Nor was the weapon "unaristocratic". The early fifteenth-century MS. *The Master of Game* of Edward, 2nd Duke of York, describes the procedure followed when the King hunted with the bow and outlines the duties of the yeomen of the King's bow.[2] *The Art of Hunting* of William Twici, huntsman of Edward II, refers to similar methods of hunting.[3] The twelfth-century *Constitutio Domus Regis* refers to the archers who carried the King's bow, each of whom received 5d. a day — a rate of pay equalled among the hunting staff only by the huntsmen and exceeded only by the knight-huntsmen.[4] These must surely have been the forerunners of the yeomen of the bow in *The Master of Game*. What of the first two earls of Pembroke, both of whom carried the name Strongbow? What of the illustrations in the fourteenth-century MS. Royal 2 B vii which show a hound dragging down a deer already wounded by an arrow?[5] Bows and hounds were clearly not mutually exclusive. And, at a later date, what of the Flodden window at St. Leonard's, Middleton (Lancs.),

---

[1] *Giraldi Cambrensis Opera*, ed. J. F. Dimock, (Rolls Series, 1868), vi. p. 54.
[2] *The Master of Game*, ed. W. A. and F. Baillie-Grohman, (London, 1904), pp. 107 ff. and plate xxx.
[3] *The Art of Hunting*, ed. A. Dryden, (Northampton, 1908), pp. 15, 24, 54-5.
[4] *Dialogus de Scaccario*, ed. C. Johnson, (London, 1950), p. 135.
[5] Reproduced in J. M. Gutch, *Lytell Geste*, (London, 1847), i. p. 195.

in which each of Sir Richard Assheton's company is represented with his bow over his shoulder and his arrows behind him? These were men of substance, some bearing the names of armigerous families; even Sir Richard himself is portrayed with arrows at his back.[6] Sir Thomas Elyot was not proposing anything novel when, in *The Governour* (1531), he recommended archery as a gentlemanly exercise. The Robin Hood of the *Gest* did not blunder when, on releasing Sir Richard atte Lee, he at once placed a bow in his hand. There need be no surprise that Robin and the King engaged in a shooting match as they rode from Sherwood into Nottingham.

Some of the differences between Mr. Keen and me reflect the distinctive features of English society. He thinks of yeomen as the upper crust of the peasantry, I as the lower ranks of the gentry and as men in official status. On this point we are both right. The Robin Hood ballads could not have developed as they did without a mixed audience; fundamentally, they are not class literature.

Other differences, however, are of Mr. Keen's own making. For example, I did not say that Robin was the "hero" of the gentry, or that the object of poaching was "sport not food", or that the ballads were concerned with questions of service and status of special interest to the gentry, or that the ballads consistently treated the knightly class with favour. My argument does not in any way require that Robin should be familiar with Border affairs, or that the ballads should contain "romantic" elements. They are not romances; neither, for example, is the *Song of Lewes*. Finally, although I dissociated the origin of the ballads from the economic causes of peasant discontent, I did not exclude the peasants of 1381 or any other peasants from Robin's audience, as my discussion of Hobbe the Robber and my reference to *How the Ploughman learned his Paternoster* show. However, I do not see that the Peasants' Revolt has any *special* significance in this context unless it can be shown that the ballads were *particularly* enjoyed by the *particular* peasants or types of peasant who revolted. As the ballads were predominantly northern and the peasant rebellions predominantly southern, this would be difficult to demonstrate.

What then is at issue? First, there is Mr. Keen's view that the rebels of 1381 did not see their grievances in economic terms and unquestioningly accepted a stratified society. This is inconsistent with established facts: the rebels demanded the abolition of villeinage, the right to rent land at 4d. an acre, the free negotiation of labour

[6] *Iter Lancastrense*, ed. T. Corser, (Chetham Society, 1845), frontispiece and pp. 38-9.

services and, according to one source, the abolition of all lordship except that of the King; they destroyed manorial records; their revolt was the most serious where the enforcement of the labour laws had been the most stringent. The Robin Hood ballads reflect nothing of all this.

Secondly, there is the question of the texts, the earliest of which is the *Gest*. My hypothesis depends, first, on the argument that the chief topics of the *Gest* — ecclesiastical usury, the forest and the sheriffs — were such, or were presented in such a way, as to appeal more to the gentry than to any other group; secondly on the argument that from this original story there developed both a more plebeian and a more aristocratic version; and thirdly on the evidence which associated the *early* Robin Hood ballads with other "gentle" literature and with a "gentle" audience. Now it is no answer to the first point to show that peasants might take an interest in some of the topics of the *Gest;* the matter is relative, not absolute. Nor, under the second point, will it do to compare the aged knight in the late seventeenth-century *Allen a Dale* with Sir Richard in the *Gest*, for this wrenches the ballads from their historical context; in any case this story was previously told of Scarlock in the early seventeenth-century prose life of Robin in which the proposed bridegroom of Scarlock's love is stated to be old and wealthy, but is not described as a knight.[7] Nor, finally, will it do simply to evade my third point.

Hence I am not disposed to abandon or alter significantly my hypothesis unless the position of the *Gest* as the earliest text and its relationship both to earlier literature and to the later ballads, as established by Child, Clowson and other scholars, is shown to be wrong. The next move — a re-examination of their work — lies with linguistic scholars.

The question of dating is a side issue. My conjectures on dating depend partly on my analysis of the *Gest* and its audience, but the converse is not true. However, if my dating is correct, the absence of J.P.s from the earlier stories of Robin may have a reason more elementary even than that suggested by Mr. Keen, namely, that they did not yet exist.

[7] Gutch, *Lytell Geste*, i. p. 381.

14. *Robin Hood*

T. H. ASTON

THE STIMULATING DISCUSSION IN *PAST AND PRESENT*, NOS. 14, 18 AND 19 [chapters 10-12 above] about the historical background and significance of the Robin Hood ballads gives considerable interest to Mr. Maurice Keen's book on *The Outlaws of Medieval Legend* (London, Routledge and Kegan Paul, 1961), as a very clear summary of the contents of the early legends from Hereward the Wake to Robin Hood; and as an attempt to put these literary outlaws in their social context. The outlaw is, in fact, something of a novelty in the writing of medieval English social history, and many of the issues raised in this book will need lengthy and careful inquiry. But a good part of the argument of the book stands or falls on the points debated in this Journal. If Mr. Holt is right, if Robin was the hero not of the peasantry but of the gentry, then much of Mr. Keen's book will need substantial modification.

One major difficulty in seeing the Robin Hood ballads as the literature of peasant discontent is, surely, the contrast between their basic acceptance of the existing social framework and the social challenge of the Peasants' Revolt. Mr. Keen's answer is not to try to make Robin into a revolutionary (except perhaps on p. 52), but to make the peasants into piecemeal reformers. They did not, he writes, demand "a review of the whole [social] system, but reform on particular points in it which bore harshly on them" (p. 162). But we need very cogent reasons for thus denying contemporary impressions, and for calling "particular" what to them seemed only too general. And given the conditions and traditions of fourteenth-century society, was the demand for the abolition of bondage and serfdom really only a "particular" point? Or for the abolition of seigneurial jurisdiction? Taken by and large, Mile End and Smithfield (different programmes indeed) — not to mention the burning of the records of existing landlordism — came passably close to denying the main economic and jurisdictional bases of what historians have meant by feudalism; and Wat Tyler would have done hardly less to the established order of the church. Again, when assessing peasant aims by the light of "establishment" reactions, it is not easy to know where real insight and true report end and "shocked imagination" (p. 168) begins: for, with men conspiring to overthrow the kingdom and much else besides in 1414 or 1431, can we be sure that those who said similar schemes were afoot in 1381 were altogether wrong?

That many of the rebels had "aims . . . bounded by local horizons" (p. 162) is true enough. The frightening novelty — for contemporaries — was that many did not.

But if the ballads do not reflect the mood and aims of 1381, normal peasant discontent did not do so either. What then of those less co-ordinated tensions in manorial society, over rent, service and tenure; over common rights (probably the most widespread and constant source of trouble) and land transfers; over the extortion of manorial officials, and so on. Of none of this is there anything whatever in the ballads. "There is not any mention of unfree peasants in the ballads. For all they tell us, the whole manorial system might have passed out of existence" (p. 139). I do not see how this simple fact can be explained away — especially if, as Mr. Keen observes, "the ballad makers were not in the habit of ignoring widespread complaint" (p. 142). To suggest (p. 139) that internal changes in the manor are the explanation[1] is surely to get those changes very much out of focus. For however much the manor changed and almost whatever we understand by the word "manor", the peasant discontent of which we hear — when not associated with royal taxation — seems overwhelmingly "manorial" up to the middle of the fourteenth century[2]; for the rest of the century, the Ordinance and Statute of Labourers[3] in particular introduced a novel element, but not an altogether "non-manorial" one since these measures were in large part designed to bolster its labour organization. Nor indeed is the currently fashionable diagnosis of this discontent — at least in the form Mr. Keen adopts — in all respects satisfactory. If, for instance, great emphasis is to be convincingly placed on increased social stratification, we need a more realistic starting point than an "average peasant" with "perhaps thirty or forty acres" *ad opus* (two or three days a week) (p. 139): we need to come to grips with the profound and widespread differentiation shown as early as 1086, confirmed more deeply two hundred years later in the Hundred Rolls

---

[1] Mr. Keen's other suggestion (pp. 154-5) supposes a lower-class acceptance of certain contemporary commonplaces which discontented peasants explicitly or implicitly often rejected in practice.

[2] It should, however, be noted that peasant discontent due to, e.g., royal taxation, prises and purveyance, royal administration in general, royal forests, or brigandage, bad harvests etc. has not yet been adequately investigated. "Non-manorial" causes may thus turn out to be relatively more important than at present appears. See, for instance, *A Lincolnshire Assize Roll for 1298*, ed. W. S. Thomson (Lincoln Rec. Soc., vol. 36).

[3] Miss Putnam's book on the enforcement of the statute is incorrectly listed in the bibliography; as are various other items, among them a book and an article by Dr. Hilton to whom is attributed Miss Levett's study of the Winchester estates.

and demonstrated in countless manorial surveys, accounts and court rolls.

None of this is to deny that peasants, discontented or otherwise, listened with relish — as do children still — to tales of the greenwood. Nor even that their disputes with their own masters — manorial lords, reeves and the like — may have whetted their appetite for stories of the triumph of right in rather romantic and gruesome vein — if only as a variant on biblical themes. What it does mean is that the primary social significance of the Robin Hood ballads does not lie in the realm of peasant discontent. Mr. Holt has (it seems to me) made out a powerful case for looking to the gentle classes; and Mr. Keen's chapter on "The Outlaw in History" seems really to point in the same direction, a direction in good harmony with the tales of Hereward, Fulk and Gamelyn. Further than that one can hardly go at the moment. We need to know much more of the real outlaws, and of crime in general; of those who passed from what we might call opposition into banditry; and of the attitudes and behaviour of those middling ranks of landowner whose discontent has yet to be put in proper perspective beside that of the baronage and peasantry. There is room enough here for a very mixed audience indeed — and for its entertainment no less than for its discontent.

15. *Lollardy and Sedition 1381-1431**

MARGARET ASTON

BEFORE 1381, THOUGH THE ENGLISH GOVERNING CLASSES HAD encountered heretics as well as rebels against society, they had never had to deal with either on a large or concerted scale. By the end of May 1382 both had been on their hands, and heresy (in the event) had come to stay. Wycliffe, who before he moved on to full consideration of the Eucharist had found employment and patronage in the highest political quarters, had already passed the watershed of his career by the time of the outbreak of the Peasants' Revolt. But nothing is heard of those adherents of his views who, though hardly perhaps his true successors, form the mainstay of the Lollard movement, until the country had been shaken by the achievements of the lower classes in the summer of 1381. Then, when Archbishop Courtenay had taken the place of the murdered Sudbury, proceedings were begun which revealed the establishment of Wycliffe's followers elsewhere than in the university, and then, too, Wycliffites appear for the first time being publicly abused as "Lollards".[1] A heretical movement and a major upheaval among the lower orders of society had arrived, in point of time, together.

Did this coincidence of timing at all affect the attitude of the government, secular and ecclesiastical, towards the double challenge? Was the reception of the heresies of Wycliffe and his followers conditioned by the shock of the unprecedented happenings of 1381, by the fears engendered in that resounding year, as well as by their inherent political implications? Was Lollardy itself in any sense a doctrine of social revolt, involved in and responsible for rebellion and sedition? And was the course of the Lollard movement influenced by the political crises and disturbances of the later

---

* I am grateful to Mr. K. B. McFarlane for his criticism and advice.

[1] *Fasciculi Zizaniorum*, ed. W. W. Shirley (Rolls Series, 1858), p. 312. On 15 June 1382 the chancellor of Oxford suspended the Cistercian, Henry Crump, and "accused him of a disturbance of the peace, because he called the heretics Lollards". The earliest official use of the word appears to be in a letter of Bishop Wakefield of Worcester of 10 August 1387; D. Wilkins, *Concilia Magnae Britanniae et Hiberniae*, (London, 1737), iii, pp. 202-3. For the meaning and derivation of the name see H. B. Workman, *John Wyclif*, (Oxford, 1926), i, p. 327, and M. Deanesly, *The Lollard Bible*, (Cambridge, 1920), pp. 70 note i, 273-4. Bishop Buckingham began proceedings against the heretics at Leicester in the early months of 1382, before the meeting of the Blackfriars Council; K. B. McFarlane, *John Wycliffe and the Beginnings of English Nonconformity*, (London, 1952), p. 121.

fourteenth and early fifteenth centuries, as well as by its "own" rebellion of 1414, and another, less recognised, attempted rising which followed? These are indeed controversial questions; it would be a rash historian who claimed to have answered any of them. But unanswerable questions are not always the least deserving of attention, particularly if they were raised by contemporaries. Lollardy was, of course, in origin and remained throughout primarily and essentially a theological movement, to which its own considerable literature and the records of ecclesiastical proceedings bear abundant witness. But the structure of medieval politics and political theory were such that extreme and penetrating statements on the nature of the church and the priesthood could hardly fail to have some bearing upon society and upon the state. And this did not pass unnoticed at the time.

*   *   *

There can be no doubt, from the views expressed on both sides of the matter, as to whether contemporaries were aware of the social and political implications of Wycliffe's teaching. From the first admonitory papal missive there appeared in official documents a number of solemn warnings that it was the whole of society, and not the church alone, whose position was at stake. Such sentiments were echoed, amplified and broadcast in the works of pamphleteers and versifiers who reflected the orthodox point of view, while on the other side, Lollard tractarians found a constant cause of complaint in the slanderous accusations to which they were being subjected. As Daw Topias put it, when defending his fellow friars against the Lollard polemic of Jack Upland:

> "But sith that wickide worme,
>   Wiclyf be his name,
>   began to sowe the seed
>   of cisme in the erthe,
>   sorowe and shendship
>   hath awaked wyde,
>   in lordship and prelacie
>   hath growe the lasse grace".[2]

Among the papal letters condemning Wycliffe's teaching which were sent from Rome in the spring of 1377, was one addressed to the archbishop of Canterbury and the bishop of London, enjoining them, among other things, to take steps to indicate to the English

---

[2] *Political Poems and Songs*, ed. T. Wright (R. S., 1859-61), ii, p. 45. These exchanges have been dated to 1401-2. ("Shendship" means disgrace or ruin).

government the danger of the views being developed in its midst. The king, his sons, the princess of Wales and other magnates and royal counsellors, were to be fully informed and shown that the condemned conclusions were not only theologically erroneous but, if properly understood, threatened to destroy the whole state.[3] It may have been no accident that the eighteen propositions chosen from Wycliffe's writings for special reprobation emphasised the subversive nature of his ideas on the question of temporal, as well as ecclesiastical, lordship: "God cannot give civil dominion to man for himself, and his heirs, in perpetuity" . . . "Charters of human invention concerning perpetual civil inheritance are impossible".[4] It is not difficult to see the radical implications of these statements, and, as the papal letter indicates, it was nothing if not easy to read into Wycliffe's philosophy ideas for a programme of devastating revolution. His theories upon dominion, on the grace of the righteous as the basis of authority, the exaltation of the power of the state over the church, and the right of temporal rulers to correct ecclesiastics, were, as the church was not slow to realise, far-reaching. And their implications, as subsequent writers and events were to demonstrate, were not confined to the church and its members. If property could be removed from a delinquent church in time of necessity, might not the same argument equally well be applied to secular owners? If tithes could be withheld from a sinful priest, could not rents and services be withheld from a tyrannical and unjust overlord? And if lay lords could and should correct churchmen, might not others in turn claim the power to correct them? Such later interpretations could be — and were — denied, but more than one prophet has made his reputation on what he did not say. We can hardly blame contemporaries for doing Wycliffe an injustice: if they were prejudiced they were also, in the main, less subtle than the great schoolman. And after the insurrection of 1381 had happened — and Pope Gregory, had he still been alive, might have pointed a certain moral — they do not seem to have been over-scrupulous in attributing the blame.

Yet, whatever the obscurities and controversies which surround his reputation and writings, Wycliffe himself was most emphatically not the advocate of revolution on the lines of 1381. After the revolt, for all his vituperance, (and he did not hesitate to draw his own deductions),[5] he showed himself as an undoubted member of

[3] *Chronicon Angliae*, ed. E. M. Thompson (R. S., 1874), p. 176.
[4] *Ibid.*, pp. 181-2.
[5] In *De Blasphemia*, written soon after the revolt, Wycliffe was saying, in effect, that if more attention had been paid to him none of this need ever have

the establishment which had suffered. The clergy were certainly to blame, indeed they deserved worse — but the people were unjustified in proceeding to murder; temporal lords had offended in the impositions they had imposed — but such things as had been done should never be attempted against them; it was treachery to God and the church for an archbishop to be chancellor — but that did not excuse the manner of his death.[6] The "reformer" himself, however abusive in language and revolutionary in theory, clearly did not envisage taking the enemies' house by such a storm, or overthrowing "Caim's Castles"[7] in one great insurrectionary outburst. Had he done so his career — and that of the early Lollard movement — might have been very different.

The St. Albans chronicler was, like Wycliffe, anxious to derive the lesson from 1381 — though in his case it was tinged with personal animosity directed towards the memory of one for whom he cherished scant respect. For the first cause of the rising to which Walsingham drew attention was the failure of the late Archbishop Sudbury to suppress the heresy of Wycliffe and his followers, who had "spread their preaching and defiled the people far and wide through the country" with their erroneous views on the Eucharist.[8] Later he tells us that John Ball, who had been preaching for over twenty years and pleasing the people by his abuse of both ecclesiastical and secular lords, himself "taught the perverse doctrines of the perfidious John Wycliffe"; and that his end was delayed by Bishop Courtenay

happened. If the temporal lords had (carefully) removed temporalities from the offending church, the people would not then have had to be taxed beyond their capacity. "Nec dubium quin moderate et prudenter predonans temporalia posset totum hoc malum faciliter extinxisse". And it was not too late. Indeed, it seemed probable that God had ordained the whole disturbance so that the kingdom might be regenerated in such a way. In the transfer of property which Wycliffe was advocating as a "theoretical remedy", the temporal lords were to have been compensated for their losses (caused by clerical usurpation), but a sufficiency was to be allowed to the clergy. "O quam gloriosa foret hec comutacio bonorum comunium, qua, reservato clero usque sufficienciam ad alimentum et tegumentum, satisfieret wulgo per bonum cleri residuum!": *Johannis Wyclif Tractatus de Blasphemia*, ed. M. H. Dziewicki (Wyclif Society, 1893), pp. 190-1, 199, 267-9. It is interesting to compare these suggestions, (and Wycliffe's intentions are, as usual, highly debatable), with those of John Ball and the rebels of 1381, who were also intending to leave churchmen "lour sustenance esement", but in their case the spoils were, apparently, to be divided among parishioners — a significant difference of emphasis: *The Anonimalle Chronicle*, ed. V. H. Galbraith (Manchester, 1927), p. 147, cf. pp. 137-8.

[6] *De Blasphemia*, pp. 189-99, 267-9.

[7] The four orders of Carmelites, Augustinians, Jacobites, (the Preachers, called after their Paris convent of St. James), and Minorites, as disparagingly referred to by Wycliffe and Lollard writers.

[8] *Chronicon Angliae*, pp. 310-11, cf. p. 117.

out of anxiety for the state of his soul.[9]   By the end of the century
the story had gained in standing.   Though less venomous and
extreme, Henry Knighton saw Ball as Wycliffe's John the Baptist,
preparing the ways for the master, "and he also, it is said, disturbed
many by his doctrine".[10]   From another source comes the (unverified)
story of how the hero of Blackheath, Wycliffe's "beloved follower",
when he was condemned publicly confessed that "he had been a
disciple of Wycliffe for two years, and had learnt from him the
heresies which he taught", and that "there was a certain company of
Wycliffe's sect and doctrine who had arranged a sort of confederacy,
and had organised themselves to go round the whole of England
preaching the matters which Wycliffe had taught, so that the whole
country should together agree to their perverse doctrine".[11]   The
chorus is so remarkably united that it may seem rather like a refrain
— but even untrue refrains may be remembered and repeated with
effect.

The chroniclers, who could afford the luxury of a certain
irresponsibility, and were habitually discriminating with their
solicitude for reputations, were prepared to be specific.   Parliament,
it seems, was not.   If, as some thought, the parliament of November
1381 expressed views about the ways in which church matters might
have affected the revolt, these were not officially recorded, but by
the following spring, with the immediate problems solved and time
to reflect, a new parliament was able to return to the question of how
to prevent the recurrence of such a catastrophe.

> "For fawte of lawe yif comouns rise,
> Than is a kyngdom most in drede".[12]

No such reminders can have been necessary.   And one of the
important outcomes of this parliament was the legislation which
gave statutory authority for the issue of commissions to sheriffs and
other local officials, upon certification of a bishop in chancery, to
arrest and imprison troublesome preachers.   No names were given,
but the terms of the statute surely leave little doubt what sort of
people its framers had in mind.   It has been found, it states,
(referring to the Blackfriars Council, where twenty-four of Wycliffe's
conclusions had just been condemned), that various ill-disposed
persons "in certain habits under the guise of great holiness" have
been going from county to county and from town to town without

---

[9] *Ibid.*, pp. 320-1.
[10] *Chronicon Henrici Knighton*, ed. J. R. Lumby (R.S., 1889-95), ii, p. 151.
[11] *Fasciculi Zizaniorum*, pp. 273-4.
[12] *Twenty-Six Political and other Poems*, ed. J. Kail (Early English Text
Society, Original Series, No. 124, 1904), p. 10.

any proper ecclesiastical licence, and preaching not only in churches and cemeteries, but also in fairs, markets, and other public places, endangering souls, the faith, the church and the whole realm. "Which persons", it continues, "preach also diverse matters of slander to make discord and dissension between the various estates of the realm, both temporal and spiritual, to the commotion of the people and the great peril of the whole realm".[13] The borrowed phraseology —taken from letters of Archbishop Courtenay[14]—makes it certain that it was intended to include among these anonymous and peripatetic speakers, Lollard preachers, whose beguiling appearance was habitually described in official pronouncements of the succeeding generation in these, or similar, words: *"sub magnae sanctitatis velamine"* became the regular advertisement to warn the unwary away from these most seductive of whited sepulchres.[15]

The charge is there — with plenty of plaintiffs. But there are no defendants. For there are no grounds to believe in John Ball's alleged association with Wycliffe, and considerable research has yielded no evidence to support the view that Wycliffe's teaching or

[13] *Rotuli Parliamentorum*, ed. J. Strachey (London, 1767-77), iii, pp. 124-5.

[14] The commissions issued after this parliament refer to the archbishop's petition pointing out the dangers of these preachers, and asking for the assistance of the lay arm. This petition has not survived, but the passage in the parliament rolls may be compared with the letter sent by the archbishop to the bishop of London on 30 May, 1382, in Wilkins, *Concilia*, iii, pp. 158-9. There is a further similarity of phraseology in a letter sent by Bishop Arundel of Ely to his official on 20 May, about the activities of false preachers, who were said to have been holding forth in churches, chapels, oratories, cemeteries, towns, villages and open spaces; Bishop Arundel's Register (Ely), ff. 41 v.-42 r. Arundel was not in London at this time, and this letter therefore suggests that the clerical plea had already taken shape at the Blackfriars meeting by about 18 May — on which day Bishop Brinton of Rochester, preaching most probably to this very council, delivered a sermon on the text *"Vigilate"*, in which he warned his clerical audience to beware of the false prophets who touched on *"subtiles materias"* in preaching to the laity, and, if necessary, to invoke the secular arm to keep such wolves out of the fold. *The Sermons of Thomas Brinton*, ed. M. A. Devlin (Camden Third Series, lxxxv-vi, 1954), ii, pp. 458-62; read 1382 for 1381, p. 458.

[15] See for example, Wilkins, *Concilia*, iii, p. 158 (the archbishop's letter of 1382); *ibid.*, p. 202 (Bishop Wakefield's letter of 1387); *ibid.*, p. 252 ("sub simulate sanctitatis colore", in the clerical petition which preceded De Heretico Comburendo). Oldcastle was described in these terms, (*Henrici Quinti Angliae Regis Gesta*, ed. B. Williams (English Historical Society, 1850), p. 6, and so were the followers of Perkins in 1431 (p. 306 below). Cf. also *Pol. Poems and Songs* i, p. 232, ("Sub sanctitatis specie Virus vomunt malitiae"), and descriptions such as those by Knighton (*Chronicon Henrici Knighton*, ii, pp. 184-5), and Gower (*Pol. Poems and Songs*, i, p. 347), which — often quoting the famous passage in Matthew vii, "beware of false prophets . . ." — stress the deceptiveness of the Lollards' outward simplicity. The fact that so many contemporaries went out of their way to make this point suggests that there were many Lollards who maintained puritanical standards.

Lollard preaching were either significant instruments, or in any way connected with the 1381 revolt.[16] Even so, it is possible to be impressed by the charge alone, for it represents a considerable and undeniable body of contemporary opinion which apparently believed, and acted on the belief, that there was such a connection. "It is noteworthy", added one writer as an afterthought, looking back on the events of 1381-2, "that so much division and dissension was created everywhere in England by John Wycliffe and his associates, that catholics were afraid that their preaching would lead to a new rising against the lords and the church".[17] Such fears were not easily dispelled. Those who had "leide heore jolité in presse"[18] when the commons began to rise could never shake it out again with quite the same abandon, and heretics were gravely compromised by the folds. Somehow, through deliberate falsification, fixed prejudice, or plausible hypothesis, the conviction seems to have become established that Lollardy was associated with revolt. And opinions once lodged are themselves historical facts: and, as such, may influence events.

If it was possible, not long after the happenings of 1381, to regard Wycliffe's followers as potential rebels and instigators of sedition, later events seemed to add substance to the interpretation. Adam Usk's memory was not very clear when, after a lapse of some thirty-five years, he came to chronicle the history of Richard II's minority, which he had seen himself as a young man, near the beginning of his career. But, having recently experienced a genuine Lollard rebellion, he entertained few doubts that Wycliffe's disciples "by preaching things pleasing to the powerful and rich, namely the withholding of tithes and offerings, and the removal of temporalities from the clergy", had sown the seed of "many disasters, plots, disputes, strife and sedition, which last until this day, and which I fear will last even to the undoing of the kingdom . . . The people of England, wrangling among themselves about the old faith and the new, are every day as it were, on the very point of bringing down upon their own heads ruin and rebellion".[19]

[16] In particular A. Réville, *Le Soulèvement des Travailleurs d'Angleterre en 1381*, (Paris, 1898); cf. C. Petit-Dutaillis, "Les Prédications Populaires, les Lollards et le Soulèvement des Travailleurs Anglais en 1381", in *Etudes d'Histoire du Moyen Age dédiées à Gabriel Monod*, ed. E. Lavisse (Paris, 1896), pp. 373-88. For another allegation of the connection see *Pol. Poems and Songs*, i, p. 235.
[17] *Fasciculi Zizaniorum*, p. 273.
[18] *Pol. Poems and Songs*, i, p. 250.
[19] *Chronicon Adae de Usk*, ed. E. M. Thompson (London, 1904), pp. 3-4.

After the first quarter of the fifteenth century the common repute of a Lollard was even less enviable than it had been a generation earlier. When Chaucer was writing the Canterbury Tales it was still a light — almost friendly — jesting matter for the host to "smelle a loller in the wind".[20] But in the summer of 1413 Margery Kempe's enemies were able to taunt her with threats of the fire, and when she was accused of Lollardy four years later (probably when Oldcastle, no longer officially Lord Cobham, was still at large), she was arrested by two yeomen of the duke of Bedford, who alleged that "she was Cobham's daughter and was sent to bear letters about the country".[21] By then the Lollards had produced open rebels and traitors, and as secular proceedings became more common, so false accusations and summary treatment of innocent persons became more easy. And, as the Lollard programme itself developed, the burden of disrepute carried in the name was cumulative. While in 1411 Lollards and heretics are mentioned alongside homicides and other malefactors,[22] in 1417 the commons, complaining of disturbances to the peace caused by violent breaking of forests, chases and parks, remarked that the offenders were "probably of the opinion of Lollards, traitors and rebels".[23] By 1425 there was no doubt that Lollardy was on a par with treason, felony, "or any such other high poynt",[24] and six years later Lollards were described as "traitors and enemies of the king".[25] To be called a Lollard — as to be called a Quaker or a Ranter — was to be abused at the outset in the very derivation of the name, but the name had grown in content. Opinion and legislation must here have reacted upon each other, and those who were deemed sufficiently dangerous to be punished as rebels and traitors naturally tended to become equated with such.

It was undoubtedly true that a Lollard might endanger a good deal more than his own and his neighbour's soul. But it is also undeniable that if current opinion represents a deformity of this truth, it was a deformity which those in authority had every reason to cultivate, and which the nature of our sources may tend to exaggerate. The

---

[20] *The Complete Works of Geoffrey Chaucer*, ed. W. W. Skeat (Oxford, 1894-7), iv, p. 165, the Shipman's Prologue. Significantly, the host's remark was provoked by the parson's objection to an oath, and accompanied by fears of a sermon. See below p. 288 and note 61.

[21] *The Book of Margery Kempe*, ed. S. B. Meech and H. E. Allen (E.E.T.S., Original Series, No. 212, 1940), pp. 33, 36, 132, 316.

[22] *Rotuli Parliamentorum*, iii, p. 651.

[23] *Rotuli Parliamentorum*, iv, pp. 113-4.

[24] *Ibid.*, p. 292.

[25] P.R.O. E.403/700, m. 11.

stress which churchmen and statesmen laid upon the seditious and treasonable aspects of certain Lollard aspirations is likely to reflect their concern to warn those in responsible positions away from dalliance with the sect. The movement certainly found adherents and patrons in high places, and long before Sir John Oldcastle is known to have given it his allegiance, two independent sources provide between them the names of ten reputed Lollard knights, (including a group attached to the royal household), some at least of whose guilt seems established.[26] Material is not lacking to show how the Lollard case was being presented to attract the support of just such persons. But, when argument was translated into action and issued in rebellion, the evidence for Lollard deeds and intentions comes almost completely from the other, and hostile, side.[27] The story can hardly be a whole one when we have to watch it at moments of crisis from an entirely adverse viewpoint. And throughout it is necessary, of course, to make a particular discount for the racy exaggerations with which — in terminology of impending disaster — men of affairs and preachers alike, were then accustomed to spice their arguments.

* * *

What were the aspects of the Lollard movement which fostered or facilitated the growth of such fears ? Lollardy was a variable creed — if indeed its heterogeneous and ill-assorted conclusions can be dignified by such a name — and seems at some points certainly to refute this contemporary interpretation. For example there is the pacifism which formed one of the twelve articles of the 1395 manifesto: objections to Christian fighting Christian, and to

[26] For the names of the suspects, and an examination of the case against them see W. T. Waugh, "The Lollard Knights", *Scottish Historical Review*, xi (1914), pp. 55-92. Cf. K. B. McFarlane, *op. cit.*, pp. 145-7. In a series of lectures delivered after the publication of his book, Mr. McFarlane reviewed both Waugh's and other evidence, and found further reasons to give weight to the chroniclers' accusations.

[27] The *Coram Rege* Rolls and the Ancient Indictments are the main sources for 1414 and 1431, and it has been shown from such evidence relating to London after the Peasants' Revolt, that these indictments might falsify the facts to make a particular case. When it comes to determining the aims and intentions of the Lollard rebels one is usually not in a position to verify the facts. If the accusations sometimes seem improbable it should be remembered that they also included much circumstantial detail, and when (as in the proceedings against those who had been in contact with Oldcastle in 1417), the jurors were themselves sympathetic, the case is not likely to have been grossly overstated. In general the presentments had at least to be credible enough to make conviction possible, and some of the more sweeping statements of the Lollards' intentions may have been derived from their own claims; see below, p. 308 and note 132.

"homicide through war or alleged law of justice in a temporal cause, without spiritual revelation",[28] could, logically, have been associated with passive resistance in domestic issues.   There were, too, Lollard teachers who (like Wycliffe himself) stressed the duty of obedience owed by the oppressed servant to the tyrannical master: "if thou be a laborer, lyve in mekenesse, and trewly and wylfully do thi labour".[29] Hard in any circumstances to construe into a doctrine of revolt.   But evangelical fervour does not tend towards systematic thinking, and if some Lollards posed so defiantly as defenders of the peace it was, in part anyway, because the dangers in the other direction were obvious.

First there is the question of temporalities, which, under John Ball's direction had assumed an ugly shape, and a prominent place in the rebels' demands, in 1381.   As a primary feature of the Lollard programme the repercussions of disendowment proposals were naturally discussed and emphasised by both supporters and opponents. Wycliffe, who like many great men, was never afraid to repeat himself, returned to the matter with relentless and exhausting insistence, and Lollards likewise (in this at least true to the spirit of the master) never tired of inveighing against the temporal endowments of the church, and of stressing the duties of lords and knights to bear up holy church "rigt as the see bereth up schippes",[30] the meaning of which they did not hesitate to elucidate — including the possible storms.   Many works made no doubt that among the first of the laity's obligations to the church was that of restoring its spiritual inheritance by relieving it of its undue load of temporal acquisitions, the which were as antipathetic as fire and water, and "rigt as water holdyng hymsilf hool in receyvyng of fier quenchith it, so seculer power igove to the clergie . . . distruyith seculer lordis, & most gendrith dyvycioun in the puple & stirith the puple to arise agen' her lordis . . ."[31]   For this same reason others after Wycliffe echoed him in thinking it therefore, "No wondur thanne thof ther ben grete discencouns in tyme of suche pristis bishopis as risyngis of the puple & comunes agen hem, & the lordis, as doolfully we sawen late".[32] The Lollard theorists had their own answers ready for the "blabering"

---

[28] *Fasciculi Zizaniorum*, p. 366.
[29] *Select English Works of John Wyclif*, ed. T. Arnold (Oxford, 1869-71), iii, p. 207.   This quotation comes from one of the large number of English Lollard writings which, without adequate foundation, have been fathered on Wycliffe.
[30] Brit. Mus. Add. M.S. 41321, f. 19 v.
[31] Brit. Mus. Add. M.S. 24202, f. 5 v. (The tract in which this passage occurs was probably written before 1389).
[32] *Ibid.*, f. 41 r.

clergy who denied the legality of the action they were advocating. Among the favourites was a *reductio ad absurdum* derived from the king's power to amerce delinquent clerks. For, it was incautiously argued, if the king were unable to fine clerks by as much as a penny or farthing, they would be free to commit what sin or treachery they pleased, "and thus no worldly lord may lette hem to conquer alle the worldly lordschipe in this londe, and forto slee alle lordis and lauedyes . . . blode".[33] Few perhaps would have been seriously frightened by the notion that "worldly clerks" were out to amortise the whole land. But it is not so hard to envisage the attraction of schemes designed to restore property to the heirs of defrauded almsgivers, and to relieve oppressed commoners of taxation. Nor was this aspect of the poor preachers' insight into their more worldly-minded lay audience lost upon contemporaries.

Arguments such as these had, in fact, an unfortunate tendency to turn into two-edged swords. While the Lollards were busy with allegations that the suppression of their virtuous proposals was a source of discord, and endangering all the lordships in the realm, those whom they chose to describe as "Antecrist and his meynee"[34] saw precisely the same points in reverse. "Thei seyen", it was bitterly complained, "that seculer lordshipis asken degrees; for yif alle weren oon, ther weren noon ordre, but ilche man mygte ylyche comaunde to other, and so seculer lordship wer fully destryed".[35] As William Wodeford wrote in the riposte commissioned by Archbishop Arundel, it followed from Wycliffe's arguments that "the people could lawfully remove the possessions of kings, dukes, and their lay superiors, whenever they habitually offended".[36] And when, soon after their appearance, the Dominican Roger Dymoke embarked on his lengthy rejoinder to the conclusions of 1395, he dwelt tellingly upon the revolutionary and destructive aspects of disendowment, depicting the promoters of the plan as setting temporal lords at loggerheads with ecclesiastical, and inciting the whole people to rise against both as misappropriators of property.[37] Removal of ecclesiastical possessions, if not carried out by legal means, which,

---

[33] *Ibid.*, f. 35 v. Cf. *Select English Works*, iii, pp. 313-4, 515-6, where the same argument appears.

[34] The title of a tract printed in *Three Treatises by John Wycklyffe*, ed. J. H. Todd (Dublin, 1851). As in most cases the insults were mutual, and the Lollards were themselves called the followers of Antichrist by their opponents.

[35] *Select English Works*, iii, p. 434.

[36] *Fasciculus Rerum Expetendarum & Fugiendarum*, ed. O. Gratius, revised E. Brown (London, 1690), i, p. 231.

[37] *Rogeri Dymmok Liber Contra XII Errores et Hereses Lollardorum*, ed. H. S. Cronin (Wyclif Society, 1922), pp. 13, 27-8.

he said, was impossible, could only damage the whole land by ending in insurrection or tyranny. For if the commons took action "it is probable that they would also usurp for themselves the lordships of others, and thus civil war would arise"; and if the lords did so "no one thenceforward in this kingdom would possess his lordships in safety, since anybody would be able to rise against another when he wished . . ."[38] Whatever the means, it seems, there could only be dire results.

Closely connected with temporalities, and also, as Adam Usk suggested, with perturbing implications, is the matter of tithes. The history of tithe disputes and the troubles attendant on them was already a long one before the Lollards made their contribution, and there were many others, apart from heretics, who held strong views on the question — capable of turning, in a later age, into an "issue of blood".[39] We do not know that any of the blood which John Ball helped to spill was lost on this account, though he, it seems, had drawn attention to the question of tithes, by directing that parishioners should withhold payment if their rector or vicar were richer, or of less virtuous life, than themselves.[40] The similarity with Wycliffe's statement that "tithes are pure alms, and parishioners may withhold them on account of the sins of their curates, and freely bestow them on others",[41] needs no elaboration. As an uncomplicated and obviously attractive proposition it was repeated, with fewer variants than many of Wycliffe's ideas, by disciples like William Swinderby, Walter Brute, William White and others, sometimes with the master's proviso that the withholding should be done with prudence.[42] But that other, and more insidious deductions could be read into it, appears from the following complaint in the Lollard tract "*Of servants and lords*".

"But yit summe men that ben out of charite sclaundren pore prestis with this errour, that servauntis or tenauntis may lawefully withholde rentis & servyce fro here lordis whanne lordis ben opynly wickid in here lyvynge. & thei maken this false lesyngis upon pore prestis to make lordis to hate hem . . . & this is a feyned word of anticristis clerkis that, yif sugetis may leffully

[38] *Ibid.*, p. 177. Another possibility which Dymoke considers is that the king should carry out such a spoliation of the church without process of law, which would have the evil result that he would "degenerate into a tyrant".

[39] As stated by General Monk; cf. M. James, "The Political Importance of the Tithes Controversy in the English Revolution, 1640-60", *History*, New Series, xxvi (1941-2), pp. 1-18.

[40] *Chronicon Angliae*, pp. 320-1.

[41] One of the twenty-four conclusions condemned in 1382. *Fasciculi Zizaniorum*, pp. 280-1.

[42] *Johannis de Wiclif Tractatus de Officio Pastorali*, ed. G. V. Lechler (Leipzig, 1863), p. 16, where Wycliffe makes this proviso; cf. *Fasciculi Zizaniorum*, p. 428, for William White's repetition of it.

withdrawe tithes & offryngis fro curatis that openly lyven in lecherie or grete othere synnes & don not here office, than servauntis & tenauntis may withdrawe here servyce & rentis fro here lordis that lyven opynly a cursed lif".[43]

One is reminded of the fears of those who, looking back from the seventeenth century to the German precedent of a peasants' rebellion, remarked in no small anxiety that "Land-lords' rent, and Tythe-rent (like Hypocrates' twins) will stand or fall both together".[44] And though in post-Reformation times these controversies were embittered by the worries of lay impropriators, the problems were essentially similar: tithes and other forms of property were at all times too closely connected for the one not to reflect upon the other.   Indeed Bishop Peacock, in his defence of ecclesiastical endowments against the arguments of the Lollards, likened tithes to "a free rente of money".[45]   Even at this period, moreover, there were circumstances in which a layman might himself be receiving tithes.[46]   "Antichrist" once again appears to have hastened to point the moral.

But the winds of alarm were stirring on account of the manner as well as the matter of Lollardy.   Wycliffe, for all his defects as a reformer, had done some radical rethinking and introduced a fundamental challenge: the deposition of the sacraments and the hierarchy for the elevation of scripture and preaching of the word. Individual interpretation was put before priestly adminstration, and every layman became the advocate of Christ: the change was a change of method as much as a change of doctrine.   But questioning based on the Bible did not begin or end with the peccability of the pope and the fallibility of the fathers, nor did it need renaissance learning and reformation experience to see that "divers naughtie and erronyous opynions"[47] secular as well as ecclesiastical, might arise

[43] *The English Works of Wyclif Hitherto Unprinted*, ed. F. D. Matthew (E.E.T.S., Original Series, No. 74, 1880), p. 229.
[44] R. Culmer, *Lawles Tythe-Robbers Discovered*, (London, 1655), p. 13.
[45] *The Repressor of Over Much Blaming of the Clergy*, ed. C. Babington (R.S., 1860), ii, p. 391.
[46] For example through tenure of the lands of alien priories, among the holders of which appears Sir John Cheyne, the suspect Lollard knight, (*Cal. Pat. Rolls*, 1399-1401, p. 111), whose anti-clericalism was feared by Archbishop Arundel in 1399; see *Annales Ricardi Secundi et Henrici Quarti*, ed. H. T. Riley (R.S., 1866), p. 290, and p. 393 for Arundel's rebuke on the subject of the alien priorities mentioned below, p. 296. Laymen might also be in receipt of tithes in lieu of a pension payable by a religious house; *The Wiltshire, Devonshire and Dorsetshire Portion of the Lewes Chartulary*, ed. W. Budgen and L. F. Salzman (Sussex Record Society, 1943), pp. 46-7.   And there were less reputable circumstances in which it could happen; Wilkins, *Concilia*, iii, p. 274, for a case of a layman illegally holding a church at farm.
[47] *Statutes of the Realm*, iii, p. 896.: 34 and 35 *Henry VIII*, c.i.

once the new approaches to belief were popularised.   Those whose learning dethroned the pope might one day try to dethrone the king. Roger Dymoke, presaging such dangers in the Lollard statement that the miracle of the sacrament induced idolatry, remarked that disrespect for the efficacy of the Eucharist tended to destroy respect for all law and authority, and thereby to undermine the unity of the state.[48]   The view that sin invalidates the sacrament, and the right — or duty — of the parishioner to judge whether the life and morals of his curate accorded with scriptural precept, ultimately indeed not only destroyed the faith, but "put all in doubt".[49]   As Archbishop Arundel, with his ripe experience of Lollard methods, asked William Thorpe in 1407, (according to the latter's account); "Why losell! Wilt not thou and other that are confedered with thee, seeke out of holie Scripture and of the sence of doctours, all sharpe authorities against lords, knights, and squiers, and against other secular men, as thou doest against priests?"[50]   Those who were actively advocating the maxims that "hooly scripture conteyneth al prophitable treuthe", and that "it is leful and nedful to the pepel for to knowe Goddis lawe and the feith of holy chirche in here langage", were well aware of what their opponents were saying, and sometimes tried to forestall criticism by refutation of the arguments "that lewed men mowe soon erre", and "that holy writ in Englische wole make cristen men at debate, and sugettis to rebelle ageyns her sovereyns".[51]

There is no doubt that the Lollards were avid in their reading, and they derived plenty of errors from the Bible.   John Purvey, Wycliffe's secretary, who may have been involved in the translation of the Bible, certainly found there the origin of his idea that "it belongs to the king to ordain bishops and priests"; he had also somehow decided that "if our kingdom elects a bastard to be king, providing he fulfills the office well, God will make him king".[52]   By 1443 Lollards in the diocese of Salisbury — whose scriptural interests were revealed by more than one bishop — had received the opportunity of familiarising themselves with the fundamental concept that "holichirche catholike is congregacioun of trewe men wiche only shulbe saved".[53]   And only a few years earlier William Wakeham

---

[48] *Rogeri Dymmok Liber*, pp. 89-92; Dymoke's answer to the fourth conclusion.
[49] *Pol. Poems and Songs*, i, p. 238.
[50] *The Acts and Monuments of John Foxe*, 4th edn., revised J. Pratt (London, 1877), iii, p. 272; cf. pp. 261-2.
[51] *The Holy Bible*, ed. J. Forshall and F. Madden (Oxford, 1850), i, pp. 49, xiv-xv, note k.
[52] *Fasciculi Zizaniorum*, pp. 396, 391.   The second of these views was derived from his theories on the sacrament of marriage.
[53] Bishop Ayscough's Register (Salisbury), f. 53 v.   (The renunciation of a heretic who was born in Bristol, had recently been living in Oxford, and had been teaching in various places, especially Windsor and Wallingford).

of Devizes, who admitted to having "gaffe entendaunce by many yerys" to English Bible readings in secret places, had been arguing with weavers in a house at Marlborough about his unusual conclusions that *"terra est supra celum"*; "the soul of man is the church of God"; and that "it is no better for laymen to say the *pater noster* in Latin than to say 'bibull babull'."[54] Such erratic thinking could develop along many channels. The Bible, as Henry VIII discovered, was too large and sage a book to leave the safely conservative hands of clerks and aristocrats. Even if the Lollards did not go to it in search of political systems there was no knowing what they might not stumble upon through intensive study in their schools and conventicles, and the archbishop who, in 1409, put controls on the translation and study of scriptural texts, was performing a service which did not benefit the church alone.

While Bible study and personal devotion were to bring men and women more closely into the fold of the church, the primary duty of their keepers was no longer to be prayer, or administration of the sacraments, but preaching. "Evangelization", Wycliffe had said, "exceeds prayer and administration of the sacraments to an infinite degree"; and it was not only "the special work of the curate"; it was also "the work of laymen".[55] Whatever else the Lollards failed in they cannot be accused of forgetting this. Though some thought that the priests of their reformed church would, like those in More's Utopia, be "of exceding holines and therefore very few",[56] they were undoubtedly to form a "godly preaching ministry", and, as far as it existed, theirs was the missionary church *par excellence*. Even if the inauguration of a priesthood of "poor preachers" — and it seems unlikely that there ever was such a conscious ceremony — was no more Wycliffe's own work than the translation of the Bible, the indirect responsibility for these devotional travellers is, equally decidedly, his.

Lay preaching had already achieved popularity during Wycliffe's lifetime: it had taken a firm hold by the time of Archbishop Courtenay's visitation of Leicester in 1389, where he found Lollards maintaining that "any layman can preach and teach the gospel anywhere".[57] The heretics' literature is full of near-theological

[54] Bishop Neville's Register (Salisbury), ff. 52 r. - v., 57 v. ("Bibull babull", idle or empty talk, prating; *Ox. Eng. Dict.*, *sub voce* Bibble-babble, gives 1532 as first reference for the expression, common in the sixteenth century).

[55] *De Officio Pastorali*, p. 33.

[56] For example, John Bath, accused of heresy in 1418, had a book which stated that "A resonable nombre taught in godd' lawe is sufficiant to do the sacrament and preche only goddis lawe in word and dede were y nowe too the churche . . ." Bishop Chandler's Register (Salisbury), f. 18 r.

[57] Wilkins, *Concilia*, iii, p. 208.

arguments justifying their frequent evasion of the law on this matter. Lay participation in the Lollard church included more, however, than preaching. Those laymen who had been educated to think that they could dispute on what seemed (to them) to be a level of equality with bishops and clerks,[58] were challenging the clergy in ways more serious. John Purvey, for instance, had taught before 1401 that "every man holy and predestined to eternal life, even if he is a layman, is a true minister and priest ordained by God to administer all the sacraments necessary for the salvation of man, although no bishop shall ever lay hands upon him".[59]

But was this ever more than a remote ideal? Had the Lollards tried to organise themselves to meet all the spiritual needs of a separate society of believers? Rare moments of vision into the Lollard underground certainly reveal direction of their preaching missions, and of the methods by which their literature was produced, circulated and advertised. The continuity of their programme, as well as the dissemination of their ideas make "some rudimentary form of organisation at least probable".[60] Contemporary authorities, at all events, were in agreement, not only as to the pastoral style affected by the Lollard missionaries, but that they were affiliated into a "sect". Numerous (and not only hostile) descriptions — among which it seems wholly probable that Chaucer's poor parson should be placed[61] — tell how the Lollards went on foot about their work, poorly clad, unshod, staff in hand. What is harder to establish is whether the chroniclers were justified, who concluded further that those who clothed themselves outwardly in gowns of poor russet cloth, as a symbol of their inward scriptural riches, did so by virtue of some sort of centralization.[62]

---

[58] Swinderby's dealings with Bishop Trefnant, (McFarlane, *John Wycliffe*, pp. 131-2), and Thorpe's with Archbishop Arundel, (Foxe, *loc. cit.*), are paralleled in the case of laymen. William Wakeham for instance, boasted to his fellow weavers that "he was before venerable men of the church, and disputed with them, and proved before them that the earth is above the sky". (Neville's Register, f. 52 v.).

[59] *Fasciculi Zizaniorum*, p. 402, cf. pp. 387-9. Purvey also renounced in 1401 the opinion that "every holy priest of God is truly a bishop, prelate, and curate of the faithful": (*ibid.*, p. 403).

[60] McFarlane, *op. cit.*, p. 179.

[61] The Lollard inclinations of the parson must strike anyone with an acquaintance of Lollard literature, as they struck the host himself, (see p. 280 and note 20 above). For an argument of the case (combined, however, with the unconvincing suggestion that the portrait is of Wycliffe) see D. V. Ives, "A Man of Religion", *Modern Language Review*, xxvii (1932), pp. 144-8.

[62] See above p. 277; also *Thomae Walsingham Historia Anglicana*, ed. H. T. Riley (R.S., 1863-4), i, p. 324, and for a more cautious version *Chronicon Henrici Knighton*, ii, p. 184.

Though it would be rash to presume upon a few examples, on occasion the Lollards did undoubtedly resort to ordination. Walsingham, who tells the story of how John Claydon had made his son (or daughter) a priest to celebrate mass in his own house for his wife, rising from childbirth,[63] was certainly not inventing — though he may unwarrantably have generalised from his news — when he recorded under the year 1389 that the Lollards had been making their own priests, *more pontificum*, in the diocese of Salisbury.[64] In July this year there appeared before Bishop Waltham in his manor house at Sonning (Berks.), a heretic by the name of William Ramsbury, who renounced a large number of errors which, he said, he had learnt from a certain Thomas Fishburn, who had tonsured him "with priestly tonsure, and invested him with a certain habit, namely a tunic of russet with a mantle of the same cloth, giving him power both to preach and to celebrate masses". There is no doubt that William Ramsbury had taken his office and its duties seriously. He had not merely practised as well as preached "that it is of greater merit for priests to go through the countryside with a Bible under their arm, preaching to the people, than to say matins, or celebrate masses, or perform other divine offices". For, during the four years before his ministry was discovered he had covered a considerable part of Wiltshire and Dorset, visiting over twenty towns and villages, where he not only expounded Lollard doctrines in churches, cemeteries, and private "confabulations" and drinking parties in taverns, but also celebrated masses according to a special unauthorised Lollard version, full of significant gaps and silences.[65]

Those with similar aspirations and temperaments, if they are not the best of friends, always make the worst of rivals. Perhaps there was too much in common between the Lollards and the mendicants, who embittered the souls of Wycliffe's successors as sorely as they had embittered the soul of Wycliffe himself. The example of William Ramsbury shows that Lollardy could seem to some suspiciously like an attempt to found a new order, and the feelings of the Franciscans cannot have been improved by the deviations of some of their own members in the same direction. The result was

[63] *Historia Anglicana*, ii, p. 307, and *The St. Albans Chronicle*, ed. V. H. Galbraith (Oxford, 1937), p. 89. Walsingham wrongly calls him William.
[64] *Historia Anglicana*, ii, p. 188. John Badby had to answer in 1410 for having held that John Rakier of Bristol had as much power to make Christ's body as any priest; Wilkins, *Concilia*, iii, pp. 326-7.
[65] Bishop Waltham's Register (Salisbury), ff. 31 r. - 32 v.

a long battle of mutual recriminations, in which the Lollards never tired of extolling and exhorting their own humble advocates of God's law, or of pouring scorn and hatred on those allies of Antichrist, the friars, who stuffed and sweetened the anecdotal substance of their sermons with "japes, lesynges and fablis" — deceits fit for no man's ear, and damaging to all. For, apart from mendicancy, preaching was the most obvious field for rivalry,[66] and here the Lollards felt that the law was a double perversion of justice: the righteous were excluded so that the evil-doers should inherit the kingdom. And (as they saw it) those hypocritical leaders of the church who feared the revelation of their own shortcomings were busy making the laws under their very eyes.

There were good reasons for this enmity. Against Lollards, as against Wycliffe, the friars were one of the church's chief bulwarks of defence. The very year after the passing of the Oxford constitutions, which tightened up the restrictions on the licensing of preachers, the four orders of the friars were given complete freedom, notwithstanding any legislation to the contrary, to preach throughout the realm.[67] Doubtless there were also personal hostilities, and one may suppose that the friars, like others since, were irritated by a certain arrogance which, to outsiders, must always seem to be inherent in the doctrine of predestination.[68] Probably then, it was for a complexity of causes that annoyance was sometimes fanned into open disturbance. The Lollardy of Peter or William Pattishall, the Austin friar whose detractions of his order caused a riot in London in 1387, and his own summons before the council, rests only on the assertion of a Benedictine chronicler, with an evident relish for the tale.[69] But Lollards were certainly involved in a similar stir, long after, in Coventry.

In November 1424 a preaching tour was given in the midlands

[66] Knighton drew attention to these rivalries, *op. cit.*, p. 188; cf. *Eulogium Historiarum*, ed. F. S. Haydon (R. S., 1858-63), iii, p. 355. Losses of alms due to hostile preaching led to proclamations in favour of the friars in September and October 1399; T. Rymer, *Foedera*, (London, 1704-35), viii, p. 87; *Cal. Cl. Rolls*, 1396-9, pp. 523-4; *Cal. Cl. Rolls*, 1399-1402, p. 1.

[67] Wilkins, *Concilia*, iii, p. 324, from which it appears that the regulations of 1409 were never intended to apply to the friars; cf. *Eulogium Historiarum*, iii, p. 417.

[68] Cf. Arundel's alleged remark to William Thorpe; "For you presume that the Lord hath chosen you only for to preach, as faithfull disciples and speciall followers of Christ"; (Foxe, *Acts and Monuments*, iii, p. 260): or William Ramsbury's statement that he "and his followers were and are in the true faith, and no others"; (Waltham's Register, *loc. cit.*). See also the remarks in Thomas Netter's *Doctrinale*, ed. F. B. Blanciotti (Venice, 1757-9), i, pp. 16-17.

[69] *Historia Anglicana*, ii, pp. 157-9; *Cal. Pat. Rolls*, 1385-9, p. 386, which shows that Pattishall had apostasised. Cf. McFarlane, *op. cit.*, pp. 138-9.

by a "brother" with heretical inclinations called John Grace, (reputed by certain of his hearers as sometime monk and friar), which created such disturbances that the Franciscans who opposed him went in fear of their lives, and here too the council intervened, with expressions of surprise that no action had been taken by the authorities in Coventry, where the matter had come to a head.[70] The mayor, for his part, was disposed to make light of the affair, as having been grossly exaggerated, but in London it was viewed differently. John Grace was arrested and imprisoned in the Tower, and the following May and June securities were taken from about fifty artisans of Coventry that they would be obedient to the mayor and bailiffs of the town, that they would not favour or sustain Lollardy or any heretical opinions, and would not make riotous congregations or illicit conventicles there, to the disturbance of the peace. More than half of these persons were also being called upon to answer for contempt of the peace by having participated in unlawful assemblies.[71]

Such happenings provide some justification for the Carmelite collector of Lollard tares, who wrote (retrospectively) of Wycliffe's early followers; "they were always spreading dissension and inciting the people to insurrection, so that it was hardly possible for any one of them to preach without their hearers being provoked to blows, and discord would arise in towns".[72] Lollards, like Cathars and earlier continental heretics, and like the friars themselves, flourished along the main roads, and found supporters among the trades-people of large towns. The midland boroughs of Coventry and Northampton (both of them being involved in 1431) can be numbered with Leicester, among the strongholds of the sect. Bristol, prominent in 1414, was another such centre. And as the movement became increasingly artisan, so it gained a footing in both rural and urban districts in the various branches of the woollen industry, where the heretics' strength probably reflects the predominance of that trade, rather than any special activity or predilection on their part. Weavers in England were never in danger of becoming synonymous for heretics as they were abroad, and Lollards were to be found in many other trades, as is witnessed by the suspect girdle-makers, shoemakers,

[70] *The Coventry Leet Book*, ed. M. D. Harris (E.E.T.S., Original Series, Nos. 134, 135, 138, 146, 1907-13), i, pp. 96-7; *Cal. Pat. Rolls, 1422-9*, pp. 275-6; F. Devon, *Issues of the Exchequer*, (London, 1837), p. 390; *Vict. County Hist. Warwicks*, ii, pp. 20-1. John Grace was called a "false prophet" but not a Lollard.
[71] P.R.O. K.B.27/655, *Rex* m. 6 v.; K.B.27/656, *Rex* mm. 6 r. - 8 v., 16 r.; K.B.27/657, *Rex* mm. 4 r., 6 v., 10 r. - v.
[72] *Fasciculi Zizaniorum*, p. 272.

escape adverse notice; they helped to make the cause resemble a treasonable scramble for property and preferment. And though there were Lollards who did not participate in these activities, the movement emerged into the open, as its opponents had long been predicting, as the rebellious enemies of the king and lay lords, not only of clerical possessioners. Nor, despite the aspirations of some of his assistants, did Oldcastle's pretensions help to refute the idea that community of property was the logical outcome of disendowment: as Hoccleve told him in 1415, after the Lollards' chief *campiductor* had gone to earth:—

> "Presumpcion of wit, and ydilnesse,
> And covetyse of good, tho vices three
> Been cause of al your ydil bysynesse.
> Yee seyn eeke: 'goodes commune oghten be'."[98]

It was possible at the time to think that Oldcastle's unknightly and "unkyndly" actions had turned the "sory sekte of lollardie" to confusion.[99] But this was not obvious, particularly to those in positions of authority, for many years to come. The aftermath of the 1414 rebellion, especially while Oldcastle was still in hiding, gave rise to a number of ill-authenticated reports. In July 1415 Lollard collaboration was supposed to have been promised in the Southampton plot. Two years later, when Lollard activity subjected several towns to house-to-house propaganda, it was stated that Henry Greyndor, described as Oldcastle's messenger, had presented the king with a bill requesting the resumption of ecclesiastical temporalities, and that the Scottish attacks on Berwick and Roxburgh were due to Lollard arrangements which included plans for the appearance of the northern version of Richard II. It may also have been hostile intent which led to the further allegation that Oldcastle himself, at the end, maintained that his liege lord Richard II was still alive in Scotland. But while his own actions, during his last days of freedom, had included a visit to north Wales to discuss matters "contrary to his allegiance" with the son of Owen Glendower,[100] more than one of his supposed adherents was accused of treacherous dealings with Scotland.

The petition of a loyal subject of Henry V advanced many years later to the council of his son, described how he had contrived the capture of Oldcastle's clerk and "chief counsellor", Thomas Payne of

---

[98] *Hoccleve's Works*, ed. F. J. Furnivall (E.E.T.S., Extra Series, Nos. 61, 72-3, 1892-7), i, p. 22.
[99] *Pol. Poems and Songs*, ii, pp. 244, 247.
[100] H. G. Richardson, "John Oldcastle in Hiding, August-October 1417", *Eng. Hist. Rev.*, lv (1940), p. 437.

Glamorgan, who having escaped unscathed in 1414, was (four or five years after) in the act of arranging to release the Scottish king from his confinement at Windsor, and escort him back to Scotland.[101] Thomas Payne spent a number of years in prison for this exploit, and — after escape and recapture — was still awaiting trial in 1422.[102] Mr. Thomas Lucas, despite his own previous spell of imprisonment, was more fortunate. Though he had certainly returned to Oxford since 1395, he may no longer have been a fellow of Merton College when he came up for trial before the King's Bench at Easter 1417, on several serious charges. It was presented that on 14 August 1416, at Westminster, he was conspiring the king's deposition and death, both by sending a letter to the Emperor Sigismund (who was then in England negotiating the Treaty of Canterbury),[103] containing among other things that religious should not have or enjoy temporal possessions, and that Richard II was alive in Edinburgh, and also by scattering bills with these suggestions in the streets of London, Canterbury and elsewhere. He was further said to have induced Richard Benet, "Wolman", John Whitlock, with other unknown persons, to destroy Henry V. And in addition, "the said Thomas was and is in agreement with, acting with, counselling and abetting, all the works of John Oldcastle, both in opinions of Lollardy and in all his other evil deeds, treacherously purposed and imagined by the said John Oldcastle towards the king".[104] Thomas Lucas put himself on the country and was acquitted. But both his alleged agents had already been brought to justice.

Benedict Wolman of London, ostler and late under-marshal of the king's marshalsea, described as a Lollard in one source, was drawn through the city and hanged at Tyburn on 29 September 1416.[105] Together with Thomas Beckering of Beckering (Lincs.), "gentleman", (who died in Newgate prison awaiting judgement), he had pleaded not guilty to a charge of conspiring in London since 18 April 1416, on

---

[101] James I of Scotland was a captive in English hands 1406-1424.

[102] *Proceedings and Ordinances of the Privy Council*, ed. N. H. Nicolas (Rec. Com., 1834-7), v, pp. 104-6; Devon, *Issues*, pp. 373, 375; *Cal. Pat. Rolls*, 1422-9, p. 186; *Rot. Parl.*, iv, p. 196; J. H. Wylie and W. T. Waugh, *The Reign of Henry the Fifth*, (Cambridge, 1914-29), iii, p. 395.

[103] Sigismund arrived at Dover on 1 May 1416; on 26 June Henry V left for Southampton and the emperor went to stay at Leeds Castle in Kent. The treaty was signed at Canterbury on 15 August 1416. E. F. Jacob, *Henry V and the Invasion of France*, (London, 1947), pp. 109-24; *Henrici Quinti Gesta*, pp. 82, 89, 93.

[104] P.R.O. K.B.27/624, *Rex* m. 9 r.

[105] *The St. Albans Chronicle*, p. 102, repeated by Capgrave, *The Chronicle of England*, ed. F. C. Hingeston (R. S., 1858), p. 316.

behalf of Thomas Ward of Trumpington, alleging him to be Richard II and in the custody of the duke of Albany in Scotland, and of having sent a petition (which Sigismund had delivered to Henry V) asking the emperor's assistance in deposing the king.[106] The third party named in Lucas' indictment had been imprisoned three months after Henry V's accession, and was brought for trial soon afterwards, in the summer of 1413.   John Whitlock, groom and yeoman of Richard II, was accused of conspiring with others against Henry IV and Henry V continuously since 1406, of adhering to the king of Scotland, the duke of Albany, and Thomas Ward of Trumpington, and escorting to Westminster Scottish envoys and with them spreading the news across England and Wales that Richard was alive, and about to return to England.   Further, Whitlock was said in the reigns of both kings to have been posting bills at Westminster and elsewhere in London, at times of parliament, in one of which produced at his trial, he declared his readiness, after long service with Richard and residence in Scotland, to prove to members that the late king was still alive.[107]

Neither Wolman nor Whitlock is known to have been officially accused of Lollardy, and Lollards were certainly neither first, nor foremost, in advocating the case of the Scottish pretender Thomas Ward, whose usefulness as a figurehead seems to have outlasted his own existence.[108]   It is possible, however, that John Whitlock's endeavours at parliamentary lobbying which were later, at least, attributed to a Lollard connection, throw some light on the anxiety of the parliament of 1406, which associated Lollards with the purveyors of lies who were accused of publishing falsely that Richard II was still alive, and of spreading false prophecies to the great commotion of the king's subjects, including that "celuy fool q'est en Escoce" was Richard himself.[109]   The Lancastrian accession,

[106] Riley, *Memorials*, pp. 638-41, *Cal. Letter-Books*, I, pp. 165-6.   A Benedict Wilman, possibly the same, was accused with others in 1410, of plotting the death of Prince Henry and his brothers, and of sending agents and letters on behalf of Richard II (allegedly in Scotland), to Scotland, France, Wales and Flanders, and to various parts of England.   P.R.O. K.B.27/595, *Rex* m. 3v.; cf. mm. 1 v. 8 r. 11 v. for similar accusations.

[107] *The Fifty-Third Annual Report of the Deputy Keeper of the Public Records*, (London, 1892), pp. 28-30; *Cal. Cl. Rolls*, 1413-19, p. 31.   Whitlock was imprisoned together with Thomas Clerk, possibly the Thomas Payne *alias* Clerk mentioned above.

[108] A reputed Lollard was associated with a plot on Ward's behalf in 1420. One of the two plotters was taken, and when questioned about the identity of Thomas Ward maintained that the matter was immaterial, since he had been dead some time.   R. R. Sharpe, *London and the Kingdom*, (London, 1894-5), i, p. 248.

[109] *Rot. Parl.*, iii, pp. 583-4, and below p. 314.

though it brought respite to several Lollards, hardly benefited the fortunes of the sect as a whole. It seemed to leave some of its members, together with other would-be legitimist plotters, on the wrong side of dynastic disputes. And no doubt Oldcastle's doings seemed to strengthen the grounds for connecting Lollardy with positive treason.

After 1417 the authorities remained watchful, and their continued vigilance was not misplaced. Oldcastle's plans died neither with his rebellion, nor with him when he went to the stake three years after. Kent, the seat of his Cobham estates, long continued to produce heretics, and some of his adherents who had escaped notice, or been pardoned in 1414, intermittently attracted attention. In 1421, when Oldcastle had been dead four years, securities not to maintain heresy were taken from John Prest who, as vicar of Chesterton (Warwicks.), had sheltered the leader of the sect two years before his capture, and also from one John Reynald, a taylor (probably of London) who undertook not to be of the assent or "covin" of the late Sir John, and not to hold or preach his opinions.[110] A decade after this, legal proceedings were still in progress against Thomas Tiperton of Cheshire, "gentleman", a member of Oldcastle's entourage, who had been appealed with others of various treasons by an approver of the previous reign.[111]

Richard Wyche, the Lollard martyr of 1440 and another of Oldcastle's probable accomplices (but not implicated in his rising), may have helped to keep the word alive in Kent, where he held livings in the 1420's and 1430's. In 1428 the archbishop of Canterbury made a determined effort to track down a large number of Kentish suspects, many of whom seem to have managed to evade him.[112] But among the heretics who were brought up in convocation that year was Ralph Mungyn, said to have been defamed of heresy for about twenty years, and to have had Lollard connections in Oxford and London (where he had been suspended from a cure of souls), as well as in Kent. Those with whom he was accused of having illicit communication included Bartholemew Cornmonger, who had already been cited by the archbishop that summer, and Nicholas Hoper, sometime servant of Sir John Oldcastle, and one of

---

[110] *Cal. Pat. Rolls*, 1416-22, p. 372; *Cal. Cl. Rolls*, 1419-22, pp. 206, 215.

[111] P.R.O. K.B.27/655, *Rex* m. 5 r.; K.B.27/680, *Rex* m. 10 v.; K.B.27/683, *Rex* m. 10 v.

[112] *Chichele's Register*, iv, pp. 297-301; but it is possible that those here referred to were caught, for a contemporary tells of a great anti-Lollard movement in the diocese of Canterbury in 1428, when the archbishop "riding several days and nights" caught and imprisoned at least thirty; *ibid.*, i, p. cxxxvii.

the twelve persons excepted from the general indemnity of March 1414.

Evidence was given at Mungyn's trial that he had made statements in the house of a citizen (late alderman) of London, to the effect that "all goods should be held in common, and no one ought to be allowed to have property".[113]   He was not the only Lollard nurturing ideas which had received special publicity in 1414. The same convocation in which he was tried heard Robert, rector of Hedgerley (Bucks.), confessor to the "notorious" thief and robber of churches, William Wawe, return a "doubtful" reply to the question of whether it was lawful for spiritual men to have temporal possessions.[114] Robert Hook, rector of Braybrooke (Northants.), whose living had been a centre of Lollard propaganda efforts in Oldcastle's rebellion, was answering for his Lollard opinions for the third time when he appeared before the convocation of 1425.   Among the errors which he agreed to abjure publicly in London and Northampton was that "lordes temporell' been holden by the lawe of god to have all' thinges in commun".[115]   Likewise renouncing his Lollardy in this assembly was Thomas Drayton, rector of Snave (Kent), who as rector of Drayton Beauchamp was another of those who failed to receive pardon in 1414, though he had submitted to a commissary of the bishop of Lincoln the following year.   One of the ways in which he had gone back on this was by associating, as he admitted, with Mr. William Taylor, who had been twice cited by Archbishop Arundel as the result of his sermon of 1406, and released on bail in 1421 after appearing before Archbishop Chicheley.   Taylor was finally condemned in 1423, in the presence of the duke of Gloucester and the earls of Warwick and Vendôme, and one of the articles for which he went to the fire sounds remarkably consistent with the views imputed to him seventeen years earlier: "civil dominion, or secular, which according to me is the same as civil, is so imperfect that in no way can it rightfully accord with priestly perfection, and in no way does Christ wish priests of the church so to rule".[116] The bishop of Lincoln testified to having heard him state also that the civil dominion of kings and temporal lords enjoyed only God's

---

[113] *Ibid.*, iii, pp. 197, 200, 202-4.

[114] *Ibid.*, iii, p. 188.   Orders for the arrest of William Wawe, who was himself suspected of heresy, as well as of consorting with heretics, were sent out in 1427; Devon, *Issues*, pp. 398-9; *Cal. Pat. Rolls, 1422-29*, p. 422.

[115] *Chichele's Register*, iii, p. 111.

[116] *Ibid.*, iii, p. 169, and above p. 296, note 90. Taylor was burnt on 2 March 1423. His long unorthodoxy on the question of temporalities, and his citation in March 1410 invite speculation on his possible connection with the 1410 proposals. But no mention of them was recorded at his trial.

permissive, but not his benevolent, approval. Lollard ideas — whose academic origin was still, though more tenuously, in evidence — could demonstrate, like Lollard preachers, disquieting obstinacy. Such continuity of personnel and opinions helps to explain the maintenance and revival of schemes for another full scale, if less distinguished, Lollard rebellion. This, discovered and repressed just as it was on the point of maturing in the spring of 1431, brought to light the foiled plans of 1414 persisting in a debased and still more subversive shape.

William Perkins' projected rising produced fewer martyrs than that of Sir John Oldcastle, but this was not because it was less ambitious, and may not have been because the cause was less popular. It lacked conspicuously, it is true, leaders of social distinction, and we only know the names of a few who died. But the subsequent indictments list, besides active participants, more than a score of others who would have benefited from the plot, and if the government of Henry VI's minority saw fit to execute only a handful or so of ringleaders, there is evidence that it felt considerable alarm — alarm which, skilfully exploited by the duke of Gloucester, provided strong grounds for a handsome annuity, not to mention other rewards.[117]

All too little, unfortunately, can be discovered of the Salisbury heretic, John Keterige, "notoriously suspect" and afterwards convicted of heresy and error, whose capture by the late mayor of that town revealed the treason and promoted the capture of John Long and William Perkins *alias* Mandeville, both of Abingdon.[118] John Long had evidently been helping to distribute the seditious Lollard leaflets by which the insurgents had been propagating their plans in London, Oxford, Coventry, Northampton and Frome, as well as Salisbury, where one of the recipients turned informer. The fuller of Abingdon and two men from Westbury who were among those accused of plotting at Salisbury, may have been similarly engaged. One of the latter, Thomas Puttok, clerk, caught in Staffordshire in July, was condemned (like a Wiltshire weaver a

[117] The duke and duchess of Gloucester received various presents on 20 May 1431, from the city of Coventry, including a silver and gilt cup, and four pipes of wine. *The Coventry Leet Book*, i, pp. 137-8.

[118] *Proceedings and Ordinances of the Privy Council*, iv, pp. 99-100. Richard Gatour, late mayor of Salisbury, duly received the £20 awarded to him for his action; (P.R.O. E.404/48/125 and E.403/700 m. 13). Orders for the proclamation promising this reward (together with half the goods of anyone convicted), for those producing the writers of seditious bills, had gone out on 13 May (*Cal. Cl. Rolls*, 1429-35, p. 123), and met with a quicker response than similar measures to secure the arrest of Oldcastle. Cf. William Warbleton's assistance in arresting Perkins, for which he too was granted £20. *Proceedings and Ordinances*, iv, pp. 107-8; Brit. Mus. Cott. Ch. iv, 24.

month before), to be hanged, burnt and quartered at Salisbury.[119]
A mercer called John Orpud, reputed to have long held heretical
opinions, but acquitted on the charge of conspiracy, came from the
village of Steventon in Berkshire, which only three years earlier
had produced a heretic defamed of spreading erroneous literature.[120]
Other suspects, likewise acquitted, included a dyer of Frome and
a labourer of Thatcham in the Kennet valley.[121] William Perkins,
the foremost leader of these and other men, who chose as his popular
pseudonym the title of "Jack Sharpe of Wigmoreland",[122] was a
weaver, and may have derived his particular hostilities towards the
abbot and monks of Abingdon from a professional connection with
the monastery.[123]

Another leader, who was executed at Tyburn nearly two months
after the deaths of Long and Perkins, is a somewhat less obscure
figure whose chequered career takes us back to the after-events of
Oldcastle's rebellion, and shows something of the workings of that
disreputable underworld of intrigue, crime, and high treason plotted
in lowly places, in which some Lollardy was sustained. John
Russell — described variously as woolman, woolmonger and
woolpacker — had been involved with the law for over fifteen years
before he finally went to his death in July 1431, and there is reason
to credit as substantially true the accusations of the jury which then
presented him as having for long held heretical opinions, and been
plotting the destruction of the king and his laws. Russell's association
with the heretical baker, Richard Gurmyn, is clearly indicated in the
action which he and two other Londoners brought at Easter 1416
against the king's escheator, for wrongful seizure of various goods
(including a box of deeds and charters), after this heretic had been
burnt on 9 September 1415. It was alleged by Russell and his

---

[119] P.R.O. K B.9/227/Pt. ii, 1-3; Devon, *Issues*, p. 413. The other rebel
condemned to be drawn, hanged, and thereafter beheaded, quartered and to
have his entrails burnt, was John Kymrygge, a weaver of Salisbury.

[120] P.R.O. K.B.27/682, *Rex* m. 18 r. Bishop Neville of Salisbury on 15 June
1428 ordered proceedings to be taken against William Fuller of Steventon,
defamed of Lollardy, of possessing heretical literature, and of publicly teaching
and preaching heretical opinions. Bishop Neville's Register (Salisbury), f. 77 v.

[121] P.R.O. K.B.9/227/154; K.B.27/686, *Rex* m. 1 v.

[122] The title — which in fact, if not by intention, commemorates a long-lasting
Lollard association with the marches of Wales, and Oldcastle's native country
— may possibly be evidence of a wish to be identified with the duke of York and
the Mortimer claim to the throne; cf. Jack Cade *alias* Mortimer in 1450. (I owe
this suggestion to Mr. McFarlane.)

[123] He is reported to have been bailiff of Abingdon; *A Chronicle of London*,
ed. E. Tyrrell and N. H. Nicolas (London, 1827), p. 119; *Fabyan*, p. 602;
cf. A. E. Preston, *The Church and Parish of St. Nicholas, Abingdon*, (*Oxf.
Hist. Soc.* xcix, 1935), p. 63.

fellow pleaders that Gurmyn had made over to them, before his conviction, all his movable and immovable possessions, which included properties in Lichfield, Shrewsbury and Shropshire, the deeds to which had been seized.[124] This connection provides an interesting link in the Lollard movement, which leads back at least to 1395, for Gurmyn's friendship and alliance with John Claydon, who went to the stake the day after him, was recorded at the latter's trial. The escheator who was attempting to enforce the crown's rights in taking possession of the goods was Thomas Fauconer who, as mayor of London, had been instrumental in the proceedings brought against Gurmyn and Claydon in the summer of 1415. In July 1416 (by which time Russell and the others had probably lost hope of winning their case), Fauconer found himself committed to the Tower and put to a fine of £1,000, on the basis of a rumoured charge that he had caused Richard Gurmyn to be burnt together with a royal pardon. Russell was running a risky course: for spreading this report he was condemned to the pillory, and then retired to sanctuary at Westminster until he confessed and submitted the following April.[125] But a year later he was back in sanctuary, and there took to false moneying, a pursuit in which he was still engaged at the time of the preparations of March 1431.

The objectives of these insurgent Lollards included, as earlier, religious disendowment. In one source there is preserved the "most evil supplication presented by John Sharpe to Humphrey duke of Gloucester, protector of the realm, to the subversion of the church".[126] The document which follows is none other than the scheme of 1410. This is the more interesting in view of the similarity between the plans of William Perkins and those of Sir John Oldcastle, as revealed in the indictments presented after the revolt had been quelled, and, though there are no doubt grounds why such present- ments should not always be taken at their face value, there is every reason for historians to consider the charges as seriously as did

---

[124] P.R.O. K.B.27/620, m. 7 r-v. Fauconer's case was that in 1407-8, when Gurmyn had been accused of heresy and was a debtor to the king and others, he was indicted for felony, and had entered into a collusive action to make over to Russell and the other two all his goods and chattels. But, it was alleged, he had never given them livery either of the goods, or of the deed of conveyance. Already before this action, in January 1416, Gurmyn's goods had been granted to a yeoman of the king's chamber; *Cal. Pat. Rolls*, 1413-16, p. 388.

[125] Riley, *Memorials*, pp. 630-4; *Cal. Letter-Books*, I, p. 180; see above, p. 294 and notes 82, 83.

[126] Brit. Mus. M.S. Harl.3775, ff. 120 r. - 121 v. Printed in *Annales Monasterii S. Albani a Johanne Amundesham*, ed. H. T. Riley (R.S., 1870-1), i, pp. 435-6. This text, like Fabian's version of the 1410 proposals, omits the suggestion for founding fifteen universities.

Henry's lieutenant, particularly in view of the known antecedents of one of the leaders. If the 1410 petition was indeed among the bills circulated by Perkins to gather his supporters he must have been ostensibly and with one hand campaigning for parliamentary disendowment, while privily and with the other, he was plotting the destruction of the very persons who would have had to carry it out. The rebels' true aims, were they in fact those described so circumstantially by the indictments, could never have had much hope of a sympathetic parliamentary hearing. But, radical as they were, one can hardly suppose that even the most foolhardy of leaders would have canvassed too openly for their realisation: "totally to destroy the estate and person of the king, as well as the estate and office of prelates and religious orders in the kingdom of England", and "to despoil both churches and religious houses of relics and other goods and chattels found in them, and to fill the said churches with secular persons of their own circle (*covina*) and opinion; and to move and make insurrection in the said kingdom, and such commotion of people between the king and his subjects against their due allegiance, that these traitors could at their own lust and will rule and kill the king, his lords, temporal and spiritual, and the religious orders".[127]

This is more than an echo of 1414. Jack Sharpe and his "meyne of rysers" were alleged to have found that the proposals for the complete destruction of religious persons and houses which they had produced, "under colour of sanctity", could not be put into effect "as long as the royal power and regal state of the king, and the state and office of prelatical dignity continued in prosperity in the kingdom".[128] Oldcastle's treason had been explained likewise. But William Perkins and his accomplices had gone a significant step beyond the known aims of 1414. They were going to be sure that there was a vested interest in their reformation, and it might have been more difficult to suppose in 1431, as Hoccleve had in 1415, that community of property was the Lollards' slogan. For though there is evidence to suggest that this conception was being advocated in London and Northampton not long before, the disciples of Robert Hook and Ralph Mungyn might have hesitated to join in the train of William Perkins and John Russell, who had not only drawn up a long list of proscribed secular and ecclesiastical lords, but had also worked out in detail the manner in which they were "themselves to take possession of the property of others of the king's faithful lieges".[129]   Secular

[127] P.R.O. K.B.9/225/2; K.B.27/681, *Rex* m. 8 r.
[128] P.R.O. K.B.27/681, *Rex* m. 8 r.
[129] *Ibid.*

disestablishment; the disendowment of lay lords together with ecclesiastical; the accession of Lollard nominees to property as well as to government: such, apparently, was the plan.

The royal uncles were the first to be done away with, as they were to have been (in a different capacity) in 1414, and on other occasions. Now, likewise honoured by inclusion in the list, were nine abbots, three priors, the dukes of Norfolk and York, and the earl of Huntingdon. Though it is clear from all accounts that Perkins was to "take upon himself as a prince"[130] the division of the spoils, we are not told what positions the leaders themselves had intended to take, and the details of the scheme, which survive in the accusations against John Russell, may have been modified by him after his fellow plotters (Perkins and Long) had gone to their deaths. At all events, the twenty or so "certain poor people" named as successors elect of those condemned were almost all Londoners — against whom no subsequent proceedings appear to have been taken, on the grounds that they were "totally ignorant" of the rôles assigned to them. Those appointed to succeed the dukes of Bedford, Gloucester and Norfolk, (holding in addition respectively, Glastonbury, Westminster, and Bury St. Edmunds), were John Byle of Chipping Norton, John Cook, a London weaver, and Richard Stowe of London. Lordships and offices were allocated in the same way to the rest of the obscure individuals predestined for sudden preferment in this territorial lottery, some of them being selected for the mysterious posts of *regis controrotulator, embasiator, custos London'*, and *capitalis hered'*, as well as two to be masters of the Lollard chancery, and one to be secretary. As in 1410 the requisitioned properties did not touch certain ecclesiastical possessioners, such as cathedral chapters, colleges, chantries, and the charterhouses, but some additions had been made, notably of London friaries, including (significantly, since it was expressly excluded in Jack Sharpe's supposed bill) that of the Crutched Friars.[131]

Careful thought seems also to have gone into the means of achieving this astonishing programme. Here, Perkins may have taken into account the experience of 1414. For, though London and Londoners featured to a large extent in the rebels' plans — meetings having been held not only at Abingdon but also continuously in March and April at Finsbury and "other hidden and suspect places" in Middlesex, where indeed the plotting probably began — the place of assembly appointed for 22 May was far distant from the capital. The "diverse unknown rebels to the number of 20 thousand men"[132] were to assemble in warlike array in a field called "Gyldynmylle" in the village of East Hendred in Berkshire. From there the first objective (before the various "armies" of rebels continued their course of destruction through the realm), was the abbot, monks and buildings of the abbey of Abingdon.[133] The irony was certainly intentional which ordained that William Perkins, after his arrest at Oxford, should be sent to be executed, with others, at Abingdon, on the very day when they were to have risen. Meanwhile in the capital (which had earned the gory spectacle of Perkins' head), hopes — or suspicions — died hard, to judge by the charge brought that autumn against Richard Leyk, holy water clerk, of Westminster, an associate of the late John Russell, of having on 26 July dispersed subversive literature, and nominated and created certain persons in the parish of St. Clement Danes to be bishops, dukes, earls and barons, including one to be treasurer of England.[134] It makes a pathetic postscript to a not very glorious affair.

The ramifications of this abortive plot were widespread, and though some of its intentions now appear wild in the extreme, the previous history both of the Lollards and of the arguments used by their opponents, help us to understand, as we cannot doubt, the anxious reactions of the government. The duke of Gloucester sent a special commissioner to deal with the heretics in Coventry, where more of them were executed, and himself returned to the midlands in the summer to make enquiry into Lollard activities, visiting both Leicester, and Coventry (where he had been in May). Meanwhile proceedings were started in Wiltshire and Somerset, and the abbot and bishop of Ely met with others in special session at Hertford[135] on the same day that John Orpud was indicted, and William Perkins executed, at Abingdon, under the direction of the king's lieutenant. It appears both from Gloucester's movements, and from the indictments, that Abingdon, Salisbury, London, and the midlands were the chief centres of the rebellion. But the royal letters sent in

---

[132] Cf. above, p. 297 for the same unrealistic figure which likewise appears in the indictments after Oldcastle's rebellion. It is possible that the number was derived from the Lollards' own claims; Walsingham says their bills in 1413 included statements that they had a hundred thousand supporters, (*St. Albans Chronicle*, p. 70), and cf. the remarks in a Lollard letter in *Snappe's Formulary*, ed. H. E. Salter (*Oxf. Hist. Soc.*, lxxx, 1924), p. 132.

[133] When Archbishop Chicheley visited the abbey of Abingdon in 1423 he found much in need of correction, and Ralph Ham, the abbot of 1431, was removed from all the offices he then held. *Chichele's Register*, iii, p. 512; A. E. Preston, *op. cit.*, pp. 60, 62.

[134] P.R.O. K.B.27/682, *Rex* m. 15 v.

[135] *Chronicon Rerum Gestarum*, in *Annales . . . Amundesham*, p. 64.

July to the alderman and bailiffs of Bury St. Edmunds, show that alarms and suspicions which were circulating that summer about "the malicious entent and purpos of goddis treitours and oures" extended further afield.[136]

Unlike 1414, no members of the landed gentry are known to have lost their lives in the venture of 1431. This does not mean to say, however, that none was thought to be implicated. There are indeed signs that one knightly family, whose name had previously been mentioned in connection with the heresy of the Lollards, was placed under particular surveillance at this time. On 19 June commissioners were sent to Buckinghamshire to arrest and bring Sir John Cheyne before the council, to seize his manors of Grove and Drayton Beauchamp, together with all his books and suspicious memoranda, and to investigate the nature of his armoury. Both Sir John and his brother Thomas Cheyne were committed to the Tower until 4 August.[137] They belonged to a family which had long been under suspicion of heresy, and which had patronised the Thomas Drayton who abjured in 1415 and 1425. And they had both been implicated in 1414, when John had gone to the Tower with their father Sir Roger Cheyne, and Thomas was excepted from the king's pardon. The treatment they now received emphasises the fact that the government looked upon these rebels as Oldcastle's successors, fearing, as the king expressed it to the townsmen of Bury, their intent to "distroie alle men of estate, thrift, and worship, as thei purposed to have do in oure fadres daies, and of ladds and lurdains wolde make lordes . . ."[138] But by the autumn, when some of them were acquitted, the "ladds and lurdains" had been put in their proper places, and the crisis was over.

No doubt as they lost influence the Lollards also lost moderation. If they lacked strong knightly support they could hardly look so hopefully to parliament, and the levels of society from which they were recruiting were perhaps less likely to do so. The more artisan the movement became, the more easily its radical elements could predominate. Those who died as rebels and traitors in these ambitious exploits may have been only a small minority of extremists, who were not at the heart of the continuing doctrinal movement. Some, strictly speaking, may not have been heretics at all. But, to those who had long been saying, or hearing, that revolution and radicalism were the likely outcome of the heretics' beliefs, the

---

[136] *Archaeologia,* xxiii (1831), pp. 341-3; (from a register of Bury St. Edmunds, now Brit. Mus. Add. M.S. 14848).

[137] *Cal. Pat. Rolls,* 1429-36, p. 153; *Cal. Cl. Rolls,* 1429-35, p. 89.

[138] *Archaeologia,* xxiii (1831), p. 342.

development and debasement of their programme and distinctions within the sect, must have mattered less than the fulfilment of unpleasantly prophetic utterances; 1431 must have seemed very much like 1381, as well as 1414, starting all over again.   If the Lollards had advocated reform, they had tried — and tried more than once — something which was more like revolution: if they had denied the authority of the pope they had also attacked the king: from making their own priests they had turned to the creation of dukes and earls. Perhaps the story does not even end with Jack Sharpe's sorry fiasco. If the Lollards avoided involvement in the rising of 1450 this does not prove that they had given up all hope of another rebellion of their own.   Indeed, as William and Richard Sparke admitted to Bishop Chedworth, Lollards in the diocese of Lincoln were still in 1457 confederating together and gathering sworn followers into a secret society, in the hope of overthrowing Antichrist.[139]   Left wing Lollards who helped to give the movement such prominence and discredit may have persisted as long as the heresy itself.

*   *   *

Lollardy did not bring England the Inquisition.   But, not surprisingly, the methods of repression were similar; an increase of episcopal powers, the assistance of the friars, and the support of the lay arm.   The rôle of the state, though the early stages of its participation have been described, remains nevertheless somewhat enigmatic.   Why, when the church seems to have made the way open, was it so long before England acquired the power which existed elsewhere to burn heretics?   And if "it is unlikely that fresh measures would be taken against heretics except upon a petition from the clergy",[140] why did three independent chroniclers on three different occasions attribute the initiative in the new proceedings to the commons?[141]   Chroniclers, unfortunately, may often seem to be getting away with an untruth or half-truth for the lack of means to prove them wrong.   Such evidence as there is, however, certainly suggests that both in 1382 and 1401 the first moves were made by ecclesiastics, and that the chronicles, if taken at their face value, are

---

[139] *Lincoln Diocese Documents*, ed. A. Clark (E.E.T.S., Original Series, No. 149, 1914), p. 92.

[140] H. G. Richardson, "Heresy and the Lay Power under Richard II", *Eng. Hist. Rev.*, li, (1936), p. 10.

[141] *Fasciculi Zizaniorum*, p. 272, (reference to a petition which, allegedly, spurred Courtenay to call the Blackfriars meeting): *Chronicon Henrici Knighton*, ii, p. 263, (a request of lords and commons in 1388): *Annales Henrici Quarti*, p. 335, (a petition of the commons in 1401).

either mistaken or misleading. But either way their words are interesting, for at the very least they provide reason to suppose that there were moments when the commons acted as the willing co-operators of the clergy. In 1401 at any rate, to judge by their petition to this parliament, the commons were anxious that an example should be made of any man or woman arrested for Lollardy, "pur legerement cesser lour malveis predications".[142] If, on the other hand, there were members of the commons who were actively hostile to the clergy, who would resent putting more power into their hands, and might even contemplate taking some away, then the passage of anti-Lollard legislation would not always have been plain sailing. Signs that some, anyway, of the commons had qualms about what was happening seem evident in a petition to the October parliament of 1382, in which they asked for repeal of the statute passed the previous May on the grounds not only that they had not agreed to it, but also because it was not their intention "to bind themselves or their successors to the prelates more than their ancestors in the past".[143] Or again, there is the request of 1410, when the commons asked to have returned a petition "touchant l'estatut nadgairs fait des Lollardes".[144] This may have been the petition which, Walsingham reports, was produced after the failure of a demand for convicted clergy to be put in royal and lordly, not episcopal prisons, and asked for modification of the procedure for heretical preachers provided in 1401. If so, it was withdrawn under a threat that if it was pressed the penalties provided would be aggravated rather than reduced. Such afterthoughts, whatever their origins, were displeasing to ecclesiastical chroniclers, who were anxious for commoners, as well as lords, to be the sound and undivided friends to a church in need. The truth was perhaps that the laymen were not considering the church's needs alone, nor attributing powers to it alone. If their views were seldom united, and varied with the times, they were most likely to approach unity when the dangers seemed most common. And if the clergy indicated the general form the legislation should take, they waited on the pleasure of statesmen to decide upon its precise terms, as well as the moment when it should be passed.

[142] *Rot. Parl.*, iii, pp. 473-4.
[143] *ibid.*, p. 141.
[144] *ibid.*, p. 623. Cf. *The St. Albans Chronicle*, p. 56. (Kingsford thought that the petition which was withdrawn was the 1410 disendowment scheme, and that this explains the latter's absence from the rolls of parliament. It seems probable, however, that there were other reasons why such radical proposals would not have been likely to find their way to formal enrolment. Cf. *Chronicles of London*, ed. C. L. Kingsford (Oxford, 1905), p. 295.)

Historians have long since noticed that Archbishop Courtenay pressed home the first successful campaign against Lollardy in the reaction following the revolt of 1381, and it can hardly have been only the advent of a new archbishop which brought the movement so prominently into view for the first time in the spring of 1382. The fact that "subverters of all kinds became suspect at a time of general subversion",[145] affected not only Wycliffe but a number of others, who found their hitherto obscure careers given a sudden and glaring publicity. When the publicity was next renewed it was by an administration which was concerned to meet the endemic fears of revolt by constructive improvements in the labour laws. The comprehensive legislation of the Cambridge Parliament of 1388 shows that the lords appellant — who had themselves come to power on a dangerous wave of rebellion, and had been told in the Merciless Parliament that there would soon be a new rising unless remedy was given for the recent "leve et rumour" of the "petitez gentz" of the realm[146] — intended to provide fully for the general maintenance of law and order. The new commissions, of laymen as well as ecclesiastics, appointed to deal with Lollardy, (several of them sent out while the Merciless Parliament was in session), would have accorded well with this interest, as well as with that of the two archbishops, one of them also chancellor and brother of one of the older appellants. Itinerant preachers, who in 1382 had been made liable to immediate arrest and imprisonment in secular prisons, now came under further lay supervision: the commissions were given the task of hunting out not only Wycliffite works, but also those teaching or studying them; at the same time local officials (sheriffs, mayors, bailiffs, etc.) were made generally responsible for assisting such enquiries. And offenders were subject to forfeiture as well as imprisonment.

If there was a background of social and political unrest to this earliest legislation against heresy, the precedents of 1382 and 1388 were fully followed on subsequent occasions. Moves in the direction of more extreme measures started in 1395, when the clergy of the southern province petitioned the two archbishops to approach the king, so that he might bring the assistance of the lay arm to deal with the Lollard sect. But though, as has been seen, Richard did not disregard Lollard activities, he took no steps to meet this plea, or another clerical request two years later, when the king and lords of parliament were asked for legislation to introduce the death penalty

[145] M. McKisack, *The Fourteenth Century*, (Oxford, 1959), p. 514.
[146] *Chronicon Henrici Knighton*, ii, pp. 266-7.

for heretics. When *De Heretico Comburendo* finally went through not only had the archbishop returned to stronger standing with a different king: the new king had also had a significant taste of political instability and disturbance.

The act which in 1401 gave England the death penalty for relapsed and impenitent heretics was also designed to meet the "damages, dangers and scandals" threatening the kingdom from the activities of the new sect, which, as the clergy pointed out to parliament, "basely instructs and informs the people, and incites them to sedition and insurrection as far as they are able, and makes great dissensions and divisions in the people . . ."[147] But Henry IV did not need instruction about the hazards of the pulpit. Already, in May 1400, writs had been sent to the sheriffs throughout England ordering proclamation to be made that no chaplains, apart from parochial chaplains in their own churches, were (under pain of imprisonment and forfeiture) to presume to preach without due licence from their diocesan, as some, it was learnt had been doing, spreading heretical views to the disturbance of the people and injury of the faith.[148] There was cause for alarm. But there long had been, and was it perhaps something more than the souls of his subjects which was causing the king this anxiety, and leading him to anticipate — if not precipitate — action in a sphere which more properly belonged to the church? 1400 was a year of widespread troubles, and Henry IV had already dealt with his first major rebellion. He may well have feared the influence of the pulpit on his own position.

To some contemporaries the restrictions imposed upon teachers of heresy in 1401, seemed quite as important as the introduction of burning which continental practice had already made familiar. The statute was framed to deal both with unauthorised preachers who escaped episcopal control by moving from diocese to diocese, and also with the holding of illicit "conventicles and confederations", meetings which had borne a sinister content at an earlier time of anxiety, twenty years back, and about which the king and some of the lords had lately expressed their concern to convocation.[149] Private Lollard study groups were certainly no new development at this time, and it is significant that they were given such prominent

---

[147] *Rot. Parl.*, iii, pp. 466-7.

[148] *Cal. Cl. Rolls*, 1399-1402, p. 185.

[149] Wilkins, *Concilia*, iii, p. 254. The word "conventicle" bore the opprobrious meaning of a private meeting for an unauthorised purpose, and was not only applied to heretical gatherings. (See Du Cange, *Glossarium*). 1381 shows its use in the sense of conspiratorial groups and assemblies. For examples see *The Peasants' Rising and the Lollards*, ed. E. Powell and G. M. Trevelyan (London, 1899).

attention at a moment when secret gatherings of any kind were liable to be viewed with suspicion.   Revolution; sedition; suspicion; and once again legislation was passed against the Lollards.   Once again, too, there had been an exchange of powers.   Transgressors who participated in the prohibited schools and conventicles of the heretics, or who preached without episcopal licence were subjected to a royal fine: but the right of immediate arrest and imprisonment of suspects was now given to the bishops.[150]

It was not long before these provisions were also found to be inadequate.   The ghost of Richard II which lingered so long, and haunted the Lancastrians in such uncomfortably material forms was already abroad in the spring of 1402.   Various mendicant preachers went to their deaths that year, not for denying the faith but for denying the rightful king, teaching that ghosts could walk, and, given sufficient support, walk back to the throne.   And as we have seen, suspicions of Lollard complicity in these matters did not take long to settle.   The parliament of 1406, which found compelling reasons for drawing attention to the danger of Lollard sermonising, ordained as a temporary measure that anyone found preaching or writing in favour either of disendowment, or of Richard II's continued existence, should be arrested and imprisoned without bail, taken before the chancellor, and brought to be judged by the king and lords in the next parliament.   The statute also empowered the lords spiritual and temporal, the justices and keepers of the peace, and all local officials to make enquiries and arrest all such persons without further commission.   When, the following year, Archbishop Arundel drafted the improvements upon the clerical machinery for licensing preachers which were published in 1409, though he brought the legislative action of the church to bear on the problem in a way which the Lollards found thoroughly objectionable, he can hardly be said to have been demonstrating ecclesiastical initiative.

The propagators of heresy, for reasons more than one, increasingly became one of the responsibilities of secular officials.   The final and logical step was taken in 1414 when parliament met at one of the centres of heresy, in a mood of little tolerance towards the heretics from whose recent traitorous purpose not only the estates and ministers of the church, but "all the temporal estates of the realm were also on the point of being finally and completely destroyed, with all manner of policy therein . . ."[151]   The outcome of these deliberations was to make heresy hunting a normal duty of the chancellor,

---

[150] *Statutes of the Realm*, ii, pp. 125-8: 2 Henry IV, c. 15.
[151] *Rot. Parl.*, iv, p. 15.

treasurer, justices, and all local officials, who were to be sworn into
this obligation when taking office. Secular courts were authorised
to receive indictments for heresy, and the justices were henceforth
to be commissioned with full powers of enquiry into the activities
of all who in sermons, schools, conventicles, congregations and
confederacies, as well as by writing, were maintaining heresy. Two
years later Archbishop Chicheley followed suit, providing for clerical
enquiries to be held twice a year in every rural deanery. The mesh
of controls which persistent heretics had to evade was now closer,
and also double. Laymen as well as churchmen were regularly
involved in the surveillance of Lollards, with all their attendant
aspirations. The legislation ends here, after the mêlée at St. Giles'
Fields, not because heretics had ceased to be a danger, but because
England had acquired a full complement of laws to deal with the
offending sect — laws which Mary Tudor re-enacted for heretics of
a different breed.

*   *   *

As it turned out the contemporary was right who wrote so
confidently:—

> "And, pardé, lolle thei never so longe,
> Yut wol lawe make hem lowte;
> God wol not suffre hem be so stronge
> To bryng her purpos so abowte".[152]

Oldcastle's revolt proved, in the end, to have been the Lollards' day
of judgement. They could nearly boast such another rebellion, but
not such another leader. Among the reasons why they never lived
to see God's doom enacted after their own desires must surely be set
the lingering echoes of an old refrain. If Lollardy emerged full
grown from the head of rebellion the church had thereby acquired
most strong defensive armour. We shall never know how many
recruits joined or left the Lollard movement not only for the stimulus
of its devotional creed, but also because it provided the promise of
rewarding but treasonable action in rebellious times. But extremism,
as the Anabaptists later showed, might discredit, if not kill reform.
"Pore phantasticals", complained Calvin, "have hyndered and
disturbed us";[153] what was needed was strong moderate influence to
win the day. Lollardy was persistent, but such hopes as it ever had of
achievement always hung upon a single thread, for the heretics no more
than their opponents needed telling that the lay lords were the keystone

[152] *Pol. Poems and Songs,* ii, p. 245.
[153] J. Calvin, *A short instruction for to arme all good Christian people
agaynst the pestiferous errours of the common secte of Anabaptistes,* (London, 1549),
from the Prologue.

to success; if they refused persuasion when living they were to do service by their deaths. The names of suspect Lollard knights are few, and there could certainly have been a number of reasons for this apart from the church's long schooling that a Lollard reformation would bring them losses and not gains. But the final outcome, as it stood, was shaped by more than hopes of the recompense or fears of the fires awaiting in a world to come.

This is not, at all, to deny that there was, throughout, a very genuine alarm for the salvation of souls, and concern for the maintenance of the orthodox faith; nor to say that this aspect of the Lollard movement was not, and is not, the first to be considered. But the nature of the heresy, of the society in which it spread, and of the government which had to deal with it, were such that its religious implications could not be considered alone. And other happenings of the period ensured that they were not. Sedition and dissent had come of age together.

NOTE, 1976

A full contemporary notice of Perkins' rising, which I only discovered after the publication of this article, is to be found in the volume of collected papers of Nicholas Bishop of Oxford (Cambridge University Library, Ms. Dd. 14. 2). Anthony Wood, who knew the collection through Brian Twyne's excerpts, described Nicholas Bishop as an author "not unworthy the taking notice of, and as yet unknown to the world".[1] Nicholas was the son and heir of Bartholomew and Isabella Bishop of Oxford, and his book was primarily a personal cartulary though it also incorporated matters of wider interest, including the brief chronicle of English kings from which the following extracts are taken.[2] The compilation can be dated from internal references to 1432. At Oxford Nicholas Bishop was situated not far from the centre of Perkins' activities, and though he remains singularly silent about occurrences in the city (including Perkins' capture), his account is valuable by reason of its proximity both in time and place to the events mentioned. The first paragraph on the rising appears to be derived from an official document but Bishop goes on to add some details not recorded else-

---

[1] *Anthony Wood's Survey of the Antiquities of Oxford*, ed. A. Clark, ii (Oxf. Hist. Soc., xvii, 1890), p. 291; cf. *Anthony Wood's Life and Times*, coll. A. Clark, iv (Oxf. Hist. Soc., xxx, 1895), p. 193.

[2] Bartholomew Bishop, whose will was dated 1395, seems to have died about 1396, and Nicholas to have been born some time after 1368. For their holdings in Oxford see H. E. Salter, *Survey of Oxford* (Oxf. Hist. Soc., N.S. xiv, xx, 1960, 1969), esp. i, pp. 22-6, 144-5.

where. From him we learn that the wife of a mayor was among those executed at Coventry,[3] while at Warwick a Chipping Norton minstrel, Hendy Clarener, lost his life having been found guilty of harbouring Lollard books and of disparaging the eucharist. Bishop also adds to the dimension of events in London, with his report of seventeen arrests including a rich man of Cheap, and the rescue of Perkins' head from London Bridge by two men who were caught in the act. He tells of a ceremonial book-burning later that same summer. And finally, this account lends weight to the view that it was suspicions of Lollard sympathies which placed members of the Cheyne family under arrest at this time.[4]

I am most grateful to Mrs. Dorothy Owen for kindly checking this transcript (in which I have extended obvious abbreviations), and thank the Librarian of the Cambridge University Library for permission to publish.

CAMBRIDGE UNIVERSITY LIBRARY MS. Dd. 14. 2.

f. 286[r-v]

In the thursday next after the closyng of Easter, in the yer regnyng of our kyng Harry the sixte the ix yer[5] at Abyngdon in the counte of Berk' bethin the kynges yerd, John Perkyn alias Sharp de Wygmorelond, John Long Couper of Chepyng Norton, a webbe of Stevynton smytsmart, Goqwyt[6] wyth hur felshyp to them i socied the numbre of xx m[l] as Lollardes fals heretikes common traytoures rysarrs conspiratours ymagined and to geders confederid oon with many tho thenn i socied and felouns of hur covyn and hur false malis before thaught as common liggers in a wayte of high weyes and the feyth of holy church to destruye there falsliche traytourlich as common traytures and felouns of our kyng lete dude wryte divers fals bulles and fals scriptures and gilful and many contraris the doctrine of christyn feyth conteynyng, and thenn to the puple of our kyng to be publich and to be comuned follysch dampnablysch in divers places that is to [f. 286[v]] wytyng in citees of London of Salebur' and of townys Coventre Marleburgh wikkydliche have set styked cast to ground, and every day so to wryte

---

[3] Cf. the report in Gregory's Chronicle about some of Perkins' followers being hung, drawn and quartered in Coventry, "and a woman was be-heddyd at the galous". *Historical Collections of a London Citizen*, ed. J. Gairdner (Camden Soc., N.S. xvii, 1876), p. 172.

[4] Cf. J. A. F. Thomson, *The Later Lollards, 1414-1520* (Oxford, 1965), pp. 60-1, 147.

[5] Marginal note: "traytours".

[6] *Sic*. The sense requires "gathered".

procureth to styke to draw to ground cessit nat ne dredith in grete
offens the high maieste of god and of dignite of corowne regal and
derision of christian feith in disturbaunce of the kynges pese and wrong
and contempt of al chistian pepele, and thenn with hur fals imaginacouns
wikkedlich by hur fore thaughtes to the world and to the multitude
xx m¹ and overe of pueple etc.

Where a pon this chevynteyns as now as instawns of Umfray Duk of
Glowcestre buth draw hanged hedyd quartered[7] and in divers countreys
hur quarteres i hanged up in tokyn here of this tresun thus for to be
eschwed fro this tyme forth. Al so a minstrell of Chepyng Norton by
name Hendy Clarener at Warewyk for this cause i drawe hanged hedid
quartered and so i send ford, as is a bove told. A womman a mayreswyf
of Coventre for this cause al so be hedyd. Al so the lord Cheyne for
thes causes is a restud and lad to the Tower of London.

f. 288ʳ

Sir John Cheyne knyght Thomas his brother sqwyer[8] for this seyd
Lollardy buth a restud and lad to the tower of London at the
comaundement of [the] Duke of Glowcestre lew tenaunt of kyng Harry
the sixt and uncle to the kyng at his wyll in the moneth of June anno ixᵒ
this was dun. Al so a worthi man and a riche of Chepe in London is
a restud for this lollardy and xvi men wyth hym a peched. Al so this
seyd Perkyn his heed fro London brigge by twey wel faryng men was
take fro thennis and soon a pon that thees twey men wer take ther with
and a rested and buth at poynt to be hange draw and quartered ther
fore, and do with as is a for seyd. Al so Hendy Clarenere a hanged
draw and quartered for be cause that he sad that godys body myght nat
be grounde in a mille and that he kept counseil in huydyng of Lollard
bokes.

f. 290ʳ

... at the same procession lollardes[9] bokes weren brend as many as
a man myght ber.

---

[7] Marginal note: "treson — traytours".
[8] Marginal note: "Henry the sixt".
[9] Seemingly that at St Paul's on 4 July 1431, referred to ff. 288ᵛ, 289ᵛ.

Index

Abbotsbury abbey (Dorset): nepotic enfeoffment at, 138

Abingdon abbey (Berks.): household knights of, 136; knights of hold villein land, 153; mercenaries enfeoffed at, 136, 159; sub-enfeoffment at, 138–9

accounting: techniques of, 65

acremen, 179

Acton, Sir Roger, 297

Adam Bell, Clim of Clough and William of Cloudesly: parallels with Robin Hood ballads, 247–8; themes of, 244, 245, 247–8

Agelwin, son of Brihtmaer, 140

Ailric, son of Agge, 186

Alexaunderstone; receipts of great sessions at (1516–7), 218

Alford, John, 209

Allen a' Dale, 261, 269

alms: given during famine, 93

Alno, Alexander de, 143

Alno, Hugh de, 143–4

alodiarii, 175

Alselin, Geoffrey, 148

Alverthorpe, Quenylda de, 24

ancient demesne, *see* demesne

Anglo-Saxon Chronicle: William I's army in, 160

Angot, Richard, 189

Annales Londonienses, 90, 92

Anticlericalism, 292; in Robin Hood ballads, 242–4, 256

arable: common rights over, 11–12, 21, 23–4, 25, 31; contraction of, 128–9, 130, 132; cropping of, 26; cultivation of, 30, 49; decline of, 85; failure, effects of, 98–102; part of common field system, 10, 37; re-allotment of, 27; strips of, 14

archery, 158, 260–1, 267–8, *see also* crossbowmen

armour: development and cost, 170

Art of Hunting, The, 267

Arundel, Thomas, archbishop of Canterbury (1399–1414), 302; defence of temporalities, 286, 295–6; and licensed preachers, 314

assarting, 40, 49; continued through agrarian crisis, 125–6; and population increase, 15

assarts: divided into strips, 22; improvement for tenant, 60

Assize of Arms (1181): armour in

Jews' possession, 171; equipment of knights, 152; two groups of fighting men, 135

Assize of Arms (1252): bow prescribed weapon, 267

Aston, Margaret, 8

avercmen, 179

bailiff: as farmer of demesne, 58; function of, 65

Baker, R. L., 104

Ball, John, 2, 237; association with Wycliffe, 276–7, 278–9; letter to rebels (1381), 241–2; and temporalities, 282; and tithes, 284

Ballard, A., 76

Bampton, Kade, 219

Barham, Lambert of: acknowledges half a knight, 163

barley: failure of (1321), 97; yields of (1315–16), 98–9; *see also* cereals, corn, grain *and under individual crops*

Barnesdale (Yorks.): and Robin Hood ballads, 226

Barnet (Herts.), 120, 122

Barnwell priory (Cambs.), 120

barons, 158; *liber homo* of Magna Carta, 175; right to judgment, 175; as sub-tenant, 136, 140

Bayeux Inquest (1133), 163

Baylly, Richard, 210

beans: yields at Bolton, 99

Beauchamp, William de: sub-tenant of Worcester, 141; commitment of knights of, 168

Bec abbey: reduction in demesne, 115

Beckering, Thomas, 299

Becket, St. Thomas, 221

Bellamy, J., 8

Bellême, Robert of: revolt (1102), 156

berewick: held by knight-service, 151; as manor, 161

Berwick, siege of, 96

besants, 82

Beveridge, Lord, 57, 83

Bible, the Lollard, 286–7

Bibury (Gloucs.), 203, 205, 211

Bigod, Roger, earl of Norfolk, 143; and lands at Bury St. Edmund's, 137, 140

Bishop, Nicholas, of Oxford: papers of, 316

Bishop, T. A. M., 24, 40, 51